T0350380

Revolutionary Applications of Blockchain–Enabled Privacy and Access Control

Surjit Singh
Thapar Institute of Engineering and Technology, India

Anca Delia Jurcut
University College Dublin, Ireland

A volume in the Advances in
Information Security, Privacy, and
Ethics (AISPE) Book Series

Published in the United States of America by
    IGI Global
    Information Science Reference (an imprint of IGI Global)
    701 E. Chocolate Avenue
    Hershey PA, USA 17033
    Tel: 717-533-8845
    Fax: 717-533-8661
    E-mail: cust@igi-global.com
    Web site: http://www.igi-global.com

Library of Congress Cataloging-in-Publication Data

Names: Singh, Surjit, 1981- editor. | Jurcut, Anca, 1984- editor.
Title: Revolutionary applications of blockchain-enabled privacy and access
  control / Surjit Singh, and Anca Jurcut, editors.
Description: Hershey, PA : Information Science Reference, an imprint of IGI
  Global, [2021] | Includes bibliographical references and index. |
  Summary: "This book provides the latest research findings, solutions and
  relevant theoretical frameworks in the area of blockchain technologies,
  information security, and privacy in computing and communication for
  professionals who want to improve their understanding of the recent
  challenges, design, and issues in these areas"-- Provided by publisher.
Identifiers: LCCN 2020047973 (print) | LCCN 2020047974 (ebook) | ISBN
  9781799875895 (hardcover) | ISBN 9781799886730 (softcover) | ISBN
  9781799875901 (ebook)
Subjects: LCSH: Blockchains (Databases)--Security measures.
Classification: LCC QA76.9.B56 R48 2021 (print) | LCC QA76.9.B56 (ebook)
  | DDC 005.74--dc23
LC record available at https://lccn.loc.gov/2020047973
LC ebook record available at https://lccn.loc.gov/2020047974

This book is published in the IGI Global book series Advances in Information Security, Privacy, and Ethics (AISPE) (ISSN: 1948-9730; eISSN: 1948-9749)

British Cataloguing in Publication Data
A Cataloguing in Publication record for this book is available from the British Library.

All work contributed to this book is new, previously-unpublished material.
The views expressed in this book are those of the authors, but not necessarily of the publisher.

For electronic access to this publication, please contact: eresources@igi-global.com.

Advances in Information Security, Privacy, and Ethics (AISPE) Book Series

ISSN:1948-9730
EISSN:1948-9749

Editor-in-Chief: Manish Gupta State University of New York, USA

MISSION

As digital technologies become more pervasive in everyday life and the Internet is utilized in ever increasing ways by both private and public entities, concern over digital threats becomes more prevalent.

The **Advances in Information Security, Privacy, & Ethics (AISPE) Book Series** provides cutting-edge research on the protection and misuse of information and technology across various industries and settings. Comprised of scholarly research on topics such as identity management, cryptography, system security, authentication, and data protection, this book series is ideal for reference by IT professionals, academicians, and upper-level students.

COVERAGE

- Technoethics
- Telecommunications Regulations
- Risk Management
- Information Security Standards
- Cookies
- Security Classifications
- Network Security Services
- Electronic Mail Security
- Computer ethics
- Security Information Management

IGI Global is currently accepting manuscripts for publication within this series. To submit a proposal for a volume in this series, please contact our Acquisition Editors at Acquisitions@igi-global.com or visit: http://www.igi-global.com/publish/.

Titles in this Series

For a list of additional titles in this series, please visit:
http://www.igi-global.com/book-series/advances-information-security-privacy-ethics/37157

Handbook of Research on Digital Transformation and Challenges to Data Security and Privacy

Pedro Fernandes Anunciação (Polytechnic Institute of Setúbal, Portugal) Cláudio Roberto Magalhães Pessoa (Escola de Engenharia de Minas Gerais, Brazil) and George Leal Jamil (Informações em Rede Consultoria e Treinamento, Brazil)
Information Science Reference • © 2021 • 529pp • H/C (ISBN: 9781799842019) • US $285.00

Limitations and Future Applications of Quantum Cryptography

Neeraj Kumar (Babasaheb Bhimrao Ambedkar University, Lucknow, India) Alka Agrawal (Babasaheb Bhimrao Ambedkar University, Lucknow, India) Brijesh K. Chaurasia (Indian Institute of Information Technology, India) and Raees Ahmad Khan (Indian Institute of Information Technology, India)
Information Science Reference • © 2021 • 305pp • H/C (ISBN: 9781799866770) • US $225.00

Advancements in Security and Privacy Initiatives for Multimedia Images

Ashwani Kumar (Vardhaman College of Engineering, India) and Seelam Sai Satyanarayana Reddy (Vardhaman College of Engineering, India)
Information Science Reference • © 2021 • 278pp • H/C (ISBN: 9781799827955) • US $215.00

Blockchain Applications in IoT Security

Harshita Patel (Vellore Institute of Technology, India) and Ghanshyam Singh Thakur (Maulana Azad National Institute of Technology, India)
Information Science Reference • © 2021 • 275pp • H/C (ISBN: 9781799824145) • US $215.00

For an entire list of titles in this series, please visit:
http://www.igi-global.com/book-series/advances-information-security-privacy-ethics/37157

701 East Chocolate Avenue, Hershey, PA 17033, USA
Tel: 717-533-8845 x100 • Fax: 717-533-8661
E-Mail: cust@igi-global.com • www.igi-global.com

Editorial Advisory Board

Table of Contents

Detailed Table of Contents

    Eranda Harshanath Jayatunga, Faculty of Engineering, University of
        Ruhuna, Sri Lanka
    Pasika Sashmal Ranaweera, Faculty of Engineering, University of
        Ruhuna, Sri Lanka
    Indika Anuradha Mendis Balapuwaduge, Faculty of Engineering,
        University of Ruhuna, Sri Lanka

The internet of things (IoT) is paving a path for connecting a plethora of smart devices together that emerges from the novel 5G-based applications. This evident heterogeneity invites the integration of diverse technologies such as wireless sensor networks (WSNs), software-defined networks (SDNs), cognitive radio networks (CRNs), delay tolerant networks (DTNs), and opportunistic networks (oppnets). However, the security and privacy are prominent conundrums due to featured compatibility and interoperability aspects of evolving directives. Blockchain is the most nascent paradigm instituted to resolve the issues of security and privacy while retaining performance standards. In this chapter, advances of blockchain technology in aforesaid networks are investigated and presented as means to be followed as security practices for pragmatically realizing the concepts.

Chapter 2

    Rochak Swami, National Institute of Technology, Kurukshetra, India
    Mayank Dave, National Institute of Technology, Kurukshetra, India
    Virender Ranga, National Institute of Technology, Kurukshetra, India
    Nikhil Tripathi, Technical University of Darmstadt, Germany
    Abhijith Kalayil Shaji, Otto von Guericke University Magdeburg,
        Germany
    Avani Sharma, Malaviya National Institute of Technology, Jaipur, India

Distributed denial of service (DDoS) attacks have been a matter of serious concern for network administrators in the last two decades. These attacks target the resources such as memory, CPU cycles, and network bandwidth in order to make them unavailable for the benign users, thereby violating availability, one of the components of cyber security. With the existence of DDoS-as-a-service on internet, DDoS attacks have now become more lucrative for the adversaries to target a potential victim. In this work, the authors focus on countering DDoS attacks using one of the latest technologies called blockchain. In inception phase, utilizing blockchain for countering DDoS attacks has proved to be quite promising. The authors also compare existing blockchain-based defense mechanisms to counter DDoS attacks and analyze them. Towards the end of the work, they also discuss possible future research directions in this domain.

Chapter 3

    Promise Agbedanu, University College Dublin, Ireland
    Anca Delia Jurcut, University College Dublin, Ireland

In this era of explosive growth in technology, the internet of things (IoT) has become the game changer when we consider technologies like smart homes and cities, smart energy, security and surveillance, and healthcare. The numerous benefits provided by IoT have become attractive technologies for users and cybercriminals. Cybercriminals of today have the tools and the technology to deploy millions of sophisticated attacks. These attacks need to be investigated; this is where digital forensics comes into play. However, it is not easy to conduct a forensic investigation in IoT systems because of the heterogeneous nature of the IoT environment. Additionally, forensic investigators mostly rely on evidence from service providers, a situation that can lead to evidence contamination. To solve this problem, the authors proposed a blockchain-based IoT forensic model that prevents the admissibility of tampered logs into evidence.

Software-defined networking (SDN) is a promising networking technology that provides a new way of network management to the customers. SDN provides more programmable and flexible network services. SDN breaks the vertical integration of control and data planes and promotes centralized network management. This unique characteristic of SDN offers security features to deal with the malicious activities. However, architectural design of SDN makes it vulnerable to several attacks. Therefore, it is important to investigate the crime through various forensic techniques. This work discusses a literature study of some possible forensic techniques. A framework is also presented for forensic investigation of SDN environment in attack scenario. The proposed framework includes the collection of evidence and preserves them against any damage. During investigation, protection of evidence and chain of custody are of utmost importance to avoid misleading of the investigators. The safe storage strategy as well as maintaining the custody link can be achieved through blockchain technology.

Technological advancements in the transportation/automotive industry are continually increasing due to competition and consumer demands. The mobile open blockchain initiative (MOBI) is one way organizations are coming together to share innovating ways to revolutionize the transportation/automotive industry. This chapter explains the events that lead to the innovation of an open consortium, MOBI, and its members and highlights some of the cutting-edge technologies and innovative methods where blockchain is being adopted by the transportation/automotive industry.

This chapter explores the drawbacks of conventional centralized share exchange frameworks, like those of higher transaction costs, central and vulnerable regulation to exploitation, and lack of revelation to business behavior and practices by introducing a revolutionary model that utilizes blockchain to establish a decentralized stock exchange and a transparent persistent economy. The suggested model utilizes exclusive contracts to implement the validity of the privileges of the owner and the proper accomplishment and settlement of the transactions, thereby mitigating the need for a centralized authority to ensure the accuracy of the stock exchange mechanism. The experimental findings convincingly demonstrate that the decentralized solution can provide lower transaction costs by progressively replacing brokerage costs and centralized officials' commissions with mining charges, which reward the miners for their backbreaking work in maintaining the system and enforcing the laws.

Blockchain is an emerging technology that is based on the concept of distributed ledgers. It allows for pervasive transactions among different parties and eliminates the need for third-party intermediaries. Several of blockchain's characteristics make it suitable for use in the agriculture sector. Some of the potential applications of blockchain include efficient management of the food supply chain and value-based payment mechanisms. The products of agriculture are usually the inputs for a multi-actor distributed supply chain, in which case the consumer is usually the final client. The food chain involves several actors including farmers, shipping companies, distributors, and groceries. This makes the entire system to be distributed with multiple actors playing different roles throughout the chain. This currently used system is inefficient and unreliable in various aspects. This project aims to leverage blockchain technology to solve and address discrepancies involved in food supply chains.

In the blockchain, the transaction hashes are implemented through public-key cryptography and hash functions. Hence, there is a possibility for the two users to choose the same private key knowingly or unknowingly. Even the intruders can follow the particular user's bitcoin transaction, and they can masquerade as that user by generating the private and public key pairs of him. If it happens, the user may lose his transaction. Generally, bitcoin technology uses random numbers from 1 to 2256. It is a wide range, but for a greater number of users, there should be one another solution. There is a possibility of digital prototyping which leads to the loss of more accounts. This chapter provides the device-specific fingerprint technology known as physical unclonable function (PUF) to be employed for authentication in a blockchain-based bitcoin environment. The random unique response from PUF ensures correct transaction. In this chapter, a new tetrahedral oscillator PUF has been introduced intrinsically. All the blockchain operations are carried out and verified with PUF response.

Chapter 9

Archana Sharma, Institute of Management Studies, Noida, India
Purnima Gupta, Institute of Management Studies, Noida, India

As the base of bitcoin, the blockchain has received widespread consideration recently. Blockchain stands for an immutable ledger which permits transactions to occur in a decentralized ways. Applications based on blockchain are numerous for instance financial services, industrial and supply chain services, legal and healthcare services, IoT and blockchain integration, bigdata analytics, and so on. Nevertheless, there are still numerous confronts of blockchain technology like security and fork problems that have to be resolved. This research highlights an inclusive indication on blockchain technology with blockchain architecture in the first phase. And in the second phase, the security challenges and problems associated with blockchain are highlighted. It further proposes and measures up to various typical consensus algorithms used in different blockchains. Research has been concluded with the potential prospects of blockchain as future trends.

Chapter 10

Ambika N., Department of Computer Applications, Sivananda Sarma
Memorial RV College, Bangalore, India

IoT is an assembly of equipment of different calibers and functionality working towards a single goal. A blockchain is a computerized record that contains the whole history of exchanges made on the system. A multi-WSN arrangement model is structured. The hubs of the IoT are isolated into base stations, group heads, and conventional hubs as per their capacities, which encourage the administration and participation of the hubs. A hybrid blockchain model is proposed. To fit the multi-WSN arrange model better, as indicated by the various capacities and energies of various hubs, neighborhood blockchain and open blockchain are sent between group head hubs and base stations individually, and a crossbreed blockchain model is framed. A shared validation plot for IoT hubs is proposed. For group head hubs, the creators utilize the worldwide blockchain for validation, and for customary hubs, they utilize the nearby blockchain for confirmation. The proposal aims in increasing reliability by 1.17% and minimizes sinkhole attack by 2.42% compared to previous contribution.

Chapter 11
Keshav Sinha, Birla Institute of Technology, India
Madhav Verma, B.I.T Sindri, Dhanbad, India

In today's world, the storage of data needs a huge amount of space. Meanwhile, cloud and distributed environments provide sufficient storage space for the data. One of the challenging tasks is the privacy prevention of storage data. To overcome the problem of privacy, the blockchain-based database is used to store the data. There are various attacks like denial of service attacks (DoS) and insider attacks that are performed by the adversary to compromise the security of the system. In this chapter, the authors discussed a blockchain-based database, where data are encrypted and stored. The Web API is used as an interface for the storage and sharing of data. Here, they are mainly focused on the SQL injection attack, which is performed by the adversary on Web API. To cope with this problem, they present the case study based on the Snort and Moloch for automated detection of SQL attack, network analysis, and testing of the system.

Preface

Nowadays, Blockchain technology is an emerging topic due to its ability to provide decentralized storage of information, transparency, immutability and to establish trust in an open networked system. It is expected that the applications using blockchain for data security and privacy will soon replace the existing technologies that provide centralized storage. There are prospects of applying blockchain technology in many industries including digital currency, Internet of Things (IoT), healthcare, supply chain management, banking, retail, insurance, logistics and public sectors. In fact, the management, access control, circulation, and sharing of any high-valued data should use blockchains.

In simple words, blockchain can be seen as a distributed database of online records on a peer-to-peer network that comprises a list of ordered blocks chronologically. Typically used in financial transactions for the Bitcoin cryptocurrency, the peer-to-peer blockchain technology records transactions without exception, in exchange to form an online ledger system. In other words, this is a decentralized and trustworthy system that is not relying on any third party. Trust relation among distributed nodes is established by mathematical methods and cryptography technologies instead of semi-trusted central institutions. The benefit of such a system is that it is distributed, permission-based and secure, hence it is called to be a public blockchain network. Distribution allows for a shared form of record keeping, meaning that each person within a business network has the possibility to verify the transaction made via the blockchain and, with permission, they can trail the record back to its source. The block is immutable, no one has sole ownership, and no one can delete the record of a transaction within the chain. It also facilitates data audit and accountability by having the capability to trace tamper-resistant historical record in the ledger. Depending on the actual deployment, data in the ledger can be stored in the encrypted form using different cryptographic techniques; hence, preserving data privacy. Further, it provides the pseudo-anonymity property, i.e. in the sense that the users are able to protect their real identities. Moreover, smart contracts (i.e. a kind of self-executing program deployed on the distributed blockchain network) can be used to support diverse functions for different application scenarios. For example, the conditions and terms of smart contract can be introduced by users and the smart contract will only be executed if these terms/ conditions are fulfilled. Hence, this hands over control to the owner of the data. Furthermore, no malware can infect the system through a node because others in the ledger will detect the attack and deny the unauthorized access. The blockchain can incorporate various classes of transactions or records, so its usability can extend beyond the initial financial scope drafted with Bitcoin cryptocurrency, to digital communications, product identification, to even customer claims.

Although research and innovation can enable businesses to use blockchain in a broad range of applications, the use of blockchain technology for information security and privacy appears to be the most obvious application area. Security and privacy are the main concern in the network and communications-based areas including IoT, 5G, Edge and Cloud Computing, Software Defined Networking, Wireless Networks and any application that is using these paradigms such as banking systems, retail, logistics and public sectors. The issues related to security include confidentiality, privacy, access control, integrity, and availability. For example, in the cloud, the data of users is stored away from their site and the users do not have direct control over it. Strong cryptographic techniques are thus needed. The controlled disclosure of personal information of the users comes under the privacy requirements. Only the authorized entities should be provided information about the cloud users. Access control is used in computer security to regulate the access to critical or valuable resources such as data, services, computational systems, storage space, and so on. The rights of users to access resources are typically expressed through access control policies, which are evaluated at access request time against the current access context. If there is any change in the stored data, the owner of data should be able to identify this change. Also, if there is any loss or corruption of stored data, there should be a way to retrieve this.

To promote the development and research of blockchain applications, to guarantee the security of these applications, and further to facilitate the research for the access control and privacy techniques, *Revolutionary Applications of Blockchain-Enabled Privacy and Access Control* (1) explains several concepts of blockchain related to WSN, CRN, SDN, Opportunistic Mobile Networks, Delay Tolerant Networks, Internet of Things (IoT), Forensic investigation; (2) provides complete coverage of the various tools, platforms and techniques used in blockchain; and (3) covers a variety of applications with real world case studies in areas such as supply chain management, stock market, banking, and attack prevention and detection techniques.

Revolutionary Applications of Blockchain-Enabled Privacy and Access Control includes 11 chapters that presents contributions from around the globe on recent advances and findings in the domain of blockchain technology, Internet of Things, networks and communication, forensic, attack detection and prevention. Chapters include theoretical analysis, practical implications, and extensive surveys with analysis on methods, algorithms, and processes for new methods development.

A brief description of the chapters of this handbook is given as follows.

CHAPTER DESCRIPTION

Chapter 1

The Internet of Things (IoT) is paving a path for connecting a plethora of smart devices together that emerges from the novel 5G based applications. This evident heterogeneity invites the integration of diverse technologies such as Wireless Sensor Networks (WSNs), Software Defined Networks (SDNs), Cognitive Radio Networks (CRNs), Delay Tolerant Networks (DTNs), and Opportunistic Networks (oppnets). However, the security and privacy are prominent conundrums seemed due to featured compatibility and interoperability aspects of evolving directives. Blockchain is the most nascent paradigm instituted to resolve the issues of security and privacy while retaining performance standards. In this chapter, advances of blockchain technology in aforesaid networks are investigated and presented as means to be followed as security practices for pragmatically realizing the concepts.

Chapter 2

Distributed Denial of Service (DDoS) attacks have been a matter of serious concern for network administrators since last two decades. These attacks target the resources such as memory, CPU cycles and network bandwidth in order to make them unavailable for the benign users, thereby, violating Availability, one of the components of cyber security. With the existence of DDoS-as-a-service on Internet, DDoS attacks have now become more lucrative for the adversaries to target a potential victim. This chapter focuses on countering DDoS attacks using one of the latest technologies called blockchain. Though in inception phase, utilizing blockchain for countering DDoS attacks has proved to be quite promising. This chapter also compares existing blockchain-based defense mechanisms to counter DDoS attacks and analyze them. Towards the end of the work, the possible future research directions in this domain are presented.

Chapter 3

In this era of explosive growth in technology, the Internet of Things (IoT) has become the game changer when we consider technologies like smart homes and cities; smart energy, security and surveillance and healthcare. The numerous benefits provided by IoT, it has become an attractive technology for users and cybercriminals. Cybercriminals of today have the tools and the technology to deploy millions of sophisticated attacks. These attacks need to be investigated; this is where digital forensics comes into play. However, it is not easy to conduct a forensic investigation in IoT systems because of the heterogeneous nature of the IoT environment. Additionally, forensic investigators mostly rely on evidence from service providers. A situation that can lead to evidence contamination. To solve this problem, this chapter proposes a blockchain-based IoT forensic model that prevents the admissibility of tampered logs into evidence.

Chapter 4

Software-defined networking (SDN) is a promising networking technology that provides a new way of network management to the customers. SDN provides more programmable and flexible network services. SDN breaks the vertical integration of control and data planes and promotes centralized network management. This unique characteristic of SDN offers security features to deal with the malicious activities. However, architectural design of SDN makes it vulnerable to several attacks. Therefore, it is important to investigate the crime through various forensic techniques. This chapter discusses a literature study of some possible forensic techniques. A framework is also presented for forensic investigation of SDN environment in attack scenario. The proposed framework includes the collection of evidences and preserve them against any damage. During investigation, protection of evidences and chain of custody are of utmost importance to avoid misleading of the investigators. The safe storage strategy as well as maintaining the custody link can be achieved through blockchain technology.

Chapter 5

Technological advancements in the transportation/automotive industry are continually increasing due to competition and consumer demands. The Mobile Open Blockchain Initiative (MOBI) is one-way organizations are coming together to share innovating ways to revolutionize the transportation/automotive industry. This chapter explains the events that leading to the innovation of an open consortium, MOBI and its members, and highlights some of the cutting-edge technologies and innovative methods blockchain is being adopted by the transportation/automotive industry.

Chapter 6

This chapter explores the drawbacks of conventional centralized share exchange frameworks, like those of higher transaction costs, central and vulnerable regulation to exploitation and lack of revelation to business behavior and practices, by introducing a revolutionary model that utilizes blockchain to establish a decentralized stock exchange and a transparent persistent economy. The suggested model utilizes exclusive contracts to implement the validity of the privileges of the owner and the proper accomplishment and settlement of the transactions, thereby mitigating the need for a centralized authority to ensure the accuracy of the stock exchange mechanism. The experimental findings convincingly demonstrate that the decentralized solution can provide lower transaction costs by progressively replacing brokerage costs and centralized officials ' commissions with mining charges which reward the miners for their backbreaking work in maintaining the system and enforcing the laws.

Chapter 7

Blockchain is an emerging technology that is based on the concept of distributed ledgers. It allows for pervasive transactions among different parties and eliminates the need for third-party intermediaries. Several of blockchain's characteristics make it suitable for use in the agriculture sector. Some of the potential applications of blockchain include efficient management of the food supply chain and value-based payment mechanisms. The products of agriculture are usually the inputs for a multi-actor distributed supply chain, in which case, the consumer is usually the final client. The food chain involves several actors including farmers, shipping companies, distributors, and groceries. This makes the entire system to be distributed with multiple actors playing different roles throughout the chain. This currently used system is inefficient and unreliable in various aspects. This project aims to leverage Blockchain Technology to solve and address discrepancies involved in Food Supply Chains.

Chapter 8

In the blockchain, the transaction hashes are implemented through public-key cryptography and hash functions. Hence there is a possibility for the two users to choose the same private key knowingly or unknowingly. Even the intruders can follow the particular user's Bitcoin transaction and they can masquerade that user by generating the private and public key pairs of him. If it happens the user may lose his transaction. Generally, Bitcoin technology uses random numbers from 1 to 2256. It is a wide range; but for a greater number of users, there should be one another solution. There is a possibility of digital prototyping which leads to the loss of more accounts. This chapter provides the device-specific fingerprint technology known as Physical Unclonable Function (PUF) to be employed for authentication in a blockchain-based bitcoin environment. The random unique response from PUF ensures correct transaction. In this chapter, a new tetrahedral oscillator PUF has been introduced intrinsically. All the blockchain operations are carried out and verified with PUF response.

Chapter 9

As the base of bitcoin, the blockchain has received widespread consideration recently. Blockchain stands for an immutable ledger which permits transactions to occur in a decentralized way. Applications based on blockchain are numerous for instance financial services, industrial and supply chain services, legal and healthcare services, IoT and blockchain integration, Bigdata analytics, and so on. Nevertheless, there are still numerous confronts of blockchain technology like security and fork problems have to be resolved. This chapter highlights an inclusive indication on blockchain technology with blockchain architecture in first phase. And in second phase, the security challenges and problems associated with blockchain. Further proposes and measure up to various typical consensus algorithms used in different blockchains. Research has been concluded with potential prospects of blockchain as future trends.

Chapter 10

IoT is an assembly of multiple equipments of different caliber and functionality working towards a single goal. A blockchain is a computerized record that contains the whole history of exchanges made on the system. A multi-WSN arrangement model is structured. The hubs of the IoT are isolated into base stations, group heads, and conventional hubs as per their capacities, which encourage the administration and participation of the hubs. A hybrid blockchain model is proposed. To fit the multi-WSN arrange model better, as indicated by the various capacities and energies of various hubs, neighborhood blockchain and open blockchain are sent between group head hubs and base stations individually, and a crossbreed blockchain model is framed. A shared validation plot for IoT hubs is proposed. For group head hubs, the creators utilize the worldwide blockchain for validation, and for customary hubs, they utilize the nearby blockchain for confirmation. The proposal aims in increasing reliability by 1.17% and minimizes sinkhole attack by 2.42% compared to previous contribution.

Chapter 11

In Today's world, the storage of data needs a huge amount of space. In meanwhile cloud and distributed environments provide sufficient storage space for the data. One of the challenging tasks is the privacy prevention of storage data. To overcome the problem of privacy the Blockchain-based database is used to store the data. There are various attacks like denial of service attacks (DoS), Insider attacks that are performed by the adversary to compromised the security of the system. This chapter discusses a blockchain-based database, where data are encrypted and stored. The Web API is used as an interface for the storage and sharing of data. Here, this mainly focused on the SQL injection attack which is performed by the adversary on Web API. To cope with this problem this chapter presents the case study based on the Snort and Moloch for automated detection of SQL attack, network analysis, and testing of the system.

This book will be of interest to graduate students, researchers, academicians, institutions, and professionals that are interested in exploring the diverse applications of the Blockchain technology, especially in the security and privacy area.

Acknowledgment

This *Revolutionary Applications of Blockchain-Enabled Privacy and Access Control* is an outcome of the inspiration and encouragement given by several people to whom we would like to express our gratitude and appreciation.

Firstly, our sincere gratitude goes to the people who contributed their time and expertise to this book. We highly appreciate their efforts in achieving this project. The editors would like to acknowledge the help of all the people involved in this project and, more specifically, the editors would like to thank each one of the authors for their contributions and the editorial advisory board/reviewers regarding the improvement of quality, coherence and the content presentation of this book.

Secondly, the editors would like to thank to Mr. Eric Whalen and Ms. Morgan Brajkovich, Assistant Development Editors; and Ms. Lindsay Wertman, Managing Director of IGI Global, USA for their continuous support and giving us an opportunity to edit this book.

Finally, we are thankful to our family members for their support during completion of this book.

Surjit Singh
Thapar Institute of Engineering and Technology, India

Anca Delia Jurcut
University College Dublin, Ireland

Chapter 1

Blockchain Advances and Security Practices in WSN, CRN, SDN, Opportunistic Mobile Networks, Delay Tolerant Networks

Eranda Harshanath Jayatunga
Faculty of Engineering, University of Ruhuna, Sri Lanka

Pasika Sashmal Ranaweera
Faculty of Engineering, University of Ruhuna, Sri Lanka

Indika Anuradha Mendis Balapuwaduge
ⓘD https://orcid.org/0000-0003-1792-2645
Faculty of Engineering, University of Ruhuna, Sri Lanka

ABSTRACT

The internet of things (IoT) is paving a path for connecting a plethora of smart devices together that emerges from the novel 5G-based applications. This evident heterogeneity invites the integration of diverse technologies such as wireless sensor networks (WSNs), software-defined networks (SDNs), cognitive radio networks (CRNs), delay tolerant networks (DTNs), and opportunistic networks (oppnets). However, the security and privacy are prominent conundrums due to featured compatibility and interoperability aspects of evolving directives. Blockchain is the most nascent paradigm instituted to resolve the issues of security and privacy while retaining performance standards. In this chapter, advances of blockchain technology in aforesaid networks are investigated and presented as means to be followed as security practices for pragmatically realizing the concepts.

DOI: 10.4018/978-1-7998-7589-5.ch001

INTRODUCTION

All the discussed variants of this chapter are the pioneer technologies that govern the emerging communication based services and their applications. These directives were formed to address lacking aspects of different existing technologies with an improved perspective for elevating performance standards. Though, each distinct directive has limitations in security, where application of cumbersome but tamper-proof security mechanisms would obviously degrade the performance of them. Thus, there is a clear trade-off between latency and applicable security level. In addition, similar to most existing communication technologies or protocols, verifiable security is only credible with Trusted Third Parties (TTPs), or certificate authorities. Blockchain, in contrast, offers a decentralized approach that eliminates the TTP dependency. Moreover, the transparent yet tamper-proof mechanism in blockchain is enabling it to be adopted for diverse applications to secure their transactions. Thus, this chapter is focusing on the technologies of WSN, oppnets, SDN, CRN, and DTNs for adopting blockchain to their security limitations. The chapter is mainly categorized into the sections of WSN, SDN, CRN, DTN and oppnets, where various prevailing blockchain adaptations are discussed summarizing the best security practices.

BACKGROUND

Wireless Sensor Networks (WSNs) are basically ad hoc networks, amalgamating small devices embedded with sensing capabilities deployed to monitor physical activities in the surrounding area of interest. These sensor nodes should have the characteristics of large coverage area, monitoring with high precision, self-organization, random deployment and fault-tolerance, etc. Due to the possibility of providing low cost solutions, nowadays Wireless Sensor Networks (WSNs) are getting more and more attention in many real-world applications. However, the dense deployment of many sensor nodes cause unique security challenges in its management. In the meantime, adaptation of many security protocols to overcome those challenges are not straightforward because of inherent limits for energy consumption at sensor nodes as well as availability of lower memory and storage space. Therefore, it is timely important researchers to discuss the trade-off between resource consumption minimization and security maximization in WSNs.

Flexibility is the key feature of Software Defined Networks (SDNs) that elevate its standards beyond the conventional networking infrastructures (Kreutz, Ramos, & Verissimo, 2013). This concept offers advanced network management capabilities to the network administrator by enabling configuration of networking instances independent of the hardware layer. Infact, diversification exhibited in networking

2

devices and their plethoric aggregate are contriving compatibility and interoperability debacles. In SDN, homogeneity of the both core and access networks are improved with standardizing the hardware specifications; and higher reliance on hardware based processing is transformed into an autonomous processing approach with software integration (Kumar et al., 2017). In fact, SDN envisages solutions for complex issues in traditional networking topologies and routing algorithms by integrating intelligence to the control plane. In addition, this is a paradigm shift for network operators that eases their issues with hardware layer and the ability to advance networking features with novel requirements to broadened avenues. Apart from flexibility, main benefits of SDN can be specified as: cost effectiveness (monetary), centralization, higher throughput, dynamic nature that support higher mobility, low communication latency, optimum network utilization, rapid and efficient load-balancing, fault tolerance, and adaptable/ context-aware security (Tomovic, Pejanovic-Djurisic, & Radusinovic, 2014; Jaballah, Conti, & Lal, 2019; Scott-Hayward, O'Callaghan, & Sezer, 2013).

Recently, research in the field of wireless communications has been focusing on the Fifth Generation (5G) cellular systems. Meanwhile, the 5G and beyond wireless network designers face challenging demands such as more capacity, higher data rates, lower latency, better connectivity for a massive number of users, lesser cost and energy, and more importantly improved quality of experience (QoE) (Munsub Ali, Liu, & Ejaz, 2020). Moreover, with the increase in the number of communication devices, the requirement for higher bandwidth is essential. However, with the limited and expensive radio spectrum resources, allocation of new frequency bands is an extremely difficult task. Therefore, efficient management of the spectrum under dynamic policies has recently become a prospective research topic.

Although Internet access has evolved as one of basic primary needs of humans, still there are many rural areas that do not have any network connectivity or sometimes intermittent. These scenarios demand the development of distributed networking techniques in an opportunistic manner to provide atleast some level of service with ad-hoc networks. Consequently, these Opportunistic Networks (oppnets) integrate diverse communication, computation, sensing, storage and other devices and resources in the surrounding. The initial set of nodes associated with an oppnet are called seed nodes. Once other nodes are invited to become potential helpers for the original oppnet, this seed oppnet nurtures into an expanded oppnet while persisting various security concerns.

The integration of blockchain with IoT provides many benefits to build a secure, trusted and robust communication prospects. But the challenge is to identify the most suitable location in placing blockchain for current IoT settings. With the amalgamation as third party to keep data in centralized data centers and later a fog layer to offload the traffic burden from the data centers, the current IoT is a three tier architecture namely IoT devices layer, Fog layer and the cloud layer. Generally, the incoming requests for access level can be divided as real-time, non-realtime and delay tolerant. Delay tolerant networks are helpful in addressing issues related to lack of infrastructure, stationary nodes and connectivity in today's heterogeneous networks by storing and forwarding facilities. Nevertheless, these networks require new authentication and trust establishing mechanisms to ensure that no adversary parties can destroy the privacy in time dependent delay tolerant network routes.

SECURITY CONCERNS IN DIVERSE NETWORKS

Security Lapses in Wireless Sensor Networks

The attacks in WSNs can be classified as host-based and network-based attacks. In host-based attacks, adversary parties always compromise with the users in the network to reveal information such as passwords or keys about the sensor nodes. This is achieved by breaking the software running on the sensor nodes or tampering the hardware to extract the program code, data and keys stored at sensor nodes. Whilst network-based attacks include all the attacks related to information transmission and/or deviations crafted on the intended functioning of protocols. The summary of inherent four-fold attacks such as interruption, interception, modification and fabrication with respect to different layers in ISO-OSI layer are shown in Table 1 (Chowdhury & Kader, 2013).

Hence, the security requirements of WSNs can be identified under four disciplines namely Confidentiality, Integrity, Authentication and Availability (CIAA). For any network, the data authenticity is required to guarantee the identities of communicating nodes whether the data has been originated from a reliable source. In the presence of malicious nodes in the network, the data at transit nodes can be tampered, altered or changed by adversaries. In order to ensure the data integrity, normally a code of message integrity is used. Since radio access technologies are open resources, sometimes passive attackers can eavesdrop messages or discover secrets in surveillance applications by collecting secret data through other compromised nodes. Consequently, encryption standards should be defined in advance to keep the confidentiality among nodes. Ultimately, the availability shall determine whether a node has the ability to use the resources and the network to transmit data (Zia & Zomaya, 2006).

Table 1. Plausible security threat in WSNs based on ISO-OSI layered architecture

Layer	Attack	Plausible Security Threat
Physical layer	Jamming	An adversary party attempts to disrupt the operation of the network by broadcasting a high-energy signal
	Tampering	Extract cryptographic keys from the captured node, tamper with its circuitry, modify the program codes or even replace it with a malicious node.
Data link layer	Continuous channel access (Exhaustion)	A malicious node disrupts the MAC protocol by continuously requesting or transmitting over the channel
	Collision	Two nodes attempt to transmit on the same frequency simultaneously
Network layer	Sinkhole	An adversary party attempts to attract almost all the traffic of other nodes through a compromised node
	Sybil	A single node attempts to demonstrate multiple identities for all other nodes in the network
	Wormhole	A low latency link is created between two portions of a network thus an attacker is able to tunnel messages to confuse the routing protocol
	Hello flood	Disrupts the process of neighbor discovery by broadcasting HELLO packets
	Acknowledge flooding	Acknowledgements are used by many link layer network routing algorithms to choose the next hop to overcome reliability issues in the network. Acknowledgments spoofing results in packets being lost when travelling along such links.
	Sniffing	An adversary node is placed in the proximity of sensor grid for interception or listen-in
Transport layer	Injects false messages and energy drain attacks	Normally sensor nodes are resource-constrained entities. As a result, attackers attempt to use compromised nodes to inject fabricated reports to generate a large amount of traffic in the network
	Flooding	An attacker generates new connection requests repeatedly to reach a maximum limit until others get exhausted
	De-synchronization	Disrupts an existing connection
Application layer	False nodes	Addition of a malicious node by an adversary party to inject malicious data as well as to lure other nodes to capture data.
	Node subversion	Revealing its information by a compromised node including disclosure of cryptographic keys thus affects the whole network.

Figure 1. Comparison of conventional and SDN networks

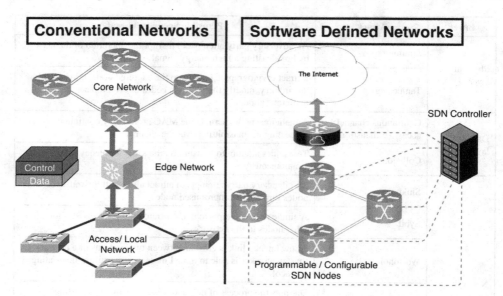

Security Lapses in Software Defined Networks

As Figure 1 indicates, conventional networks are mainly partitioned into access or local, edge, and core networks; where the nodes or devices operating at each level are different in terms of their build, system specifications (processing, storage, memory, energy requirement, access interfaces and amounts), financial cost, operating cost, embedded protocols, and operational complexity. In fact, the complexity of the devices are dependent on the layer in which the device is operating in the Open System Interconnection (OSI) or TCP/IP protocol stacks. Typically, local network devices are operating at Layer 2 (Data-Link) while edge and core network devices are extending to the rest of the layers above Layer 2 (Network to Application in OSI). Directives such as Multi-Protocol Labeled Switching (MPLS), and Virtual Private LAN Service (VPLS) have been introduced to improve the packet forwarding efficiency and security at edge and core networks (Liyanage, Ylianttila, & Gurtov, 2016). Upgrading the holistic network into such directives require the replacement of networking nodes, so that they are compatible with the pursuing updates. This is an obvious drawback with the existing networks that restricts the application of advancements to real-world networks. In addition, control/signalling information, and data forwarded through the network are carried through separate channels; which make bandwidth utilization arduous due to the dedicated signalling channels. Traffic load balancing has become a static and standalone process that can be monitored and administered only via the control channels remotely. Since the load balancing algorithms/ mechanisms/ protocols should be executed at the device level, managing the control signals and statistics has become overly de-centralized beyond the acceptable controlling domains. This is an important aspect of novel services that require more control over the traffic management with the prescribed Quality of Service (QoS) and Quality of Experience (QoE) classifications.

The SDN architecture is categorized into 3 layers or planes as illustrated in Figure 2. Application layer launches the applications and services specified in the networking context. The application instances are generating the flow rules and convey the requirements to the controller via the Northbound Application Programming Interfaces (APIs) or plugins (Feghali, Kilany, & Chamoun, 2015). The infrastructure layer consists of network elements that have a controller logic embedded to it. As specified above, these network elements can be configured into different network functions. The control layer is the most important aspect of this architecture that centralizes the complete network. The controller is responsible for the functions of network visualization, service provisioning, network management, and trac engineering. These functions are carried out by the Network Operating System (NOS) and an instance of each network service is deployed at the controller. High-level policies can be formed at the controller supporting security and dependability (Kreutz et al., 2013). OpenFlow (OF) protocol is employed to establish the communication channel between the controller and the network elements while NOX, POX, Faucet, Floodlight, ONOS, Open vSwitch, Cherry and Beacon are most commonly used controllers. The controller is reaching the network elements via the resource abstraction layer from southbound APIs. In addition to the three common layers, there is a management and administration layer that interacts with all other layers. In fact, management abstraction layer is interacting with: application layer on Service Level Agreements (SLAs) for each service instance, control layer for updating configuration policy and monitoring performance, and infrastructure layer for setting up and launching network elements.

The same benefits of SDN, network programmability and centralized control logic, are exposing the IT networks towards nascent threats (Kreutz et al., 2013). The allowance granted for application layer entities to engage with control plane elements (i.e. for improving the flexibility) is exposing the rest of the architecture towards unauthorized access control, and malicious network rule insertion threats (Tselios, Politis, & Kotsopoulos, 2017). Centralized nature of the paradigm is compromising the holistic network in case the SDN controller becomes infiltrated. The softwarized approach in SDN is no longer operating standalone network devices, where connected nature is improving the odds for adversaries to instill malicious content or interpose such links (Aujla et al., 2020). Since conventional networks were mostly based proprietary devices as in Cisco, Juniper, and NEC, the attackers were tasked with revealing vulnerabilities specific to each vendor. This is an arduous task, which meant one revealed vulnerability is only applicable to devices of a specific vendor. Though with SDN, for maintaining compatibility and interoperability, a generic standardization and a set of protocols should be utilized.

Figure 2. Typical SDN architecture

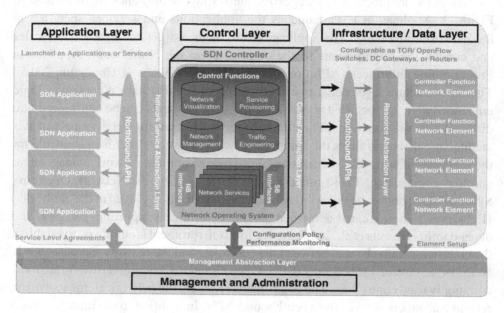

Figure 3. Threats in a typical SDN deployment

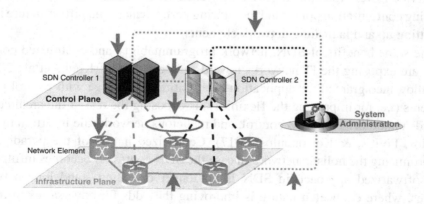

This fact is increasing the vulnerability level of the SDN, where Advanced Persistent Threats (APTs) can be targeted to gain access.

Figure 3 indicates diverse threats exploitable by an adversary in a typical SDN deployment scenario. The connectivity between the SDN networks elements are the most probable threat for an attacker. This link can be subjected to Man-in-the-Middle (MitM), Relay, or APT attacks that result in various consequences. Such consequences can be Malicious code injection, Eavesdropping, Sybil, Spoong, Denial of Service (DoS), or malware instilling. Due to its dynamic nature in the SDN environment, network elements can be subjected to side channel type attacks (Liu, Reiter, & Sekar, 2017). Further, a malicious node injected as a network element can be exploited to perform either sinkhole or wormhole attacks to manipulate the traffic flows (Tselios et al., 2017). In addition, a compromised node can sabotage the performance of the entire data plane devices by forging other nodes or cloning; while SDN controllers can be exploited appearing as a legitimate node. Multiple and simultaneous impersonation attacks can result in a Distributed DoS (DDoS) threat that delay the traffic flows while disrupting the provisioned services. The access to SDN controllers by physical means are improbable due to their placement in secure premises. Their access can be gained from exploiting the vulnerabilities of the OF protocols. Appearing as a legitimate network device and authenticating to secure the access is an obvious approach for any attacker. Once the access is gained, the SDN controller can be overloaded via DoS type attacks. Further, a compromised network controllers can delude the controllers in other domains. A resourceful attacker capable of launching an impersonation attack as the administrator can infiltrate both control and infrastructure planes. The main issue with the SDN environment is its lack of trust and accountability model for guaranteeing security of consumers.

Security Lapses in Cognitive Radio Networks

According to the spectrum utilization statistics, a large amount of spectral resources in all over the world are still either partially or completely unused at different times across geographical areas, and therefore, inefficient. Although different technologies and techniques have been identified as solutions for spectrum underutilization in future wireless networks, integration of cognitive radio (CR) technology will provide an effective solution for spectrum scarcity issues faced in the future 5G and beyond networks (Hindia et al., 2020). The main objective of CR technology is to sense the spectrum from the real time environment and discover the non-utilized spectrum. Cognitive radio networks (CRNs) are intended to be able to opportunistically exploit those spectrum holes in order to adapt their radio parameters accordingly. To facilitate this task, CR needs accurate and reliable spectrum sensing.

Figure 4. Main components in a CR node

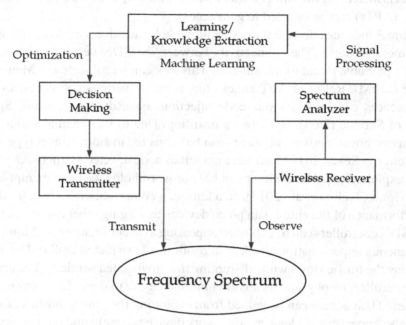

Therefore, a cognitive radio transceiver consists of different components to implement those functionalities as shown in Figure 4. In order to detect the channel occupancy of licensed users and to find vacant or available channels for unlicensed access spectrum analyzer is used. For an effective identification of available and occupied spectrum bands efficient signal processing techniques need to be supported in a CR node. Based on the analyzed spectrum details, CR node's learning and knowledge extraction unit functions to identify spectrum usage patterns of licensed users by adopting machine learning techniques. From this correct identification, the decision on accessing the spectrum has to be made by the decision making unit by applying optimization theory.

In a CRN, CRs have the capability of adapting their transmission parameters according to the environmental conditions and make changes based on their communication capabilities. However, the security is susceptible in case of wireless networks compared to wired networks. Spectrum management and sensing in CRNs involve various control messages. During this process, malicious users may eavesdrop on those information, thereby leading to the serious statistical information leakage of both licensed and unlicensed users. Consequently, malicious activities need to be prevented within the CRN. For instance, a malicious secondary user can eavesdrop other users' signal information and based on that, pretend a false interference level.

On the other hand, some malicious secondary users may masquerade as a primary user to obtain the resource of a given channel by using Physical layer attacks (Nanthini S., Hemalatha, Manivannan, & Devasena, 2014). A summary of several security issues, network layers involved, as well as possible reasons for those issues are listed in Table 2.

Table 2. Security issue in CRNs

Attack Type	Target Layer	Reason/Description
Jamming (Primary user or secondary user)	Physical	The attacker maliciously sends out packets to hinder legitimate participants in a communication session from sending or receiving data
Increase interference by malicious nodes	Network	When negotiating with malicious nodes
Ripple effect	Network	Due to incorrect information about channel occupancy
Primary user emulation attack (PUE)	Physical	Malicious secondary user emulating a primary user to obtain the resources of a given channel
Spectrum sensing data falsification	Data Link	The CR receivers make false spectrum-sensing decision if an attacker sends incorrect local spectrum sensing results to its neighbors
Lion attack	Transport	Uses the PUE attack to disrupt the Transmission Control Protocol (TCP) connection

In 5G networks, where a massive number of users are expected to be handled in heterogeneous networks, the above mentioned security issues may not be overcome effectively by using existing cryptographic methods. Indeed for above mentioned technological fields, the spectrum management and the security mechanisms should not rely on a centralized controller. This due to the fact that the fixed spectrum allocation, operator controlled resource sharing algorithms and security mechanisms will not be scalable for 5G and beyond applications when a large number of small cells are deployed to support Millions of mobile users.

BLOCKCHAIN ADVANCES AND SECURITY PRACTICES IN DIVERSE NETWORKS

Blockchain Advances for Enhancing Security in WSNs

Malicious node detection and isolation in the application layer, key management and secure routing implementations in network layer, and link layer encryption performed at the data link layer are the most commonly available techniques. In addition, use of adaptive antennas and spread spectrum techniques have been considered as physical layer solutions. However, in the current IOT paradigm, WSNs are open, distributed and dynamic multi-hop routing technology is used to transmit aggregated data from integrated sensor nodes to a central location via agreed routing protocol. Hence, it is required many judgments on security, privacy, connectivity and data requirements. The existing cryptography mechanisms are simply capable of detecting and defending node compromise to some extent. On the other hand, multi-hop routing is exposed to several malicious or selfish attacks solely depends on encryption algorithm and authentication mechanism. When there is a malicious attack, conventional routing algorithms cannot distinguish a malicious node from other routing nodes. The malicious node can discard packets thus creates a data "black hole" in the network. Hence, a trusted, decentralized and self-organizing third-party intermediary is mandatory to overcome the aforesaid security issues.

Consequently, blockchain is perceived as a decentralized or distributed network that is capable of Peer-to-Peer Networking (PPN), Distributed File Sharing (DFS) and Autonomous Device Coordination (ADC) functions, allowing the IoT systems to track the massive number of connected and networked devices. Mainly it enhances the privacy and reliability of IoT systems having robust transactions among devices in coordination.

Blockchain Based Malicious Node Detection in WSNs

Threats generated in WSNs follow two customs as the external attacker to the network or an internal node which becomes malicious after being invaded. Therefore, malicious node detection is key in WSNs to assure the security in operation. It has been comprehended using either based on developing trust models or based on introducing new WSN protocols. In the former method, trust models were developed by accounting trust values with neighbor-weight trust determination (NWTD) algorithm, D-S (Dempster-Shafer) evidence theory or fuzzy based multi-attribute trust model, etc. Enhanced LEACH protocol to detect energy consumption, distance and malicious nodes to ensure the robustness, and new multi-valued trust routing protocol (MTR) are some examples for new protocols used for malicious detection (She, et al., 2019). Despite the behavioral-based trust models that can be used to monitor the network and detect malicious nodes, they are still exposed to malicious attacks due to inaccurate location estimates. In order improve the accuracy as well as to record the detection process of malicious nodes for later traceability, a hybrid blockchain based trust evaluation method of behavioral- and data-based has been proposed in (Kim, et al., 2019) as shown in Figure 5. This rejects malicious sensor nodes in network and thus enhances trust relationships among beacon nodes. First, a trust value of each beacon node is computed taking into account the metrics such as closeness, honesty, intimacy and frequency of interaction and then it is broadcast to base stations to generate blockchain of trust values. The beacon values with least trust values are discarded eventually. Simulated results reveal that the proposed algorithm outperforms the existing algorithms in terms of False Positive Rate (FPR), False Negative Rate (FNR) and Average Energy Consumption (AEC) though most trusty beacon nodes were used to estimate localization process of unknown nodes. However, it is recommended that Bayesian statistics, Maximum likelihood estimation, reinforcement learning based trust evaluation and the complexity associated with the length of blockchain should be tested further to determine the completeness of the method.

Figure 5. Hybrid blockchain-based trust management model

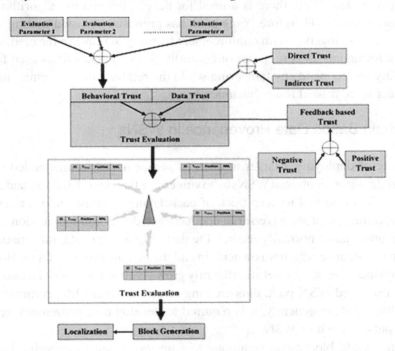

Trusted Routing Schemes Using Blockchain and Reinforcement Learning

In order to enhance the trustworthiness among routing nodes, conventional WSNs use cryptographic systems, trust management, centralized routing decisions, etc.

Although many researchers have suggested third-party intermediaries or management centers to resolve the security issues, most of the routing schemes in multi-hop distributed WSNs are failed to identify untrusted behaviors of routing nodes dynamically. Meanwhile, there is still no effective way to prevent malicious node attacks. Therefore, as a trusted, decentralized, self-organizing ledger system, the blockchain has shown improved solutions for the security and fairness. By replacing the traditional public key infrastructure (PKI) with a blockchain protocol, Gómez-Arevalillo et al. has proposed blockchain based public key management framework (SBTM) to remove central authentication and to provide a decentralized inter-domain routing system. Smart blockchain based contract routing (BCR) has been used in (Ramezan & Leung, 2018) to record routing nodes with malicious behaviors and thus to help routing nodes for finding trusted routes. However, it seems that there is no assurance to stop packet forwarding to a malicious node that claims with a BCR token. Therefore, there is a need for developing routing algorithms with self-adaptive nature. Therefore, Yang et al. has proposed a trusted routing scheme using blockchain together with reinforcement learning to improve the credibility of routing information. In here, proof of authority (PoA) blockchain is used for easy traceability and to avoid any tampering while the reinforcement learning model is used select more trusted route dynamically.

Blockchain Based Data Provenance in WSNs

The nature of deploying a larger number of sensor nodes in unattended or even adversarial environments lead WSNs to be vulnerable for network failures and attacks. Therefore, it is essential to keep track of packets among sensor nodes to evaluate the trustworthiness, probe adversarial conducts and detect communication failures. The data provenance normally records the data origin trace back information of a packet in accordance with both ownership and the actions taken on them. However, the provenance size of a packet significantly grows with the number of transmission hops in a selected WSN path, thus creating issues in battery life, communication bandwidth, etc. Consequently, it is required to develop data provenance schemes itself or outside the host WSN.

A lightweight blockchain technique to empower against tampering has been proposed in (Tiberti, et al., 2020) to detect compromised nodes. In this approach, the sensor network consists of several motes and a sink node, a constrained node which serves as the gateway towards the external networks. In the monitoring process, the sink node collects and stores data from other nodes before forwarding them to other networks. A blockchain based hash computation is used to provide an immutable and tamper-resistant storage at the sink node. Another compression free blockchain based data provenance scheme (BCP) has been proposed in (Zeng,et al.,

2018) where provenances are stored distributively on the high performance nodes (H-nodes) deployed above or nearby the network along the packet path. Base stations can retrieve the provenance on demand through a query process.

Figure 6. Layered architecture for blockchain framework in WSNs

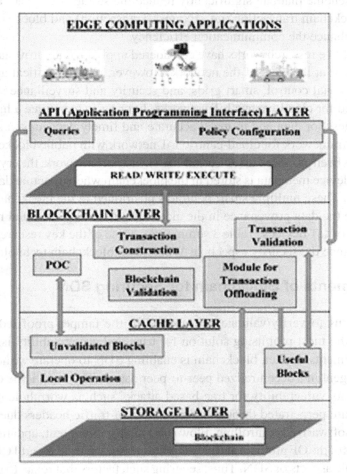

Although non-repudiation and non-tampering properties can be adopted with blockchain based schemes in WSNs, the implementation of these schemes is still a challenge due to resource-limited edges. A green blockchain framework for big data sharing in collaborative edges to overcome the challenges arising from the properties of edge computing has been proposed by Chenhan Xu et al. They have divided the framework into four layers, Application Programming Interface (API) layer, cache layer, blockchain layer, and storage layer based on the reduced computational, storage, and network resource requirements for big data sharing in collaborative edges as shown in Figure 6. The key findings of the this works are; 1) PoC (Proof-of-Collaboration) based consensus mechanism with low computation complexity which provided low computation capacity, 2) blockchain transaction filtering and offloading scheme that can significantly reduce the storage overhead, and 3) new types of blockchain transaction (i.e., Express Transaction) and block (i.e., Hollow Block) to enhance the communication efficiency.

All the above research works have considered applying data provenance within the network or at the edge of the network. However, mission-critical applications such as industrial control, smart grids, and security and surveillance systems are still preferred for cloud-centric IoT networks. In order to guarantee a high level of trustworthiness for data and to make accurate and timely decisions, a secure data provenance framework for cloud-centric IoT network with public blockchain smart contracts has been proposed in (Ali, et al., 2018). In this framework, the cryptographic hash of the device metadata is stored in the blockchain whereas actual data is stored in the cloud. These multiple smart contracts positioned in the blockchain are used to guarantee the data provenance in the cloud thus allowing more and more dense deployment of IoT devices. Table 3 summarizes some of the key research literature used to enhance the security aspects of WSNs with blockchain technology.

Advancements of Blockchain for Securing SDN

The consensus to verify/validate and append to the tamper-proof ledger makes blockchain the most promising solution for trust and accountability issues in the SDN deployments. In fact, blockchain is enabling SDN to operate without a third-party trust agent in a decentralized peer-to-peer nature. The main issue of the SDN networks is its vulnerability for trac based attacks such as wormhole or sinkhole threats that are perpetrated through manipulation of traffic headers due to its over reliance on softwarized controlling. Flow rules tables, its content, updating process, and specifics of the OF protocol and its integration issues with TLS and TCP protocols are vulnerable aspects of SDN. Thus, securing such factors that relate to routing and trac engineering processes with instilled traceability and verification capabilities is a prime requisite. Blockchain being a data structure that its elements (i.e. blocks) are linked or chained with cryptographic hashes imprinted on timestamps and a record of all the transactions conducted in the ledger (Tselios et al., 2017). This approach makes the blockchain immutable and incorruptible. Such features of the blockchain technology are well suited for securing flow/ routing tables, and protocol mechanisms that offer a transparent and rapid applying abilities. Thus, this subsection is explicating various approaches blockchain can be applied for securing SDN.

Table 3. Blockchain based security practices for WSNs

Reference	Blockchain Based Security Practice	Preventable Security Threats/ Attacks	Feature of the Solution
She, et al., 2019)	A malicious node detection blockchain trust model (BTM)	Data tampering, Malicious node detection	Uses hash values and hash pointers to connect the previous block thus to meet the needs of blockchain integrity
(Kim, et al., 2019)	Base station generates blockchain with trust values of individual beacon nodes for trust management.	Malicious node detection	Interactions and collaborations among beacon nodes are used to evaluate trust values based on node location information, node behavioral trust and data trust
(Yang et al., 2019)	Queries network state information through blockchain	Tracing and tampering of routing information	Preliminary obtains the routing information of routing nodes on the blockchain and uses reinforcement learning to improve the routing security
(Ramezan & Leung, 2018)	A decentralized Ethereum blockchain-based contractual routing (BCR)	Blackhole and Greyhole attacks by malicious devices	Routing protocol for the IoT with much lower routing overhead
(Cui, et al., 2020)	A consortium blockchain with the PoA consensus mechanism to be jointly managed by several authoritative nodes	False nodes, Node subversion	Decentralized network with high provenance security including integrity and authenticity
(Ali, et al., 2018)	A hybrid blockchain model consists of both local blockchain and public blockchain	Collisions, Flooding, De-synchronization	Adaptation of the network to eliminate private blockchain nodes that need to be authenticated to join the network, while are at different base stations
(Haseeb, et al., 2019)	A trustworthy device registration and identity provenance smart contracts via blockchain	Discrepancies in the traffic behavior	Ensures the device integrity and provenance in cloud-centric IoT network
(Xu, et al., 2019)	A blockchain transaction filtering and offloading scheme that can significantly reduce the storage overhead	Traffic issues	Longer network lifetime with lightweight secure data routing between mobile IoT devices based on WSNs

Blockchain for SDN Node Identity Verification

Injecting malicious packets into a traffic flow of the OF switch is a most common infiltration method for SDN attackers. In (Aujla et al., 2020), flow tables and packets are secured using permissioned blockchain where the function of contriving blocks and aggregating into a chain are restricted to the controller. This approach is extended to verify and validate the OF switches' identity in the authentication phase using zero knowledge proof concept. The switch identities are linked into a blockchain. This research further demonstrates prevention of DoS/ DDoS attacks perpetrated at the immediate connected nodes at the infrastructure plane, finally targeting the controller. The final solution can be visualized as blockchain as a service approach for SDN.

A Blockchain Layer for SDN Architecture

A monolithic blockchain based security mechanism is proposed by (Jiasi, Jian, Jia-Nan, & Yue, 2019), that decentralizes the SDN control plane to avoid single point of failure while guaranteeing authenticity, traceability, and accountability. In the proposed architecture, a blockchain layer is appended in between the control and data planes; where Attribute Based Encryption (ABE) is employed for interactions with the application plane and One-pass High Performance Diffie-Hellmann (HOMQV) protocol is utilized for interactions between the blockchain layer and the data plane. This blockchain layer is creating a secure zone for all the transactions conveying within control and data planes.

Applying Blockchain for SDN Flow Rules Tables

Load balancing is a key aspect of SDN, where the conveyed control statistics and network states should be secured in transit. The (Faizullah, Khan, Alzahrani, & Khan, 2020) proposes a permissioned blockchain based approach for securing the load balancing process of SDN, that enables it as a suited solution for Internet of Things (IoT) applications. The SDN flow rules tables are secured with blockchain based transactions. A flow rule table update process is used to evaluate the proposed system where accuracy, scalability, security, and efficiency are compared with public blockchain based and OF based SDN; where the proposed system proved to be better performing.

The DistBlockNet scheme proposed in (Sharma, Singh, Jeong, & Park, 2017) is a novel method for updating the flow rules table employing blockchain with a verification strategy. Version verification, validation, and downloading the flow rules table to the IoT devices can be achieved with this system. One of the major concerns of SDN is its reliance on administrator manual engagement for reviewing and applying proliferating amounts of security policies and recommendations. DistBlockNet offers adaptability towards the considered threat landscape, where complete autonomous decision making and application can be realized in the real-time context. Each SDN controller-local network view is composed of OrchApp, controller, and shelter components. Both OrchApp and Shelter modules are focusing on security attacks perpetrated at application and data layers. In terms of functionality, OrchApp is responsible for access controlling with threat intelligence; while shelter is updating the flow rules table in a distributed blockchain network. Thus, application of blockchain in this solution is focused on the trac policy within the SDN controller network.

Blockchain Enabled SDN Approaches for Emerging Applications

Emerging technologies such as Internet of Vehicles (IoV) or Vehicle-to-Vehicle (V2V) have considered applying SDN based networking infrastructure to achieve the envisaged requirements stated under 5G based use cases. The architecture proposed in (Gao et al., 2019) employs SDN to manage the networking within the fog zones and mobile access networks for Vehicular Ad-Hoc Network (VANET) deployments. The data extracted from the on-board units are forwarded to the backhaul or cloud, via the fog zones in the edge equipped with radio resources. The SDN model enables the softwarized trac handling of fog zones utilizing the OF protocol and leveraging the capacity of the fiber optic backhaul link. Blockchain is adopted for handling authentication, access control, data management, and policy management in the control plane. The block structure is formulated with timestamp and Merkle root embedded in the header while transaction stats are encapsulated as a separate eld. This solution contrives a trust model for VANET peers that enable rapid and secure communication.

Handover process is an inconvenient aspect of any mobile or wireless networks that exposes the radio channels for interception intended adversaries. This is an unavoidable factor of such networks that require re-authentication of the mobile device at each handover instance. The issue becomes severe when corresponding wireless cells become heterogeneous, where authentication mechanisms and protocols are distinct for each underlying technology. Therefore, (Yazdinejad, Parizi, Dehghantanha, & Choo, 2019) proposes a SDN based internal network for tackling the heterogeneous nature with 5G while a blockchain approach is adopted for securing the handover mechanism. A blockchain centre where Ethereum based ledger technology is employed, handles the authentication control incorporation with the SDN controller. The primitives generated for each mobile device are recorded at the blockchain centre where they can be leveraged to verify its identity during a handover administered by the SDN controller. This approach eliminates the requirement for re-authentication and discourages infiltrations.

Various methods are adopted for integrating blockchain for SDN networks as perceived in the previous sub section. Classification of such approaches is imperative for realizing the successful adaptation of these two technologies in a pragmatic context. Thus, Table 4 specifies the classified best practices for blockchain enabled SDN implementations.

Table 4. Blockchain based security practices for SDNs

Applicable SDN Layer	Reference	Blockchain Based Security Practice	Preventable Security Threats/ Attacks	Features of the Solution					Intrusion Detection
				Adaptability	Flexibility	Authenticity	Accountability	Traceability	
Application	(Steichen et al, 2017)	Blockchain firewall application for SDN	Virus, malware, warms						×
Control	(Faizullah et al., 2020) (Sharma et al., 2017)	Employing blockchain to secure flow rules tables and their update process	Traffic engineering		×		×	×	
Control	(Gao et al., 2019)	Authentication, access control, and data management of VANETs	attacks, wormhole, sinkhole		×	×		×	
	(Yazdinejad et al., 2019)	Securing mobile handover process in heterogeneous networks	Intervening attacks such as MitM, Relay, APT	×	×	×		×	
Infrastructure/ Data	(Jiasi et al., 2019)	Introducing a blockchain layer between control and data layers	DoS/ DDoS attacks on controller, impersonation threats			×		×	
	(Aujla et al., 2020)	Blockchain for OF switch identity verification	Malicious node injection, rouge node			×	×	×	

Advancements of Blockchain for CRNs

Meanwhile Blockchain technology is introduced as an effective solution for security issues in wireless networks which consists of distributed databases that can be securely and iteratively updated. Blockchain technology implements a distributed ledger: a secure decentralized form of a database where no single party has control (Werbach, 2018). Thus, blockchains can be considered as tamper resistant digital ledgers implemented in a distributed manner without a central source.

Note that the records stored on blockchain's distributed ledger can be related to any data type. Then, information about spectrum access rights and spectrum usage and their dynamic changes can be recorded on this distributed ledger. Meanwhile, the spectrum can be dynamically managed using smart contracts. Consequently, with respect to a CRN, they enable CR users to record spectrum sensing details and QoS requirements and true identities in a shared ledger within the relevant group of CRNs, such that under normal operation of the blockchain network no information can be changed in malicious ways.

Secure Blockchains for DSA in Moving CRNs

In (Kotobi & Bilen, 2018), a blockchain verification protocol is proposed and evaluated as a technique for enabling and securing spectrum sharing in CRNs. In order to verify and secure spectrum sharing between mobile CRs a decentralized blockchain database is maintained. The general concept behind this proposed work is that spectrum licensees announce the auction of a particular spectrum band to the other parties, i.e., secondary users. For this, a common control channel is utilized to advertise the available channels and the auction information. The bidder(s) who won the bid can purchase the corresponding spectrum via a virtual currency known as Specoins. By making the blockchain or through direct exchange, secondary users can receive this currency. For instance, A CR can earn Specoins via updating the blockchain by utilizing its processing power. In addition, the proposed scheme permits conversion of real currency into Specoins by considering the secondary users who have a large amount of data to transmit however without enough Specoins.

Secondary users' transactions using Specoins are recorded in the blockchain. Note that this distributed database is visible by all participating parties according to the blockchain concept. The nodes which can update the database are known as miners. Once the secondary network transactions occur, it is updated by miners. After that the blockchain is used to validate the transactions. According to the simulation results obtained, the proposed blockchain-based spectrum allocation scheme in (Kotobi & Bilen, 2018) outperforms the conventional CR systems, in terms of the amount of transmitted data. However, this throughput improvement is achieved at a cost of higher power consumption. An interesting observation made in (Kotobi & Bilen, 2018) is that the proposed scheme can provide a higher throughput than the existing schemes even at the presence of fading conditions. This study provides a basic way of looking into the application of blockchains over the CRNs. It needs further improvement in terms of power consumption of battery-powered devices.

A CR Technique for Blockchain-Enabled IoV

Vehicular ad-hoc networks (VANETs) enable communication among on-road vehicles to provide safety to drivers in a vehicular environment by collecting and sharing traffic status with other vehicles. Since future VANETs are equipped with cognitive sensors and intelligent communication units, CRN-based Internet of vehicle (IoV) will provide a smart solution for high reliable and safety vehicular communications. Since secure communication is an essential feature to achieve high reliability, in (Rathee et al., 2020), a decision-making technique is developed to provide the security to IoV during spectrum sensing and information transmission using CRNs. Therein, in order to maintain transparency among the vehicles during data sharing, a Blockchain mechanism has been used.

In (Rathee et al., 2020), a fusion center (FC) is adopted to collect the spectrum sensing data of cognitive users (CUs). The FC analyzes the security and privacy measures of submitted data reports. In addition, the FC conducts an independent assessment of CUs' performance, analyzing the availability of ideal channels. The decision-making model can be represented hierarchically as shown in Figure 7 consisting of this decision-making scheme known as Technique for Order Preference by Similarity to the Ideal Solution (TOPSIS), and Blockchain framework. In this figure, $[\![CU_{ij}]\!]$ _ denotes the jth security parameter of ith CU. In the blockchain part, the records from each CU is stored on a network which will be further traced and analyzed by all the users. Therein, the records and data modifications by intruders can be identified by legitimate CUs. In order to increase the number of miners who perform the block verification, the proposed decision model provides various incentives in the form of extra credits or high trust ability.

Figure 7. Hierarchical model of Blockchain-based IoV proposed in (Rathee et al., 2020)

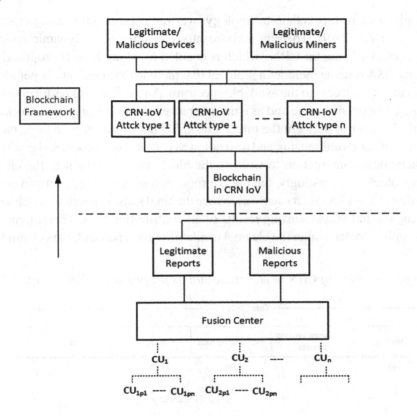

According to the simulation results analyzed based on a real-world dataset of San Francisco, the detection rate of malicious IoT devices is significantly higher when the proposed method is adopted than to a baseline (existing) method. The main reason for having a higher detection rate could be the identification process of legitimate IoT devices based on various interaction parameters such as interaction frequency, energy consumption, and the positive and negative interactions by legitimate or malicious devices and transmission time. Moreover, the results in (Rathee et al., 2020) shows that denial-of-service (DoS) threats can easily be measured by the proposed method through the blockchain mechanism. Due to the fact that the proposed approach is based on blockchain in the back-end the impact of the intrusion is also limited as the devices are unable to delete or alter the data. Furthermore, it is shown that when the network consists of a large number of IoT devices, the proposed phenomenon can provide better performance due to the parametric evaluation.

Blockchain Enabled Cooperative Spectrum Sensing

The application of blockchain technology over radio spectrum sensing is studied in (Weiss et al., 2019). Therein, a cooperative-sensing-based dynamic spectrum access (DSA) scheme for CRNs which is enabled by blockchain is proposed. The proposed DSA scheme includes a protocol that includes a time-slotted operation by the SUs to get an access to the available spectrum. An SU needs to perform the both roles, i.e., as a sensing node and as a miner or a verifier in the proposed blockchain network. In order to perform the miner's task, SU nodes gather up a large number of records of spectrum sensing and utilization as can fit into a block, and go through a mathematical computation to validate the block and combine it to the chain of previous blocks. Interestingly, the paper proposes a cooperative spectrum sensing mechanism for the secondary network where the final sensing result is concluded by analyzing the individual sensing results of all contributing SUs. Therein, majority rule is applied to determine the channel availability for a particular spectrum band.

Figure 8. Operation of CRN in each time slot as proposed in (Weiss et al., 2019)

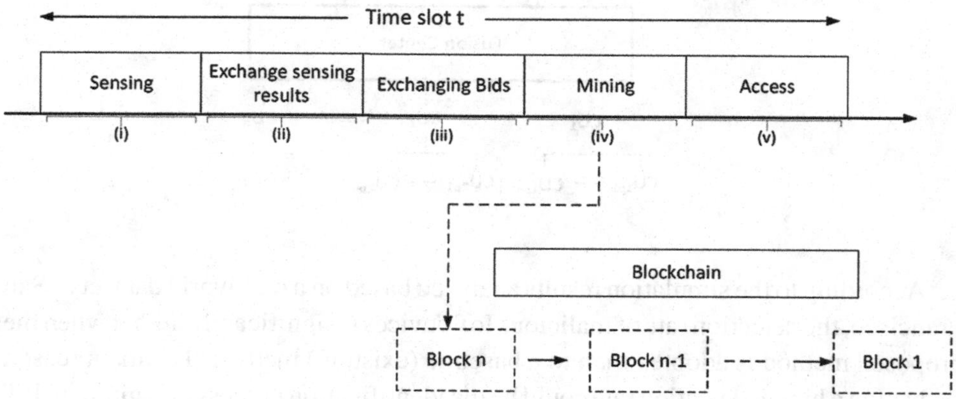

As shown in Figure 8, the cooperative spectrum sensing details are recorded in a blockchain after exchanging bids for spectrum access and performing proper verifications. In order to motivate the SUs to perform mining tasks, SUs who participate in the cooperative spectrum sensing will be rewarded with tokens that can be later utilized to bid for the spectrum access.

As already pointed out, when blockchains are enabled in the dynamic spectrum access, it is observed an increase of the power consumption as a major cost to achieve a higher throughput of CR networks. To further analyze this cost, a metric called sensing-mining energy efficiency is introduced in (Weiss et al., 2019) which measures the average transmission rate per unit of energy consumption used for sensing and mining. According to the obtained simulation results, it is observed that the sensing-mining energy efficiency does not grow monotonically with the increase of the sensing probability of SUs. Indeed, an optimal value of sensing probability corresponding to a given maximum energy efficiency can be noticed. Therefore, blockchain-enabled CRNs need to configure spectrum sensing related parameters of CRs without causing higher cost in terms of power consumption.

Deep Reinforcement Learning in CR-based Blockchain Networks

Different from the previously discussed research work, (Luong et al., 2019) proposes a deep reinforcement learning approach to derive an optimal transaction transmission policy for the secondary users in a CR-based blockchain network. Due to the lack of transparency and traceability as well as the limited security, traditional ways of maintaining IoT data in a CRN will not help to achieve 5G level service requirements. Therefore, to avoid those drawbacks, (Luong et al., 2019) adopts blockchain technology for collecting, storing, and processing the sensing data from the SUs. However, in order to make optimal decisions, only blockchain enabled secure mechanisms may not be sufficient. Consequently, the authors proposed a deep neural network (DNN) and Q-learning based machine learning approach to take optimal transmission decisions and channel selection.

In the proposed network model, an SU selects required channels and sends a transaction message which contains sensing data of the SU and a transaction fee that the SU is willing to pay to the blockchain mining pool via a base station. On the other hand, the adopted reinforcement learning method learns the environment with the objective of maximizing the number of successful transaction transmissions and minimizing the channel cost and the transaction fee. Furthermore, considering more practical situations, (Luong et al., 2019) does not completely neglect double-spending attacks in which transactions in a block can be maliciously modified during the transmission. During the performance evaluation, it can be noticed that the proposed machine learning approach enables the SU to achieve the higher number of successful transaction transmissions under a lower cost.

CRNs are susceptible for different kinds of threats and security problems that will affect the performance of the network. With blockchain technology, new security practices can be realized in the management of this CR spectrum. The goal of this section is to investigate the utility of blockchain in CRNs by referring to recently performed research work. A summary of the above discussed blockchain-based security practices in CRNs is listed in Table 5.

Table 5. Blockchain-based security practices in CRNs

Applicable Layer in CRNs	Reference	Blockchain Based Security Practices	Preventable Security Threats/ Attacks
MAC	(Weiss et al., 2019)	Eliminate the need for trusted third party for spectrum sensing	Tampering of sensing data
MAC, Network	(Kotobi & Bilen, 2018)	Blocking the access for malicious users to the network	Single-point attacks
Application, Network	(Rathee et al., 2020)	Secure data sharing process among each other and validate the legitimacy of new users	Denial-of service (DoS) attack, False report generation, Malicious nodes identification
Application, MAC	(Luong et al., 2019)	Enhance the security and guarantees the data integrity	Double-spending attack is analyzed, however, did not overcome completely

Blockchain Advances and Security Practices in DTNs

R.H. Memon et al. has proposed a blockchain-based DualFog-IoT architecture which segregates the Fog layer as Fog Cloud Cluster and Fog Mining Cluster. In here, the Fog Cloud Cluster entertain real-time and non real-time application requests similar to existing IoT architecture whereas Fog Mining Cluster is dedicated to perform the mining operations and to maintain the distributed ledger for delay tolerant blockchain application requests as shown in Figure 9.

Figure 9. Model for DualFog-IoT architecture

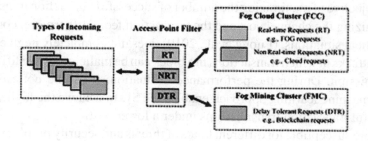

In machine-to-machine (M2M) communication, machine-type communication Devices (MTDs) are connected and communicated without any human intervention. Therefore, applications such as intelligent meters, environmental monitoring and e-health systems can allow relatively longer delays in data traffic. As an example, deploying smart meters may require data uploads or downloads that happen periodically. However, since the MTDs are equipped with limited battery power, data computing tasks cannot be cached, processed and executed solely on the local devices. Therefore, the best option to offload some of the storage and computation requirements at the edge of the network. On the other hand, security and reliability is also a prime concern for sensitive data of MTDs. Meng Li et al has proposed a joint optimization framework to make optimal decisions about caching servers and computing servers as well as to ensure the security in M2M communication networks based on dueling deep Q-network (Li,et al., 2020).

Blockchain Advances and Security Practices in OPPNETs

Normally, the mobile IoT oppnets are frequently suffer from to bandwidth and latency issues in cloud computing mainly due to poor wireless connectivity between the device and cloud. Rather than depending solely on centralized cloud platforms, it is vital to seek solutions that is plausible execute same network operations or services closer to the devices. Referring to that, an opportunistic collaborative mobile IoT design has been proposed in (Chamarajnagar & Ashok, 2018), to provide distributed computing solutions at the edge of the mobile IoT network using the blockchain framework. Similar to the previous work, in order to meet the stringent latency and bandwidth requirements of next-generation mobile networks, Fog-based Radio Access Network (F-RAN) has been proposed in (Jijin, Seet, & Joo Chong, 2019). However, this is not entirely identical to conventional F-RAN and virtual Fog Access Points (v-FAP) or service nodes formed dynamically with devices placed at the local edge are monitored by pre-defined physical or seed nodes. The integrations of Opportunistic Fog RAN (OF-RAN) with blockchain smart contracts guarantees the verifiable automation of physical processes at edge nodes.

FUTURE RESEARCH DIRECTIONS

It is evident that state-of-the art of blockchain technologies have made a huge impact to enhance the security in field such as healthcare, logistics, smart cities or energy management. However, these blockchain based IoT settings demand numerous technical requirements that differ from implementation of crypto-currencies to different aspects like energy efficiency of resource-constrained hardware or the need for specific architectures. Hence, it still needs to discover innovative research directions regarding seamless authentication, data privacy, easy deployment and self-maintenance along with safeguarding blockchain based networks against security attacks as stated below.

- **Data Management and Privacy, and Security Solutions:** The traditional online payments are usually visible to only transacting parties and to a distributor. But, since all transactions are shared by users in blockchain technique, it needs to ensure the privacy of transactions while nurturing the transparency.
- **Energy Efficiency:** Generally, blockchain based transactions use power-hungry mining processes and request more power requirement to setup point-to-point (P2P) links among edge devices. Therefore, ensuring the energy efficiency in blockchain based applications are utterly important characteristic.
- **Multi-chain Management:** The possibility of dealing multiple networks simultaneously would enable to provide more flexibility in network management.
- **Sustainability of the Blockchain Protocols:** More and more protocol suits are requisite to attract the claims of diverse applications by optimizing the throughput and latency of blockchain networks while regulating the blockchain size, bandwidth and infrastructure required.
- **Big Data and Artificial Intelligence:** The adaptation of artificial intelligence solutions backed by blockchain can be used to exploit smart contracts as well as routing autonomous drones for allowing real-time implementations.

CONCLUSION

Modern and future communication networks will grow up to billions of interactions among machines and sensors. Moreover, future wireless networks are becoming increasingly heterogeneous and complicated due to a growing need for ubiquitous access for various data sources, which is enabled by advances in modern technologies. Since those networks highly utilize the existing wireless sensor technologies, inherently it remains exposed to privacy as well as security threats. Wireless nodes in SDNs, WSNs as well as CRNs characteristically are considered to be prone to attacks such as distributed denial-of-service. Moreover, intelligent wireless nodes in those networks are mostly controlled on cloud environments. Such centralized architecture also undergoes single point of failure and further adds to vulnerability.

However, prevention of the drawbacks associated with security, privacy and vulnerability aspects has become one of the main challenges for those networks. This chapter explores existing studies which discuss how to add blockchains to distributed systems implemented in SDNs, WSNs and CRNs which can make network operations more secure, autonomous, flexible, and profitable. Blockchain provides those networks security, anonymity, and data integrity without the involvement of a third party.

In addition, blockchain applications over delay tolerant and opportunistic mobile networks are also discussed in brief. The research works presented in this chapter show that blockchain can serve as a method to log data in a form highly resistant to tampering and as a way to combat the introduction of malicious users into SDN, WSN and CRN networks.

REFERENCES

Ali, S., Wang, G., Bhuiyan, M. Z. A., & Jiang, H. (2018). Secure data provenance in cloud-centric internet of things via blockchain smart con-tracts. In 2018 IEEE Smart-world, Ubiquitous Intelligence Computing, Advanced Trusted Computing, Scalable Computing Communications, Cloud Big Data Computing, Internet of People and Smart City Innovation (smart-world/scalcom/uic/atc/cbdcom/iop/sci) (pp. 991-998). Academic Press.

Aujla, G. S., Singh, M., Bose, A., Kumar, N., Han, G., & Buyya, R. (2020). BlockSDN: Blockchain-as-a-service for software defined networking in smart city applications. *IEEE Network, 34*(2), 83–91. doi:10.1109/MNET.001.1900151

Chamarajnagar, R., & Ashok, A. (2018). Opportunistic mobile Iot with blockchain based collaboration. In *2018 IEEE Global Communications Conference* (pp. 1-6). 10.1109/GLOCOM.2018.8647756

Chowdhury, M., Kader, M. F., & Asaduzzaman, A. (2013). Security issues in wireless sensor networks: A survey. *International Journal of Future Generation Communication and Networking, 6*(5), 97–116. doi:10.14257/ijfgcn.2013.6.5.10

Cui, Z., Xue, F., Zhang, S., Cai, X., Cao, Y., Zhang, W., & Chen, J. (2020). A hybrid blockchain-based identity authentication scheme for multi-WSN. *IEEE Transactions on Services Computing, 13*(2), 241–251. doi:10.1109/TSC.2020.2964537

Faizullah, S., Khan, M. A., Alzahrani, A., & Khan, I. (2020). *Permissioned blockchain-based security for SDN in IoT cloud networks.* arXiv preprint arXiv:2002.00456.

Feghali, A., Kilany, R., & Chamoun, M. (2015). SDN security problems and solutions analysis. In *2015 International Conference on Protocol Engineering and New Technologies of Distributed Systems* (pp. 1-5). Academic Press.

Gao, J., Agyekum, K. O.-B. O., Sifah, E. B., Acheampong, K. N., Xia, Q., Du, X., & Xia, H. (2019). A blockchain-SDN-enabled Internet of vehicles environment for fog computing and 5G networks. *IEEE Internet of Things Journal, 7*(5), 4278–4291. doi:10.1109/JIOT.2019.2956241

Gómez-Arevalillo, A. de la R., & Papadimitratos, P. (2017). Blockchain-based Public Key Infrastructure for Inter-Domain Secure Routing. In *International Workshop on Open Problems in Network Security* (pp. 20-38). Academic Press.

Haseeb, K., Islam, N., Almogren, A., & Ud Din, I. (2019). Intrusion prevention framework for secure routing in wsn-based mobile internet of things. *IEEE Access: Practical Innovations, Open Solutions, 7*, 185496–185505. doi:10.1109/ACCESS.2019.2960633

Hindia, M. N., Qamar, F., Ojukwu, H., Dimyati, K., Al-Samman, A. M., & Amiri, I. S. (2020). On platform to enable the cognitive radio over 5G networks. *Wireless Personal Communications, 113*(2), 1241–1262. doi:10.100711277-020-07277-3

Jaballah, W. B., Conti, M., & Lal, C. (2019). *A survey on software-defined vanets: benets, challenges, and future directions.* arXiv preprint arXiv:1904.04577.

Jiasi, W., Jian, W., Jia-Nan, L., & Yue, Z. (2019). *Secure software-defined networking based on blockchain.* arXiv preprint arXiv:1906.04342.

Jijin, J., Seet, B., & Joo Chong, P. H. (2019). Blockchain enabled opportunistic fog-based radio access network: A position paper. In *2019 29th International Telecommunication Networks and Applications Conference* (pp. 1-3). Academic Press.

Kim, T., Goyat, R., Rai, M. K., Kumar, G., Buchanan, W. J., Saha, R., & Thomas, R. (2019). A novel trust evaluation process for secure localization16 using a decentralized blockchain in wireless sensor networks. *IEEE Access: Practical Innovations, Open Solutions, 7*, 184133–184144. doi:10.1109/ACCESS.2019.2960609

Kotobi, K., & Bilen, S. G. (2018). Secure blockchains for dynamic spectrum access: A decentralized database in moving cognitive radio networks enhances security and user access. *IEEE Vehicular Technology Magazine, 13*(1), 32–39. doi:10.1109/MVT.2017.2740458

Kreutz, D., Ramos, F. M., & Verissimo, P. (2013). Towards secure and dependable software-defined networks. In *2nd ACM SIGCOMM Workshop on Hot Topics in Software Defined Networking* (pp. 55-60). 10.1145/2491185.2491199

Kumar, R., Hasan, M., Padhy, S., Evchenko, K., Piramanayagam, L., Mohan, S., & Bobba, R. B. (2017). End-to-end network delay guarantees for real-time systems using SDN. In *2017 EEE Real-Time Systems Symposium* (pp. 231-242). 10.1109/RTSS.2017.00029

Li, M., Yu, F. R., Si, P., Wu, W., & Zhang, Y. (2020). Resource optimization for delay-tolerant data in blockchain-enabled iot with edge computing: A deep reinforcement learning approach. *IEEE Internet of Things Journal, 7*(10), 9399–9412. doi:10.1109/JIOT.2020.3007869

Liu, S., Reiter, M. K., & Sekar, V. (2017). Flow reconnaissance via timing attacks on SDN switches. In *2017 IEEE 37th International Conference on Distributed Computing Systems* (pp. 196-206). 10.1109/ICDCS.2017.281

Liyanage, M., Ylianttila, M., & Gurtov, A. (2016). *Improving the tunnel management performance of secure VPLS architectures with SDN. 2016 13th IEEE Annual Consumer Communications & Networking Conference.*

Luong, N. C., Anh, T. T., Binh, H. T. T., Niyato, D., Kim, D. I., & Liang, Y.-C. (2019). Joint transaction transmission and channel selection in cognitive radio based blockchain networks: A deep reinforcement learning approach. In *IEEE International Conference on Acoustics, Speech and Signal Processing* (pp. 8409-8413). 10.1109/ICASSP.2019.8683228

Memon, R. A., Li, J. P., Nazeer, M. I., Khan, A. N., & Ahmed, J. (2019). Dualfog-Iot: Additional fog layer for solving blockchain integration prob-lem in Internet of things. *IEEE Access: Practical Innovations, Open Solutions, 7,* 169073–169093. doi:10.1109/ACCESS.2019.2952472

Munsub Ali, H., Liu, J., & Ejaz, W. (2020). Planning capacity for 5G and beyond wireless networks by discrete fireworks algorithm with ensemble of local search methods. *EURASIP Journal on Wireless Communications and Networking, 185,* 1–24.

Nanthini, S. B., Hemalatha, M., Manivannan, D., & Devasena, L. (2014). Attacks in cognitive radio networks (CRN) - a survey. *Indian Journal of Science and Technology, 7*(4), 530–536. doi:10.17485/ijst/2014/v7i4.18

Ramezan, G., & Leung, C. (2018). A Blockchain-Based Contractual Routing Protocol for the Internet of Things Using Smart Contracts. *Wireless Communications and Mobile Computing, 4029591,* 1–14. Advance online publication. doi:10.1155/2018/4029591

Rathee, G., Ahmad, F., Kurugollu, F., Azad, M. A., Iqbal, R., & Imran, M. (2020). *CRT-BIoV: A cognitive radio technique for blockchain-enabled Internet of vehicles. IEEE Transactions on Intelligent Transportation Systems.*

Sharma, P. K., Singh, S., Jeong, Y.-S., & Park, J. H. (2017). Distblocknet: A distributed blockchains-based secure SDN architecture for IoT networks. *IEEE Communications Magazine*, *55*(9), 78–85. doi:10.1109/MCOM.2017.1700041

She, W., Liu, Q., Tian, Z., Chen, J., Wang, B., & Liu, W. (2019). Blockchain trust model for malicious node detection in wireless sensor networks. *IEEE Access: Practical Innovations, Open Solutions*, *7*, 38947–38956. doi:10.1109/ACCESS.2019.2902811

Steichen, M., Hommes, S., & State, R. (2017, September). ChainGuard—A firewall for blockchain applications using SDN with OpenFlow. In 2017 Principles. Systems and Applications of IP Telecommunications. Academic Press.

Tiberti, W., Carmenini, A., Pomante, L., & Cassioli, D. (2020). A light weight blockchain-based technique for anti-tampering in wireless sensor networks. In *2020 23rd Euromicro Conference on Digital System Design* (pp. 577-582). Academic Press.

Tselios, C., Politis, I., & Kotsopoulos, S. (2017). Enhancing SDN security for IoT-related deployments through blockchain. In *2017 IEEE Conference on Network Function Virtualization and Software Defined Networks* (pp. 303-308). 10.1109/NFV-SDN.2017.8169860

Weiss, M. B. H., Werbach, K., Sicker, D. C., & Bastidas, C. E. C. (2019). On the application of blockchains to spectrum management. *IEEE Transactions on Cognitive Communications and Networking*, *5*(2), 193–205. doi:10.1109/TCCN.2019.2914052

Werbach, K. (Ed.). (2018). *The blockchain and the new architecture of trust*. MIT Press. doi:10.7551/mitpress/11449.001.0001

Xu, C., Wang, K., Li, P., Guo, S., Luo, J., Ye, B., & Guo, M. (2019). Making big data open in edges: A resource-efficient blockchain-based approach. *IEEE Transactions on Parallel and Distributed Systems*, *30*(4), 870–882. doi:10.1109/TPDS.2018.2871449

Yang, J., He, S., Xu, Y., Chen, L., & Ren, J. (2019). A Trusted Routing Scheme Using Blockchain and Reinforcement Learning for Wireless Sensor Networks. *Sensors (Basel)*, *19*(4), 970. doi:10.339019040970 PMID:30823560

Yazdinejad, A., Parizi, R. M., Dehghantanha, A., & Choo, K.-K. R. (2019). Blockchain-enabled authentication handover with ecient privacy protection in SDN-based 5G networks. *IEEE Transactions on Network Science and Engineering*.

Zeng, Y., Zhang, X., Akhtar, R., & Wang, C. (2018). A blockchain-based scheme for secure data provenance in wireless sensor networks. In *2018 14th International Conference on Mobile Ad-hoc and Sensor Networks* (pp. 13-18). 10.1109/MSN.2018.00009

Zia, T., & Zomaya, A. (2006, October). Security issues in wireless sensor networks. In *2006 International Conference on Systems and Networks Communications (ICSNC'06)* (pp. 40-40). 10.1109/ICSNC.2006.66

ADDITIONAL READING

Banerjee, M., Lee, J., & Choo, K.-K. R. (2018). A blockchain future for internet of things security: A position paper. *Digital Communications and Networks*, *4*(3), 149–160. doi:10.1016/j.dcan.2017.10.006

Casino, F., Dasaklis, T. K., & Patsakis, C. (2019). A systematic literature review of blockchain-based applications: Current status, classification and open issues. *Telematics and Informatics*, *36*, 55–81. doi:10.1016/j.tele.2018.11.006

Chanson, M., Bogner, A., Bilgeri, D., Fleisch, E., & Wortmann, F. (2019). Blockchain for the IoT: Privacy-preserving protection of sensor data. *Journal of the Association for Information Systems*, *20*(9), 1274–1309. doi:10.17705/1jais.00567

Dai, H., Zheng, Z., & Zhang, Y. (2019). Blockchain for internet of things: A survey. *IEEE Internet of Things Journal*, *6*(5), 8076–8094. doi:10.1109/JIOT.2019.2920987

Jiasi, W., Jian, W., Jia-Nan, L., & Yue, Z. (2019). Secure software-defined networking based on blockchain.

Minoli, D., & Occhiogrosso, B. (2018). Blockchain mechanisms for IoT security. *Internet of Things*, *1-2*, 1–13. doi:10.1016/j.iot.2018.05.002

Mohsin, A., Zaidan, A., Zaidan, B., Albahri, O., Albahri, A., Alsalem, M., & Mohammed, K. (2019). Blockchain authentication of network applications: Taxonomy, classification, capabilities, open challenges, motivations, recommendations and future directions. *Computer Standards & Interfaces*, *64*, 41–60. doi:10.1016/j.csi.2018.12.002

Raju, S., Boddepalli, S., Gampa, S., Yan, Q., & Deogun, J. S. (2017). Identity management using blockchain for cognitive cellular networks. *In 2017 IEEE International Conference on Communications* (p. 1-6) 10.1109/ICC.2017.7996830

KEY TERMS AND DEFINITIONS

Consensus Mechanism: An agreement in relation to a single data value made by all members in a group of a blockchain based system such as with crypto-currencies.

Crypto-Currency: This a digital currency which is used to acquire services through online. Therfore, a decentralized ledger is used to verify and execute online transactions securely.

Data Provenance: A piece of metadata or records that can be used to trace the validity of source data including all transition steps from the origin to the current location.

Fog Computing: This enables computing functions at the edge of network or closer to the source of data, as a result, it allows to get rid of the necessity for cloud based storing requirement.

Reinforcement Learning: An area of Machine learning used by software agents to maximize or determine the best possible solution based on cumulative reward in a specific environment.

Software-Defined Networking: This a centralized controller that enables the management of network functions using software applications by separating the control plane by the data plane.

Spectrum Sensing: A periodic monitoring process regarding a specific frequency band to determine whether to identify status of the presence or absence of primary users.

Chapter 2
Towards Utilizing Blockchain for Countering Distributed Denial-of-Service (DDoS)

Rochak Swami
National Institute of Technology, Kurukshetra, India

Mayank Dave
 https://orcid.org/0000-0003-4748-0753
National Institute of Technology, Kurukshetra, India

Virender Ranga
 https://orcid.org/0000-0002-2046-8642

National Institute of Technology, Kurukshetra, India

Nikhil Tripathi
Technical University of Darmstadt, Germany

Abhijith Kalayil Shaji
Otto von Guericke University Magdeburg, Germany

Avani Sharma
Malaviya National Institute of Technology, Jaipur, India

ABSTRACT

Distributed denial of service (DDoS) attacks have been a matter of serious concern for network administrators in the last two decades. These attacks target the resources such as memory, CPU cycles, and network bandwidth in order to make them unavailable for the benign users, thereby violating availability, one of the components of cyber security. With the existence of DDoS-as-a-service on internet, DDoS attacks have now become more lucrative for the adversaries to target a potential victim. In this work, the authors focus on countering DDoS attacks using one of the latest technologies called blockchain. In inception phase, utilizing blockchain for countering DDoS attacks has proved to be quite promising. The authors also compare existing blockchain-based defense mechanisms to counter DDoS attacks and analyze them. Towards the end of the work, they also discuss possible future research directions in this domain.

DOI: 10.4018/978-1-7998-7589-5.ch002

INTRODUCTION

Distributed denial of service (DDoS) is considered one of the most devastating attacks nowadays. DDoS attacks attempt to disrupt the normal working of the network by targeting a server, service, or network (Mirkovic et al., 2004). It forwards a massive flood of internet traffic towards the target and makes the normal users suffering from denying the service of the network's resources. DDoS attacks target the system's resources, such as bandwidth, CPU, and memory. These attacks can be utilized in both wired and wireless network scenarios. DDoS attacks can create massive destruction in the network in a short duration. Therefore, providing efficient defense solutions against these attacks to secure the network is very important. Recently, several defense mechanisms have been proposed (Elsayed et al., 2020; Tripathi et al., 2016; Tripathi et al., 2018). DDoS attacks are increasing rapidly with time. The average size of DDoS attacks was 26.37 Gbps in 2018 as per a DDoS attack statistics report provided by Lawrence Abrams (Abrams, 2018). The largest DDoS attack had been reported on "Github" with a very high rate of 1.35 Tbps before 2020 in the history (Sam Kottler, 2018). However, the year 2020 is proving itself a more successful year for DDoS attackers and hackers. In February 2020, Amazon Web Services (AWS) was targeted with a rate of 2.3 Tbps DDoS attack that was defended by AWS shield – a security service to protect against DDoS attacks (Cimpanu, 2020). This attack has been reported as the largest DDoS attack ever in history. In 2020, DDoS attackers have become more active that increased the chances of attacks. DDoS attackers are also taking advantage of exploiting the global pandemic "COVID-19" (Wikipedia, 2020). Most of the people are working on a remote basis that requires online or internet access. Every person/organization is dependent on online services for their daily life routine. These attacks target the online services and overwhelm it with a large volume of network traffic. Government and educational organizations have also been targeted during COVID-19 lockdown with higher rates (Palmer, 2020). In March 2020, servers of an agency "US department of health and human service (HHS)" were exhausted for a duration of time (Bannister, 2020). Preventing DDoS attacks completely may not always be possible, but the impact of the attack can be reduced. Research work should be done to mitigate these destructive attacks and efficient attack defense systems should be developed. In the last few years, a new trending technology named "blockchain" (Li et al., 2020) has been introduced to prevent and mitigate the DDoS attack. Blockchain is basically a collection of records. These records are also called blocks and hence the reason for its name that is blockchain. The blocks are interconnected with each other using cryptographic techniques. Blockchain and DDoS work in the opposite way. Blockchain is a distributed technology, whereas DDoS attack is based on centralized server. As blockchain is a distributed/decentralized technology, it allocates the information to the different nodes, which makes it difficult for attackers to destroy the functioning of the whole network by targeting a specific system. Attackers have to gain access to the nodes to make the attack successful. This process makes the attack launching difficult and time-consuming. Another advantage of blockchain in reducing the success of DDoS attacks is that it stores the information/data on ledgers, which uses encrypted blocks. This feature denies the third party to access or make any updating, which makes it more secure. Blockchain uses key management (private keys) to permit the users for communicating with each other. Therefore, blockchain can play an important role in mitigating DDoS attacks.

This chapter presents various existing blockchain-based defense mechanisms against DDoS attacks and possible research challenges. The remaining chapter is organized as follows. Section 2 defines DDoS and its various types. A study related to blockchain and its different types are explained in Section 3. Section 4 discusses various existing blockchain-based defense mechanisms against DDoS. Section 5 presents some possible research challenges in the blockchain-based defense mechanisms. Lastly, the chapter is concluded in Section 6.

DISTRIBUTED DENIAL OF SERVICE ATTACKS

Definition of DDoS Attack

A distributed denial-of-service (DDoS) (Swami et al., 2020) attack is a malicious attempt to disrupt regular traffic of a targeted server, service, or network by overwhelming the target or its surrounding infrastructure with a flood of internet traffic. These attacks achieve high throughput by utilizing multiple compromised computers or networked resources like IoT devices (Cloudflare, 2020). Most of the targeted resources are bandwidth, CPU usage, and memory of the system (server). It aims to deny the services for legitimate customers, which degrades the performance of the network system. Figure 1 shows a general structure of DDoS attack.

The primary goal of DDoS attack is to exhaust or overload the resources of the target. The impact of DDoS varies from a minor inconvenience to severe financial losses for enterprises that rely on their online availability. The attackers' motivations are diverse, ranging from simple fun (hacktivist) to financial gain (business competition) and ideology (political, terrorist, etc.) (Radwire ltd, 2019). DDoS attack accounts for around 8% of all cyber-attacks in the previous year. From recent studies, the trend shows that DDoS is continuously evolving in terms of frequency, volume, and duration. For example, over 80 percent of DDoS attacks in 2018 were of short durations and lasted less than 10 minutes, but of these attacks around, 20 percent of DDoS victims were targeted again within 24 hours. The size of DDoS attacks increased 73 percent in Q1 2019 versus Q1 2018 (Infosec newsflash, 2019). One reason for the increase in the volume of the attacks is the availability of weekly secured end devices, IoT devices, and underground marketplaces offering for sale access to compromised systems. Table 1 presents some of the most famous and recent DDoS attacks.

Figure 1. Structure of DDoS Attack

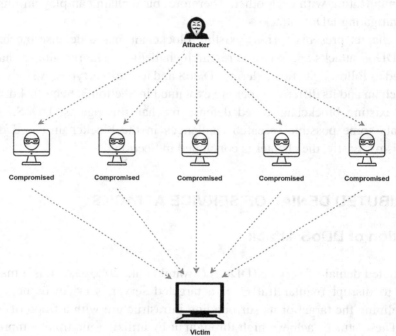

Some Major Reasons and Motivations Behind DDoS Attacks

There are various reasons for DDoS attacks. Some common reasons are discussed here (Douligeris et al., 2004; Mirkovic et al., 2004).

- **Limited Internet Resources:** Every internet component, like network, host, or service has, limited power and size of resources. The resources are utilized by several users that may cause DDoS attack.
- **Interdependent Internet Security:** Each system is connected with different systems on the network via internet. A particular system may be highly secured. However, the possibility that a particular system is being targeted by a DDoS attacker completely depends on the global internet security.

- **Many against a few:** In case of attackers having more resources than the resources of the victim, there are higher chances of DDoS attack.

Table 1. Some of the Most Recent DDoS attacks

Attack Month/Year	Attack Name	Victim Website	Attack Description	Attack Impact
February, 2020	AWS attack	Amazon Web Services	CLDAP reflection attack with a massive volume of 2.3 Tbps	3 days of elevated threat within a week before it was mitigated
June, 2019	Telegram attack	Telegram (an encrypted messaging service)	Attack measuring 200-400Gbps. DDoS type not available	Messaging services of over 200m users across the Americas as well as in some other countries were affected
February, 2018	GitHub attack	GitHub (a coding website for software developers)	DDoS with a traffic rate of 1.3Tbps with packet rate of 126.9MPPS. Amplification type attack using memcached over UDP was used.	GitHub.com was unavailable for several minutes before it was mitigated by the Github DDoS protection service.
October, 2016	Dyn Attack	Dyn – a domain name service (DNS) provider	Botnets created by malware mira was utilized to target Dyn, a major DNS provider. TCP Syn flood was used to target 20 data centers of Dyn.	Created service disruption for many sites, including AirBnB, Netflix, PayPal, Visa, Amazon, The New York TImes, Reddit, and GitHub
December, 2015	BBC attack	BBC news website	Attack of about 602 Gbps in size was directed towards BBC servers.	The services of BBC was unavailable for 24 hours, even though the attack lasted less than 20 minutes only.
March, 2013	Spamhaus	Spamhaus (an anti-spam organization)	Layer 3 attack was devised against spamhouse datacenter. DNS reflection attack with Initial traffic of 10Gbps and peak of up to 120Gbps was attained.	Spamhouse data centers access to internet was blocked for hours. The attackers came with full force around 48hours later and the service was disrupted until the Cloudflare Anycast based load balancing was implemented.

- **Competitive Advantage:** Some online serviced oriented business companies launch DDoS attacks towards their competitive business to slow down their websites. This results in crashing the website, dropping the legitimate customer's requests that cause a financial loss and tarnishing the image of that brand. In that case, customers approach the competitive website.

- **Political Issues:** Nowadays, DDoS attacks are happening between countries and governments. The new battlefield is "Web". The government sites can be targeted in the same country or other countries. It is trending to use the web for communicating by different political parties or governments. Therefore, government targets other opposing parties via DDoS attacks. Citizens also target their government websites if they are not happy with the government's work.

- **Personal Enjoyment:** Some hackers use different types of latest DDoS attack tools to launch the attack and to show their hacking skills. Whereas, some hackers target the websites for their personal fun and to disturb the functioning of the website.

Classification of DDoS Attacks

There are different types of DDoS attacks utilized for various purposes. Figure 2 presents a classification of DDoS attacks. DDoS attacks are classified as per the type of consumed resources, i.e., bandwidth depletion and resource depletion (processing power and memory) (Swami et al., 2019)

- **Bandwidth Depletion:** The bandwidth depletion attack is an important category of DDoS attacks. As per the attack, a huge amount of network traffic is sent to the network that consumes the network bandwidth. The consumed bandwidth drops the requests from the legitimate users and degrades the performance of the network. Bandwidth depletion attacks are classified into two different types that are direct flood attack and amplification attack.
  - **Direct Flood Attack:** This is one of the most common and easy to perform type of DDoS attacks. In this kind of attack, the attackers send a large number of packets to the target device to exhaust its bandwidth or send a large number of packets to a network segment with the aim of creating network congestion. The availability of IoT devices and botnets for rentals have made this attack type a more common type. UDP flood and ICMP flood are types of direct flood attack.
  - **Amplification Attack:** This kind of DDoS attack involves an amplification factor with which the attack gets multiplied. This occurs when a user sends several requests to a server and the server replies with a much larger number of replies to the target device. Typically, the attacker will spoof the source IP in the packet headers, resulting in a large volume of data packets to the victim. Some examples of amplification attacks are smurf, fraggle, NTP, and DNS amplification.

- **Resource Depletion:** This category of DDoS attacks targets the major resources of the system such as memory, CPU (processing power), etc. Resource depletion attacks try to consume the resources completely so that normal users will have to suffer due to the unavailability of the resources. There are two different types of resource depletion attacks that are protocol exploitation and malformed packet attack.

    ○ **Protocol Exploit Attack:** This kind of attack targets the weakness of the protocols in L3 and L4 of the TCP/IP stack. The attackers exploit a specific feature or bug in the protocol installed on the target device in order to exhaust its resources. There are some examples of protocol exploit attacks that are push + ack, tcp-syn, http flood, and sip flood.

    ○ **Malformed Packet Attack:** In this kind of attack, the attackers transmit IP packets, which are either malformed or incomplete to the target device, thereby causing the target device to perform abnormally or even crash while processing it. Examples of malformed packet attacks are teardrop, ping of death, and UDP fragmentation.

Figure 2. Taxonomy of DDoS Attacks

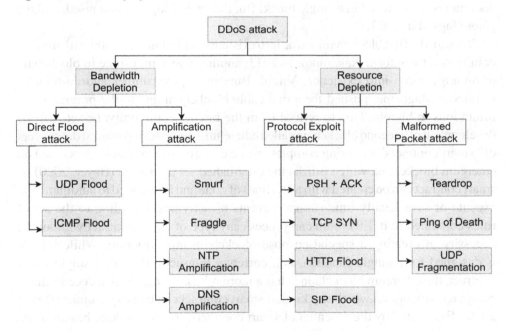

BLOCKCHAIN TECHNOLOGY

The blockchain is an undeniably ingenious invention. It is a system of recording information in which the history of any digital asset is unalterable and transparent by the use of decentralization and cryptographic hash technology. A blockchain alias distributed ledger is a digital ledger of transactions that is duplicated and distributed among the computer systems in the entire blockchain network (Euromoney, 2020). Each block in the blockchain contains several transactions, and once a new block is added to the blockchain, a copy is added to every participant's ledger. The working flow of blockchain is explained in Figure 3. The birth of blockchain is generally considered to be in late 2008 with the publishing of a whitepaper introducing a decentralized P2P electronic cash system called bitcoin using the pseudonym Satoshi Nakamoto. The introduction of Bitcoin was clearly a significant milestone and provided further advancement in the field of P2P and blockchain itself. But like many other innovations, bitcoin is also built on previous technologies (Beyer, 2020).

The concept of blockchain was first described in 1991 (17 years before the bitcoin paper) by scientists Stuart Haber and W. Scott Stornetta. They introduced a system using a cryptographically secured chain of blocks to store time-stamped documents, which in 1992 was further enhanced with Merkel trees (Haber et al., 1991). This enhancement improved the efficiency of the system by allowing multiple documents to be stored in a single block. But this technology went unused, and the patent lapsed in 2003.

Bitcoin, the first blockchain, came into existence on 3rd January 2009 with the first coin mined by Satoshi Nakamoto. In 2013, another major milestone in blockchain technology came into existence. Vitalik Buterin, a programmer and co-founder of bitcoin Magazine, pushed for a malleable blockchain due to the programming limitations in bitcoin. Due to refusal from the bitcoin community, he sets off the development of a second blockchain called ethereum. Ethereum introduced the concept of "smart contracts" - a turing complete piece of software that can be processed on ethereum blockchain, which fulfills the established set of criteria (Beyer, 2020). A smart contract can be created with a few lines of code and is intended to automatically execute or save legally time-stamped events or activities according to the set of rules contained in it. Ethereum can process any type of smart contract without the necessity of creating a special-purpose blockchain infrastructure. While bitcoin is designed for a single function, i.e., currency transactions, with a single smart contract, the ethereum blockchain is has a more robust design using a decentralized computer network on which any kind of smart contract can be programmed (Beyer, 2020). Fascinated by the potential of smart contracts, this technology has attracted the attention of many major IT giants. Enterprise Ethernet Alliance is one such formal organizations formed by members from leading IT companies for further advancement of the technology (Medium, 2020).

Figure 3. Working of Blockchain

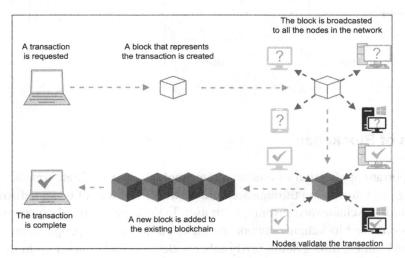

Blockchain architecture is very broadly used in the financial industry. However, these days, this technology is widely applied not only for cryptocurrencies but also for fields like Insurance, Blockchain Internet-of-Things (IoT), Asset Management, Supply Chain Sensors, etc. The structure of blockchain is a back-linked list of blocks of transactions in a particular order. These lists can be stored as a flat file (.txt format) or in the form of a simple database. Two vital data structures used in blockchain are:

- **Pointers** - value simply refers/points to another value stored somewhere else. Hash Pointer just adds the hash of the value along with reference to make the data temper proof.
- **Linked list** - is a data structure to store a sequence of blocks where each block stores some data and the blocks are linked using a pointer.

Figure 4 presents the structure of blockchain, which is based on two data structures, i.e., pointer and linked list.

Figure 4. Blockchain structure

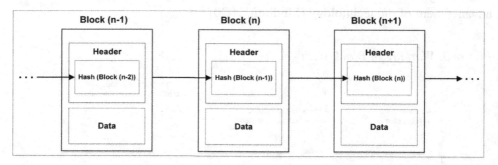

Types of Blockchain

An important application of blockchain technology is to facilitate transactions or exchange of information through a secure network. The way of using a distributed ledger or blockchain varies from user to user. In the case of digital cryptocurrency like bitcoin, the blockchain network should be public because people from all over the world can become a node, verify other nodes and trade bitcoins. On the other hand, network in baking sector should be restricted towards the users to maintain the confidentiality of information. Broadly, blockchain is classified as public and private blockchain. To get advantages of both public and private blockchain, researchers have started working over consortium/hybrid model.

1. Public Blockchain

It is a permission-less and restriction-less distributed ledger system of transaction blocks in which any user, having accessibility to internet, can enter into the blockchain system to be its part and authorized entity. The users can also access the previous and present transaction records, involve in proof-of-work for transaction verification, and mine the blocks. The basic application is to mine and exchange cryptocurrency. It is a secure system where users have to follow security rules and policies. However, security breaches when participants deny obeying the security protocols. Some of the examples of public blockchain are Bitcoin, Ethereum, and Litecoin. A comparison study of Bitcoin, Ethereum, and Litecoin is shown in Table 2.

Table 2. Comparative Study of Bitcoin, Ethereum, and Litecoin

Blockchain	Bitcoin	Ethereum	Litecoin
Founder	Satoshi Nakamoto	Vitalik Buterin	Chris Larsen & McCaled
Description	Decentralized cryptocurrency used in a peer to peer network	Decentralized platform that runs smart contracts	Like Bitcoin, it is a peer-to-peer cryptocurrency and open source software project released under the MIT/X11 License
Founded	January 2009	January 2014	October 2011
Market cap(approx)	56%	13%	3%
Maximum amount	21 million Bitcoins	18 million	84 million units
Transactions made via	Blockchain/mining	Decentralized program/Smart Contract	Mining based on less-complex algorithms
Transaction Time	10 minutes	12-14 seconds	2.5 minutes
Hashing Algorithm	SHA-256	Ethash	Scrypt
Mining	Processor intensive	Memory Intensive	Memory Intensive
Price per USD (till 2018)	BTC/USD: 17,571	Eth/USD: 610	LTC/USD: 332

(SEPA, 2017)

2. Private Blockchain

The private Blockchain is a permissioned and restrictive network which is generally used within an enterprise/organization. In this, only selected members are involved in the blockchain activities. To maintain and manage the permission and authorization, a controlling entity is deployed. Generally, such a type of network is used for the voting systems, digital identity, and supply chain management. Examples are Multichain and Hyperledger that are compared in Table 3.

3. Consortium Blockchain

Consortium blockchain has semi-decentralized behaviour, which is managed by a group of entities. They work in a slightly different manner from private blockchains. The key difference between private and consortium blockchain is that former are handled by multiple organizations, but the latter is handled by a single organization. Multiple organizations work as a single node and can exchange data. This type of blockchain technology is used by banking sectors and government agencies.

Table 3. Comparison between Multichain and Hyperledger

Blockchain	Multichain	Hyperledger Fabric
Description	Open platform for blockchain applications	An open source initiative to advance blockchain technology
Founded	June 2015	December 2015
Model	Adaptive runtime	Endorsement
Language	Javascript	Go+Java+Javascript
Speed	~1s	~10s
Hash & DS	SHA-256, ECDSA (secp256k1)	SHA-256, ECDSA (p-256, p-385, p-521)

(Ismailisufi et al., 2020; Cachin et al., 2016)

4. Hybrid Blockchain

It combines features of both private and public blockchain. In such type of system, participants have control over access permission for the stored data in blockchain. Instead of making all the data public, only a selected part of information/data is made public, keeping the confidential one as private. Verification of transactions that happened in a private region is done in the same area. However, users have the privilege to send the transactions to the public network for verification. An example of a hybrid system based blockchain is Dragonchain.

BLOCKCHAIN-BASED DDoS MITIGATION APPROACHES

Blockchain is one of the most trending technologies, which is being used in the field of cyber-security for preventing attacks. Researchers are using blockchain due to its distributive architecture that can help in reducing the chances of DDoS attacks. Mostly, existing works based on blockchain have utilized public blockchain. In this section, some major works for defending DDoS attacks using blockchain are discussed.

Rodrigues et al. (2019a) proposed a collaborative mechanism between autonomous systems and customers for the mitigation of DDoS attacks. The main components of this approach are Autonomous systems and Customers, a part of the SDN concept, and Smart contracts from blockchain technology. In this implementation, the Ethereum blockchain is chosen as infrastructure for signaling due to its features like publicly available, smart contract generation is possible as well and a new block is created every 14 seconds. OpenFlow protocol of SDN is used as a monitoring framework at gateways to analyze the traffic. The participants of this system need to create a smart contract initially. While customers have the right to write into the blockchain, the ASes possess both writing and reading rights of the blockchain. If any AS or customer comes under DDoS attack, the list of IP addresses of the attackers is stored in the smart contract. The updated list of addresses will be received to the subscribed ASes to confirm the authenticity of the attack by analyzing the traffic and verifying the authenticity of the target. Once the addresses are confirmed, different mitigation strategies can be applied to prevent the attack according to the policies of the domain. The authors suggest near-source mitigation as an ideal strategy in these scenarios for the better health of the internet. This prevents the cost of forwarding packets, as a DDoS attack involves massive useless packets. An incentive mechanism is also proposed for mitigation in near-source to prevent domains from taking advantage of the cooperative defense.

Javaid *et al.* (Javaid et al., 2018) proposed a DoS/DDoS mitigation framework using blockchain for IoT devices. The proposed framework is based on Ethereum blockchain for the attack defense. The Ethereum blockchain is integrated with smart contract for defense. In this framework, IoT devices are registered to the servers for communicating with other IoT devices. A gas limit is assigned to the IoT device for working. The IoT device does not work on the expired limit. The server may deregister an IoT device anytime if it does not work correctly or its gas limit expires. The server also manages the creation and registration of smart contract. The address of a registered smart contract is broadcast to all the available IoT devices in the network. The contract maintains a trusted list that includes the registered IoT devices. The gas limit for each transaction in the contract is fixed at the time of smart contract initialization. The smart contract being the main component checks the IoT devices timely. The smart contract performs the authorization of the IoT devices. When an IoT device sends a message, smart contract checks its trusted node list. If the smart contract finds the address of IoT device in the trusted list, then only that IoT node's message is stored in the blockchain otherwise, the message is dropped.

The main advantage of the proposed framework is that the architecture has a distributed control. It means that a collapsed node cannot affect the working of the remaining system. The distributed architecture also decreases the burden of servers. The proposed system is capable of securing the server from flooding DDoS attacks. It works on the idea that the server does not get exhausted even if all the devices send the traffic at one time at the gas limit. If any of the IoT devices are compromised and acts as an attacker, it cannot work beyond the gas limit. The system provides both detection and mitigation.

Kataoka et al. (Kataoka et al., 2018) proposed a blockchain-based DDoS mitigation architecture using IoT devices. The mitigation mechanism is based on a trust list for traffic management. Trust list integrates the blockchain with SDN technology. It consists of three modules: (1) IoT servers, gateways, and validators, (2) IoT applications and devices, (3) edge networks. Trust list is preserved in the blockchain. It gives a feedback mechanism between all three components. The trust list allows only the trusted devices to be communicated. The trust list defines whether the device is trusted or not. It maintains two types of profiles, i.e., service profiles and device profiles. These profiles are spread in the network. The service profile stores the information related to the trusted IoT server, gateways, and validator. The information of trusted IoT applications and devices is placed in the device profile. SDN switches are connected at the edge network, which filters the malicious network traffic. The controller maintains synergy with the blockchain and accesses the information related to services and devices' profiles. IoT server, gateways, and validators maintain the data related to trusted services and devices. The controller sends flow rules to the switches to update them to block or allow the IoT traffic. The purpose of using a validator is to check the authenticity of the IoT devices. Therefore, it makes the DDoS attack restricted at the edge network. However, in the case of spoofed attack there may be security concerns.

Rodrigues et al. (Rodrigues et al., 2017b) proposed a new mechanism "Blockchain Signaling System" (BloSS) for DDoS defense in a cooperative network defense system. BloSS includes two major components, i.e., Smart contract (SC) and decentralized applications (dApp). SC shows how information is interchanged among autonomous systems. dApp defines how an autonomous system interacts in a cooperative defense. Blockchain maintains a trust in the autonomous systems. The BloSS architecture is integrated with Software-defined networking (SDN). It consists of three layers: Smart contract that is deployed in ethereum blockchain; dApp, interfaces with blockchain to extract the addresses; Ryu controller for monitoring the traffic and updating flow rule in the switches. In the blockchain layer, a central SC is used to configure SCs of autonomous systems and to update the information on the IP networks. The dApp layer is responsible for a connection of local client to ethereum blockchain. A hardware testbed used for the experimental purpose includes OpenFlow Zodiac FX switches, Ryu as an SDN controller.

Gruhler et al. (Gruhler et al., 2019) proposed a reputation management scheme for DDoS mitigation. The authors have primarily focused on the design, implementation, and evaluation of the proposed reputation scheme for BloSS. The key idea behind the proposed scheme is to use incentive design for dealing with malicious activity by proposing a reputation and a basis to reward schemes. A reputation scheme basically gives power to the contributors and consumers of the network to rate entities that request protection in a cooperative defense. The proposed scheme consists of three modules, namely Mitigation task Index, Storage of Reputation Data, and implementation of reputation metrics. The scheme is evaluated on ethereum blockchain and it is shown that DDoS attacks are mitigated effectively. The main advantage of this scheme is that the reputation management scheme overcomes the problem of "false-reporting" and "free-riding" in the cooperative defense. In addition, it also prevents Sybil and collusion attacks. The main limitation of this scheme is that it uses Proof-of-Work (PoW), which leads to variable block creation times. This limitation can be handled by using Proof-of-Authority (PoA). The proposed scheme can be improved to detect ballot stuffing and bad-mounting attacks.

Kumar et al. (Kumar et al., 2020) proposed a distributed intrusion detection system (IDS) based on the sfog computing paradigm for smart contracts. The authors have first proposed two artificial intelligence-based attack detection models, and then proposed an interplanetary file system for managing data load balancing and distributed file storage for IoT. For the development of detection models, Random Forest and XGBoost are used. The proposed IDS is evaluated on BoT-IoT dataset. The main aim of integrating smart contracts with machine learning based IDS is to prevent anomalous transactions in blockchain-IoT systems. The proposed solutions have the following steps: (1) the incoming traffic is analyzed by IDS, (2) in case the packet is normal the transaction is executed according to the logic included in smart contracts, after execution the transaction gets permanently added to the blockchain, (3) in case the packet is found to be malicious the then an alert is reported to the administrator who takes necessary actions, (4) if the IDS raises a false alarm, then it's the administrator responsibility to decide whether to send transaction to smart contract or not. The experimental results indicate that the proposed IDS outperforms state-of-the-art solutions. The main advantages of the IDS are: it achieves detection rate of up to 99.99% using less features, distributed file storage removes actual data hurdle, and maintains off-chain storage of IoT data. The main limitation of the proposed IDS includes its integration with smart contracts in fog nodes.

Abou El Houda et al. (Abou El Houda et al., 2019) proposed a blockchain-based mechanism "Cochain-SC" for DDoS mitigation. It involves two levels of mitigation that are intra-domain and inter-domain. Authors proposed DDoS mitigation based on SDN for intra-domain level. This mitigation method contains three procedures: intra entropy-based, intra bayes-based, and intra-domain mitigation. Intra entropy-based procedure is used for measuring the random behavior of the data in the domain. Intra bayes-based procedure is responsible for classifying attack and non-attack (legitimate) flows using the entropy variations. To mitigate the attack flows in the same domain, an intra-domain mitigation procedure is used. For DDoS mitigation for inter-domain, a blockchain-based DDoS mitigation approach was proposed by authors. This mechanism utilizes smart contracts of ethereum blockchain for mitigating the attacks among the different SDN domains. For this purpose, an approach is developed to allow secure communications among the other SDN domains and attack information exchange in a distributed way. Thus, it is observed that an integration of inter-domain and intra-domain DDoS mitigation approaches that is "Cochain-SC" makes it possible to provide efficient mitigation of an ongoing DDoS attack. The proposed approach has been implemented as a first mitigation approach for considering intra and inter-domain DDoS mitigation using SDN and smart contracts. For the implementation purpose, an emulator "mininet" is used for creating a real network scenario of SDN. sFlow-RT is used for monitoring the network flows and Floodlight is used as an SDN controller. It also reduces the cost of sending the packets to different domains and avoids single-point-of-failure. The proposed approach provides evaluation results with high accuracy for attack detection and flexibility.

Yeh et al. (Yeh et al., 2019) proposed a mechanism based on blockchain for sharing an IP list of DDoS attacks. This sharing of malicious IP lists is done to prevent the attacks ongoing on the different nodes. Consortium blockchain is used for monitoring the malicious behavior. IP lists are compared to identify malicious IPs using smart contracts. The proposed system confirms all the security principles (confidentiality, integrity, and availability) of CIA model. Elliptic curve cryptography is used for ensuring data confidentiality and integrity.

Yeh et al. (Yeh et al., 2020) proposed a mechanism "SOChain" for an information exchange related to DDoS attacks as an extended work proposed by Yeh et al. (2019). The proposed mechanism utilized consortium blockchain. All the nodes are required to be authenticated to share the information related to DDoS attacks. The proposed mechanism is comprised of four modules that are smart contract, swarm, security operation center (SOC), and decentralized oracle service. Smart contracts are used to control the complete flow on the platform. Swarm is responsible for storing logs of encrypted IP lists of DDoS attacks. SOC is used for monitoring any malicious activity in the network. Decentralized oracle service are used for handling the events raised from smart contracts to take any action for privacy protection. The goal of the proposed mechanism in terms of security is to maintain the confidentiality and integrity of IP lists of DDoS attacks. Each SOC can behave like an uploader, buyer, and data verifier to share the security information with other SOC. For this purpose, some DDoS coins as virtual coins and two kinds of reputation points, i.e., positive reputation and negative reputation are used. These coins and points are managed by SOCs. Further, the proposed system includes two phases, namely upload phase and purchase phase. In the upload phase, whenever a DDoS attack is detected, SOC uploader uploads the IP list of detected attack to the swarm. The uploading of IP list is done in an encrypted form. In the purchase phase, buyer receives an IP list of DDoS after going through security checks and decrypt the IP list to access it.

These blockchain-based defense solutions are summarized in Table 4.

Table 4. Blockchain-based defense solutions against DDoS

Authors	Mechanism	Type of Blockchain	Implementation Details	Advantage	Limitation
Rodrigues et al. (2017a)	Blockchain-based collaborative mechanism using smart contracts	Ethereum	Only proposed framework has been provided	Can be incorporated as a supplementary scheme with the existing security mechanisms	No practical details including SDN has shown
Javaid et al. (2018)	Integrated defense system of blockchain and IoT	Ethereum	Ethereum development package and Go client nodes (for IoT devices).	Avoids single-point-of-failure, reduces burden on servers	Scalability issues
Kataoka et al. (2018)	Trust list based mechanism using SDN and blockchain	Ethereum	Ryu controller,	Provides attack prevention and defensive action	Scalability issues in terms of cost, and trust lists are nit encrypted
Gruhler et al. (2019)	Reputation management scheme for BloSS	Ethereum	Testbed	overcomes the problem of "false-reporting" and "free-riding" in the cooperative defense	Variable block creation time due to PoW
Rodrigues et al. (2017b)	BloSS- a cooperative mechanism with SDN	Ethereum	Testbed (Zodiac FX SDN switches, Ryu controller and Raspberry-Pi)	Provides higher trust	-
Kumar et al. (2020)	Distributed IDS	Ethereum	-	99.99% detection rate, distributed file storage	Integration with smart contract is challenging task.
Abou El Houda et al. (2019)	Cochain-SC (based on intra-domain and inter-domain mitigation approach)	Ethereum	Mininet, Floodlight controller, an official network "Ropsten" of ethereum	Deal with intra-domain and inter-domain both using SDN and smart contract. Reduces cost of transferring packets to different domains and also avoids single-point-of-failure.	Information shared among devices in SDN is also required to be secured against attacks.
Yeh et al. (2019)	Based on sharing malicious IP list with other nodes using token and bloom-filters	Consortium	No implementation details available	More scalable than existing approaches of sharing IP list.	-
Yeh et al. (2020)	SOChain- an extension of Yeh et al. (2019)	Consortium	wolfSSL library	Reduces encryption time, increases level of trust.	No implementation details have been shown in detail

RESEARCH CHALLENGES AND FUTURE DIRECTIONS

There are some research challenges in blockchain technology. Figure 5 shows a list of these challenges and future directions in blockchain-based defense solutions.

- **Cost:** Blockchain-based defense systems face cost issues as per two perspectives. Blockchain alone is not capable enough to provide security solutions. It has to have collaborated with some other networking technologies. For example, it can be analyzed that recently blockchain technology is being integrated with a trending networking paradigm, i.e., software-defined networking (SDN). SDN provides the monitoring of the malicious traffic flows in the network and dynamic dealing with any anomalous activity after its detection. Blockchain is utilized to publish information related to attack or trust. This integration of these two technologies can be used for defending the network against attacks such as DDoS. These integrated defense solutions increase the overall cost of the complete system. As it is known that blockchain is in its early stages of development and innovation. Therefore, replacing it with the existing conventional systems and its collaboration makes the process costly.

The adoption of blockchain technology in securing the network involves high energy consumption. Most of the existing blockchain-based mechanisms are based on bitcoin infrastructures and proof-of-work (PoW) as a consensus technique to validate the transactions. These techniques need higher computing power to solve complex computational problems for the defense solutions. The computer systems that are used for solving complex computations, require a higher amount of energy. Therefore, there is a need of cooling down these computer systems, which increases the costs of the process.

- **Scalability:** Scalability is one of the major challenges of blockchain. In the case of public blockchain, scalability is a bigger issue than for private blockchain. Scalability issues can be in terms of time, speed, and cost. In the current scenario, most of the systems prefer public blockchain to use. Traditional transaction networks are able to process transactions at higher speeds. But some blockchains like bitcoin and ethereum have a lower speed of transactions. Private blockchains do not suffer from these kinds of scalability issues. In the private blockchains, the processing of transactions is directly done with less computational power for validating the blocks.

Figure 5. Research challenges

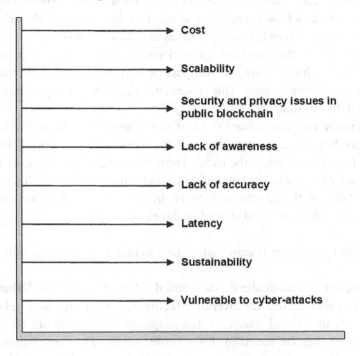

- **Security and Privacy issues in public blockchain**: Most of the existing solutions use public blockchain. There is a difference between public and private blockchains in terms of privacy/confidentiality. In a public blockchain, the information is open to access. It can have privacy issues. Blockchain does not provide any transactional guarantee. Also, blockchain can be targeted by cyber-attacks. Private blockchain can be considered to keep the information and transaction details confidential. To make the information confidential, limited access should be there. Therefore, such mechanisms should be developed to provide privacy to the sensitive information and deal with other cyber-attacks.
- **Lack of Awareness:** One of the main challenges of using blockchain is lack of awareness. Different organizations and academia are not well aware enough of blockchain technology and its applications. It is not introduced in many institutions that make working with blockchain more difficult and time taking. Organizations should be familiar with the blockchain technology to propose more efficient blockchain-based defense solutions.
- **Lack of accuracy:** A DDoS defense system should try to provide more efficient results. The validation of the defense systems is measured in terms

of accuracy, false alarm, etc. An efficient defense system offers more accurate results with less false positives. But most of the proposed blockchain-based solutions do not care for false positives and false negatives.

- **Latency:** Blockchain technology works in a distributed infrastructure. In the distributed infrastructure, all the parties have to update their information, which can take much time. This process increases the latency in the blockchain based defense solutions.

- **Vulnerable to cyber-attacks:** Most of the solutions use public blockchain such as bitcoin, ethereum that utilizes PoW as a consensus method for defending the actions of the users. These blockchains are attracted to various cyber-attacks. Therefore, such defense systems should be designed that can make mitigate the attacks in blockchain systems. For this purpose, a more secure consensus method should be developed.

Some of the promising research directions in this domain are as follows:

- **Developing a Full-fledged Automated Blockchain based DDoS defense tool:** In order to test the overall effectiveness of a proposed scheme, it is important that a tool based on that proposed scheme should be developed, which can then be tested in different test cases. Thus, we believe that the interested researchers in this domain should develop a full-fledged automated blockchain based DDoS defense tool. Subsequently, the effectiveness of the proposed tool should then be tested against a wide variety of well-known DDoS attacks.

- **Adapting Blockchain to counter Slow Rate DoS Attacks** (Tripathi et al. 2016 and Tripathi et al. 2018): The popularity of Slow Rate DoS attacks, among other types of application layer DoS attacks, is on continuous rise since last decade. These attacks can bring down servers with huge computational power even using a small number of computers. A variety of defense mechanisms have been proposed in the litereature to counter these attacks however, all the known mechanisms come with their own set of limitations. Thus, we believe that it would be interesting to pursue research in this direction and analyze if the blockchain based defense mechanisms can effectively counter these attacks.

CONCLUSION

DDoS is one of the most powerful attacks that aim to consume the resources (bandwidth, CPU power, and memory) by flooding a huge amount of network traffic towards a system. DDoS attacks can cause a massive destruction to the network. Even when the whole world is facing a global pandemic "COVID-19" and trying to deal with this, the DDoS attackers have come in an active state. All the works related to daily routine, professional, institutional, or health are being handled via online services. DDoS attackers have the best chance to crash or slow down all the services. These attacks should be handled on time before it makes the service entirely down. Many prevention solutions have been proposed by researchers and organizations. One of the trending technology, "blockchain" is also used for DDoS defense. In this chapter, DDoS attacks have been explained in detail with its different types. The chapter also discusses the different types of blockchain, and blockchain-based defense works against DDoS. Blockchain provides many advantageous features to deal with cyber-attacks, whereas it also makes itself vulnerable to attacks. Blockchain has some challenges that should be explored. Therefore, some of the important research challenges present in the existing blockchain mechanisms have been explained in the chapter. The major issue with the field of blockchain is lack of awareness and understandability. Blockchain is such a technology that cannot be utilized in the existing networking paradigms with less knowledge of its concepts. This is why most of the existed research works are lacking in implementations and simulations. Thus, blockchain should be studied widely for taking the benefits that can help in preventing the cyber-attacks such as DDoS.

REFERENCES

Abou El Houda, Z., Hafid, A. S., & Khoukhi, L. (2019). Cochain-SC: An intra-and inter-domain Ddos mitigation scheme based on blockchain using SDN and smart contract. *IEEE Access: Practical Innovations, Open Solutions*, 7, 98893–98907.

Abrams, L. (2018). *Dramatic Increase of DDoS Attack Sizes Attributed to IoT Devices.* https://www.bleepingcomputer.com/news/security/dramatic-increase-of-ddos-attack-sizes-attributed-to-iot-devices/

Bannister, A. (2020). *DDoS suspicions: US health department investigating 'significant increase' in traffic.* https://portswigger.net/daily-swig/ddos-suspicions-us-health-department-investigating-significant-increase-in-traffic

Beyer, S. (2020). *Blockchain Before Bitcoin: A History | Block Telegraph. Block Telegraph.* https://blocktelegraph.io/blockchain-before-bitcoin-history

Cachin, C. (2016, July). Architecture of the hyperledger blockchain fabric. In *Workshop on distributed cryptocurrencies and consensus ledgers* (Vol. 310, No. 4). Academic Press.

Cimpanu, C. (2020). *AWS said it mitigated a 2.3 Tbps DDoS attack, the largest ever.* https://www.zdnet.com/article/aws-said-it-mitigated-a-2-3-tbps-ddos-attack-the-largest-ever/

CloudFlare. (2020). *What is a DDoS Attack?* https://www.cloudflare.com/learning/ddos/what-is-a-ddos-attack/

Douligeris, C., & Mitrokotsa, A. (2004). DDoS attacks and defense mechanisms: Classification and state-of-the-art. *Computer Networks, 44*(5), 643–666. doi:10.1016/j.comnet.2003.10.003

Elsayed, M. S., Le-Khac, N. A., Dev, S., & Jurcut, A. D. Ddosnet: A deep-learning model for detecting network attacks. In *2020 IEEE 21st International Symposium on "A World of Wireless, Mobile and Multimedia Networks" (WoWMoM)* (pp. 391-396). IEEE.

Euromoney.com. (2020). *Blockchain Explained: What Is Blockchain? | Euromoney Learning.* https://www.euromoney.com/learning/blockchain-explained/what-is-blockchain

Gruhler, A., Rodrigues, B., & Stiller, B. (2019, April). A reputation scheme for a blockchain-based network cooperative defense. In *2019 IFIP/IEEE Symposium on Integrated Network and Service Management (IM)* (pp. 71-79). IEEE.

Haber, S., & Stornetta, W. (1991). How to time-stamp a digital document. *Journal of Cryptology, 3*(2), 99–111.

Infosec newsflash. (2019). *Cyber Security Statistics for 2019 By InfoSec Newsflash.* https://www.cyberdefensemagazine.com/cyber-security-statistics-for-2019/

Ismailisufi, A., Popović, T., Gligorić, N., Radonjic, S., & Šandi, S. (2020, February). A Private Blockchain Implementation Using Multichain Open Source Platform. In *2020 24th International Conference on Information Technology (IT)* (pp. 1-4). IEEE.

Javaid, U., Siang, A. K., Aman, M. N., & Sikdar, B. (2018, June). Mitigating IoT device based DDoS attacks using blockchain. In *Proceedings of the 1st Workshop on Cryptocurrencies and Blockchains for Distributed Systems* (pp. 71-76). Academic Press.

Kataoka, K., Gangwar, S., & Podili, P. (2018, February). Trust list: Internet-wide and distributed IoT traffic management using blockchain and SDN. In *2018 IEEE 4th World Forum on Internet of Things (WF-IoT)* (pp. 296-301). IEEE.

Kottler, S. (2018). *February 28th DDoS Incident Report.* https://github.blog/2018-03-01-ddos-incident-report

Kumar, P., Kumar, R., Gupta, G. P., & Tripathi, R. (2020). A Distributed framework for detecting DDoS attacks in smart contract-based Blockchain-IoT Systems by leveraging Fog computing. *Transactions on Emerging Telecommunications Technologies*, ▪▪▪, 4112.

Li, X., Jiang, P., Chen, T., Luo, X., & Wen, Q. (2020). A survey on the security of blockchain systems. *Future Generation Computer Systems*, *107*, 841–853. doi:10.1016/j.future.2017.08.020

Medium. (2020). *Blockchain Architecture Basics: Components, Structure, Benefits & Creation.* https://medium.com/@MLSDevCom/blockchain-architecture-basics-components-structure-benefits-creation-beace17c8e77

Mirkovic, J., & Reiher, P. (2004). A taxonomy of DDoS attack and DDoS defense mechanisms. *Computer Communication Review*, *34*(2), 39–53. doi:10.1145/997150.997156

Mlsdev.com. (2020). *Mlsdev.* https://mlsdev.com/blog/156-how-to-build-your-own-blockchain-architecture

Radware. (2019). *DDoS Attack Definitions - DDoSPedia.* https://security.radware.com/ddos-knowledge-center/ddospedia/dos-attack/

Rodrigues, B., Bocek, T., Lareida, A., Hausheer, D., Rafati, S., & Stiller, B. (2017a). A blockchain-based architecture for collaborative DDoS mitigation with smart contracts. In *IFIP International Conference on Autonomous Infrastructure, Management and Security* (pp. 16-29). Springer.

Rodrigues, B., Bocek, T., & Stiller, B. (2017b). *Enabling a cooperative, multi-domain DDoS defense by a blockchain signaling system (BloSS).* Semantic Scholar.

SEPA for Corporates. (2017). *The Difference between Bitcoin, Ethereum, Ripple & Litecoin.* https://www.sepaforcorporates.com/thoughts/difference-bitcoin-ethereum-ripple-litecoin/

Swami, R., Dave, M., & Ranga, V. (2019). Software-defined networking-based DDoS defense mechanisms. *ACM Computing Surveys*, *52*(2), 1–36. doi:10.1145/3301614

Swami, R., Dave, M., & Ranga, V. (2020). DDoS Attacks and Defense Mechanisms Using Machine Learning Techniques for SDN. In *Security and Privacy Issues in Sensor Networks and IoT* (pp. 193–214). IGI Global. doi:10.4018/978-1-7998-0373-7.ch008

Tripathi, N., & Hubballi, N. (2018). Slow Rate Denial of Service Attacks against HTTP/2. *Computers & Security*, *72*, 255–272. doi:10.1016/j.cose.2017.09.009

Tripathi, N., Hubballi, N., & Singh, Y. (2016). How secure are web servers? An Empirical Study of Slow HTTP DoS Attacks and Detection. In *2016 11th International Conference on Availability, Reliability and Security (ARES)* (pp. 454-463). IEEE. 10.1109/ARES.2016.20

Wikipedia. (2020). *COVID-19 pandemic*. https://en.wikipedia.org/wiki/COVID-19_pandemic

Yeh, L. Y., Huang, J. L., Yen, T. Y., & Hu, J. W. (2019, August). A Collaborative DDoS Defense Platform Based on Blockchain Technology. In *2019 Twelfth International Conference on Ubi-Media Computing (Ubi-Media)* (pp. 1-6). IEEE.

Yeh, L. Y., Lu, P. J., Huang, S. H., & Huang, J. L. (2020). SOChain: A Privacy-Preserving DDoS Data Exchange Service Over SOC Consortium Blockchain. *IEEE Transactions on Engineering Management*.

Chapter 3
BLOFF:
A Blockchain–Based
Forensic Model in IoT

Promise Agbedanu

https://orcid.org/0000-0003-2522-891X
University College Dublin, Ireland

Anca Delia Jurcut
University College Dublin, Ireland

ABSTRACT

In this era of explosive growth in technology, the internet of things (IoT) has become the game changer when we consider technologies like smart homes and cities, smart energy, security and surveillance, and healthcare. The numerous benefits provided by IoT have become attractive technologies for users and cybercriminals. Cybercriminals of today have the tools and the technology to deploy millions of sophisticated attacks. These attacks need to be investigated; this is where digital forensics comes into play. However, it is not easy to conduct a forensic investigation in IoT systems because of the heterogeneous nature of the IoT environment. Additionally, forensic investigators mostly rely on evidence from service providers, a situation that can lead to evidence contamination. To solve this problem, the authors proposed a blockchain-based IoT forensic model that prevents the admissibility of tampered logs into evidence.

DOI: 10.4018/978-1-7998-7589-5.ch003

1. INTRODUCTION

In this era of explosive growth in technology, the Internet of Things (IoT) has become the game changer when we consider technologies like smart homes and cities; smart energy, security and surveillance and healthcare. In a report, Statista predicted that the number of IoT device will reach 75 billion in 2025 (Statista, 2019). The integration of real-world objects with the internet does not only bring numerous advantages but also bring cybersecurity threats to our life, through our interaction with these devices (A. Jurcut et al., 2020). Like any computing technology, IoT is threatened by security issues. Many researchers and device manufacturers are exploring various techniques to ensure the security of IoT devices as well as protect the data generated by these devices. However, according to (Atlam et al., 2017), it is difficult to secure data produce in IoT environments because of the heterogeneity and dynamic features deployed in these devices. It is therefore not surprising that the security of IoT, ranging from the physical security of the devices through to the security of their architecture has become an important area of research for a lot of researchers (A. D. Jurcut et al., 2020).

Currently, several works are being done to ensure data confidentiality, access control, authentication, privacy and trust in IoT environments (Borhani et al., 2020; Braeken et al., 2019; A. Jurcut et al., 2009, 2012; A. D. Jurcut, 2018; A. D. Jurcut et al., 2014; Kumar et al., 2019; Xu et al., 2019). Although a lot of success has been made in the security of IoT using the parameters mentioned above, attackers still find ways to exploit the vulnerabilities that exist in IoT systems (A. D. Jurcut et al., 2020). These billions of IoT devices contain sensitive data, an attribute that makes them attractive to cyber-attacks. The number and the cost of cyber-attacks have been increasing over the years. According to a report by (Morgan, 2017), the damages caused by cybercrimes will cost a whopping 6 trillion dollars by 2021. These attacks need to be investigated; this is where digital forensics comes into play.

Digital forensics helps in acquiring legal evidence that can be used to know more about these attacks, prevent future attacks and most importantly prosecute the perpetrators of these crimes. However, it is not easy to conduct a forensic investigation in IoT systems. According to (Perumal et al., 2015), the heterogeneity and dynamic nature of IoT systems make it practically difficult to use the same frameworks used in traditional digital forensic in IoT environments. It is therefore expedient to develop frameworks that can be used in IoT environments considering their dynamic and heterogeneity nature.

In this chapter, we discuss a blockchain-based model that ensures the verifiability of logs produced in IoT environments. The main idea of this model is to ensure the credibility and authenticity of logs produced by IoT devices during forensic investigations. Our model uses the decentralized approach and the immutability property of blockchain to ensure that logs and other pieces of evidence produced in IoT environments can be verified by forensic stakeholders. Our proposed model prevents Cloud Service Providers (CSPs) or Law Enforcement Agencies (LEAs) from tendering in false evidence during forensic investigations or court proceedings. The proposed model brings the court, LEAs, CSPs and other stakeholders under one umbrella where each stakeholder can verify the authenticity of the evidence presented by any of them. The model also ensures that pieces of evidence are not tampered with during the chain of custody. We start this chapter by providing an introduction to digital forensics in IoT and blockchain. We then continue by describing our proposed model. The benefits of our model are discussed and then we present our conclusion.

2. BACKGROUND

In this section, we present a background of digital forensics, IoT forensics and blockchain.

2.1 Digital Forensics

Several definitions have been given for digital forensics. (Bellegarde et al., 2010) defined computer forensics as "the preservation, identification, extraction, interpretation, and documentation of computer evidence to include the rules of evidence, legal process, the integrity of evidence, factual reporting of the information and providing expert opinion in a court of law or other legal and/or administrative proceedings as to what was found." The concept of digital forensics and computer forensics are closely related with the latter being the subset of the former. The most widely accepted definition of digital forensics is the one proposed during the first digital forensic research workshop and was stated by authors in (James et al., 2015) as "The use of scientifically derived and proven methods toward the preservation, collection, validation, identification, analysis, interpretation, documentation and presentation of digital evidence derived from digital sources to facilitate or further the reconstruction of events found to be criminal, or helping to anticipate unauthorized actions shown to be disruptive to planned operations." Digital forensics involves the application of scientific methods in investigating cyber-crimes (Carrier, 2003). According to (Sumalatha & Batsa, 2016), the methodologies employed in digital forensics to handle electronic evidence has its stems springing out from forensic science.

2.1.1 Digital Forensic Process

There are various stages that digital forensic artifacts undergo before finally being presented in a court for prosecution purposes. (Daniel & Daniel, 2012) stated that the digital forensic is made up of four processes. These processes are identification, collection, organization, and presentation. Similarly, (Zawoad et al., 2015) enumerated the stages of digital forensics as identification, preservation, analysis, and presentation. According to (Hemdan & Manjaiah, 2018), digital forensics involves the application of scientific processes in identifying, collecting, organizing and presenting evidence. Ken Zatyko, the a former director of the US Defense Computer Forensics Laboratory outlined an eight-step process that makes digital forensic a scientific process (Zawoad et al., 2015). These eight steps include (Zawoad et al., 2015): obtaining the search authority, documenting the chain of custody, imaging, and hashing of evidence, validating tools used in the forensic process, analysing evidence, repeating and reproducing to ensure quality assurance, report by documenting the procedures used in the forensic process and then finally, present an expert witness in a court of law.

2.1.2 Evidence Identification

This is the first stage of the forensic process. This stage involves two steps. The first is the identification of the incident and the second is the identification of the evidence. There must be a direct correlation between the incident and the evidence being identified (Daniel & Daniel, 2012).

2.1.3 Evidence Collection

This stage involves the extraction of evidence from different media. The extraction methods may include imaging the original copy of the evidence. This stage also involves preserving the integrity of the evidence (Daniel & Daniel, 2012).

2.1.4 Organization

This stage has two main steps including evidence examination and evidence analysis. Some researchers separate these two steps distinctively. During the evidence examination, the investigator performs a thorough inspection of the data being used as evidence (Daniel & Daniel, 2012). This inspection may involve the use of different forensic tools. These tools are used for extracting and filtering data that is of interest to the investigator and relevant to the investigation process (Zawoad & Hasan, 2015). The analysis phase involves reconstructing events by analysing the data collected. The rationale behind the evidence analysis is to discover any evidential material which will aid the technical as well as the legal perspective of the case (Ademu et al., 2011).

2.1.5 Evidence Presentation

The evidence, after the identification, collection and organization; needs to be presented to a court of law. This stage includes the investigator preparing an organized report to state the findings he or she made during the investigation process (Daniel & Daniel, 2012). These findings are then presented to a court of law with the investigator serving as an expert witness if there is a need to testify (Ieong, 2006).

2.2 IoT Forensics

Unlike the traditional digital forensics, IoT forensics is a new and unexplored area by both industry and academia. Although the purpose of both digital and IoT forensics, is to extract digital information using a scientific approach; the scope available when it comes to information extraction is wider in IoT forensics. According to (Atlam et al., 2017; Raghavan, 2013), IoT forensics is made up of the cloud, network and the device level forensics. Similarly, (Stoyanova et al., 2020) defined IoT forensics as an aspect of digital forensics with the identification, collection, organization, and presentation of evidence happening within the IoT ecosystem. They also broke IoT forensics into Cloud, Network, and Device-level forensics.

2.3 Blockchain

Blockchain, also known as distributed ledger technology is a decentralized and distributed ledger that contains chains of blocks of various transactions joined together by cryptographic hashes. According to (Gaur et al., 2018), the blockchain is "an immutable ledger for recording transactions, maintained within a distributed network of mutually untrusted peers." Any transaction coming from a node is validated by other participating nodes in the blockchain network. After the validation, the set of transactions is added to the block by special nodes called miners as in the case of bitcoin. A miner is a node with sufficient computational power to solve a cryptographic puzzle. Blockchain uses a peer-to-peer (P2P) network. This architecture makes it possible for each node to communicate with a set of neighbour nodes, then each of these nodes also communicate with their neighbour nodes and the communication goes on and on. The blockchain is designed in such a way that any node can join and leave the network at will. Certain key elements are needed in the design and implementation of blockchain technology. These elements are:

1. **Timestamping:** This means that the problem of double-spending in the case of cryptocurrency applications like bitcoin is avoided. Timestamping is achieved by collecting pending transactions into the block and then calculating the hash of the block. This can prove that a transaction existed at the time of creating the block since it is hashed onto the block.

2. **Consensus:** Because new blocks are created and broadcasted by mining nodes, all nodes need to agree on a single version of the block. A distributed consensus helps to decide on which block out of the several variants generated by different nodes would be added to the blockchain.

3. **Data security and integrity:** This property or attribute prevents a malicious node from creating a fake transaction since each transaction is signed by a node or a user using their private key. Similarly, (Gaur et al., 2018) also identifies four blocks within a blockchain framework. These blocks are: the shared ledger, cryptography, consensus, and the smart contracts.

Mining also called proof-of-work (PoW) is used to achieve consensus and to ensure data security and integrity. Mining is done based on the sequence of transactions; a situation can only be changed by redoing the proof-of-work. Mining introduces the difficulty in block generation. There are other methods available ensuring data security and integrity. Some of these methods are proof-of-authority (PoA), proof-of-existence (PoE) and proof-of-concept (PoC). A blockchain can either be permissionless or permissioned. A permission-less blockchain also known as public blockchain allows any node to join and leave at any point in time, whereas private or permissioned blockchain allows nodes to be authenticated before joining the network.

3. RELATED WORK

In this section, we explore some works that are closely related to ours. Blockchain has been widely used in the area of IoT security. However, the concept is still in its exploratory stage when it comes to IoT forensics. (Meffert et al., 2017) proposed a framework that helps evidence acquisition in IoT forensic. Using a centralized approach, the framework is deployed in three nodes namely; controller to IoT device, controller to cloud and controller to controller. Although, the proof of concept used in this work showed that the proposed framework can pull forensic data from IoT devices. However, the centralized nature of their approach makes it difficult to authenticate the evidence captured by the framework. (Li et al., 2019) also used a digital witness approach that allows people to shared logs from IoT devices with guaranteed privacy. The authors used the Privacy-aware IoT Forensics (PRoFIT) model proposed in their earlier work to deploy their digital witness model. The method proposed in their work is to help collect digital evidence in IoT environments as well as ensuring that the privacy of the evidence collected is maintained. The proposed method supports 11 privacy principles captured (Nieto et al., 2018) in their PRoFIT methodology. In their work, (Nieto et al., 2017) proposed a distributed logging scheme for IoT forensics. In this work, the authors used a Modified Information Dispersal Algorithm (MIDA) that ensures the availability of logs generated in IoT environments. The logs are aggregated, compressed, authenticated and dispersed. The distributed approach used in this work only focuses on how logs are stored but not how they are verified. Leveraging the immutability property of blockchain technology, (Noura et al., 2020) proposed an IoT forensics framework that uses a permissioned-based blockchain. This framework enhances the integrity, authenticity and non-repudiation of pieces of evidence.

4. PROPOSED MODEL

In this section, we present our blockchain-based forensic model for IoT (BLOF). In IoT environments, there are three layers. These are the cloud, network and the device layer. Our model leverages the decentralized property of blockchain to ensure that the logs produced in IoT environments are stored on the network and are available for the verification by any of the participating nodes in the network. There are several artefacts to be considered when conducting a forensic investigation. However, our model focuses only on system and event logs. The entities in our model are the Cloud Service Providers (CSPs), Network Devices and the IoT devices. The entities serve as the blockchain nodes in the network. New nodes are added to the network through a key generation process. The public key of a node is appended to a transaction before it is written onto the block. New nodes generate a pair of keys. The CSPs act as the miners in the network. Their computational capacity of CSPs makes them ideal candidates for mining. Our model is made up of a Blockchain Centre (BC), Log Processing Centre (LPC) and User Centre (UC). In the preceding subsections, we discuss each of these components into details. The proposed model is shown in Figure 1.

4.1 Blockchain Centre

The blockchain centre is made up of a distributed ledger where each log is written onto a block after processing. The distributed ledger is made up of all blocks that have been committed to the network. Each block contains a transactional value of hashed values computed from logs. The logs are extracted from the various entities, hashed and written onto the blockchain network as transactions. The nodes in the

BC are made up of forensic stakeholders, network and IoT devices and cloud service providers. The blocks are proposed after a consensus has been reached by the nodes.

4.2 Log Processing Centre

This component of our model handles the log processing. The LPC is an Application Programming Interface (API) that sits between entities and the blockchain network. The LPC extracts the logs from the IoT devices, network devices and the cloud layers. The extracted logs are hashed using a SHA-256 hash function and the hashed values are written onto the block as a transaction. We chose to hash the logs because these logs may contain sensitive information. Therefore, it is not advisable to store the logs as plaintext. Secondly, hashing the logs reduces its size which eventually reduces the time needed to process the logs.

$$Transaction = hash\left(\log\right)$$

4.3 User Centre

The user centre is made up of the courts and the forensic investigators. This component of the model makes it possible for forensic investigators to verify the authenticity of logs presented to them by service providers. Additionally, forensic investigators can verify the authenticity of logs even as they are passed on from one investigator to another during the chain of custody. Furthermore, the court can also verify the authenticity of logs presented by prosecutors and decide if such a piece of evidence (log) must be admitted or not. This prevents investigators from tampering with logs to either incriminate innocent people or to exonerate criminals.

5. VERIFICATION OF LOGS

Unlike the traditional digital forensics, investigators solely depend on the CSPs, network and the IoT devices for evidence when it comes to the IoT forensics. This dependence on CSPs may lead to compromising pieces of evidence. Our proposed model does not only ensure the integrity of logs through the use of a decentralized ledger but also allows logs tendered in as evidence to be verified by various stakeholders in the forensic process.

In our proposed model, the forensic investigator still falls on the CSP and IoT devices for the evidence. However, the evidence which in this case is the various logs generated by the cloud instances, network and the IoT devices are hashed after a forensic investigator receives such evidence from a CSP. The hashed value is then compared to the hashes stored as transaction values on the blockchain network. The investigator then searches for the hashed value on the blockchain network. If the hash value exists on the blockchain then the log is accepted by the investigator and forwarded to the court as credible evidence. On the other hand, if the hash value does not exist on the blockchain network then the log is rejected. When the court receives a log from a forensic investigator, the court can determine the credibility of the log by similarly hashing the log and comparing the hashed value to the hash values on the blockchain network. If the value exists, the evidence is accepted by the court. Otherwise, it is rejected. The verification process of our propose model is shown in Figure 2.

For example, Bob who is a forensic investigator receives logs from a CSP intending to present the evidence to a court to prosecute an attacker called Elvan. However, Bob is not sure if the logs provided by the CSP has been tampered with or not. Since the hash of all logs is processed and stored in our blockchain-based model; Bob can verify the authenticity of the logs. Bob first runs the log through a SHA-256 hash function and gets a value (x). He then searches for the transaction (x) on the blockchain network. Bob is one of the participating nodes on the network. If he finds the value (x) as a valid transaction on the network; then the log is genuine and he can then proceed to court and present the log as a piece of evidence. However, if the value (x) is not a valid transaction then Bob must discard that log and rather investigate who made changes to the log. After Bob is presenting the log to the court, the court can also verify the authenticity of the log. The assumption here is that Bob might try to implicate Elvan as the perpetrator of a crime he is innocent of. Similarly, the court runs the log through a SHA-256 hash function and then search for the exact value on the blockchain network. If the transaction value exists, then the court admits the log as evidence and proceeds with hearing the case. Otherwise, the court rejects the evidence and dismisses the case.

Figure 1. Our proposed blockchain-based IoT forensic model

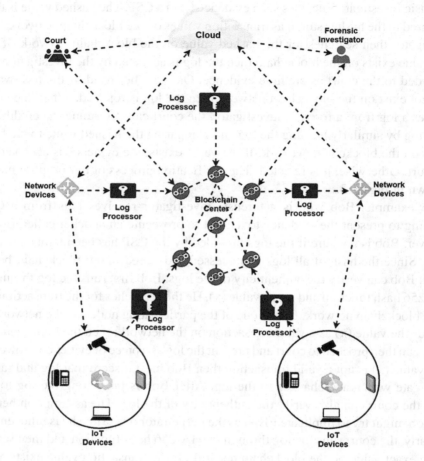

6. DISCUSSION

In this section we discuss the advantages of our proposed model, the possible impact it may have on the performance of IoT forensics and then we compare our model to the current existing ones.

Firstly, our proposed model is based on blockchain, making the model a fully decentralized one as compared to a centralized approach discussed in (Meffert et al., 2017). The decentralized characteristic of our model ensures that logs can be verified to determine their authenticity or otherwise. It also prevents service providers and forensic investigators from tampering with logs without being detected. Our model uses the immutability property of blockchain as a leverage to ensure the integrity of logs produced in the IoT environment.

Figure 2. Verification process of our proposed model

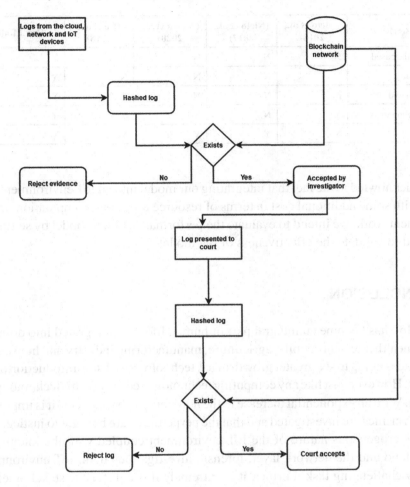

Further, our model offers the advantage of verifiability. This advantage gives the possibility for the forensic stakeholders to verify the authenticity of the logs produced in IoT environments - an advantage that is either not available or not fully explored in the existing related work (Nieto et al., 2018; Nieto et al., 2017; Nieto et al., 2017; Le et al., 2018).

We compare our model with the current work that is closely related to ours, using the following parameters: blockchain-based, verifiability, decentralized, evidence integrity and privacy. In the instance where a model satisfies a parameter, we mark it as a Yes (Y). If it does not satisfy that parameter then we mark it as a No (N). The comparison is shown in Table 1.

Table 1. Comparing our model to other existing models

Metric	(Nieto et al., 2018)	(Nieto et al., 2017)	(Noura et al., 2020)	(Le et al., 2018)	Our Model
Blockchain-based	N	N	N	Y	Y
Verifiability	N	N	N	N	Y
Decentralized	N	N	N	Y	Y
Evidence integrity	Y	N	Y	Y	Y
Privacy	Y	Y	Y	Y	Y

We acknowledge the fact that integrating our model into an IoT environment will come with some additional cost in terms of resource usage and computation. In our subsequent work, we intend to evaluate the performance of our model by setting up a testbed to validate the effectiveness of the model.

7. CONCLUSION

Today, IoT has become an integral part of human life. It is integrated into domains such as healthcare, automobile, agriculture, manufacturing industry and household. The world is going to see greater growth in IoT technology with the introduction of 5G network. However, just like any computing technology security of this technology is a concern. With an exponential increase in the number of cyber-attacks, it is important that such crimes are investigated and that the perpetrators are brought to justice. Due to the heterogeneous nature of the IoT environment coupled with the integration of the cloud and the network layer, forensic investigations in an IoT environment is a very challenging task. Further, it is extremely difficult for the stakeholders to determine the authenticity of the evidence they deal with, since in most cases they have to depend on service providers for these pieces of evidence. To ensure that logs presented to forensic investigators are authentic and tamper-free, we proposed a blockchain forensic model that uses a decentralized approach to keep the hashed values of logs produced in IoT environment as transactional records. The proposed model allows any forensic stakeholder to verify the authenticity of the logs they are working with. This model ensures that innocent people are not framed up and culprits are not exonerated by interested parties during a forensic investigation. For future work, we seek to perform an experimental validation to ascertain the computational impact our model will have in an IoT environment. Additionally, exploring ways of storing logs within our model is another area that is of interest to us.

REFERENCES

Ademu, I. O., Imafidon, C. O., & Preston, D. S. (2011). A new approach of digital forensic model for digital forensic investigation. *International Journal of Advanced Computer Science and Applications*, 2(12), 175–178.

Atlam, H. F., Alenezi, A., Walters, R. J., Wills, G. B., & Daniel, J. (2017). Developing an adaptive Risk-based access control model for the Internet of Things. *2017 IEEE International Conference on Internet of Things (IThings) and IEEE Green Computing and Communications (GreenCom) and IEEE Cyber, Physical and Social Computing (CPSCom) and Ieee Smart Data (SmartData)*, 655–661. 10.1109/iThings-GreenCom-CPSCom-SmartData.2017.103

Bellegarde, M., Orvis, M., & Helba, S. (2010). *Ethical Hacking and Countermeasures: Attack Phases*. EC-Council Press.

Borhani, M., Liyanage, M., Sodhro, A. H., Kumar, P., Jurcut, A. D., & Gurtov, A. (2020). Secure and resilient communications in the industrial internet. In *Guide to Disaster-Resilient Communication Networks* (pp. 219–242). Springer. doi:10.1007/978-3-030-44685-7_9

Braeken, A., Liyanage, M., & Jurcut, A. D. (2019). Anonymous lightweight proxy based key agreement for iot (alpka). *Wireless Personal Communications*, 106(2), 345–364. doi:10.100711277-019-06165-9

Carrier, B. (2003). Defining digital forensic examination and analysis tools using abstraction layers. *International Journal of Digital Evidence*, 1(4), 1–12.

Daniel, L., & Daniel, L. (2012). Digital forensics for legal professionals. *Syngress Book Co*, 1, 287–293.

Gaur, N., Desrosiers, L., Ramakrishna, V., Novotny, P., Baset, S., & O'Dowd, A. (2018). *Hands-On Blockchain with Hyperledger: Building decentralized applications with Hyperledger Fabric and Composer*. Packt Publishing. https://books.google.co.za/books?id=wKdhDwAAQBAJ

Hemdan, E. E., & Manjaiah, D. H. (2018). *CFIM : Toward Building New Cloud Forensics Investigation Model*. Academic Press.

Ieong, R. S. C. (2006). FORZA–Digital forensics investigation framework that incorporate legal issues. *Digital Investigation*, 3, 29–36. doi:10.1016/j.diin.2006.06.004

James, J. I., Shosha, A. F., & Gladyshev, P. (2015). Digital Forensic Investigation and Cloud Computing. In *Cloud Technology* (pp. 1231–1271). IGI Global., doi:10.4018/978-1-4666-6539-2.ch057

Jurcut, A., Coffey, T., & Dojen, R. (2012). Symmetry in Security Protocol Cryptographic Messages—A Serious Weakness Exploitable by Parallel Session Attacks. *2012 Seventh International Conference on Availability, Reliability and Security*, 410–416. 10.1109/ARES.2012.39

Jurcut, A., Coffey, T., Dojen, R., & Gyorodi, R. (2009). Security Protocol Design: A Case Study Using Key Distribution Protocols. *Journal of Computer Science & Control Systems, 2*(2).

Jurcut, A., Niculcea, T., Ranaweera, P., & LeKhac, A. (2020). *Security considerations for Internet of Things: A survey.* ArXiv Preprint ArXiv:2006.10591.

Jurcut, A. D. (2018). Automated logic-based technique for formal verification of security protocols. *Journal of Advances in Computer Network, 6,* 77–85. doi:10.18178/JACN.2018.6.2.258

Jurcut, A. D., Coffey, T., & Dojen, R. (2014). Design requirements to counter parallel session attacks in security protocols. *2014 Twelfth Annual International Conference on Privacy, Security and Trust*, 298–305. 10.1109/PST.2014.6890952

Jurcut, A. D., Ranaweera, P., & Xu, L. (2020). Introduction to IoT Security. *IoT Security: Advances in Authentication*, 27–64.

Kumar, T., Braeken, A., Jurcut, A. D., Liyanage, M., & Ylianttila, M. (2019). AGE: Authentication in gadget-free healthcare environments. *Information Technology Management*, 1–20.

Le, D.-P., Meng, H., Su, L., Yeo, S. L., & Thing, V. (2018). Biff: A blockchain-based iot forensics framework with identity privacy. *TENCON 2018-2018 IEEE Region 10 Conference*, 2372–2377.

Li, S., Choo, K.-K. R., Sun, Q., Buchanan, W. J., & Cao, J. (2019). IoT forensics: Amazon echo as a use case. *IEEE Internet of Things Journal, 6*(4), 6487–6497. doi:10.1109/JIOT.2019.2906946

Meffert, C., Clark, D., Baggili, I., & Breitinger, F. (2017). Forensic State Acquisition from Internet of Things (FSAIoT): A General Framework and Practical Approach for IoT Forensics Through IoT Device State Acquisition. *Proceedings of the 12th International Conference on Availability, Reliability and Security*, 56:1-56:11. 10.1145/3098954.3104053

Morgan, S. (2017). *Cybercrime Report, 2017*. Academic Press.

Nieto, A., Rios, R., & Lopez, J. (2017). A methodology for privacy-aware IoT-forensics. *2017 IEEE Trustcom/BigDataSE/ICESS*, 626–633.

Nieto, A., Rios, R., & Lopez, J. (2018). IoT-forensics meets privacy: Towards cooperative digital investigations. *Sensors (Basel)*, *18*(2), 492. doi:10.339018020492 PMID:29414864

Noura, H. N., Salman, O., Chehab, A., & Couturier, R. (2020). DistLog: A distributed logging scheme for IoT forensics. *Ad Hoc Networks*, *98*, 102061. doi:10.1016/j.adhoc.2019.102061

Perumal, S., Norwawi, N. M., & Raman, V. (2015). Internet of Things(IoT) digital forensic investigation model: Top-down forensic approach methodology. *2015 Fifth International Conference on Digital Information Processing and Communications (ICDIPC)*, 19–23. 10.1109/ICDIPC.2015.7323000

Raghavan, S. (2013). Digital forensic research: Current state of the art. *CSI Transactions on ICT*, *1*(1), 91–114. doi:10.100740012-012-0008-7

Statista, R. D. (2019). *Internet of Things-Number of connected devices worldwide 2015-2025*. Statista Research Department. Statista. Com/Statistics/471264/Iot-Number-of-Connected-Devices-Worldwide.

Stoyanova, M., Nikoloudakis, Y., Panagiotakis, S., Pallis, E., & Markakis, E. K. (2020). A Survey on the Internet of Things (IoT) Forensics: Challenges, Approaches and Open Issues. *IEEE Communications Surveys and Tutorials*, *22*(2), 1191–1221. doi:10.1109/COMST.2019.2962586

Sumalatha, M. R., & Batsa, P. (2016). Data collection and audit logs of digital forensics in cloud. *2016 International Conference on Recent Trends in Information Technology (ICRTIT)*, 1–8. 10.1109/ICRTIT.2016.7569587

Xu, L., Jurcut, A. D., & Ahmadi, H. (2019). Emerging Challenges and Requirements for Internet of Things in 5G. *5G-Enabled Internet of Things*.

Zawoad, S., & Hasan, R. (2015). A trustworthy cloud forensics environment. *IFIP Advances in Information and Communication Technology*, *462*, 271–285. doi:10.1007/978-3-319-24123-4_16

Zawoad, S., Hasan, R., & Skjellum, A. (2015). OCF: an open cloud forensics model for reliable digital forensics. *2015 IEEE 8th International Conference on Cloud Computing*, 437–444.

Chapter 4
Forensic Investigation–Based Framework for SDN Using Blockchain

Sonam Bhardwaj
National Institute of Technology, Kurukshetra, India

Rochak Swami
National Institute of Technology, Kurukshetra, India

Mayank Dave
ⓘ https://orcid.org/0000-0003-4748-0753
National Institute of Technology, Kurukshetra, India

ABSTRACT

Software-defined networking (SDN) is a promising networking technology that provides a new way of network management to the customers. SDN provides more programmable and flexible network services. SDN breaks the vertical integration of control and data planes and promotes centralized network management. This unique characteristic of SDN offers security features to deal with the malicious activities. However, architectural design of SDN makes it vulnerable to several attacks. Therefore, it is important to investigate the crime through various forensic techniques. This work discusses a literature study of some possible forensic techniques. A framework is also presented for forensic investigation of SDN environment in attack scenario. The proposed framework includes the collection of evidence and preserves them against any damage. During investigation, protection of evidence and chain of custody are of utmost importance to avoid misleading of the investigators. The safe storage strategy as well as maintaining the custody link can be achieved through blockchain technology.

DOI: 10.4018/978-1-7998-7589-5.ch004

INTRODUCTION

Networking has become an essential part of our daily lives as per the business requirements and personal experience. There are two major conceptual models in the networking technology, i.e., data plane and control plane. These planes describe the handling of network traffic or packets. The data plane consists of different networking and forwarding devices such as routers, switches, etc. The networking devices handle the forwarding of the packets. Therefore, the data plane is also known as forwarding plane having the forwarding functionality. The control logic for the forwarding decision making used by the data plane devices is placed in the control plane. In conventional networks, data and control planes are coupled with each other. These networks work in a distributed and static manner. The control logic is implemented in each networking device of the network. When a new mechanism or policy is required to add in the existing mechanism, the changes are done in all the networking devices. To overcome such limitations, a new networking paradigm has been developed, i.e., Software-defined networking (SDN). SDN is a unique networking technology that offers simplified and programmable network management to the users as per the requirements. SDN has attracted both academia and industry communities due to its flexible and programmable nature of handling the networking services. In the case of SDN, the control logic is separated from the data plane devices (Kreutz et al., 2015; Hakiri et al., 2014). This separation is the prime feature of SDN. In SDN, data plane includes SDN-specific switches and the control plane comprises a controller. The controller controls the forwarding devices and provides a global view of the complete network. The controller is the most important and intellectual component of SDN, which offers a centralized networking architecture. The data plane devices communicate with the control plane via a standard protocol - "OpenFlow" (McKeown et al., 2008; Lara et al., 2013). OpenFlow came into existence in 2008, which was developed by Open Networking Foundation (ONF) (Goransson et al., 2013). There may be required to add or update any existing policy in the network, then the changes are made in the control plane only (Kim et al., 2013). SDN makes this process cost-effective and less time-consuming over conventional networks. SDN also offers security features such as global visibility of malicious traffic in the network and updating a policy immediately to deal with malicious activities on the detection of an attack. Whenever or whichever networking technology is used, there are always chances of security issues. Similarly, SDN attracts several attacks like man-in-the-middle, sniffing, DDoS, saturation attacks, etc., because of its centralized control and separation of control-data planes (Swami et al., 2019; Swami et al., 2020). Out of all the SDN components, control plane is the most sensitive entity to the attacks, which may cause a single point of failure due to its centralized architecture. By exhausting the controller, the complete network can be collapsed that degrades the network's performance for normal users. Therefore, it is necessary to secure the network against cyber-attacks by analyzing the malicious activities periodically. Investigating such attacks in SDN is a challenging task. For this purpose, a branch of digital forensics - "Network Forensics" is used in the network to investigate network traffic and all the network activities.

Network forensics plays a vital role in locating the source of attacks and to find out the type of attacks. The investigation process involves collection, acquisition, and attribution of the attacks, which is done systematically, requiring the investigators to identify digital evidence sources as their first priority (Liu et al., 2018). The investigation is purely based on evidence, and there is a need to preserve the evidence and protect them against any damage or tampering. Therefore, a strong evidence preservation model for investigation is proposed for the SDN environment employing a famous technology known as "Blockchain". The investigation of the network is done in several phases that are documented in a clear way. Since all the data that is examined needs to be safe and secure, blockchain based framework allows the data storage in the form of transactions. The data is stored in the blocks as evidence and to maintain the chain of custody, the blocks are linked through cryptographic links. In order to preserve the victim device and the device under examination, the SDN controller maintains the smart contracts between the data collection module, switches, and hosts to avoid any unauthorized access to any system connected to the network.

This chapter introduces an overview of the different forensic investigation techniques and their required working components. The chapter is structured as follows. Section 2 discusses the Blockchain and SDN architecture with their working. In Section 3 a taxonomy on various forensic investigation techniques are presented and summarized. The proposed framework based on forensic investigation for SDN is introduced in Section 4. In Section 5 open research challenges in this area are discussed. Finally, the chapter is concluded in Section 6.

BACKGROUND

In this section, we discuss the basic concepts and architecture presented in this chapter related to Blockchain technology and SDN. A great detail is provided on how these technologies work and further how they can be integrated.

Blockchain Technology

Blockchain is substantially a data management technology that stores an entire list of committed transactions and digital traces in a sequence of blocks managed by a cluster of entities rather than a single computer. These entities are linked cryptographically to each other as shown in figure 1 over a peer-to-peer (P2P) network with each block containing three primary elements being data, a hash value of the current block, and the previous block hash value. The first block of the chain is referred to as the "genesis block" which marks the beginning of the block chain. Every block stores the data related to the transaction amount, sender, and receiver of the amount. The hash stored is useful in proving the identity of an individual block serving as a fingerprint. Therefore, any modification in the content of the block causes the hash to change its value making it easier to identify any invalid transaction and thereby discarding it from the chain (Zheng et al., 2018).

Figure 1. Blockchain Architecture

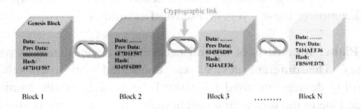

There are three types of Blockchain based on transaction management and availability: public, private, and consortium (Lu, 2018). In public Blockchain, it is almost impossible to tamper the data because the records can be validated by large number of participants and the transactions are visible to public making blockchain prominent for passing digital information. This digital information is shared between users with electronic cash in the form of Bitcoin, validating and transmitting the cryptocurrency securely in a decentralized and peer-to-peer manner.

The committed transactions are approved and verified by every participant creating irrefutable records, thus avoiding data tampering and ensuring ledger consistency. This unique feature of blockchain motivates to integrate this technology with the cybersecurity solutions to attain sustainability and robustness in different network environments.

Software-Defined Networking

Software-defined networking (SDN) is a networking technology that provides a flexible and easily reconfigurable networking environment to the customers. The prime characteristic of SDN is the separation of the data plane and control plane. The data plane consists of different networking devices such as routers, switches, etc. A controller is placed in the control plane, which provides a global view of the whole network. This property of the controller makes the SDN a centralized networking architecture (Swami et al., 2019). With the help of a global view and separation of data and control planes, any new policy can be easily implemented to the existing policy. This modification has to be done in the control plane only. Therefore, the process becomes less time-taking and cost-effective as compared to conventional networks (non-SDN). Due to these advantages of SDN, it is rapidly replacing the conventional networks.

SDN Architecture

The architecture of SDN is made up of three layers (planes) that are data plane, control plane, and application plane. figure 2 describes the different layers of SDN. A brief explanation of these layers is discussed as follows:

- **Data Plane:** It consists of several networking devices such as routers and switches. The different devices are connected with each other. These forwarding devices are used to forward the network traffic from a host to another. Due to the forwarding functionality, the data plane is also known as data forwarding plane. SDN works on switches as a data forwarding device generally. Each SDN switch has flow tables that store the entries of network packets. Each entry has three main components that are rule, action, and counter. Rule maintains different header values for incoming packets, i.e., source IP address, destination IP address, protocol, source port, destination port, Ethernet source, Ethernet destination, priority, etc. These header values are used for matching with header values of the incoming new packets. Action component decides which action should be taken under what condition. The actions include forwarding the packet to controller, forwarding to the destined host, or dropping the packet. Each flow table has a counter field that keeps track of statistics related to the packets. It can be determined how many packets have been dropped, forwarded, or sent to controller of a particular flow. Data plane devices communicate with the controller via a standard protocol, "OpenFlow". When a packet comes at the switch, it doesn't get any matching entry in the flow table, then it is forwarded to the controller for taking appropriate action.
- **Control Plane:** Control plane comprises controller that may be single or multiple in quantity. The controller controls and manages all the forwarding devices (SDN switches) and the complete working of the network. That is why the controller is considered as a "brain of SDN". It decides what action should be taken when a packet is sent to the controller due to an unmatched entry. Also, the controller sends a flow modification rule to the switches for

updating its flow table. A controller provides a global view of the complete network. There are some examples of centralized controllers, i.e., Ryu, POX, etc. OpenDaylight, Floodlight, ONOS are types of distributed controllers that support a multi-controller scenario. In the case of multi-controller control plane, the controllers are connected via east-west bound interfaces. A multi-controller environment is used if a single controller is not capable of handling a large number of switches. An individual controller controls a group of switches.

- **Application Plane:** The application layer includes different applications such as routing, security, load-balancing, traffic monitoring, and many more. The applications are placed over the control plane. These applications make the logic for forwarding decisions. In the controller, the control logic is implemented in the controller with the help of the application, which is used by the forwarding devices for making forwarding decisions. The application layer communicates with the control plane via a northbound interface such as REST.

Packet Forwarding Between Controller and Switch

In SDN, when a packet arrives at the switch, it checks its flow table to check the installed rules. Then if the header fields of the incoming packet match with the rules in the flow table, the packet is forwarded towards the destined host. In case of not matching flow rules, a packet_in message with the required header fields of the packet is transferred to the controller. The controller decides an appropriate action for the packet, defines a new rule, and sends a flow modification rule "FlowMod" to all the switches. All the switches update the flow modification rule in their respective flow tables.

In the case of attacks or any malicious activities, the normal processing of packet forwarding in SDN gets disrupted, and the entire network collapsed. The normal users suffer from such kind of malicious activities and the performance of the network degrades.

Figure 2. SDN Architecture

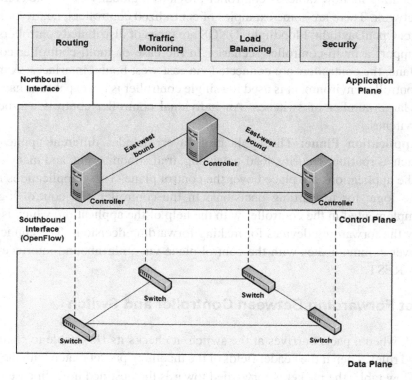

Vulnerable Target Points in the SDN Architecture

There are various vulnerable points in the SDN architecture (Swami et al., 2019). The controller is the most sensitive target of the attackers. The major potential targets of SDN architecture are discussed in brief.

- **SDN switch:** SDN switches have flow tables to store the track of incoming network packets. These flow tables have a limited size of memory, so it is an issue for security purposes.
- **Links between SDN switches:** Switches forward the network packets to other switches for delivering it to the destination host. The forwarded packets carry important information that can be intercepted by the attackers.
- **SDN controller:** SDN controller is the centralized entity that manages the whole network. It can suffer from a single point of failure.
- **Link between controller and switch:** The link between controller and switch is used to send the essential messages like packet in and flow modification

rules as per the requirement. When the flow rules are sent from the controller to the switch, they may have interfered and malicious rules can be added.

- **Links between controllers:** Controllers share sensitive information with each other. The attacker can target the controller to gain knowledge and source of information. In the case of multi-controller environment, cascading failure of controllers may have happened.

- **The applications:** Various applications are implemented in the controller via north bound interface as per the requirements. Attackers can obtain access to the applications and may add malicious activities.

A TAXONOMY OF INVESTIGATION TECHNIQUES IN NETWORK FORENSICS

The investigators must follow a systematic and timely investigation of the crime so that the collected evidence doesn't lose their credibility. To handle the evidence, various preservation methods (Brotis et al., 2019) are followed that make the evidence secure. The investigation team should not just follow a strategic plan for securing the evidence but also adopt standard network forensic techniques to further investigate. The adaption of any technique has to fulfill the requirement of being valid and acceptable in the court of law. Some of the techniques with their respective forensic approaches are delineated in figure 3. The techniques have their own framework and methodology (Khan et al., 2016) intended to achieve a particular objective like determining an attack, monitoring logs, or maintaining the evidence's integrity. A few of the existing techniques are discussed below:

- **Traceback based NFT:** Trace-backing techniques are used when the investigators need to identify the origin of the packets in a network. The identification of origin signifies the source from where the attack is generated. Traceback stands as a useful technique that traces the packets' origin for DDoS attack and IP Spoofing attacks (Dou et al., 2012) a different distributed network. The distributed networks collaborating with the Internet also attract bot-master for different attacks (Mizoguchi et al., 2011). To enhance the security of the network system and to overcome such attacks, Traceback mechanisms must be effectively incorporated into the system. A few of the forensic approaches used in the Traceback mechanisms are discussed below:

  ○ **Hash Correction Codes:** In this approach, fragments of IP addresses are used to traceback the source/origin of the attack (incident) by performing the hash coding at the victim node. This approach is effective for tracing back the DoS and DDoS attacks in Topology assisted Deterministic Packet Marking (TDPM) scheme (Wang and Wang, 2010). The router uses hash values inside a packet, which is then compared at the victim node. The victim node bears the responsibility of identifying ingress router (generating malicious packets) using BFS (breadth-first search). Later, the received hash fragments from other routers are compared with the ingress router hash fragments to investigate malicious packets.

- ○ **Authenticated Evidence:** This approach also makes use of a packet marking scheme for Traceback as in TDPM, which provides integrity to the collected evidence. The authentication to the collected evidence is provided by the trustful operators that manage the collected data and relieve the edge routers (maintaining time label for each record) from traffic management overhead, hence improving overall network performance (Ma et al., 2020).

- ○ **Flow-based selection marking scheme:** The approach is adopted by Network Forensic Evidence Acquisition (NFEA) that follows a packet marking scheme (Kim and Kim, 2011). It Traceback the origin of the Intruder with an appropriate tracking range. The effective tracking range is improved by looking into packet header and router information. The critical aspect of this approach can be seen finding the origin when the attacker hides its MAC address.

- ○ **Light-Weight IP Traceback (LWIP):** The scheme investigates large DDoS attacks in a network using Time-To-Live (TTL) field of IP header by finding and reconstructing the attack paths. The approach uses tree analysis algorithm and routing filter algorithm to Traceback an attack along with TTL value decrementing with packet movement from one router to another towards the victim node (Saurabh and Sairam, 2016).

- ○ **Hopping based Spread Spectrum (HBSST):** This technique is based upon Frequency hopping direct spread spectrum, code hopping direct sequence spread spectrum, and time hopping direct sequence spread spectrum (Gomes et al., 2018). In HBSST, a secret pseudo-noise code is sent with the normal traffic that is hidden from the intruders and can be monitored by investigators for their malicious activities.

Figure 3. Network Forensic Investigation Techniques and their approaches

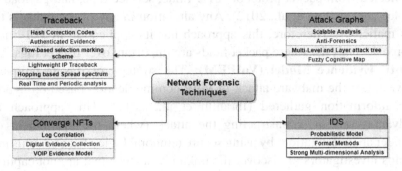

- **Real-time and periodic analysis:** This approach is used by IP Traceback protocol to determine the origin of the intruder performing real-time and periodic analysis on the traffic that runs through the router (Tian et al., 2018). The real-time analysis is performed for the router hash tables. In contrast, periodic analysis is carried for the compress hash table stored in the database for further investigation of the traffic.
  ○ **Converge NFTs:** This indicates the identification of digital pieces of evidence in converge networks, specifically in VoIP communication (Khan et al., 2014), where signals are divided into frames eventually embedded in data packets as voice codes. Later these data packets are sent over the IP network just as a normal voice packet. The transmitted voice packet is exploited and changed to a malicious packet by intruders due to unencrypted fields in the voice packets. The intruders may perform attacks including flooding, buffer overflow, hijack calls, degrading call integrity, man-in-the-middle, and privacy leakage. Therefore, to deal with such attacks various forensic approaches that may be considered are:
- **Log Correlation:** The key approach for Pattern based network Forensics (PBNF), guides in discovering and stopping attacks, determines the traces of intruders, and aids in collecting evidence against the intruder. The two modules playing a vital role in the success of this approach are VoIP evidence collector and VoIP evidence analyzer. The former collects the attack packets in a real-time environment based on the filter rule set applied on the voice traffic. The latter collects the data from the forensic server and analyzes it based on log correlation and normalization.
- **Digital evidence collection:** The usefulness of this approach lies in the identification of malicious packets in network traffic. Malicious packets are also categorized as abnormal traffic against which digital evidence is

collected from packet protocol, TTL value, service type, and payload of the voice packet (Len et al., 2012). Any alteration in any of the fields is treated as malicious. Therefore, this approach has its application in VoIP network forensic analysis, where packet fields are important over packet logs.

- **VoIP Evidence Model (VoIPEM):** The strategy of this technique is to investigate the malware attack in VoIP communication based on hypothesis on information gathered (Ibrahim et al., 2012). This approach stands advantageous in reconstructing the attack (where the insufficient details hinder an investigation) by using secure temporal logic of action. This method helps investigators to discover the unknown attacks that are not captured by the system. The reconstruction of the attack scenario is done to identify the time, location, and procedure of the attack.
  - **Attack Graphs based NFT:** Attack Graph approach is followed to track and visualize all the possible paths an intruder followed to perform an attack in a network. All the possible paths can be identified by analyzing networks, hosts, and other security devices. The attack graph (Ou et al., 2006) consists of vertices representing attack nodes and edges denoting the state transition between those vertices (nodes). Such visualization is used in network forensic investigation to determine the worst attack paths and help the network administrator to improve the defense system before an attack occurs.
- **Scalable Analysis (SA):** SA determines a class of alerts so as to measure the impact of malicious activities for current and future attacks in a large network traffic environment. SA provides a framework for real-time situations to process a huge amount of raw data (Albanese et al., 2011). At first, the attack graph is generated to determine the network components and their relationship among themselves. After determining the components, the attack graph is distributed over a time span to capture probabilistic temporal behavior of the intruder. The probabilistic behavior aids the construction of attack scenarios to gather services and vulnerabilities exploited by the attack so that dependencies can be integrated with the graphs.
- **Anti-Forensics:** This approach is adopted for forensic investigation in the scenarios when the intruder may delete or alter the traces by using various anti-forensic techniques. Hence, Attack Graph for Forensic Examination (AGFE) employs anti-forensic nodes with the attack graph to monitor the malicious activities and store the same on anti-forensic database. This stored information helps the investigators for monitoring malicious activities and identify the traces for any injected alteration in traces (Chandran and Yan, 2014).

- **Multi-level and layer attack tree (MLL-AT):** MLL-AT determines the system risks in multi-stage network attacks. The system risk is calculated by employing the multi-attribute utility theory, and nodes are assigned with some weightage in the attack tree. After the system risk is calculated, the attack sequence is generated, and unwanted nodes are removed from the attack tree (Soleimani and Ghorbani, 2012).

- **Fuzzy Cognitive Map (FCM):** FCM is constructed from an attack graph that uses genetic algorithm to identify attack paths (Luo et al., 2019). It identifies the worst attack paths only instead of finding all attack paths. It performs identification of the worst path by assigning weights to concept edges (edges in FCM solution) based on concept nodes (nodes in FCM solution). These concept nodes and edges are stored in an adjacent matrix based on which the genetic algorithm determines the worst attack from the collection of attack behaviors.

  ○ **Intrusion Detection Systems (IDS) based NFT:** The IDS monitors the network for any malicious activities by an intruder trying to exploit the network and trigger alert messages to inform the management system. IDS helps in investigating for any breaches in the network and reporting them to the administrator to act on it accordingly.

- **Probabilistic Model:** This approach is employed in Analytical Intrusion Detection Framework (AIDF) to integrate alert information from IDS Sensors and forensic analysis for intrusion detection (Kamthe and Deisenroth, 2018). The hidden information is uncovered by the probabilistic approach adopted for modeling and detecting intruder attacks. Snort (Shah and Issac, 2018) is used as a probabilistic inference to trigger a rule if there is a match of network traffic with the pattern encoded in the signature rule. These rules help in detecting and understanding attacks so that investigators can take necessary action for preventing such attacks in the future.

- **Formal methods:** These forensic methods are used in Intrusion tolerance system for analyzing and modeling a dynamic forensic system (Belta et al., 2017). The intrusion tolerant system basically means that the system must be able to withstand the failure condition resulting from attacks conducted by intruders to bring the system into malicious state. The security attributes of such systems can be evaluated using steady state probability for Markov model that uses finite state machine to build a dynamic forensic system.

- **Strong Multi-Dimensional Analysis:** Such an analysis approach is used to build the framework for network forensics based on intrusion detection static as well as dynamic analysis. The approach is used to perform behavioral analysis on the captured data in offline mode by matching patterns based on library traces and carrying out protocol analysis for detecting malicious behavior (Dernbecher and Beck, 2017).

Table 1. Summary of the Network Forensic Techniques in different Network Environments

Technique	Approach	Network Environment	Data Integrity	Authentication	Confidentiality	Chain of Custody	Evidence Protection
Traceback based NFT	Hash Correction Codes	Distributed Networks	Yes	Yes	No	No	Yes
	Authenticated Evidence:	Distributed Networks	Yes	Yes	No	No	Yes
	Flow-based selection marking scheme	Data Centric networks	Yes	No	No	Yes	No
	Light-Weight IP Traceback (LWIP)	Wireless sensor networks	No	No	No	Yes	No
	Hopping based Spread Spectrum (HBSST)	Wireless LAN	No	No	Yes	No	No
	Real-time and periodic analysis	Wireless mesh networks	No	No	No	Yes	No
Converge NFTs	Log Correlation	VOIP Networks	No	No	No	Yes	Yes
	Digital evidence collection	VoIP networks	Yes	No	No	Yes	Yes
	VoIP Evidence Model (VoIPEM)	VoIP	Yes	No	No	Yes	Yes
Attack Graphs based NFT	Scalable Analysis (SA)	Real- time networks	Yes	No	No	Yes	No
	Anti-Forensics	Honeypot network	Yes	No	Yes	Yes	Yes
	Multi-level and layer attack tree (MLL-AT)	Multi-stage networks	No	No	No	Yes	No
	Fuzzy Cognitive Map (FCM):	Fuzzy cognitive networks	Yes	No	No	Yes	No
Intrusion Detection Systems (IDS) based NFT	Probabilistic Model	Social Networks	No	Yes	Yes	No	No
	Formal methods	Wireless Sensor Networks	Yes	No	No	Yes	Yes
	Strong Multi-Dimensional Analysis	Real time network	No	Yes	Yes	No	Yes

Table 1 summarizes the network forensic techniques in different but not limited to different network environments. The techniques are better in terms of their performance but together lack to impose CIA (confidentiality, integrity, and availability) triad properties along-with chain of custody and evidence protection. Therefore, it urges for an investigation framework in the SDN environment to collectively provide strong protection for the evidence by incorporating the mentioned security traits.

FORENSIC INVESTIGATION BASED FRAMEWORK FOR SDN

The reconfigurable SDN has its base on the data plane devices and the SDN controller. The data plane contains the switches that handle the data forwarding task from one host to another. The numerous hosts are connected to the network with the help of switches that forward the packets to the controller based on the flow rules. The rules in the switches' flow tables, which do not have the ability to identify malicious unknown nodes among the connected hosts. Therefore, with the flow of data towards the SDN controller, malicious traffic also enters the network and try to exploit the vulnerabilities of the network. The unauthorized access to the network may harm the security principles (data integrity, confidentiality, and availability) and perform malicious activities in the form of attacks. SDN alone fails to identify these suspicious activities. Hence, it requires a network investigation module to identify the attacks and report them to the SDN controller to improve its defense mechanism in the framework presented in figure 4. The data gathered at the controller is passed to the data collection module using network monitoring tools as shown in figure 5. In the data collection module, blockchain mechanism is applied to preserve the data and store them in the form of blocks. The crypto-preservation system of the blockchain technology keeps the data secure and helps in maintaining the chain of custody. The proposed framework combines supervision and data access control based on smart contracts using blockchain technology, which provides a secure and trusted environment for data sharing. The framework applies 3-step preservation of data, firstly, in the data collection module using blockchain. The first preservation is done for storing the raw data and maintaining its integrity. Secondly, at the time of seizure while investigating an incident by creating hash of the seized data and lastly, at the time of acquisition of the evidence in network investigation module to confirm that the data is accurate and verifiable.

Figure 4. Forensic investigation in SDN network

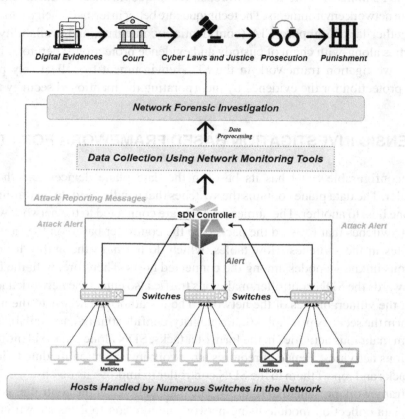

During the data collection, the preprocessing or filtering is applied on the data to get rid of ambiguity and integrating data from different switches. A detailed forensic investigation is carried out on the digital data received by the network investigation module taking the form of digital evidence. This digital evidence passes through numerous thorough investigation phases from identification of the incident to reporting the incident as an attack. As soon as the attack is confirmed, an attack reporting message with the supporting details of the attack are sent to the SDN controller. The controller issues alert to the data plane in the network and propose defense action against the attack. The report generated by the network investigation module are supported with the laws to be presented in front of jurisdiction against the cybercriminals. All the mechanisms of the framework are supported by the blockchain technology. It not only provides security to the framework but a decentralized transaction based system to store the evidence in a manageable form with a high degree of protection for data. The whole framework is supported by laws and legal ethics ultimately presented in front of the judiciary for the criminal prosecution.

Figure 5. Blockchain based Data Collection Module

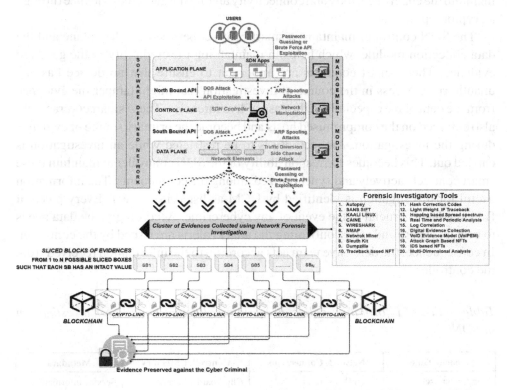

Components of Proposed Framework

- **Data Collection Module (DCM):** The basic principles of data collection are to gather the data, plan the unified process of data selection, collection, and analysis. The collection module in the proposed framework is based on decentralized blockchain technology that employs smart contracts between the DCM and switches ensuring that any data collected is valid, reliable, and credible. It is equally important that ethical issues are considered while an investigation is made.

The data is gathered using various network monitoring and collection tools that help in feeding data to DCM along with the meta-data. As soon as the data enters the DCM, the data is distributed in blocks as in the form of pieces of evidence sliced in different blocks. To ensure integrity, blocks containing evidence are connected with the cryptographic link. The block of evidence is preserved using SHA-256 cryptography. The idea of storing the evidence in the form of transactions is to maintain the chain of custody and connectivity among the gathered evidence through a cryptographic link.

The SDN controller maintains a smart contract between the data plane and the data collection module, which helps in maintaining the credibility of the gathered evidence. These smart contracts are important to ensure that no device has any unauthorized access in the course of investigation that might tamper the evidence from the data plane especially in the case of live forensics. These smart contracts are also enforced on the compromised hosts and become the primary source of evidence during the investigation. Any activity is to be restricted while an investigation is carried out. This becomes the responsibility of the SDN controller to maintain these smart contracts actively and synchronized among the components. The information useful for investigation is identified by DCM as listed in Table 1. Every piece of flowing data is crucial in the event of any cybercrime. Accordingly, the data needs to be kept secure and after confirming the attack, alerts are issued by the controller. In consequence, the defensive team acts according to the information received from the controller.

Table 2. List of information collected by data collection module for investigation in SDN

System Time	Network Connections	Controller Memory	Metadata
Logged-on-user	Open flow rules	Clip-board contents	Service information
Type Of Controller	Process information	Driver information	Command history
Protocols used	Type of switch	Mapped drives	Shared resources
Network Information	Process-to-port mapping	Open files	Type of switch
Process memory	Network status	Controller logs	Memory dumps

The DCM in the proposed framework allows for controlled access to the information and provides better security to the raw evidence collected. The synchronization between smart contracts ensures the proper and trustful functioning of the network by reducing the security risks.

- **Network Forensic Investigation:** The investigation in the SDN network is carried out based on the modified generic model of network forensics (Pilli et al., 2010), containing six phases as illustrated in figure 6. The proposed work modified this model for the SDN network and handing over the investigation task to controller. The data collection module transfers the collected data to the network investigation module, which acts on the data in the defined phases.

- ○ **Identification:** The network events monitored by the tools are identified for the incident (attack) and all the sources from where the piece of evidence can be gathered are determined based on the confirmation of attack. The recognition of the evidence is the first task in the investigation. In the SDN network, the primary source of evidence is the data plane having all the networking devices and associated data and flow rules stored on these devices. Since the memory of devices is limited, the volatile data is transferred immediately to the control plane for further investigation.

- ○ **Seizure, Hashing, and Preservation:** As soon the identification of the attack is made, seizure of devices and data take place based on the seizure principles. These principles govern the investigation to safely create data image, which cannot be written back and tampered. The data is seized based on the suspicious activity in the network and collecting the suspicious data for investigation. The investigators must also be aware of the running processes in the "ON" state machine, shared and mapped device, registry, and event logs. The collected data needs to be preserved immediately so that no tampering of evidence is possible. The protection of data is basically done by applying hashing, which is an irreversible process that converts the block of data into fixed size string (MD5, SHA-1, SHA-256, or HMAC) and storing the hash values corresponding to the data. At the end of this phase, a seizure report is generated containing various details about the system configuration, hash values, transfer, and storage media.

Figure 6. Forensic Investigation Module with two-step evidence Preservation

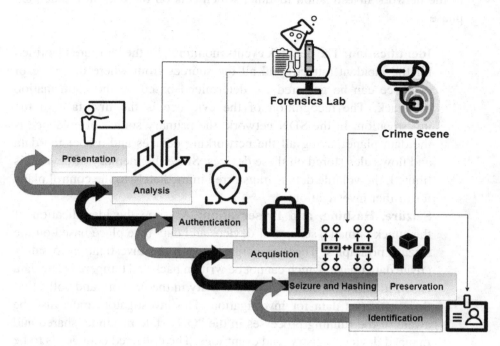

- **Acquisition:** This is the most essential phase of an investigation that converts the collected original digital evidence into a bit stream image and is written in a trusted block where it needs to be stored safely (write blocker). The seized evidences cannot be directly processed because of maintaining the credibility and integrity of the evidence. The image of the collected evidence must be taken in a device that must have sufficient storage than the source so as to hold the data image for examination. The acquisition report consists of the hash of the original evidence and the hash of blocks of hashes where the image was taken. The hash of original evidence is verified with the one in the seizure report. If the match is a true match, the report is considered to be trusted and aids in further investigation.
- **Authentication:** The preservation of the evidence holds the priority as soon as an incident is reported and piece of evidence is collected. The authentication of the evidence must be done, confirming the truth. The evidence needs to follow simple rules to prove their genuineness that are:
  - Admissible: The collected evidence can be used in court or elsewhere to prove the happening of the incident or cybercrime.
  - Authentic: The shreds (evidence) must not divert the incident in any other direction. It must relate to the incident in a relevant way.

- ○ Complete: There should not be any tunnel vision or exculpatory evidence for alternative suspects.
- ○ Reliable: Evidence is collected to prove a crime against a suspect. Hence, there should be no question regarding authenticity and veracity.
- ○ Believable: It is the responsibility of the investigators to gather the evidence, which are clear, easy to understand, and believable by jury.

Therefore, in the investigation process, the authenticity of the evidence is accepted if the evidence follows the above-mentioned rules and verifies the pre-acquisition hash value. At the time of examination, the hash value of the actual data is calculated and verified with the pre-acquisition hash value. If the hash values make a true match, the authenticity is confirmed by the examining authority.

- **Analysis:** The investigators analyze the verified data to discover the relevant information and figure out the patterns of attack. The router information, flow rules applied, the meta-data, and PCAP files of the southbound traffic serve as the essential data for analysis. This critical phase serves the purpose of identifying the attack behavior, what vulnerabilities are exploited, unlock the attack patterns, report any unknown attack, and issue an analysis report to improve the defense mechanism. The integrity of the analyzed data is assured by the blockchain mechanism, which is maintained through the process.
- **Presentation:** Every phase of the investigation is documented in detail to prepare the report of the investigation that is supported by law to be presented in the court. The presentation of the evidence must be recognizable and clearly depicts the facts relevant to the incident. In the case of a network attack, the evidences are presented in the form of evidence graphs that are generated based on attack graphs. Each evidence is provided with a probability score for an attack and all possible paths are determined based on that score. These graphs help in visualizing an attack and predict the attacker's behavior to avoid futuristic attacks.

OPEN RESEARCH CHALLENGES

This section discusses the challenges being envisaged for effective protection of evidence using block-chain technology in SDN so as to carry out a forensic investigation.

- **Management of Data Volume:** In a network, the amount of traffic flowing through the network is tremendous and every unit of traffic is essential from the point of investigation. The network flows may also contain multimedia files or log files that require sufficient storage. The memory of the devices in the data plane is limited. Therefore, the volatile data that is important might be short-lived due to the limited memory (Azmoodeh et al., 2019). Therefore, necessary storage service must be provided, thereby storing only the hash of the data in the blocks and rest of the data in a write blocker disk.

- **Data Extraction Location:** Extracting information from an appropriate location in a network with high speed transmissions is a challenge for network forensics. In huge networks, reconstructing and investigating each attack path becomes difficult for the investigators. It is of utmost importance for an investigation to determine right device, right location, and the right time to collect relevant information. To overcome this problem, a log repository can be maintained by grouping similar logs in the same blocks and providing centralized access to these blocks for carrying analysis centrally.

- **Access to IP addresses:** The identification of the source of the packet is essential to identify the intruder in a network. The IP addresses of the intruders are mostly hidden through various techniques (IP spoofing). These techniques are usually adopted to conduct DDoS attacks in SDN by bombarding the controller with a huge number of packets that are beyond the controller's capacity to process them and hence making the system collapse. Therefore, a source address validation can be employed, which stores the addresses of the same uplinks in the same block. This helps in the reduction of IP spoofing attacks and binds the source IP and MAC address in the same block.

- **Event Timelines and Chronology:** To maintain the chain of custody, timeline of the events must be respected. The data acquisition and order of events are the key to determining the patterns and group similar incidents, so as to, avoid such incidents in future. The high rate of data in SDN makes it a challenge to record events in time and storing logs in limited storage. The blockchain timestamps and hashes ensure that the evidence was collected at a specific moment and not modified.

- **Understandable forensic reports:** The use of blockchain in SDN provides benefits, such as the verifiable and provision of data flows. The knowledge retrieving and creating reports belong to a different phase. In this context, even if the reports and outcomes are automated, they must be understandable in court. Hence, even if blockchain helps to accomplish this task, research has to be done providing a link forensic procedure, SDN flow rules and their explanation.

- **Intelligent forensic tools:** Traditional forensic tools monitor and record traffic by capturing a complete packet, which faces usual time delays in storing and processing the packets. Hence, intelligent tools are needed to capture the traffic based on investigational situations in the emerging SDN infrastructure. This will overcome the storage, resources, and time delay problems with a quick incident response mechanism. The blockchain hash transactions can be applied to the traffic in the form of rules and generate automated reports, thereby providing security to the intelligent systems (Krivchenkov et al., 2018).

CONCLUSION

SDN offers more flexible and programmable network services to users over conventional networks. The centralized global view and programmability to deploy the security policies immediately on detection of malicious behavior makes the SDN trending in the networking field. However, its design characteristics also attract various attacks that can disrupt the working of the entire network. Hence, to secure the centralized SDN forensic investigation plays an important role in analyzing the network activities and identifying the source of the malicious activities. Therefore, various forensic investigation techniques have been discussed in this work. Further, a forensic investigation framework has also been proposed for SDN that collects the data, carryout investigation, and issues alert in the network to activate the defense system.

The work discusses different modules of the framework and their detailed functionalities. The framework securely keeps the gathered data with the three-step preservation method using blockchain hence avoiding any kind of tampering in the collected evidence. The investigation process enforces judiciary laws to act against cybercriminals by presenting evidence in a way acceptable by the court. To make the evidence credible, blockchain allows the data to be stored securely, maintaining integrity and chain of custody.

In future work, the focus will be on developing a blockchain based automated forensic framework for SDN, which enables the controller agent to collect heterogeneous digital evidence. The controller agent will also integrate the forensic tool that carries investigation and encrypt the report to be transferred on the network.

REFERENCES

Albanese, M., Jajodia, S., Pugliese, A., & Subrahmanian, V. S. (2011). Scalable analysis of attack scenarios. In *European Symposium on Research in Computer Security* (pp. 416-433). Springer.

Azmoodeh, A., Dehghantanha, A., & Choo, K. K. R. (2019). Big data and internet of things security and forensics: challenges and opportunities. In *Handbook of Big Data and IoT Security* (pp. 1–4). Springer. doi:10.1007/978-3-030-10543-3_1

Belta, C., Yordanov, B., & Gol, E. A. (2017). *Formal methods for discrete-time dynamical systems* (Vol. 89). Springer. doi:10.1007/978-3-319-50763-7

Brotsis, S., Kolokotronis, N., Limniotis, K., Shiaeles, S., Kavallieros, D., Bellini, E., & Pavué, C. (2019, June). Blockchain solutions for forensic evidence preservation in IoT environments. In *2019 IEEE Conference on Network Softwarization (NetSoft)* (pp. 110-114). IEEE. 10.1109/NETSOFT.2019.8806675

Chandran, R., & Yan, W. Q. (2014). Attack Graph Analysis for Network Anti-Forensics. *International Journal of Digital Crime and Forensics*, *6*(1), 28–50. doi:10.4018/ijdcf.2014010103

Dernbecher, S., & Beck, R. (2017). The concept of mindfulness in information systems research: A multi-dimensional analysis. *European Journal of Information Systems*, *26*(2), 121–142. doi:10.105741303-016-0032-z

Dou, W., Chen, Q., & Chen, J. (2013). A confidence-based filtering method for DDoS attack defense in cloud environment. *Future Generation Computer Systems*, *29*(7), 1838–1850. doi:10.1016/j.future.2012.12.011

Gomes, P. H., Watteyne, T., & Krishnamachari, B. (2018). MABO-TSCH: Multihop and blacklist-based optimized time synchronized channel hopping. *Transactions on Emerging Telecommunications Technologies*, *29*(7), e3223. doi:10.1002/ett.3223

Goransson, P., Black, C., & Culver, T. (2016). *Software defined networks: a comprehensive approach*. Morgan Kaufmann.

Hakiri, A., Gokhale, A., Berthou, P., Schmidt, D. C., & Gayraud, T. (2014). Software-defined networking: Challenges and research opportunities for future internet. *Computer Networks*, *75*, 453–471. doi:10.1016/j.comnet.2014.10.015

Kamthe, S., & Deisenroth, M. (2018). Data-efficient reinforcement learning with probabilistic model predictive control. In *International Conference on Artificial Intelligence and Statistics* (pp. 1701-1710). Academic Press.

Khan, S., Gani, A., Wahab, A. W. A., Shiraz, M., & Ahmad, I. (2016). Network forensics: Review, taxonomy, and open challenges. *Journal of Network and Computer Applications*, *66*, 214–235. doi:10.1016/j.jnca.2016.03.005

Khan, S., Shiraz, M., Abdul Wahab, A. W., Gani, A., Han, Q., & Bin Abdul Rahman, Z. (2014). A comprehensive review on adaptability of network forensics frameworks for mobile cloud computing. *TheScientificWorldJournal, 2014*, 2014. doi:10.1155/2014/547062 PMID:25097880

Kim, H., & Feamster, N. (2013). Improving network management with software defined networking. *IEEE Communications Magazine, 51*(2), 114–119. doi:10.1109/MCOM.2013.6461195

Kim, H. S., & Kim, H. K. (2011, May). Network forensic evidence acquisition (NFEA) with packet marking. In *2011 IEEE Ninth International Symposium on Parallel and Distributed Processing with Applications Workshops* (pp. 388-393). IEEE. 10.1109/ISPAW.2011.27

Kreutz, D., Ramos, F. M., Verissimo, P., Rothenberg, C. E., Azodolmolky, S., & Uhlig, S. (2015). Software-defined networking: A comprehensive survey. *Proceedings of the IEEE, 103*(1), 14–76. doi:10.1109/JPROC.2014.2371999

Krivchenkov, A., Misnevs, B., & Pavlyuk, D. (2018, October). Intelligent Methods in Digital Forensics: State of the Art. In *International Conference on Reliability and Statistics in Transportation and Communication* (pp. 274-284). Springer.

Lara, A., Kolasani, A., & Ramamurthy, B. (2013). Network innovation using openflow: A survey. *IEEE Communications Surveys and Tutorials, 16*(1), 493–512. doi:10.1109/SURV.2013.081313.00105

Liu, C. H., Lin, Q., & Wen, S. (2018). Blockchain-enabled data collection and sharing for industrial IoT with deep reinforcement learning. *IEEE Transactions on Industrial Informatics, 15*(6), 3516–3526. doi:10.1109/TII.2018.2890203

Lu, Y. (2018). Blockchain: A survey on functions, applications and open issues. *Journal of Industrial Integration and Management, 3*(04), 1850015. doi:10.1142/S242486221850015X

Luo, C., Zhang, N., & Wang, X. (2019). Time series prediction based on intuitionistic fuzzy cognitive map. *Soft Computing*, 1–16. doi:10.100700500-019-04321-8

Ma, J., Huang, X., Mu, Y., & Deng, R. H. (2020). Authenticated Data Redaction with Accountability and Transparency. *IEEE Transactions on Dependable and Secure Computing*, 1. doi:10.1109/TDSC.2020.2998135

McKeown, N., Anderson, T., Balakrishnan, H., Parulkar, G., Peterson, L., Rexford, J., Shenker, S., & Turner, J. (2008). OpenFlow: Enabling innovation in campus networks. *Computer Communication Review, 38*(2), 69–74. doi:10.1145/1355734.1355746

Mizoguchi, S., Takemori, K., Miyake, Y., Hori, Y., & Sakurai, K. (2011, June). Traceback framework against botmaster by sharing network communication pattern information. In *2011 Fifth International Conference on Innovative Mobile and Internet Services in Ubiquitous Computing* (pp. 639-644). IEEE. 10.1109/IMIS.2011.152

Ou, X., Boyer, W. F., & McQueen, M. A. (2006, October). A scalable approach to attack graph generation. In *Proceedings of the 13th ACM conference on Computer and communications security* (pp. 336-345). 10.1145/1180405.1180446

Pilli, E. S., Joshi, R. C., & Niyogi, R. (2010). A generic framework for network forensics. *International Journal of Computers and Applications*, *1*(11), 1–6. doi:10.5120/251-408

Saurabh, S., & Sairam, A. S. (2016). Increasing Accuracy and Reliability of IP Traceback for DDoS Attack Using Completion Condition. *International Journal of Network Security*, *18*(2), 224–234.

Shah, S. A. R., & Issac, B. (2018). Performance comparison of intrusion detection systems and application of machine learning to Snort system. *Future Generation Computer Systems*, *80*, 157–170. doi:10.1016/j.future.2017.10.016

Soleimani, M., & Ghorbani, A. A. (2012). Multi-layer episode filtering for the multi-step attack detection. *Computer Communications*, *35*(11), 1368–1379. doi:10.1016/j.comcom.2012.04.001

Swami, R., Dave, M., & Ranga, V. (2019). Software-defined networking-based DDoS defense mechanisms. *ACM Computing Surveys*, *52*(2), 1–36. doi:10.1145/3301614

Swami, R., Dave, M., & Ranga, V. (2020). DDoS Attacks and Defense Mechanisms Using Machine Learning Techniques for SDN. In *Security and Privacy Issues in Sensor Networks and IoT* (pp. 193–214). IGI Global. doi:10.4018/978-1-7998-0373-7.ch008

Tian, Z., Cui, Y., An, L., Su, S., Yin, X., Yin, L., & Cui, X. (2018). A real-time correlation of host-level events in cyber range service for smart campus. *IEEE Access: Practical Innovations, Open Solutions*, *6*, 35355–35364. doi:10.1109/ACCESS.2018.2846590

Wang, X. J., & Wang, X. Y. (2010). Topology-assisted deterministic packet marking for IP traceback. *Journal of China Universities of Posts and Telecommunications*, *17*(2), 116–121. doi:10.1016/S1005-8885(09)60456-8

Zheng, Z., Xie, S., Dai, H. N., Chen, X., & Wang, H. (2018). Blockchain challenges and opportunities: A survey. *International Journal of Web and Grid Services*, *14*(4), 352–375. doi:10.1504/IJWGS.2018.095647

Chapter 5
The Mobility Open Blockchain Initiative:
Identity, Members, Technologies, and Future Trends

Loreen M. Powell
Bloomsburg University of Pennsylvania, USA

Jessica Schwartz
University of the Cumberlands, USA

Michalina Hendon
University of the Cumberlands, USA

ABSTRACT

Technological advancements in the transportation/automotive industry are continually increasing due to competition and consumer demands. The mobile open blockchain initiative (MOBI) is one way organizations are coming together to share innovating ways to revolutionize the transportation/automotive industry. This chapter explains the events that lead to the innovation of an open consortium, MOBI, and its members and highlights some of the cutting-edge technologies and innovative methods where blockchain is being adopted by the transportation/automotive industry.

DOI: 10.4018/978-1-7998-7589-5.ch005

1. INTRODUCTION

Despite Blockchain being a relatively new concept, there are many initiatives currently in existence (Cao, Wang, Li, Gu, and Chen, 2019). Once such initiative is the MOBI (Bothos, Magoutas, Arnaoutaki, and Mentzas, 2019). This initiative was founded by a few leading automakers and launch in early May of 2018 at the Dubai Future Blockchain Summit (Russell, 2018). Today, MOBI is a thriving consortium for blockchain innovation in the mobility industry with many prestigious academic institutions and global organizations including, but not limited to, IBM, Accenture, and ConsenSys. (Lannquist, 2018; Polluck, 2019). By using blockchain technology, this potential initiative hopes to make mobility safe, secure, cheaper, and greener through the creation of blockchain use cases and technology standards for automotive applications (Bothos et al., 2019; Griffin, 2019; Lannquist, 2018). Additionally, MOBI hopes to make mobility more accessible, especially to those currently with issues in obtaining such technology. While MOBI has partnered with many prestigious academic institutions, more partnerships are needed. However, finding and identifying possible Blockchain researchers is not an easy task (Cao et al., 2019). Many IT or business educators struggle with the basic understanding of Blockchain, in general (Zheng, Xie, Dai, Chen, and Wang, 2018). This chapter discusses MOBI via identity, customers, competition, technology, and trends. This work has practical implications for IT programs and faculty wishing to explore or adopt Blockchain or MOBI within their curriculum. This chapter provides future MOBI researchers with an overview of its evolution, members, technology, and reveal points on which special efforts should be explored in the near future. The remainder of this paper is structured as follows. A brief overview of the transformation of the automotive industry and blockchain is introduced in section 2. Section 3 presents MOBI and its members. Blockchain technologies are explored in section 4. This area specifically discusses internet of things (IOTs), cloud computing, smart products and objects, along with smart contracts, sensors, and peer-to-peer (P2P) systems. Section 5 provides insights on upcoming trends and section 6 concludes the paper.

2. RELATED WORK

This section combines theory and technology to explain the recent state of the transportation industry, the use of blockchain and the velocity of MOBI. Over the past two decades, transportation has dramatically transformed with the advent of smart cars autonomous vehicles (AVs), and connected cars (Jeong, Youn, Jho & Shin, 2020). Furthermore, the mobility and innovation of transportation has also experienced tremendous growth and extensive research.

Originally, smart cars integrate global various type of innovated technology to enhance the driving experience. For example, global positioning systems (GPS) and geographical information systems to aid in vehicle navigation and location. Sensors aid with blind spots, braking, and many other vehicle safety measures. However, there is limited simultaneous integration with other public or private systems outside of the smart car. As a result, AVs emerge as they leveraged Mobility as a Service (MaaS) to gain a more completive advantage by using multiple public and private systems to feed information into the vehicle (Bothos et al., 2019; Jeong et al. 2020).

The work proposed by Li and Liu (2020) explored the existing literature on management of AVs. In their paper, the authors explain the importance of using real-time sensors and connecting with other systems. They caution the accuracy and security of the data.

More recently, Jeong et al. (2020) explored the connected cars because of their two-way communication network between the car and the connected data points throughout it's entire infrastructure. They proposed a blockchain data marketplace model. This allowed for system security to be handled on- and off the chain via a data-owner attributed based encryption (DO-ABE). Thus, the data owner can better control their data.

The transportation/automotive research based on blockchain technology is new, vast, and evolving. Du, Gao, Wu, Wong & Bi (2020) argue that there is little research on the sustainability impact on utilizing blockchain across multiple intelligent transportation systems and their stakeholder. They explained how blockchain-based intelligent transportation is attracting world-wide attention within the automobile and transportation industry. Utilizing the fuzzy, DEMATEL and ISM set theories, they created a theorical framework of an intelligent transportation system to explain blockchain as a sustainable and secure system among multiple stakeholders. Their framework also elaborated upon how blockchain is very secure but computationally expensive to implement. They believed that regardless of the limited research and high cost, the blockchain within the transportation industry will rapidly expand.

Similarly, Jones, Wollschlaeger, and Stanley (2018), conducted international research for IBM Institute for Business Value in collaboration with Oxford Economics on automotive blockchain use. Utilizing an online survey instrument, they examined 1,314 automotive executives' perspectives regarding their exportation with blockchain. Participants were from 10 functional areas throughout 10 different countries. Results revealed that 62% of the executives believe that blockchain will be a "disruptive force". Additionally, more than half of the executives anticipate new business models will influence their blockchain plans within the next few years. More importantly, 54% indicated their first commercial blockchain network will be within the next three years.

2.1 Blockchain

Blockchain, is often described as decentralized, traceable, trustworthy, and transparency among users. It is often referred to as a disruptive technological innovation which is steering to novel global changes (Appelbaum & Smith, 2019; Cao, et al., 2019; Du et al., 2020; Hawlitschek, Notheisen, and Teubner, 2018). It is a decentralized database utilizing distributed storage, consensus, encryption algorithms, and smart contracts. Data is digitally signed, and time stamped as every block is added to the blockchain. Each block on the blockchain is connected or joined via a hash. The blockchain is housed on distributed storage which allows for data sharing (Du et al., 2020).

One of the benefits of using blockchain technology is that the organizations do not have to store data in third-party data warehouses. Instead they can distribute the data on interlinked electronic devices to create a network. Thus, if a hack occurs on one electronic device, the whole interlinked network can halt acceptance of new data or changes to data (Kestenbaum, 2017).

Additionally, a blockchain system, typically provides an additional layer of security. Huh and Seo (2018) state that blockchain is understood to be the best level of security. Knowing that blockchain possesses a secure state of data, it has become an attractive technology for many to explore implementation. However, many organizations are still unsure about the use of blockchain technology. As a result, the development of MOBI emerged.

3. MOBILITY OPEN BLOCKCHAIN INITIATIVE (MOBI)

3.1. Identity

MOBI is a rapidly developing consortium for blockchain innovation in the mobility industries. Numerous academic institutions and global organizations are members of MOBI (Lannquist, 2018; Polluck, 2019). The common goal of MOBI is to share innovative ways to utilize blockchain to benefit the transportation/automotive industry. Currently, the identity of this mobility initiative is focused on the transportation industry and mobility (i.e. access to data wherever, whenever, from any device). Many automakers plan to develop a proof of concept for a blockchain-based vehicle identity platform.

3.2 Members

Currently, MOBI has many interested customers. Because one of the biggest projected uses of this type of blockchain initiative, one goal is to allow businesses and consumers sovereignty over driving data, including ride-share and vehicle usage information. Therefore, one of the main types of customers for this initiative would be the top automotive companies around the globe. Another key customer are ride-share companies and their employees. The goal of, this paper is to focus on automotive companies and not ride-share companies.

The founding members of the MOBI Consortium include companies such as:Ford Motor Company, Renault, General Motors, and BMW (Bayerische Motoren Werke). The automakers started the initiative to support the exploration of the use of blockchain in their business model. The transportation organizations are using blockchain both in their automobiles as well as their supply chain.

3.2.1 Bayerische Motoren Werke (BMW)

BMW (Bayerische Motoren Werke), the German automobile manufacturing company, joined the MOBI initiative and are using the blockchain to drive the transparency within their supply chain. The use of blockchain allows for optimization of the process, which includes secure data sharing within the value chain (BMW AG, 2020). Another example would be the use of blockchain to track raw material through a supply chain verification, which tracks any tampering with the material as it flows through the supply chain.

3.2.2. Ford Motor Company

Ford uses blockchain technology to secure and track their material within the supply chain, as well as implementing the blockchain technology into the car. The FordPass Connect is a plug-in device that allows for geofencing, as well as incorporating blockchain capabilities. Once a vehicle equipped with FordPass enters a controlled zone, the car's electric-drive mode is triggered and tracked to record the zero-emission driving time (Ford, 2020). The recording of the zero-emission is secured through the blockchain.

3.2.3 Renault

The French automobile company Renault is focused on being recognized as a sustainable mobility provider. One method of providing sustainable mobility is to include smart cities to include the use of car-sharing, rentals, and carpooling Renault has been using blockchain technology since 2015 and has 20 projects to date that are established on blockchain technology for the security and traceability of transactions, supply chain communication with suppliers, and the use of communication within their vehicles (Groupe Renault, 2020).

3.2.4 General Motors (GM)

General Motors (GM) is using blockchain technology in the identification and payment system for automobiles. GM has applied for a patent for a "Decentralized Distributed Map Using Blockchain," as well as implementing a Vehicle Intelligent Platform (General Motors, 2020). Specifically, GM is using blockchain to provide secure dynamic feedback, creation of mapping of geographic locations, as well as using the navigation for autonomous cars (Pollock, 2020).

3.2.5 Dealer Market Exchange (DMX)

Dealer Market Exchange (DMX) is one of the fasted growing enterprise mobility start-up companies. DMX provides platforms for most of the automotive industry. Recently they implemented their first blockchain technology and the vehicle identification number i.e VINblock. The VINblock is one of the many new initiates that aid multiple stakeholders over the lifetime of any vehicle. Specifically, it keeps record of all activities of a registered through their VINnumber on the DMX blockchain. The VINblock starts with setting the vehicle as a minimum representation of that vehicle's creation. From there, subsequent vehicle identification phases will be added to include product definition, history of ownership, and important events in the vehicle's life (such as accidents, body work, recalls, and more). While this is newly created, guidance is needed on and off-chain data. Thus, all the VIN information should be collected (Adams, 2020).

As noted within each of the automobile manufacturers highlighted, the MOBI consortium has provided a meeting space for each of the organizations to expand their use of blockchain technology in different ways in order to accomplish their personally set organizational goals and mission alignments. The future development of technology to increase mobile open blockchain can expand the sustainability, convenience, security, and allow for advances in the transportation.

4. TECHNOLOGIES

Since blockchain is open source, it is suitable to be the key technology for the mobility initiative. A goal of this initiative with regards to technology is to stimulate scalable adoption of technology by companies developing autonomous vehicle and mobility services. Using blockchain technology will ensure to eliminate mileage fraud because it will establish a transparent, anonymous, and tamper-proof database. Thus, it is important to explain on-chain and off the chain governance when explaining MOBI technologies.

Blockchain governance is a process that allows a decision-making process to provide for permissions on and off the block (Kampik & Najjar, 2020). Not all data included within a transaction needs to be computed on the blockchain. Transactions on the blockchain are expensive for both storage and authorization. Authorization through a third party of translational acceptance governance is required to accept the transaction to the chain. Off-chain computation bypasses the permissions needed for blockchain transactional acceptance from outside approval; rather, it uses established and authorized individuals on the network for consensus finding as well as allowing for trust within the storage system (Eberhardt & Tai, 2017). The future of off the chain use is still constrained, keeping the information on block, but off-chain allows data to be protected and restricted from public view. Therefore, the current research is combining blockchain with distributed storage to keep data storage low and allow the system to focus on the approval of the data that needs the protection of the chain (Kawaguchi, 2019).

4.1 Blockchain Technology

Blockchain technology is an amalgamation of different technologies and their integrations. Blockchain technology can meld the internet of things (IoT), cloud computing, smart products, smart objects, sensors/RFID as well as artificial intelligent (AI) machines. As Schinckus (2020) defines, "blockchain technology refers to the idea that information and transactions can systematically be recorded through a cryptographic process in a public database so that all stakeholders involved in the network can contribute to the validation of the information" (p.1). The technology that allows the "information" and "transactions" to be processed is dependent upon the support of the communication and analytical platform. This section will limit its focus on mobile blockchain technologies and will not delve into the financial sector's use of blockchain.

4.2 Internet of Things (IoT)

The term the IoT is thought to be coined in 1999 by Kevin Ashton during a Proctor and Gamble conference presentation (Ashton, 2009). When first defined, the term IoT was meant to describe the need of human interaction for computers to gain information. Since then, IoT has assumed many different roles and descriptions such as a paradigm, concept, network along as many other terms. Thus, as a paradigm, IoT is a new way of interconnection of technology to the internet. As a concept, IoT is that small computing devices or "things" can communicate with other "things" via wireless connectivity. As a network, the IoT is paving the way to use the IoT to connect devices, sensors, or smart objects to create their own IoT system (Arellanes & Lau, 2020).

The network that an IoT can create for data exchange includes sensor data to a control system. A control system can receive and accumulate the data sent by the devices but can also process sending commands in response to the data sent (Sabir et al., 2020). This information, once received, can also be sent to cloud for storage. As Chanson et al. (2019) asserts, cloud solutions and sharing sensor data are becoming more of a common practice which can allow more collaboration throughout the organizational technology ecosystem. The collaboration of IoT sharing of data can intertwine the blockchain technology.

One of the concepts that MOBI aims to promote within the motor vehicle manufacturing industry is the IoT. According to Griffin (2019), MOBI believes that the use of IoT can enable cars to verify their identities autonomously, maneuver complex rules, and interact effectively with other automobiles and road infrastructure. As a result of this technology, motor vehicles will become safer and more efficient. Additionally, MOBI's business platform also includes mobility management software, computers, wearables, and IoT sensors ("MOBI Launches Grand Challenge for Blockchain in Transport Sector", n.d.). Essentially, the use of these digital devices and strategies has enabled the consortium to better integrate with unified endpoint management (UEM) (Mearian, 2018). These technologies have further enhanced MOBI's proficiency in the management of mobility services.

The advancement of IoT has provided users with another use of blockchain technology. With regards to MOBI, IoT sensors calculate the parking charges for the parking duration, and the billing takes place directly through the crypto wallet (Subramanian et al., 2020). The integration of IoT in blockchain technology has facilitated the real-time detection of vehicles and the determination of the available parking space. IoT has widened the scope of blockchain technology as it allows for the innovation to disrupt and redefine operations in the automotive industry, especially those relating to autonomous vehicles.

4.3 Cloud Computing

Cloud computing technology allows for a multiplicity of on-demand data, storage centers, computer resources, and services available to organizations via the internet (Zhu et al., 2020). The use of cloud technology allows for blockchain to be used and produces a decentralized and distributed storage (Cearnau, 2019). The use of blockchain infrastructure and cloud infrastructure can be comparatively similar and can both be run on decentralized applications. The use of blockchain in the cloud provides networking, machine algorithms, and storage. The networking power that the cloud platform can provide can access large bandwidth. Machine algorithms can provide an enhanced level of security and encryption. Finally, the ability to use cloud storage allows for scalability to meet the needs of the user in order to facility the blockchain usage.

The incorporation of cloud computing technology in the motor vehicle manufacturing industry is also part of MOBI's ambitions. MOBI aims to use cloud computing to provide on-demand digital systems resources, such as data storage and enhancing computing power to eliminate the need for users' direct and active management of these systems (Lannquist, 2018). Cloud computing has been particularly useful in the vehicle identification and data tracking; due to the sensors and RFID tags that are fitted on blockchain manufactured vehicles, the authenticity of each component can be verified easily and effectively (Kucinski, 2019). MOBI plans to create convenient, standard, and digital ways of paying for mobility services, motor vehicle identification, managing trips, and secure exchange and monetization of data in ways that protect property rights and privacy ("MOBI Launches Grand Challenge for Blockchain in Transport Sector", n.d.). In doing so, MOBI will revolutionize the operations of the automotive manufacturing sector.

4.4 Smart Products

Smart products can be viewed as both an artifact and a mixture of technology. They include sensor connection, software communication, and storage to use and optimize data interaction (Rijsdijk & Hultink, 2009) Smart products can be categorized as semiautonomous or autonomous. A smart product that is semiautonomous requires human input to function, whereas autonomous smart products can function without any human input to function (Kahle et al., 2020). The ability of a Smart product to be used in an antonymous fashion lends itself to security issues. For example, a hacker can gain entry to an autonomous smart product that stores information to the cloud regarding the user or products behavior (Riel et al., 2018)

MOBI is renowned for promoting smart products. The consortium has been working with its partners to procure smart contracts and experiment with blockchain technology ("MOBI Launches Grand Challenge for Blockchain in Transport Sector", n.d.). MOBI also focuses on enhancing the confirmation of vehicle identity, as well as tracking their history, supply chain data, transparency, and efficiency (Kucinski, 2019). Autonomous vehicle payments and secure mobility ecosystem trade are other smart products from MOBI ("MOBI Launches Grand Challenge for Blockchain in Transport Sector", n.d.). The consortium also manages related services such as usage-based mobility pricing, motor vehicle insurance, energy production and consumption, environmental pollution, and improvement of road infrastructure (Zoria, 2019). According to Griffin (2019), MOBI is also trialing the application of blockchain technology in paying for car parking tickets as well as highway tolls. Therefore, it is evident that MOBI's goals stretch beyond creating a greener automotive industry. This idea is evidenced by the consortium's plans to use blockchain to create a smart future for the road transportation sector.

4.5 Smart Objects

Smart objects are assorted in relation to the capacity to only sense and store data, while other objects have data processing capabilities. Smart objects are similar to smart products but do benefit more fully with the data sharing connection through an IoT. Smart objects have the ability to be self-autonomous but are more frequently seen within the semi-autonomous division, whereas the data is needed from the user interaction to accumulate and learn from the user's behavior (Perez Hernandez & Reiff-Marganiec, 2015). Smart objects can benefit blockchain as Lee, Rathore, Park, and Park (2020) found by placing blockchain technology at the gateway of smart objects (especially in the case of smart home objects and devices) to secure the data exchange.

The paradigm aspect of IoT has created an appropriate framework for incorporating smart objects into MOBI technology. For instance, connected and intelligent smart objects enable functionality that can be divided into four areas, including autonomy, monitoring, optimization, and control (Yang et al., 2018). Smart objects will act without human intervention, which means that their functionality will be optimized through the algorithms and commands used to control the object remotely. Therefore, the incorporation of MOBI has created a centralized system for addressing the gap between IoT and smart objects and increasing the accuracy of the decisions made by smart objects. MOBI has created a framework for verifying and tracing all decisions made by smart objects in various industries, including the automotive industry; since for IoT and smart objects to succeed, a transparent and secure system has to be implemented to increase its reliability and prevent privacy violations.

4.6 Sensors and RFID

Both sensors and RFID play an intricate role within IoT networks. Sensors are used to gather and ascertain computing environments. The IoT architecture that is provided through sensors allow the computation and computing to adjust into various computing situations. The data can also be filtered upon connection to cloud storage; however, the data flow can restrict the data that is unnecessary or restricted

(Rao & Clarke, 2020). Sensors and RFID's using end-to-end encryption such as blockchain allow for sensitive data to flow to cloud storage with an enhanced level of security using blockchain application.

Blockchain inspired-RFID information architecture has increased the efficiency of MOBI in achieving real-time monitoring. For example, RFID provides a unique identity of the product and the sensor data, which helps in real-time quality monitoring (Kaiser et al., 2019). In the automotive industry, the development of MOBI has prompted the adoption of sensors and RFID to incorporate trackers in vehicles and navigate autonomous vehicles because of real-time detection or monitoring capabilities. A technology goal of the MOBI initiative is to stimulate scalable adoption of technology by companies developing autonomous vehicle and mobility services. Using blockchain technology will help eliminate mileage fraud since MOBI will establish a transparent, anonymous, and tamper-proof database.

4.7 Smart Contracts

Smart contracts are terms of a contracts built digitally within a self-executing protocol of blockchain technology (Allam, 2018). Smart contracts used within the framework of blockchain technology stipulate contract terms to be digitally verified as well as provide digital security (Christidis & Devetsikiotis, 2016). Smart contracts on the blockchain are stored within the blocks internal ledger and identified through the contracts address (Fotiou et al., 2019).

Smart contracts' usage will help encourage automation in many ways, such as allowing settlements to happen much quicker and behind the scenes over traditional methods. For example, the transactions that happen in a smart contract are processed by the Blockchain, which means they can be sent automatically without a third party (Kaiser et al., 2018). Similarly, it will automate the formation of contractual agreements since smart contracts are negotiated and completed using computer codes. Smart contracts have automated various aspects because they are automatically executed when the predetermined conditions and terms are met. The integration of smart contracts into MOBI has automated the sale of vehicles and parts in the automotive industry. It has also geared towards making autonomous vehicles a reality in the industry.

4.8 Peer-to-Peer Systems

Blockchain uses peer-to-peer (P2P) distributed ledger technology to establish trust and form consensus within a decentralized network (Cao et al., 2019). This decentral system is most frequently used for monetary transactions to eliminate the need for a middleman, rather the use of machine consensus is employed. Currently a P2P consensus is also utilized to share the storage of the block. The sharing of storage of the blockchain can range from the whole block to a single transaction. Trending is the use of P2P to tap into users underutilized storage with an arrangement of trade in the form of network usage or cryptocurrency. The importance of the P2P system is the redundancy of data to ensure that the pieces of the block can be retrieved from more than one entity.

At conception, MOBI innovators considered building a peer-to-peer system in order for stakeholders to easily access and share relevant records, including with insurance policies, new buyers, and quite possibly ride-share passengers. Ultimately, MOBI innovators went that route and built a peer-to-peer system by creating a network of interconnected computers that does not rely on a central party to facilitate interaction (Wang et al., 2019). For example, it has integrated IoT to increase the connection between computer systems to facilitate virtual transactions. The initiative has created an autonomous computer system that supports mobile payments, car-wallet applications, and seamless information sharing between parties.

5. TRENDS

Blockchain has revolutionized the operations in various industries across the globe. Besides its existing applications, new trends are emerging in the scope of blockchain technologies to increase their reach and applications in the world. One of the trends is the Blockchain as a Service (BaaS), which is designed to facilitate the creation of a complete blockchain-based infrastructure. Other trends include digital products such as decentralized applications (Dapps) and other services that can work without any setup requirements of the complete blockchain-based infrastructure (Banafa, 2019). The emerging trends in Blockchain are designed to increase the MOBI initiative's functionality and improve the relevance of peer-to-peer systems in the automotive industry.

5.1 Hyperledger Framework

Another use of blockchain technology is found within the architecture of a Hyperledger framework. Hyperledger technology can be used for the supply chain within the MOBI initiative. It has facilitated the creation of a system that supports transshipment and run-cross border transactions. It is built on a modular architecture that separates transaction processing into three phases: increasing performance, scalability, and improving trust level in supply chain operations. The three phases are distributed logic processing and agreement, transaction ordering, and transaction validation, and commitment (Subramanian et al., 2020). The integration into MOBI has focused on creating a reliable transaction system for supporting financial operations in various industries. Hyperledger is ideal for MOBI as it hosts a variety of developing business blockchain technologies that support cross-industry transactions.

5.2 Future of MOBI

The future of MOBI will rely heavily on the diversification of their operations. The consortium has recognized this need, which is evidenced by its investment in the use of cryptocurrency. Mearian (2018) conveys that cryptocurrency has been fundamental in the development of blockchain technology in the recent past. As the future of the Bitcoin industry grows uncertain, the experts in this field have projected that distributed ledger technology will be critical to the growth of various industries (Zoria, 2019). According to Zoria (2019), the future of blockchain technology will be primarily driven by consortia and related open innovation working strategies. Furthermore, Mearian (2018) opines that the consortiums should also address competitive privacy and security issues in order to boost their chances of achieving their goals. However, MOBI's blockchain technology will face stiff competition from fellow blockchains in the near future.

6. CONCLUSION

In the past few decades, there have been growing concerns about environmental pollution across the world. Consequently, national governments, companies, and humanitarian organizations globally have been making efforts to improve environmental conservation. In response to this initiative, several renowned motor vehicle manufacturing companies came together in 2017 to create the MOBI, a non-profit consortium that seeks to improve operations in this sector. In essence, MOBI's objective is to make motor vehicle transport safer, greener, more affordable, and more accessible ("Mobility Open Blockchain Initiative ", 2020). According to Boucherat (2020), most automotive manufacturers concur with the fact that a lack of scale and harmonized production standards make it more difficult to establish and benefit from blockchains. The current automotive companies that are members of MOBI include BMW, Ford, General Motors, Honda, Groupe Renault, Bosch, and Hyundai; the consortium also has several partners from outside the automotive industry, such as IBM, Hyperledger, Accenture, Bigchain, Exasys, Vestella, Fetch, AI, AAIS and Quant (Industry Week Staff, 2018). The collaboration of these companies, via MOBI, will make more realistic to enhance technology in the automotive sector and friendlier to the environment.

By focusing on the transportation industry, MOBI will be less complex, but also will provide a framework for the other industries to follow in creating a blockchain mobility platform. As an example, this initiative could be applied to the education industry, where people could potentially store their education history, degrees, courses, diplomas, dates, schools, etc. on the blockchain easily accessible by the mobility initiative. This could help future employers or future educational institutions to quickly and easily verify education history for the person.

By utilizing cutting edge technology, especially around the transportation industry at this time, the initiative will be successful. It gives the flexibility to not only adopt new technology but be a leader in creating cutting edge technology. Additionally, by using new technology and being an innovator in technology and blockchain, the initiative will stay competitive. Even though this initiative will set the stage for other industries and companies to adopt a blockchain mobility platform, the transportation industry is quite large and will continue to grow for the years to come. If this initiative keeps up with the latest technology and makes updates as required, the need for this platform will continue to be relevant and competitive. Just as the start of the internet set the stage for many new technologies and ways of connecting twenty years ago, we believe that this initiative will be setting the stage for new ideas yet to come.

REFERENCES

Adams, J. (2020). *DMX Announces VINblock™ — Blockchain for Everyday Car Business*. https://www.businesswire.com/news/home/20181211005898/en/ DMX-Announces-VINblock%E2%84%A2-%E2%80%93%E2%80%93-Blockchain-Everyday-Car

Allam, Z. (2018). On smart contracts and organizational performance: A review of smart contracts through the blockchain technology. *Review of Economic and Business Studies*, *11*(2), 137–156. doi:10.1515/rebs-2018-0079

Appelbaum, D., & Smith, S. (2018). Blockchain basics and hands-on guidance: Taking the next step toward implementation and adoption. *The CPA Journal*, *88*(6), 28–37.

Arellanes, D., & Lau, K.-K. (2020). Evaluating IoT service composition mechanisms for the scalability of IoT systems. *Future Generation Computer Systems*, *108*, 827–848. doi:10.1016/j.future.2020.02.073

Ashton, K. (2009). That "Internet of Things" Thing. *RFID*. https://www.rfidjournal.com/that-internet-of-things-thing

Banafa, A. (2019). *Ten Trends of Blockchain in 2020*. Open Mind. Retrieved from https://www.bbvaopenmind.com/en/economy/finance/ten-trends-of-blockchain-in-2020/

BMW AG. (2020). *How blockchain is changing mobility.* https://www.bmw.com/en/innovation/blockchain-automotive.html

Bothos, E., Magoutas, B., Arnaoutaki, K., & Mentzas, G. (2019). Leveraging Blockchain for Open Mobility-as-a-Service Ecosystems. In *Proceedings of the IEEE/WIC/ACM International Conference on Web Intelligence - Companion Volume (WI '19 Companion)*. Association for Computing Machinery. 10.1145/3358695.3361844

Boucherat, X. (2020). Interview: Chris Ballinger, CEO, Mobility Open Blockchain Initiative (MOBI). *Automotive World.* https://www.automotiveworld.com/articles/interview-chris-ballinger-ceo-mobility-open-blockchain-initiative-mobi/

Cao, J., Wang, X., Li, Z., Gu, Q., & Chen, Z. (2019). The evolution of open-source blockchain systems: An empirical study. In *Proceedings of the 11th Asia-Pacific Symposium on Internetware (Internetware '19)*. Association for Computing Machinery. 10.1145/3361242.3361248

Cearnau, D. C. (2019). Block-Cloud: The new paradigm of cloud computing. *Economy Informatics Journal, 19*(1), 14–22. doi:10.12948/ei2019.01.02

Chanson, M., Bogner, A., Bilgeri, D., Fleisch, E., & Wortmann, F. (2019). Blockchain for the IoT: Privacy-preserving protection of sensor data. *Journal of the Association for Information Systems, 20*(9), 1271–1307. doi:10.17705/1jais.00567

Christidis, K., & Devetsikiotis, M. (2016). Blockchains and Smart Contracts for the Internet of Things. *IEEE Access: Practical Innovations, Open Solutions, 4*, 2292–2303. doi:10.1109/ACCESS.2016.2566339

Du, X., & Gao, Y. (2020). Blockchain-based intelligent transportation: A sustainable GCU application system. *Journal of Advanced Transportation*, (1), 1–14. https://downloads.hindawi.com/journals/jat/2020/5036792.pdf

Eberhardt, J., & Tai, S. (2017). On or Off the Blockchain? Insights on Off-Chaining Computation and Data. In F. De Paoli, S. Schulte, & E. Broch Johnsen (Eds.), *Service-Oriented and Cloud Computing* (Vol. 10465, pp. 3–15). Springer International Publishing., doi:10.1007/978-3-319-67262-5_1

Ford. (2020). *Ford Sustainability Report 2019/20.* https://corporate.ford.com/microsites/sustainability-report-2020/assets/files/sr20.pdf

Fotiou, N., Pittaras, I., Siris, V. A., Voulgaris, S., & Polyzos, G. C. (2019). *Secure IoT access at scale using blockchains and smart contracts.* doi:10.1109/WoWMoM.2019.8793047

General Motors. (2020). *GM Digital Vehicle Platform Enables Adoption of Future Technologies | General Motors.* https://www.gm.com/content/public/us/en/gm/home/masthead-story/digital-vehicle-platform.html

Griffin, B. (2019). *MOBI explained: the consortium that's bringing blockchain to vehicles. Decrypt.* https://decrypt.co/10770/mobi-mobility-open-blockchain-initiative-vehicles-explained

Groupe Renault. (2020). *Shared and urban mobility services—Groupe Renault.* https://group.renault.com/en/innovation-2/mobility-services/

Groupe Renault. (2020, May 14). *Groupe Renault has been working on blockchain technology since 2015 to have real-time and secured transactions.* https://group.renault.com/en/news-on-air/news/the-blockchain-transformation-vector-for-the-future-of-the-automotive-industry/

Hawlitschek, F., Notheisen, B., & Teubner, T. (2018). E limits of trust-free systems: A literature review on blockchain technology and trust in the sharing economy. *Electronic Commerce Research and Applications, 29*(1), 50–63. doi:10.1016/j.elerap.2018.03.005

Huh, J.-H., & Seo, K. (2018). Blockchain-based mobile fingerprint verification and automatic log-in platform for future computing. *The Journal of Supercomputing, 75*(7), 3123–3139.

Industry Week Staff. (2018). *Major automakers, startups launch Mobility Open Blockchain Initiative.* IndustryWeek. https://www.industryweek.com/leadership/companies-executives/article/22025584/major-automakers-startups-launch-mobility-open-blockchain-initiative

Jeong, B.-G., Youn, T.-Y., Jho, N.-S., & Shin, S. U. (2020). Blockchain-based data sharing and trading model for the connected car. *Sensors (Basel), 20*(3141), 1–20. doi:10.339020113141 PMID:32498273

Jones, M., Wollschlaeger, D., & Stanley, B. (2018). *Daring to be first - How auto pioneers are taking the plunge into blockchain.* IBM Institute for Business Value, IBM Corporation. https://newsroom.ibm.com/2018-12-12-IBM-Study-Blockchain-Brings-Trust-to-How-Companies-Consumers-and-Cars-Connect

Kahle, J. H., Marcon, É., Ghezzi, A., & Frank, A. G. (2020). Smart Products value creation in SMEs innovation ecosystems. *Technological Forecasting and Social Change*, *156*, 120024. doi:10.1016/j.techfore.2020.120024

Kaiser, C., Steger, M., Dorri, A., Festl, A., Stocker, A., Fellmann, M., & Kanhere, S. (2018, September). Towards a Privacy-Preserving Way of Vehicle Data Sharing–A Case for Blockchain Technology? In *International Forum on Advanced Microsystems for Automotive Applications* (pp. 111-122). Springer.

Kampik, T., & Najjar, A. (2020). Simulating, off-chain, and on-chain: Agent-based simulations in cross-organizational business processes. *Information (Basel)*, *11*(1), 34. doi:10.3390/info11010034

Kawaguchi, N. (2019). Application of Blockchain to Supply Chain: Flexible Blockchain Technology. *Procedia Computer Science*, *164*, 143–148. doi:10.1016/j.procs.2019.12.166

Kestenbaum, R. (2017). Why bitcoin is important for your business. *Forbes*. https://www.forbes.com/sites/richardkestenbaum/2017/03/14/why-bitcoin-is-important-for-your-business/#44c5d84741b5

Kucinski, W. (2019). *MOBI rolls out the first blockchain-enabled Vehicle Identity (VID) mobility standard*. SAE Mobilus. https://saemobilus.sae.org/automated-connected/news/2019/07/mobi-rolls-out-the-first-blockchain-enabled-vehicle-identity-vid-mobility-standard

Lannquist, A. (2018). Introducing MOBI: The Mobility Open Blockchain Initiative. *IBM Blockchain Blog*. https://www.ibm.com/blogs/blockchain/2018/06/introducing-mobi-the-mobility-open-blockchain-initiative/

Lee, Y., Rathore, S., Park, J. H., & Park, J. H. (2020). A blockchain-based smart home gateway architecture for preventing data forgery. *Human-centric Computing and Information Sciences*, *10*(1), 1–14. doi:10.118613673-020-0214-5

Li, Y., & Liu, Q. (2020). Intersection management for autonomous vehicles with vehicle-to-infrastructure communication. *PLoS One*, *15*(7), 1–12. https://doi-org.proxy-bloomu.klnpa.org/10.1371/journal.pone.0235644 PMID:32614893

Mearian, L. (2018). MOBI adds UEM reporting with new desktop, IoT management tools. *Computerworld*. https://www.computerworld.com/article/3313046/mobi-adds-uem-reporting-with-new-desktop-iot-management-tools.html

MOBI launches Grand Challenge for blockchain in transport sector. (n.d.). *Internet of Business*. https://internetofbusiness.com/mobi-grand-challenge-for-blockchain-in-transportation-launches/

Mobility Open Blockchain Initiative. Home. MOBI. (2020). https://dlt.mobi/

Pérez Hernández, M. E., & Reiff-Marganiec, S. (2015). Autonomous and self controlling smart objects for the future internet. *Proceedings from 2015 3rd International Conference on Future Internet of Things and Cloud*, 301–308. 10.1109/FiCloud.2015.89

Pollock, D. (2020, April 3). General Motors applies for decentralized blockchain map patent. *Forbes*. https://www.forbes.com/sites/darrynpollock/2020/04/03/general-motors-applies-for-decentralized-blockchain-map-patent/

Polluck, D. (2019). *BMW Opens Its Doors for Mobility Open Blockchain Initiative's First European Colloquium*. Available at: https://www.forbes.com/sites/darrynpollock/2019/02/15/bmw-opens-its-doors-for-mobility-open-blockchain-initiatives-first-european-colloquium/#618b0c127f1d

Rao, A. R., & Clarke, D. (2020). Perspectives on emerging directions in using IoT devices in blockchain applications. *Internet of Things*, *10*, 100079. doi:10.1016/j.iot.2019.100079

Riel, A., Kreiner, C., Messnarz, R., & Much, A. (2018). An architectural approach to the integration of safety and security requirements in smart products and systems design. *CIRP Annals*, *67*(1), 173–176. doi:10.1016/j.cirp.2018.04.022

Rijsdijk, S. A., & Hultink, E. J. (2009). How today's consumers perceive tomorrow's smart products. *Journal of Product Innovation Management*, *26*(1), 24–42. doi:10.1111/j.1540-5885.2009.00332.x

Rosic, A. (2020). *What Is hashing?* [Step-by-Step Guide-Under Hood of Blockchain]. https://blockgeeks.com/guides/what-is-hashing/

Russell, J. (2018). *BMW, GM, Ford and Renault launches blockchain research group for automotive industry*. Techcrunch.

Sabir, B. E., Youssfi, M., Bouattane, O., & Allali, H. (2020). Towards a New Model to Secure IoT-based Smart Home Mobile Agents using Blockchain Technology. *Engineering, Technology & Applied Scientific Research*, *10*(2), 5441–5447.

Schinckus, C. (2020). The good, the bad and the ugly: An overview of the sustainability of blockchain technology. *Energy Research & Social Science*, *69*, 101614. doi:10.1016/j.erss.2020.101614

Subramanian, N., Chaudhuri, A., & Kayıkcı, Y. (2020). Blockchain applications and future opportunities in transportation. In *Blockchain and Supply Chain Logistics* (pp. 39–48). Palgrave Pivot. doi:10.1007/978-3-030-47531-4_5

Wang, S., Ouyang, L., Yuan, Y., Ni, X., Han, X., & Wang, F. Y. (2019). Blockchain-enabled smart contracts: Architecture, applications, and future trends. *IEEE Transactions on Systems, Man, and Cybernetics. Systems*, *49*(11), 2266–2277. doi:10.1109/TSMC.2019.2895123

Yang, W., Garg, S., Raza, A., Herbert, D., & Kang, B. (2018, August). Blockchain: Trends and future. In *Pacific Rim Knowledge Acquisition Workshop* (pp. 201-210). Springer.

Zheng, Z., Xie, S., Dai, H. N., Chen, X., & Wang, H. (2018). Blockchain challenges and opportunities: A survey. *International Journal of Web and Grid Services*, *14*(4), 352–375. doi:10.1504/IJWGS.2018.095647

Zhu, Z., Qi, G., Zheng, M., Sun, J., & Chai, Y. (2020). Blockchain based consensus checking in decentralized cloud storage. *Simulation Modelling Practice and Theory*, *102*, 101987. doi:10.1016/j.simpat.2019.101987

Zoria, S. (2019). *How is Blockchain Technology impacting the automotive industry*. Medium. https://medium.com/datadriveninvestor/how-is-blockchain-technology-impacting-the-automotive-industry-728875a7c940

ADDITIONAL READING

Abbade, L. R., Ribeiro, F. M., da Silva, M. H., Morais, A. F. P., de Morais, E. S., Lopes, E. M., Alberti, A. M., & Rodrigues, J. (2020). Blockchain applied to vehicular odometers. *IEEE Network*, *34*(1), 62–68. doi:10.1109/MNET.001.1900162

Ebert, C., Louridas, P., Fernández-Caramés, T. M., & Fraga-Lamas, P. (2020). Blockchain technologies in practice. *Software IEEE*, *37*(4), 17–25. doi:10.1109/MS.2020.2986253

Fraga-Lamas, P., & Fernández-Caramés, T. M. (2019). A review on blockchain technologies for an advanced and cyber-resilient automotive industry. *IEEE Access: Practical Innovations, Open Solutions*, *7*(1), 17578–17598. doi:10.1109/ACCESS.2019.2895302

Holotescu, C. (2018). Understanding blockchain opportunities and challenges. In *Proceedings of 14th International Conference on eLearning and Software for Education.* (vol. 14, pp. 275-283). National Defence University Publishing House.

Jabbar, R., Kharbeche, M., Al-Khalifa, K., Krichen, M., & Barkaoui, K. (2020). Blockchain for the internet of vehicles: A decentralized IoT solution for vehicles communication using ethereum. *Sensors (Basel), 20*(14), 3928. doi:10.339020143928 PMID:32679671

Kandah, F., Huber, B., Skjellum, A., & Altarawneh, A. (2019). A Blockchain-based trust management approach for connected autonomous vehicles in smart cities. In *Proceedings of the 9th Annual Computing and Communication Workshop and Conference.* (pp. 0544-0549). IEEE Digital Library. 10.1109/CCWC.2019.8666505

Kasten, J. E. (2020). Engineering and manufacturing on the blockchain: A systematic review. *Engineering Management Review IEEE, 48*(1), 31–47. doi:10.1109/ EMR.2020.2964224

Uhlemann, E. (2018). Time for autonomous vehicles to connect. *IEEE Vehicular Technology Magazine, 13*(3), 10–13. doi:10.1109/MVT.2018.2848342

KEY TERMS AND DEFINITIONS

Centralized Network: A main computer on the network in which all devices and transactions are controlled.

Decentralized Network: Networked computers with multiple trustworthy nodes and subsets which aid in providing consensus of data.

Distributed Storage: Networked computers in which every node interacts with each other to allocate and share the storage of the data.

Mobile Open Blockchain Initiative: New collaborative consortium with the goal of using blockchain to further enhance various sectors of the automobile industry.

Off Block: Data connected to a block on blockchain but, cannot be viewed by the public or others.

On Block: Data on a blockchain that can be view but all parties involved or the public.

Smart Contracts: A transaction protocol or program that allows for the auto tracking and execution of specific digital terms to be upheld throughout the transaction.

Smart Products: Innovated digital technologies that allow the product to digitally interact and adapt to various triggers and environments.

Technology Sensors: Innovative technologies that can be placed upon products to allow real-time data interaction and collection.

Chapter 6
Revolutionizing the Stock Market With Blockchain

Namrata Dhanda
Amity University, Noida, India

Anushka Garg
Amity University, Noida, India

ABSTRACT

This chapter explores the drawbacks of conventional centralized share exchange frameworks, like those of higher transaction costs, central and vulnerable regulation to exploitation, and lack of revelation to business behavior and practices by introducing a revolutionary model that utilizes blockchain to establish a decentralized stock exchange and a transparent persistent economy. The suggested model utilizes exclusive contracts to implement the validity of the privileges of the owner and the proper accomplishment and settlement of the transactions, thereby mitigating the need for a centralized authority to ensure the accuracy of the stock exchange mechanism. The experimental findings convincingly demonstrate that the decentralized solution can provide lower transaction costs by progressively replacing brokerage costs and centralized officials' commissions with mining charges, which reward the miners for their backbreaking work in maintaining the system and enforcing the laws.

DOI: 10.4018/978-1-7998-7589-5.ch006

INTRODUCTION

A stock exchange is a platform in which stock brokers and dealers may purchase and exchange assets such as stock and bond shares as well as other investment funds. These security measures and financial activities including the payment of profits and dividends can be given and repaid by shares markets as well. To start a company, we need some amount of capital or income (Donald, 2012). For this purpose, the business is split into small parts that are called inventories and are sold legally, which is referred to as shares. The individual who owns the stock is deemed an investor or a shareholder. Thus they would be considered as a tiny part of the company. The exchange and management of stock therefore is conducted out in the Share / Stock Market. The auctioning process was manual before the advent of Internet but now it's all digital (Bala, 2013).

There are two prominent markets where all of the stock exchanges take place –

- NSE – National Stock Exchange
- BSE – Bombay Stock Exchange

NSE is the youngest stock market of India but currently the biggest market as it uses the electronic systems for investments while the BSE is the oldest stock market of India. Fluctuation indexes in NSE are referred to as NIFTY, while the BSE index is referred to as SENSEX.

HOW DOES A STOCK EXCHANGE FUNCTION?

If one wants to invest in the share market, he/she must have a good idea about the stakeholders that exist in the share market. The major entities in the stock market include the investors or the traders, stock brokers, exchanges and the clearing corporations. A broker is a person that acts an intermediary between the investor and the exchange. The companies that raise money by issuing shares to the public get listed on the exchanges. Through the IPO (Initial Public Offering), shares are issued to the investors in the primary market and once IPO gets over, the company is listed on the exchange that gives an opportunity for trading in the shares. For instance if one wants to purchase the shares of a company say like Colgate or Royal Enfield, he can buy it from the exchange any time once the IPOs are conducted only for a period of 3 days. After that duration, one can trade in shares only through the secondary market. It is the place where all shares get traded and the stock markets are regulated by SEBI (Securities and Exchange Board of India). It is essential for any trader or investor to understand what is NSE and BSE in share market and the difference between the two before putting a step in the stock market. NSE and BSE are the major national exchanges in India. We can trade in stocks by opening a demat or trading account with a depository participant or stockbroker. The organization establishes itself at BSE / NSE in the first place. If the shareholder has enough industry experience, it will directly contact the dealer through the marketplace to purchase the shares and if the consumer has the inadequate industry knowledge, they would require the help of third party financial advisor who may charge some amount and further help them in transacting in the shares accordingly.

VULNERABILITIES IN THE CURRENT SCENARIO

The functioning of stock market follows more of a traditional pattern which include the following risk while investing:

1. Financial Broker acting as the middle man.
2. Stock Market handling.
3. Financial Security.

Financial Broker Acting as the Middle Man

The Financial Broker or the Stock Broker is the one who has comprehensive understanding and access to the market. He can study and guide people in appropriate ways to invest in the market according to ones' requirements and preferences, thus preventing one from exhausting legal work. Financial analysts can save us from a lot of financial liabilities. For this to be done the broker may charge some amount of fees. But apart from this positive aspect, there are some negatives also. Suppose the broker gets an incentive from a specific lender for selling their shares (Brunnermeier & Pedersen, 2009), then the brokers' ultimate goal would be to sell that share first and get the incentive without being considerate to the investor. There will also be a situation where the financial advisor finds the best value for money according to him and you wouldn't find it worth the money. Investing with the help of a broker may blur the portrait of what is genuinely the market value and profit margin of the share and what is the commission of the share, and therefore sometimes you probably end up paying far more additional money than actually investing. Brokers also do not offer forecasts, which may result in a lossy investment. Sometimes in the final analysis, some corporations don't function with brokers, they sell their shares on their own, and you might even never know about them and end up investing something that may not be worth enough.

Stock Market Handling

Several unethical practices in the Indian equity market ultimately resulted in the tragic loss of shareholders assets. Many activities, such as fake companies, emerging or newly born markets and guaranteeing stakeholders highly liquid returns while subsequently employing it for their internal purposes. Such activities betray customers and by the end of the day resulting in events like bankruptcy, ultimately causing financial losses to the people. Some of the firms have artificially higher share prices before the privileges were allegedly issued by circular trading (Gupta, 1992). There is, furthermore, a lack of genuine traders, as the number of investors is speculators, which can effectively be observed by the fundamental fact that they reluctantly produce a revenue profit from short-term volatility not really for investment purposes. Investors are often naïve and hence they fail to notice that the share certificate they have got is fraudulent. Inside trading seems to remain a widespread phenomenon in the marketplace, i.e. responsible individuals from within may come to know any valuable information and therefore advertise and purchase it at nominal rates, thereby causing an appalling loss to the leading vendor. Although many legal steps have been promptly taken and also many rules and bureaucratic regulations are being formulated but then too it is the widespread practice scrupulously observed. Unofficial trading typically comprises.

Financial Security

While investing wisely in the stock market, concerned investors genuinely need to be very careful as transactions should not fail in between otherwise a hefty amount as the counterfeit money would fall in crooked hands. The financial security undoubtedly holds a primary concern as the capital market is not so transparent and building up trust is crucial. Any possible breach can occur due to an apparent lack of profound knowledge (Adrian & Shin, 2010) & (Adrian et al., 2014). Therefore, for a modern market, we demand something that may help tremendously to establish a trustful and transparent platform so that one can invest freely and hence support the economic growth. Trust is not gained in a day but is developed over a period of time. This mutual trust can befriend us to build up by **Blockchain.**

INTRODUCTION TO BLOCKCHAIN

Blockchain is one of the evolving technology worldwide. It helps to maintain trust and additionally provides transparency in a system. It maintains mutual trust by decentralizing the system by using peer to peer network. Blockchain is principally a chain of Blocks that are connected to one and another consequently crafting a piece of persistent information. Every logical block possesses a common data, its hash and also the hash of the previous block to maintain a block (Sutcliffe, 2017). The data of the block typically depend on the specific type of Blockchain we want to efficiently create. Let's examine an example of the BITCOIN – it typically holds the detail of the sender, receiver, amount, date and time, etc. The hash value is created by traditionally using a hash function that encrypts the data in a particular form that if ever the hash of the data is allegedly breached it cannot sufficiently restore the sensitive data from the hash. It is principally of 128 bits. It gallantly helps to positively identify the data and therefore maintain the uniqueness of the key block. Thus for Blockchain, we can say that it requires precisely sufficient proof of work. It intentionally slows down the effective mechanism of addition of irrelevant and making it steady and reliable (Asharaf & adarsh, 2017). Thus we can say, *"Blockchain is a decentralized, distributive, public ledger."*

IMPLEMENTING BLOCKCHAIN IN STOCK MARKET FOR ENHANCING SECURITY

In today's world full of technology, we have already implemented Blockchain in various field like in (Miraz & Ali, 2018) –

- Money Transfer giving birth to the cryptocurrency – BITCOIN (Karame & Androulaki, 2016).
- Smart Contracts as in emergence of the SOLIDITY PROJECT which is a decentralized platform which eliminated the fraud, censorship, downtime and third party interference (Narayanan et al, 2016).
- Notary service as in UPROOV.
- Cloud Storage as in STORJ etc.

Blockchain is also tremendously useful in the field of financial management systems. The ambitious people are now becoming more magnetized towards reliable networks in banking, investing wisely in successful cryptocurrency. It has at present induced a significant change in technology. Financial Security is the key priority when we discuss about any legitimate transaction or unsustainable debt. The stock market as a financial market deals totally with the money which includes excessive risk and also high returns. Blockchain technology can effectively be used in the stock market and can minimize the potential threats as discussed above to a great extent. Through decentralization and automation, it will encourage us to engage in optimal stock exchanges effectively. Several stock markets around the globe are switching towards it and a massive difference can be observed which takes transaction technology to the next level that is more secure and transparent. Some independent countries are diligently preparing for it. Its stable platform generously provides a vast potential for monitoring stock funding, leverage borrowing, and network risk surveillance.

In decentralized market systems, Blockchain can be the solution to significant information sharing, uniformity, potential reliability, and accountability problems. A lengthy mechanism (that involves 3 + days for executing transaction process, mostly because of the involvement of middlemen, functional transaction clearing and deliberative procedures) is expected for stock exchange stakeholders, including the alleged dealers, vendors, concerned investors, brokers, regulators, and precipitous banks.

Through computerization and decentralization, Blockchain will render stock exchanges far more absolute. It would inescapably lead to minimizing the substantial expenses of commissioning on prominent consumers while accelerating quick transactions arbitration procedures.

The elevated platform can indeed be feasible for official clearance and successful resolution, along with automating post-trade procedures securely, facilitating trade documentation and the gradual transition of rightful possession of valuable assets.

Blockchain can to a considerable extent eradicate the fundamental need for a third party control board because unconstitutional laws and regulations are adequately incorporated into knowledgeable lease agreements and imposed by each exchange into the registration of transactions through the Blockchain channel behaving as all transactions process a regulator.

DECENTRALIZED SHARE MARKET

This engaged segment tentatively proposes a decentralization approach to apparently address the above-mentioned shortcomings by offering a thorough decentralized blockchain system: global agreement for all transaction processing, self-implemented authentication by smart contracts, consistency of practices through means of intelligent agreement codes and reduced cost via competition.

A smart contract is an official document that typically includes various business laws that must be carefully reviewed and settled upon (Satyavolu & Sangamnerkar, 2016). Therefore, an evidentiary arrangement can be accurately interpreted as a unique set of standard protocols. As with contracts, such agreements are recorded in the blockchain. In the future, transaction requests will activate them, which will wisely decide whether each entity updates its status, based on the possible outcomes accomplished by the smart contract. But even if the word ' contract' is used, the intelligent contracts can be considered as representatives that can be sufficiently established and operated on and activated sometime through effective implementation. Intelligent contracts aim to substitute actual-world third-party individuals (judge, authorized officers, escrows, etc.) with a rational entity operating efficiently under a predefined set of fundamental laws (Abeyratne & Monfared, 2016). The distinctive features of an intelligent contract are very reliant on its context. At present, NXT (Aitzhan & Svetinovic, 2016), Side Chain (Hendricks & Singhal, 2009), Hyper-ledger and Ethereum (Sajana et al., 2018) remain by far the most standard booklets that generously offer ample opportunity to establish smart contracts. Ethereum is among them the most experienced and technologically advanced in smart contract research. It is a distributed ledger framework that offers several remarkable improvements in computer algorithms and Ethereum blockchain architectures for consensus.

Besides, further to define the Decentralized Exchange Platform, the Stock Market contract, which serves as just an updated order book, is created. The following items are described as smart contract states:

- **Symbol -** The name of the valuable resource transacted.
- **Owned inventories -** Mapping of the presidential address of the key vendor to the considerable sum of the capital investments made.
- **Market value –** Appropriate measure of the specific product of the most recent action.
- **Bids –** Request all recorded and has not yet been executed selling acts in an ordered array.
- **Ask –** Request a comprehensive list of all recorded and yet not performed buying acts.

The smart contract describes what behavior for the transaction as a framework which contains information about:

- The actor's address.
- The time signature on the device when the operation has been registered.
- The sum of properties that were transacted.
- The rate at which the participant is prepared to sell or purchase.
- The transaction service portion of the contract (OrderSide: Sale or Purchase) determines the response side.
- The order type suggesting demand requirements (OrderType –determine the order type: restrict or market).
- Methods are available for the order availability (OrderAvailability –a form of availability specifies: OPEN FOK or IOC).

Apart from this extensive documentation, each cooperative agreement to typically print a modern order appropriately includes a sealed sum of guaranteed money (eth) for compensation purposes.

The chain-business Stock Market promptly recognizes each legitimate holder's considerable shares. The cognitive mapping of the owner's address and the number of shares is a shared depository that carefully tracks all unique properties and replicates details through the extensive network. Moreover, every necessary adjustment to the depository is subject to consensus among peers, and any form of assaulting is unachievable because of the tamper-proof of the depository status held in blocks. Besides this sufficient paperwork, a secured sum of pledge money (eth) is appropriately included for reimbursement purposes in every mutual arrangement to produce a modern invoice.

The validity of the order is positively reviewed on the official website prior to its successful implementation once the mutual agreement of the order is willingly exchanged among the peers. Which node in the network can examine the validity of the order by ensuring successful implementation if there is a similar request if it executes the tasks of a Decentralized Clearing House? It shall be confirmed for each buying transaction if the sender has locked ample money to pay the capital assets during the transaction.

Depending on the specific type of order (the Sale contract should have zero cash locked.), this will be verified for the required amount. The substantial amount of money to be spent by locking into the deal, hence eliminating the need for escrow. The capital will be secured and managed by the mutual agreement from this key moment onwards and transferred to the seller once the order has been satisfactorily completed. In the same manner, the network can search for the Decentralized Depository entries whenever a Sale transaction is launched whether the seller has the number of shares that he is willing to sell.

The validity of the order is reviewed on the website prior to its implementation once the orders agreement is exchanged among the peers. Which node in the network can check the validity of the order by ensuring successful implementation if there is a similar request, if it executes the tasks of a decentralized clearing house. It shall be confirmed for each buying transaction if the sender has locked ample money to pay the assets during the transaction.

Depending on the type of order (the Sale contract should have 0 cash locked), this will be tested for the required amount. The actual amount of money to be spent by locking into the deal, hence eliminating the need for escrow. The capital will be secured and managed by the agreement from this moment onwards and transferred to the seller once the order has been completed. In the same manner, the network can search on the Decentralized Depository entries whenever a Sale transaction is launched whether the seller has the quantity of shares that he is willing to sell.

In the blockchain network, the authentication processes maintain track of all these necessary modifications and at every stage confirm the status updates of each bid/offer the key participant gets. Because the Share market contract is equitably distributed across all network nodes, each network node substantiates each incoming transaction (market actions) in a continuous chain. To powerfully build a legitimate block it must additionally include the current account status, in our case the Stock market deal, together with legitimate transactions. After the series of behavior shown by transactions deposited in this block is added, the last states are decided by the miner. When a miner wins a competition, the block is circulated for test and acceptance into the entire system. That network node receives this newly mined block and validates the state change, executes all transactions as far as the status of the prior block is known and compares the results between the block obtained from the miner and its records. If and only if the confirmation is right, the proposed amendment is adopted; otherwise, the block is rejected and new block proposals are approved.

Therefore, the system offers a completely distributed and extremely reliable decentralized implementation, in which each knot is accountable for validating the validity of the affirmative actions taken: valuable property purchased, deals and proposals, market prices, price set, and others. Simultaneously, a consensus mechanism is adequately established, which can be applied by each of the actors involved hence establishing a democratic system. The more reasonable costs accomplished by replacing the broker representatives that act on behalf of consumers represent a significant change for the network. Such payments are superseded by the mineral costs required by justly rewarding the experienced miners for their conscientious work and guarantee the assured safety and excellent reputation of the successful operation.

BENEFITS OF BLOCKCHAIN MODEL

1. Intermediary Elimination

Within stock buyers and sellers, there, in general, are several arbitrators. A significant business could forcibly incorporate stockbrokers, potential investors, leading banks and brokerage firms. On numerous instants these intermediaries undoubtedly make capitalism works easier, but most of them aren't necessary. Some blockchain applications facilitate micro-investment and compensate for more reluctant stakeholders or are unable to invest complete assets.

Evolutionary investment networks powered by blockchain do not provide the guidance and strategies that a skilled broker can offer These are also not as appropriate for the complex portfolios many investors are looking for. But the future of blockchain-based trading networks is a skylight. They typically aim to progressively reduce investment costs by radically reducing whoever takes cut for each transaction.

2. Incorporated Regulation

Users of Blockchain may build up an accounting system by the password vault vaguely. Traders may carefully preserve capital by enabling authorities to accurately track prime brokerages empowered by blockchain. Potential investors with every level of practical experience and financial ability can, in realtime, escape unexpected constitutional implications. Increased surveillance can also endorse accountable trade practices.

3. Events / Settlement Simplification for The Post-Trade

The extensive scale of the global investment industry mankind cannot perceive. On the typical day of the economic exchange (T+0) or the following day (T+1), successful transactions shall settle. The essential need to have more sustainable development and guaranteed income is demanded to realistically achieve these ideologies. Many genuinely think that knowledgeable contracts driven by blockchain have become an efficient manner to do it with impunity.

Innovative, expensive human supervision in blockchain-driven transaction frameworks may substitute intelligent contractual technologies. Mutual agreements shall be executed as long as certain basic requirements are satisfied like a price point decided by the potential buyers and willing sellers. Faster buying and selling means reduced delays in time. The needed money required to continue wheeling and dealing is freer for a shorter time.

4. Mechanisms for Automated Regulation

A key role in regulating the finance industry is efficiently performed by the Securities and Exchange Commission (SEC). They prevent the nation's economy from ever being paralyzed. Modern technology Blockchain can empower bureaucrats to carry out their remarkable job more efficiently. Several crooked stakeholders, fortunately, escape straightforward crime. Despite repeated notices, nevertheless, they dwelled fondly unflagged. SEC cannot regulate all the ultimate ends alone but reasonably demands valuable assistance to track continuously fumbling stocks. The Commission may encounter apparent miracles by properly implementing innovative technologies to universally recognize manifest irregularities, fraudulent activity, and illegal trade.

The responsible supervisor of financial transactions is crucial for human regulatory authorities, but Blockchain-based trade systems can generously help with suspect negotiation processing. Active traders who can tacitly acknowledge suspect trends and liberally educate flagging systems to use blockchain would safeguard an immeasurable asset and they don't indeed end up taking a reimbursement.

5. Setting Up a Secured Token Market

Many labels 2018 the "Privacy Token Era." SEC-compatible tokens endure a great deal, but still common. The economic sustainability of supplementary trading and the persistent legal uncertainty undoubtedly continue being unresolved pertinent questions. Such evident confusion has not barred leading companies from selling security token offerings (STOs) and they earn money for an accomplished purpose.

STO generously provided protective tokens that retain strong appeal. Start-ups and creditors consider it now for their economic dividends as a convenient way to change funding. But in some form or other, often protective tokens are unconstitutional. STOs would be given more legitimacy in a marketplace like a stock exchange for verified safety tokens. Consider this as the unique distinction between the debt and the New York Stock exchanges (NYSE). The Wild West of capital investment traditionally represents the Penny stock—that's up to you if you get burnt. Regulatory authorities in the NYSE are much more aggressive. The determined STOs' cause would be extremely promoted by this honorable market.

6. Increased Liquidity

Blockchain can minimize perverse incentives by automating, which also reduces the operational cost and thereby removes regulatory barriers which invariably add to an enhanced market base. Individuals who are incapable to promptly break into the capital market due to various cost constraints, fierce competitiveness and innovations would eventually be improved.

7. Mutual Funds and Crypto ETFs Fueled by Blockchain

The exchange-traded fund (ETF) is a "marketable infrastructure that adequately monitors a stock market index, effective means of economic exchange, bond funds, or equity basket." By striking contrast, a mutual fund is "an asset class composed of a sum of money gathered from several shareholders to spend inequities like shares, bond funds, money market tools, and some other investments."

The exchange-traded fund (ETF) is a "marketable infrastructure that adequately monitors a stock market index, effective means of economic exchange, bond funds, or equity basket." By striking contrast, a mutual fund is "an asset class composed of a sum of money gathered from several shareholders to spend inequities like shares, bond funds, money market tools, and some other investments."

Even though they both contain diversified types of tangible equity, ETFs trade as common shares. Mutual funds behave identically to a venture capital firm — your earned cash is in it, and yields are up to the beneficial owner.

Thoroughly consider that those investments or ETFs consisted of tokens and blockchain-reliant businesses. Repackaging of distributed equities may generously offer unprecedented opportunities through the unifying theme of blockchain technology. Tokenized ETFs and mutual funds may progressively reduce the entry cost for investment firms horrendously overpriced from valuable assets. Micro-investment is a remarkable phenomenon that will potentially influence ETFs and mutual funds.

The CEE Services Head of Microsoft, Norbert Biedrzycki, has currently published a paper on how blockchain can carefully turn the share market to data-driven buyers (Bouri et al., 2017). The modern world's stock exchange that, in specific, because the effective regulation of financial capital transfers has subtly changed over the last two to three decades little, presenting with Norbert Blockchain.

He states –

Today's investor relies on a traditional system of buying, selling and accounting for transactions that are old enough to be called ossified. The system generates considerable costs and adds to the time needed to close transactions. This is because trading in financial assets requires multiple entities arranged in a complex web of intermediaries, settlement systems and business partners. Whether they are investors, brokers, depositaries, stock exchange management or central supervisory bodies, all actors taking part in asset trading – buying, selling, or transferring – are obliged to generate messages, receive authorizations, and continuously update transaction status records.

As this economic system involves modifying financial procedures such as stock issuing, trading, clearance, and compulsory arbitration, decentralized based blockchains can be handled directly and without any congestion as a distributed ledger.

He claims Blockchain would provide an opportunity for a potential stock exchange. On an exchange based on a blockchain, turbulent transactions would subsequently become a gruesome relic of the past. Exclusive smart contracts might debunk significant doubt about the correctness of settlements. Supervisory systems are no longer necessary –which is currently required, although ineffective.

Apart from that, in collaboration with IBM, the London Stock Exchange Group has already started experimenting with a blockchain-based platform that facilitates the absolute digitalization of legitimate transactions of small to medium-sized businesses. The LSEG Italian regulator, Borsa Italiana, performs these critical examinations. By the end of this challenging year, the Australian Securities Exchange is expected to wisely conclude a two-year process of developing a sensitive system to progressively improve accountability so strengthen the welfare of concerned customers. Ultimately, he sincerely believes stock markets will enthusiastically embrace blockchain.

CONCLUSION

In this chapter, we give the Indian Stock Exchange a decentralized approach for addressing the weaknesses of the Centralized Framework and growing trade prices for traders and primary authorities (Dannen, 2017). We seamlessly combine stock market components with associated intelligent contracts into a blockchain system to guarantee the successful self-implementation of released directives. A comprehensive framework for confirming and properly checking the design architecture was adequately incorporated in Solidity (Hofmann et al., 2017). The study shows that perhaps the blockchain approach possesses a significant advantage to charge reduced rates for partially filled order books.

In comparison, the decentralized solution for finished order books nevertheless produces better results than the centralized method for orders costing more than US$ 2,500, when the processing costs go below brokerage charges. But the blockchain-based system demands much lower fees than traditional stock markets for a persona customer who transacts hundreds of thousands of dollars. To allow more changes in the future, we plan to explore how the government channel incorporation will give the device millions of transactions per second to optimization, while simultaneously reducing costs nearly nil.

REFERENCES

Abeyratne, S. A., & Monfared, R. P. (2016). Blockchain ready manufacturing supply chain using distributed ledger. *International Journal of Research in Engineering and Technology*, 5(9), 1–10. doi:10.15623/ijret.2016.0509001

Adrian, T., Etula, E., & Muir, T. (2014). Financial intermediaries and the cross-section of asset returns. *The Journal of Finance*, 69(6), 2557–2596. doi:10.1111/jofi.12189

Adrian, T., & Shin, H. S. (2010). Liquidity and leverage. *Journal of Financial Intermediation*, 19(3), 418–437. doi:10.1016/j.jfi.2008.12.002

Aitzhan, N. Z., & Svetinovic, D. (2016). Security and privacy in decentralized energy trading through multi-signatures, blockchain and anonymous messaging streams. *IEEE Transactions on Dependable and Secure Computing, 15*(5), 840–852. doi:10.1109/TDSC.2016.2616861

Asharaf, S., & Adarsh, S. (Eds.). (2017). *Decentralized Computing Using Blockchain Technologies and Smart Contracts: Emerging Research and Opportunities: Emerging Research and Opportunities*. IGI Global. doi:10.4018/978-1-5225-2193-8

Bala, A. (2013). Indian stock market-review of literature. *Trans Asian Journal of Marketing & Management Research, 2*(7), 67–79.

Bouri, E., Molnár, P., Azzi, G., Roubaud, D., & Hagfors, L. I. (2017). On the hedge and safe haven properties of Bitcoin: Is it really more than a diversifier? *Finance Research Letters, 20*, 192–198. doi:10.1016/j.frl.2016.09.025

Brunnermeier, M. K., & Pedersen, L. H. (2009). Market liquidity and funding liquidity. *Review of Financial Studies, 22*(6), 2201–2238. doi:10.1093/rfs/hhn098

Dannen, C. (2017). *Introducing Ethereum and solidity* (Vol. 1). Apress. doi:10.1007/978-1-4842-2535-6

Donald, D. C. (2012). *The Hong Kong stock and futures exchanges: Law and microstructure*. Sweet & Maxwell.

Gupta, L. C. (1992). *Stock exchange trading in India: Agenda for reform*. Society for Capital Market Research and Development.

Hendricks, K. B., & Singhal, V. R. (2009). Demand-supply mismatches and stock market reaction: Evidence from excess inventory announcements. *Manufacturing & Service Operations Management, 11*(3), 509–524. doi:10.1287/msom.1080.0237

Hofmann, E., Strewe, U. M., & Bosia, N. (2017). *Supply chain finance and blockchain technology: the case of reverse securitisation*. Springer.

Karame, G. O., & Androulaki, E. (2016). *Bitcoin and blockchain security*. Artech House.

Malik, S., Kanhere, S. S., & Jurdak, R. (2018, November). Productchain: Scalable blockchain framework to support provenance in supply chains. In *2018 IEEE 17th International Symposium on Network Computing and Applications (NCA)* (pp. 1-10). IEEE.

Miraz, M. H., & Ali, M. (2018). *Applications of blockchain technology beyond cryptocurrency*. arXiv preprint arXiv:1801.03528.

Narayanan, A., Bonneau, J., Felten, E., Miller, A., & Goldfeder, S. (2016). *Bitcoin and cryptocurrency technologies: a comprehensive introduction.* Princeton University Press.

Sajana, P., Sindhu, M., & Sethumadhavan, M. (2018). On blockchain applications: Hyperledger fabric and ethereum. *International Journal of Pure and Applied Mathematics, 118*(18), 2965–2970.

Satyavolu, P., & Sangamnerkar, A. (2016). Blockchain's smart contracts: Driving the next wave of innovation across manufacturing value chains. *Cognizant 20–20 Insights.*

Sutcliffe, M. (2017). *An overview of Blockchain applications—this is just the beginning!* Academic Press.

Chapter 7
Blockchain–Based Food Supply Chain Management

Dhana Srinithi Srinivasan
PSG College of Technology, India

Karpagam Manavalan
ⓘ https://orcid.org/0000-0002-0015-200X
PSG College of Technology, India

Soundarya R.
PSG College of Technology, India

Thamizhi S. I.
PSG College of Technology, India

ABSTRACT

Blockchain is an emerging technology that is based on the concept of distributed ledgers. It allows for pervasive transactions among different parties and eliminates the need for third-party intermediaries. Several of blockchain's characteristics make it suitable for use in the agriculture sector. Some of the potential applications of blockchain include efficient management of the food supply chain and value-based payment mechanisms. The products of agriculture are usually the inputs for a multi-actor distributed supply chain, in which case the consumer is usually the final client. The food chain involves several actors including farmers, shipping companies, distributors, and groceries. This makes the entire system to be distributed with multiple actors playing different roles throughout the chain. This currently used system is inefficient and unreliable in various aspects. This project aims to leverage blockchain technology to solve and address discrepancies involved in food supply chains.

DOI: 10.4018/978-1-7998-7589-5.ch007

CASE STUDY

The food industry plays a vital role in providing necessities that support the growth of various human activities. Once harvested or produced, it undergoes various stages like processing, transportation, distribution, storage and delivery. Reports say that about one-third of the produced food has either been abandoned or wasted every year (approximately 1.3 billion tons). Two-third of the wasted food (about 1 billion tons) occurs during phases in the supply chain like harvesting, shipping and storage. Perishable goods including fruits and vegetables were wasted by 492 million tons worldwide in 2011 due to inefficient and ineffective food supply chain management.

Food supply chain management differs from other supply chains such as furniture logistics in that, the importance reflected by factors like food quality, safety, and freshness within a limited time, which makes the underlying supply chain more complex and difficult to manage. This gets more complex when it comes to perishable products where their traversal time through the food supply chain, which includes the use of warehouses or buffers, needs to be quite limited.

One of the major difficulties faced by farmers is the need for middlemen to sell their agricultural goods. In certain cases, the farmers are forced to sell their goods at a price quoted by these so-called middlemen. In countries like India, poor infrastructure in crop-producing regions enables these middlemen to deceive farmers as to the true value of the produce they are selling. Most of the warehouses are near the cities, which increases post-harvest losses due to rotting.

A report from Label Insight and the Food Marketing Institute (FMI) revealed that shoppers are increasingly demanding transparency and a closer connection to their food so much so that 75% say they will switch to a brand that provides more in-depth product information, beyond what is provided on the physical label. These factors emphasize the need for a more transparent food supply chain that alleviates the toil faced by the farmers at least up to an extent and ensures that the information regarding the origin of a product is made available for the end-users.

LITERATURE REVIEW

The purpose of this survey is to place each work in the context of its contribution to understanding the research problem being studied. It defines data sources that other researchers have used. Literature review helps in viewing what came before, what did and did not work for other researchers. It also provides evidence to support our findings.

Features of Blockchain

In 2016, Yuan, Y. Wang conducted a preliminary study of the Blockchain-based Intelligent Transportation System. The study outlines an Intelligent Transportation System oriented, a seven-layer conceptual model for blockchain and presents a case study for blockchain-based real-time ride-sharing services. The study talks in brief about the pros and cons of blockchain technology. Once a new block is validated and added into the chain, this addition is permanent and can't be tampered or removed and this feature of blockchain is known as immutable. This feature of blockchain leads to increased security in the network and is the easiest accountability of the network. In 2017, Zibin Zheng et al. presented a comprehensive overview on blockchain technology and blockchain architecture comparing some typical consensus algorithms used in different blockchains and also analysing the technical challenges of blockchain and recent advances.

Blockchain is described as "a revolutionary picture which has generated thousands of clones across computer networks" (Zibin Zheng et al., 2017). Bitcoin, Ethereum blockchains and smart contract implementations form the core of the development of cryptocurrencies. Dr.Gavin Wood (2014) discussed various features of the Ethereum blockchain by outlining how blockchain technology is implemented in a generalized manner in this framework and provided deep explanations about the design, implementation, issues encountered during implementation of blockchain, the various opportunities it provides and the future hurdles in the framework. In 2018, Dejan Vujičić et al. focused on providing a brief introduction into several aspects and evolutions in the field of Blockchain, also elaborating outlines about Bitcoin, Ethereum blockchains and smart contract implementations.

Applications of Blockchain

Blockchain has a wide range of applications in various sectors like cryptocurrency, healthcare, advertising, insurance, copyright protection, energy, societal applications to list a few. Wubing Chen et al. (2013) surveyed several blockchain applications throughout the years in different domains. The purpose of this survey was to motivate the creation of more blockchain-based applications.

Blockchain technology can empower various paths of Big Data areas with novel solutions (E.Karafiloski,2017). When searching for the best way to deal with Big Data to store, organize and process the data, the Blockchain technology comes in as a significant choice of input. Its proposed solutions about decentralized management of private data, digital property resolution, IoT communication and public institutions' reforms are having significant impact on how Big Data may evolve (see Blockchain Solutions for Big Data Challenges,2017, for more).

Blockchain in Food Supply Chain Management

A food supply chain involves several actors including, farmers, shipping companies, distributors, and groceries. This makes the supply chain management system to be distributed with multiple actors playing different roles throughout the supply chain. Nir Kshetri (2018) examined how blockchain will impact supply chain management objectives by focusing on linking the objectives of food supply chain management to the features of blockchain such as transparency and accountability. IoT can play a major role when incorporated into blockchain-based food supply chain management (see, Blockchain's roles in meeting key supply chain management objectives,2018, for more).

In 2018, Miguel Pincheira Caro et al. presented a fully decentralized, blockchain-based traceability solution for Agri-Food supply chain management. Miguel Pincheira Caro et al. provided two blockchain implementations, using Ethereum and Hyperledger Sawtooth. The performance of both of these deployments was then compared.

Food security is the situation when "all people, at all times, have physical, social and economic access to sufficient, safe and nutritious food that meets their dietary needs and food preferences for an active and healthy life" (Food and Agriculture Organization (FAO)). Attaining such an objective is not an easy task, especially during times of crises, natural calamities and violent political climate. In such situations, blockchain could turn out to be an indispensable resource in ensuring the transparent delivery of international aid, removing intermediaries from the delivery process, making authentic resources accessible and responding more rapidly and efficiently in the wake of emergencies.

Food safety involves processing, managing and storing food in hygienic ways. Illnesses caused due to food contamination are a prevalent issue in today's world. Blockchain would most certainly be an efficient solution because of its ability to ensure transparency at every level in the food supply chain, hence improving the traceability of food regarding its safety. Tian (2017) proposed a system that facilitates the integration of blockchain with Internet of Things for real-time monitoring of physical data and tracing based on the HACCP system has recently. This system will be critically important for the maintenance of cold-chain in the distribution logistics of spoilable food products. ZetoChain is a system which focuses on environmental monitoring in each and every link of the cold chain, based on IoT devices (Zeto, 2018). Problem identification and reporting are done rapidly in order to take immediate measures to control the damage. A mobile application is suggested for usage by consumers to scan Zeto labels on products in order to locate the product's history.

Food integrity is about a reliable exchange of food within the supply chain. Each actor has the responsibility to deliver complete details about goods, right from the origin to production. By means of blockchain, food companies can mitigate food fraud by quickly Identifying and linking outbreaks back to their specific sources is an essential step in assuaging fraud by rapid identification and resolving of outbreaks. This system is being adopted by several organizations and institutions.

TERMS AND TERMINOLOGIES

- Blockchain - A blockchain is a data structure that holds transactional records and ensures security, transparency and decentralization. It is like a chain of records stored in the form of blocks which are not controlled by any central authority.
- Public blockchain - A public blockchain is a globally open network where anyone can participate in transactions and execute consensus protocol to determine which blocks get added to the chain and maintain a shared ledger.
- Private blockchain - Private blockchain is a closed network where the participants require a verification process. There may be a limit to the number of participants in a private blockchain.
- Distributed Ledger - A database that is consensually distributed and ownership is shared across multiple parties. The data is replicated and stored synchronously on every node across the system.
- Transaction - Transaction refers to the transfer of cryptocurrency or data between different nodes. Every transaction in a blockchain generates a hash.
- Ethereum - A public blockchain network and a decentralized software platform upon which developers build and run their applications.
- Cryptocurrency - A digital currency that is based on mathematical function and uses cryptographic encryption techniques to regulate the creation of units of currency. It also verifies the transfer of funds.
- Gas - In Ethereum, Gas measures how much work an action takes to perform. It is a measure of the computational steps required for a transaction on the Ethereum network which is then equated to a fee for the users.
- Gas limit - A limit set for each transaction which states the maximum amount of Gas that can be consumed by that particular transaction.
- Ether - Ether is the native currency of the Ethereum blockchain network. It functions as a fuel of the entire Ethereum ecosystem by behaving as the medium of incentive and form of payment for different nodes or participants to execute essential operations.
- Block - A collection of transactions on a blockchain network is gathered onto a set called a block which is hashed and added to the blockchain.
- Genesis block - The initial block within a blockchain system

- Cryptographic Hash function - A function that returns a unique fixed-length string for every unique input. It creates a digital identification or a digital thumbprint.
- Hash - Hash is the output of a cryptographic hash function. It is also known as a digital fingerprint. Hashes confirm transactions on a blockchain.
- Smart Contract - A self-executing contract with the terms of agreement written into the code. They are automated actions that can be coded and executed once a set of conditions is met.
- Solidity - Solidity is a contract-oriented programming language which is used for writing smart contracts.
- Token - A representation of a digital asset that is built on an existing blockchain system.
- Bitcoin - It is the first cryptocurrency based on Proof of Work blockchain.
- Proof of Work - A protocol for establishing consensus across a system that ties mining capacity to computing power. Hashing a block requires each miner to solve for a difficult variable known as a set, which results in a competition among the miners to solve for a set. For each hashed block, the process of hashing would have taken an amount of time and computational effort. This hashed block is considered Proof of Work.
- Consensus - When a majority of participants of a blockchain network agree on the validity of a transaction that happens within the blockchain system
- Authentication - The process of recognizing a user's identity by associating an incoming request with a set of identifying credentials.
- Digital trust - It is the participant's confidence in a blockchain network's ability to protect and secure data.
- Threat - A threat is any incident that can cause damage to a system by creating a loss of confidentiality, availability or integrity. It can be accidental or deliberate.
- Vulnerability - Vulnerability is a latent weakness in a system which can be exposed by a threat.
- Attack - An attack is a deliberate unauthorized action on a system. It could be active or passive.
- Spoofing - A spoofing attack is an event in which a malicious user or a program successfully identifies as another by falsifying its identity to gain illegitimate access or advantage. In the blockchain technology, spoofing refers to the ability of the attacker to masquerade as another on the blockchain network.
- Tampering - Tampering attack refers to deliberately modifying data through unauthorized channels in order to violate the integrity of the data.
- Repudiation - A repudiation attack is an event when a system does not adopt controls to efficiently track and log the actions of the nodes or users and

thereby allowing illegitimate manipulation or forging the identification of new actions.

- Information Disclosure - Information disclosure attack is aimed at acquiring specific information from a system by an illegitimate user. This information will most likely be classified as sensitive. Breaches of confidentiality fall under information disclosure.
- Elevated privileges - Elevated privileges attack is when a user manages to get unauthorized levels of control over the system. The user may be an authenticated user who is denied access to sensitive information of the system.
- Blockchain network - A blockchain network is the underlying network that the nodes use to communicate. The network defines the protocol that states how communication occurs within the blockchain ecosystem.
- Node - Any computer which is connected to the blockchain network is called a node. It is a copy of the ledger which is operated by a legitimate user on the blockchain system. A full node is a computer which can fully validate transactions and download the entire data of a specific blockchain. A lightweight node does not download the entire data and uses different validation mechanisms.
- Encryption - A process that combines plaintext with a shorter string of data known as key to produce a ciphertext. The ciphertext can be decrypted into the original plaintext by someone who has the key.
- Nonce - A number used only once in a cryptographic communication process. It often includes a timestamp.
- DDoS Attack - A cyber-attack in which the attacker tries to make a machine or a network resource unavailable to legitimate users by temporarily or indefinitely disrupting the services.
- 51% attack - A situation in which a majority of miners in a blockchain system launch an attack on the rest of the nodes which allows for double-spending.
- Double spending - The event during which someone in a blockchain system tries to send a specific transaction to two different recipients at the same time.
- Big data - Big data is the compilation of massive datasets. It is the field that treats ways to analyze and extract information from datasets that are too complex to be dealt with traditional data processing techniques.
- IoT - Internet of Things refers to a network of connected devices that are capable of collecting and exchanging data with one another.

PROPERTIES OF BLOCKCHAIN

Blockchain offers several properties that make it a widely sought and suitable technology for several use cases and business solutions. Every blockchain has a chain of blocks that store information. Each block holds information about transactions and the values appertaining to these transactions are hashed and stored in the blocks. This elemental working of blockchain institutes several properties that ensure integrity, confidentiality and transparency of the data pertaining to the various transactions. Listed below are the properties of a blockchain that makes it suitable for several use cases.

Immutability

Immutability means something that cannot be changed or altered. Each block of information, such as facts or transaction details, proceeds using a cryptographic principle or a hash value. That hash value consists of an alphanumeric string generated by each block separately. Every block not only contains a hash or digital signature for itself but also for the previous one. This ensures that blocks are retroactively coupled together and unmodified. This functionality of blockchain technology ensures that no one can intrude upon the system. This feature also ensures that the network will be intact and unaltered throughout.

Every block in a blockchain has the hash of the previous block. Hence, tampering of data in a particular block requires strenuous efforts and is almost impossible to succeed. Changing the value of a block changes its hash value and therefore the 'previous block's hash value' of the next block. Since this hashing is quite complex, it is impossible to reverse it. This property of blockchain ensures the integrity of data.

Decentralization

The entire blockchain network is decentralized in that, a group of nodes maintains the network and there is no centralized governing authority involved. Due to the absence of a governing authority, anybody can access the network and deposit their assets in it. Every user will have their own private key with which they can directly access the data stored that they stored. This feature offers several advantages.

No Single Point Failure

Since the data is stored in several nodes and because of the absence of a centralized authority, there will be no single point failure

Expensive to Attack

Attacking the network will be an expensive task as it involves attending to more than one node.

No Third Parties

Users can have direct access to their assets without having to approach any third parties.

User Control

With decentralization, users have complete control over their properties. They do not have to rely on any third party to maintain their assets.

Distributed Ledger

Blockchain is a decentralized as well as an open ledger. Ledger is a record or log of the transactions done. Since it is visible to everyone in the blockchain system, it is called an open ledger. No individual or any institution is in charge of the transactions. Each and every node in the blockchain network has the same copy of the ledger. This feature offers several advantages.

No Malicious Modifications

Since Blockchain is a distributed ledger, it responds really well to any suspicious activity or tamper. As no one can change the ledger and everything updates real fast, tracking what's happening in the ledger is quite easy with all these nodes. Since it is an open ledger, blockchain ensures that any change made is visible to everyone on the network, making it too risky and hard for the hackers to make modifications.

Ownership of Verification

In a blockchain system, each node acts as a verifier of the ledger. If a user wants to add a new block, others would have to verify the transaction first and then give an approval. This makes each user a fair and safe participant.

Equal Privileges

No one on the network can get any special favors from the network. Everyone has to go through the usual channels and then add their blocks. There is no hierarchy of privileges in a blockchain system. The decentralization property of a blockchain makes the blockchain network a peer to peer network. This property allows the blockchain to involve only two parties, the sender and receiver, thereby totally eliminating a third-party authorization. Every node in the network can authorize itself.

Transparency

The decentralized nature of the blockchain technology ensures a high degree of transparency. A transparent profile is created for every participant. Every change on the blockchain is viewable and is ultimately established more concretely. Every transaction made is recorded and is viewable by every participant in the network. This underlying nature of blockchain ensures that the changes are concrete and makes it a good fit for applications encompassing the need for making storages and transactions visible to all stakeholders. In a public blockchain, everyone in the blockchain network can see the transactions, so it is super transparent. On the other hand, a private or federated blockchain could be the best choice for enterprises who want to remain transparent among staff and protect their sensitive information along the way from public view.

Consensus

A consensus mechanism/algorithm is crucial when multiple participants need to validate a transaction taking place in the network, especially in public blockchains that operate as decentralized, self-regulating systems working on a very large scale without any single authority. They involve contributions from a vast number of participants who work on verification and authentication of transactions occurring on the blockchain. The architecture is cleverly designed and consensus algorithms are at the core of this architecture. Every blockchain has a consensus to help the network make decisions. A consensus ensures that all the transactions occurring in the chain are legitimate and all of the stakeholders agree upon the state of the distributed ledger.

Security

The records on a blockchain are secured through cryptographic algorithms, including hashing techniques, which is a cardinal aspect of the blockchain technology. Each participant holds a unique private key that they can use to access their assets and hence acts as a personal digital signature. If a record is altered, the hash will become invalid and the peer network will know right away about the discrepancies. This ensures that once the transaction blocks get added on the ledger, no one can just go back and change it. Thus, any user on the network won't be able to edit, delete or update it. The risks in a supply chain management system may arise from attacks by external or internal entities. One of the big advantages of using blockchain for supply chain management is that it promises to eliminate intermediaries or any third party authentication, instead, it enables peer-to-peer interaction and exchange of data. This quality of a blockchain makes the network a steady and secure environment.

MATHEMATICAL MODEL

The underlying mathematical model of blockchain technology involves a cryptographic concept called the Elliptic Key Cryptography (ECC). It is a type of asymmetric cryptography that is widely used in the implementation of Blockchains, especially to validate transactions and to ensure that the transactions are authorized to execute. There are two main ways ECC in which ECC can be used:

- Elliptic Curve Digital Signature Algorithm (ECDSA)
- Elliptic Curve Diffie-Hellman key exchange (ECDH)

ECDSA is used to generate signatures for transactions, whereas ECDH is used to encrypt the message that needs to be transacted. Blockchain and its applications including Bitcoins, widely use the ECDSA to validate and authorize transactions. ECC relies on mathematics to ensure that a transaction is secure.

An elliptic curve is a plane curve defined by an equation of the form,

$$y^2 = x^3 + ax + b$$

The values of a and b determine the shape of the elliptic curve and different values a and b result in different elliptic curves. Elliptic curves have numerous properties, one such property is that when a nonvertical line intersects two non-tangent points in the curve, it will always intersect a third point on the curve.

Figure 1. Elliptic Curve Digital Signature Algorithm Graph
Note. *P and Q are two distinct points on an elliptic curve, and P is not -Q. To add the points P and Q, a line is drawn through the two points. This line intersects the elliptic curve in exactly one more point, R`. The point R` is reflected in the x-axis to point R. The law for addition in an elliptic curve group is P + Q = R. From https://medium.com/dataseries/explaining-the-math-behind-blockchain-algorithms-98d06e06c2e3*

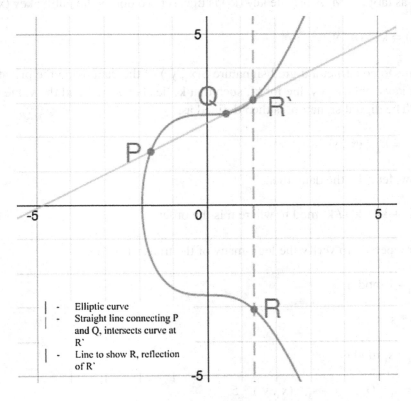

The points P and Q on the curve, as seen in Figure 1, are added to find the corresponding third point R. For instance, consider two points, $P(x_1, y_1)$ and $Q(x_2, y_2)$. To find the sum of the points P and Q, define,

$$\lambda = (y_2 - y_1)/(x_2 - x_1) \bmod M$$

Then the sum $R(x_3, y_3) = P(x_1, y_1) + Q(x_2, y_2)$ is given by,

$$x_3 = \lambda - x_1 - x_2 \bmod M$$

$$y_3 = \lambda (x_3 - x_1) + y_1 \bmod M$$

This is the concept with which blockchains are implemented. In practical real-world scenarios, M is chosen to be a prime non-zero integer. Then, a base point (x_1, y_1) is chosen such that the number of times the point (x_1, y_1) can be added to itself before it fails due to division by zero is a prime number, this is called order, and a value that is as large as M. A private key (k_1) is then set. To obtain the public key (x_3, y_3),

$$(x_3, y_3) = k_1 * (x_1, y_1)$$

Now, to construct a digital signature $S(x_4, y_4)$ of the data using the private and public keys, choose a value for k_2, such that k_2 lies between 0 and the value of the order. The digital signature is then defined as,

$$(x_4, y_4) = k_2 * (x_1, y_1)$$

Now, let Z be the data, then,

$y_4 = (Z + x_4 * k_1) / k_2$ mod n, where n is the order

For a person to verify the legitimacy of the transaction, let,

$s_1 = y_4 - 1$ mod n

$s_2 = Z * s_1$ mod n

$s_3 = x_4 * s_1$ mod n

$(t_1, t_2) = s_1 * (x_1, y_1) + s_3 * (x_3, y_3) * 5$

Finally, verifying if t_1 is equal to x_4 will yield the result of the verification of the transaction's legitimacy.

CONTEXT OF RESEARCH

Figure 2. Context of Research
Note. *Various options available for the implementation of blockchain systems and the chosen methodologies are highlighted.*

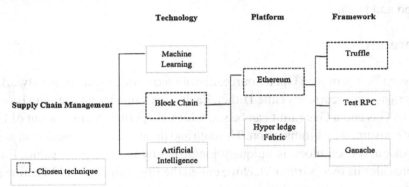

Food Supply Chain Management can be implemented by leveraging several technologies and tools. The chosen ones are highlighted in Figure 2.

Based on the conclusions drawn from the literature survey, the software technologies and platforms for implementing different functionalities of the proposed system have been selected. The major considerations for the selection process include ease of usability, maintaining efficiency and ensuring transparency.

Blockchain Technology

There are certain key features that are expected out of a Food Supply Chain Management system especially when the products involve perishable goods. Each participant in the Supply Chain is responsible for delivering a consumable product to the final end customer. For such use cases, immutability, transparency and traceability become indispensable factors. Blockchain Technology is used in this system because of its ability to support and provide such features.

Why Not Artificial Intelligence or Machine Learning?

By definition, Artificial Intelligence represents the ability of a digital computer or computer-controlled robot to perform tasks commonly associated with intelligent beings. Machine learning is an application of AI-based around the idea that machines should be given access to data and let them learn for themselves. However advanced, no technology is ideal. One incorrect prediction by an Artificial Intelligent robot, for example, prediction of the health of a food product in a food supply chain management, will lead to health as well as business concerns. Additionally, Artificial Intelligence involves automation rather than the manual entry of data. This requires the developer to have deep knowledge about factors that will determine the spoilage of food and so on.

Ethereum

Ethereum Platform is an Open Source, distributed public blockchain network which has its own cryptocurrency called Ether. Each transaction in an Ethereum Blockchain requires Gas and a Gas Limit can be set, which is the maximum amount of Gas that can be consumed by a transaction. The data and details about a transaction are stored in blocks and each block is uniquely identified by using a hash value. Ethereum also provides its own Virtual Machine called the Ethereum Virtual Machine (EVM) which can be used to run the smart contracts.

Why Not Hyperledger?

Hyperledger Fabric is a modular blockchain framework that acts as a foundation for developing blockchain-based products, solutions, and applications using plug-and-play components that are aimed for use within private enterprises. There are no significant disadvantages to be discussed about Hyperledger. Although, Ethereum has significant advantages over Hyperledger for Supply chain management. Ethereum is transparent which is necessary for a supply chain management system. It has a built-in cryptocurrency called Ether, unlike Hyperledger. Ethereum runs smart contracts with the purpose of being decentralized and for mass consumption. While Hyperledger leverages blockchain technology for business with high confidentiality. Hence, with this proper supporting evidence, it is obvious that Ethereum is more suitable for supply chain management applications.

Truffle Framework

The Truffle Framework provides an entire suite of tools for building and testing a blockchain. It provides features for compiling, linking and deploying smart contracts and all of these are in-built within the framework. Additionally, it uses Node Package Manager or Ethereum Package Manager for package installation, version management, and dependency management. The Truffle Framework consists of three primary development frameworks for Ethereum smart contracts and decentralized application development called Truffle, Ganache, and Drizzle. Hence, it was chosen for the development of this prototype.

Truffle

Truffle is made for building dApps using the Ethereum Virtual Machine (EVM) by providing a development environment, testing framework

Ganache

Ganache is a personal blockchain that allows developers to create smart contracts, dApps, and test software that is available as a desktop application and command-line tool

Drizzle

Drizzle is a JavaScript-based front-end development library that is capable of automatically synchronizing contract and transaction data

PROPOSED SYSTEM

The architecture adopted in this system is the Layered Architecture. Each of the components within the system is organized into horizontal layers, with each layer performing a specific function within the application. Each layer has a specific responsibility which contributes to the proper functioning of the system.

The Application Layer, Interface Layer, Transaction Layer, Blockchain Layer and Physical Layer interact with each other in an orderly fashion and form their own abstraction around the work that needs to be done in order to satisfy a request.

Layered Architecture improves the maintainability, scalability and flexibility of the entire system as each layer is concerned with only a particular task and thereby makes a contribution in satisfying a request.

Figure 3. Conceptual Architecture
Note. The various layers considered for the Food Supply Chain using Blockchain is shown.

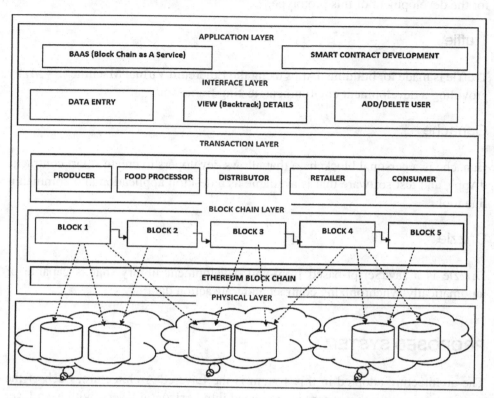

The conceptual architecture visually describes, at a high level, the particulars of the Food Supply Chain Management System. The purpose of this Conceptual Architecture is to provide information that cannot be easily conveyed through words. The architecture considered for implementing Food Supply Chain using Blockchain is layered.

Application Layer

The topmost layer of the Architecture, as shown in Figure 3, is the Application Layer which emphasizes the deployment of the Smart Contracts and provides the entire Food Supply Chain Management as a Service to the users. In this layer, the smart contracts are brought into action by deploying them onto the underlying blockchain.

Interface Layer

The Interface Layer focuses on three major aspects. Each aspect satisfying the different functionalities of the system. The various stakeholders including the farmer, distributor, retailer and customer are registered within the system using the interfaces in this Layer. Additionally, interfaces for the traceback option provided to a registered customer. The various participants enter details specific to their role including factors such as humidity, temperature, price and so on. Additionally, the interface also provides a provision for removing stakeholders from the system.

Transaction Layer

This layer shows various levels of users involved in the transaction. A 20-byte address represents the account or stakeholder that initiates the transaction. Gas Limit is the maximum amount of Gas a user is willing to pay for a transaction. A typical simple transaction usually requires a gas limit of 21000. A value should be assigned to each gas which is basically the value a user is willing to pay for each gas unit.

Blockchain Layer

This layer is where the blocks are created and managed. Each block stores information about a transaction, the various participants involved in a transaction, the gas used up to perform the transaction and the data exchanged between the participants. Each block has a hash value that uniquely identifies the block. The blocks connect with one another by referring to the hash value of the previous block.

Physical Layer

The last layer, as shown in Figure 3, is the Physical Layer. The blocks created in the previous step are stored in Databases in the Physical Layer. In Ethereum, a block can hold up to 20 to 30 kb of data.

REQUIREMENTS

This section attempts to highlight the functional and non-functional requirements that are generally expected out of a Food Supply Chain Management system. Functional requirements explain the various elements that constitute a basic workflow of a supply chain management system, whereas non-functional requirements highlight the abstract and implicit factors that are inherently expected out of such systems.

Functional Requirements

User Accounts

Truffle provides us 10 different user accounts with some permissible amount of composition levels. These accounts are used by the different kinds of users like farmers, distributors, retailers, processors for making transactions and appending them to the blockchain.

Appending the Details at Each Phase

A farmer saves details of grown-up crops like origination, type of crop, the procedure used for sowing, storage info and so on using the mobile app. The information stored by farmers can be accessible by all involved stakeholders within the system. Once the crops are ready, the farmers distribute them to the food processing companies or refineries for further processing. After receiving food items from the farmers, refineries or food processing companies start processing and store the information related to the refining of crops on the public blockchain. After processing the food items, processing companies transport the processed food to the wholesalers and update transportation details on the blockchain. The wholesaler hires logistic service providers to distribute the items to different retailers. Transporting processed food through IoT-enabled vehicles or trucks help to keep the food items safe under controlled environments. The sensors built in the IoT vehicles send information related to the temperature of food items and real-time location to the blockchain.

Traceback

Information stored on the blockchain helps retailers or consumers verify if the food has been appropriately processed or not. From source to destination, the information such as farm origination details, batch numbers, transportation details, storage temperature, expiration details, are linked digitally to the food items within the supply chain blockchain. An end-consumer backtracks the food supply chain blockchain and ensures if the food is safe or not.

Non-Functional Requirements

Usability

The application is designed with a simple user interface along with needed instructions to ensure that the user has a comfortable experience. The internal working of the blockchain are totally abstracted from the user to make it completely user friendly.

Integrity

The data regarding the goods are stored in a blockchain thus making it tamper-proof. The information regarding the supply of the goods is also stored in the blockchain thus those records become immutable. This prevents the denial of purchase by the distributors or denial of supply by the farmers.

Confidentiality

This feature is about a reliable exchange of food within the supply chain without interference from unsolicited third parties. Each actor has the responsibility to deliver complete details about goods, right from the origin to production. By means of blockchain, food companies can mitigate food fraud by quickly identifying and linking outbreaks back to their specific sources is an essential step in assuaging fraud by rapid identification and resolving of outbreaks. This system is being adopted by several organizations and institutions for fraud prevention.

SETUP

Installation

As discussed in the Context of Research, for this application, the Truffle Framework is used for developing and compiling smart contracts and for deploying it in the Ethereum blockchain. Setting up this framework involves installing and configuring a set of tools and frameworks both as a dependency and for ease of usage as the development phase begins. Truffle Framework requires NodeJS and an operating system which is one among Windows, Linux or Mac OS X. NodeJS comes with its own package manager called Node Package Manager(NPM) which can be used for installing and managing packages. The installation and basic setup of the Truffle Framework, in a Windows machine, is explained in detail in the following subsection.

1. Install NodeJS for the respective operating system. This can be done by downloading the executable file from https://nodejs.org/en/ or using software management automation software like Chocolatey.
2. Setup NPM on the computer.
3. Install Truffle using the Node Package Manager by typing the following command in the terminal,

```
npm install -g truffle
```

4. Once, Truffle is successfully installed, a new project needs to be created. This can be done in two ways,

    a. Create an empty project using the command,

```
truffle init
```

    b. Create a project with existing code using the command,

```
truffle unbox metacoin
```

Metacoin is a Truffle Box which acts as a boilerplate code to ease out the process of getting started with Truffle. Several such boxes are available in the Truffle website that helps focus on specific needs and applications.

Structure of a Project in Truffle

Truffle offers a wide range of functionalities to deal with compiling, testing, deploying and accessing smart contracts for a wide range of applications that use the Ethereum Blockchain. Truffle also provisions for several packages for easy building of a user interface and allows for interaction with the smart contracts in a simplified manner, both in terms of development and usage. A folder created for a Truffle project contains a number of subfolders including Contracts, Migrations and Test. It also consists of a configuration file. Each of these files and folders plays a role starting from the development of smart contracts up to its deployment and also for building a user interface for the distributed application. The functionalities of each of them are listed below.

Contracts Folder

The Contracts folder is where all the smart contracts required by the dApp are stored. In addition to the user-specific smart contracts, it also holds one called Migration.sol. The primary purpose of this contract is to keep track of all the migrations that take place in the network. It basically acts as as an interface to manage the deployments

Migrations Folder

Migrations involve deploying contracts to the Ethereum network. As the project changes and scales up as the development furthers, new migration scripts need to be created. The Migration folder holds JavaScript files that deploy Migrations.sol to the blockchain. As more number of migrations are incorporated, the Javascript files in the Migrations folder increases by count.

Test Folder

Truffle has a built-in automated testing framework that can be leveraged to test smart contracts. When running tests against Ethereum clients like Ganache or Truffle Develop, Truffle ensures that the various test files do not share state with each other. Test codes can either be written in Solidity or JavaScript.

Running Smart Contracts

In Solidity, a contract is basically a set of code and data that is stored at a particular address on the Ethereum blockchain. The steps to run a smart contract are listed below.

Compiling Smart Contract

The first step in running a smart contract is compilation. To compile a Truffle project, change to the root of the directory where the project is located. For compiling smart contracts, the following command needs to be used,

```
truffle compile
```

During the first run, all contracts will be compiled. During subsequent runs, Truffle will compile only the contracts that have been changed since the last compile. To override this behavior, the following command needs to be used,

```
truffle compile --all
```

Artifacts. Artifacts of the compilation will be placed in the build/contracts/ directory, relative to your project root.

Dependencies. Contract dependencies can be declared via the import command in 2 ways:

- Importing dependencies via file name,

```
import "./importContract.sol"
```

- Importing contracts from an external package,

```
import "externalpackage/externalContract.sol"
```

Running Migration

Migrations are JavaScript files that help in deploying contracts to the Ethereum network. These files are responsible for staging the deployment tasks, and they're written under the assumption that the deployment needs will change over time. The command to run the migration is as follows,

```
truffle migrate
```

This will run all migrations located within the project's migrations directory. This command will start execution from the last migration that was run, running only newly created migrations. If no new migrations exist, it won't perform any action at all. To run all the migrations from the beginning, the following command needs to be executed,

```
truffle migrate --reset
```

Structure of a Migration File

- **artifacts.require().** To tell Truffle which contracts to interact with. The specified name should match the contract definition name inside that source file.
- **module.exports().** All migrations must export a function via the module. exports syntax. The first parameter of the function exported by each migration should be a deployer object.
- **Deployer.** Deployer is used by a migration file to stage deployment tasks.

Testing Contracts

Truffle has a standard automated testing framework. This framework allows writing simple and manageable tests in two different ways.

- In Javascript and TypeScript, for exercising the contracts from an external application.
- In Solidity, for exercising the contracts in advanced, bare-to-the-metal scenarios.

All the test files should be present in the ./test directory. Additionally, it is also possible to mention the path of the test file next to the command. The command to run a test is as follows,

```
truffle test
```

A stack trace is a list of method and function calls made by an application while an exception was thrown. Solidity stack traces can be obtained for failed or reverted transactions with,

```
truffle test --stacktrace
```

Executing this command will produce stack traces for transactions and deployments made via Truffle Contract during the tests if one of them reverts and thereby causes the test to fail. This option is still experimental, and stack traces are not currently supported for calls or gas estimates.

Writing Tests in Solidity

Solidity test contracts are saved as .sol files. When truffle tests are run, they will be included as a separate test suite per test contract. These contracts provide a clean-room environment per test suite, direct access to the deployed contracts and the ability to import any contract dependency.

Solidity Test Structure

The structure for the solidity test contract contains several parts each of which has a special functionality. By using these test contracts, the working of each function within the smart contract can be tested in terms of several parameters. The various components that make up a test contract are discussed below.

- **Assertions**. Assertion functions can be from a default assertion library like Assert.equal() or can be created.
- **Deployed Addresses.** The addresses of contracts that were deployed as part of the migrations are available through the truffle/DeployedAddresses.sol library.
- **Test Contract Names.** All test contracts must start with Test, using an uppercase T.
- **Test Function Names**. All test functions must start with test, t lowercase. Each test function is executed as a single transaction, in order of appearance in the test file.
- **Before/After Hooks**. These hooks can be used to perform setup and teardown actions before and after each test, or before and after each suite is run.

Ethereum Clients

An integral tool required for building a dApp in Truffle is the Ethereum client. There are many Ethereum clients available. Suitable clients can be chosen depending on whether the purpose is developing or deploying.

Ganache

Ganache is a personal blockchain for Ethereum development that runs on a local desktop. Ganache is part of the Truffle Suite. It simplifies dApp development by placing the contracts and transactions front and center. Ganache helps the developer to quickly see how the application interacts with the blockchain, and introspect details like accounts, balances, creations of contracts and gas costs. Ganache, when launched, runs on http://127.0.0.1:7545. It will display the first 10 accounts and the mnemonic used to create those accounts. Mnemonics can also be inputted by the developer.

Truffle Develop

Truffle Develop helps in setting up an integrated blockchain environment with a single command,

```
truffle develop
```

Execution of this command runs the client on http://127.0.0.1:9545. It will display the first 10 accounts and the mnemonic used to create those accounts. The difference from Ganache is that the mnemonic will persist across restarts of Ganache, whereas in Truffle Develop it will generate a random mnemonic that will persist for that user account alone, that is, unique to the particular user account.

Once Truffle Develop is launched, it will provide you with a console you can use to run all available Truffle commands. These commands are input by omitting the truffle prefix. For example, to compile the smart contracts, instead of typing,

```
truffle compile
```

```
compile
```

Ganache CLI

Ganache has a command-line interface which is a great choice for automated testing and continuous integration environments. Ganache CLI runs headless and can be configured to serve all the development needs. Ganache CLI can be used to test if code works quickly as it processes transactions instantly instead of waiting for the default block time. It also tells immediately when the smart contracts run into errors, and integrates directly with Truffle to reduce test runtime up to 90% compared to other clients.

Drizzle

Drizzle automatically syncs chain data to a Redux store minimizing the effort required from the developers' side. Drizzle can be configured to either sync chain data on each and every block or only when there are changes to contract data the end application is listening to. It covers contract state, events and transactions.

A Truffle Box is available for Drizzle that combines a Create React App setup with Drizzle and Drizzle React Components package. The Truffle Box can be downloaded by this command,

```
truffle unbox drizzle
```

This automatically sets up the required folders and contracts required for user interface development and integration with the underlying architecture.

Remix IDE

Remix provides an integrated environment that can be used to write, compile and debug Solidity code. Remix IDE can be accessed using the online version via a web browser, from a locally installed copy or via Mist, am Ethereum Distributed applications browser. It provides various options for injecting a blockchain instance into the browser. Out of the different options, JavaScript Virtual Machine has certain perks in that, it ignores gas limits, it gives the user an unlimited amount of ether to play with, and it offers tools to speed up the entire debugging process. The current version (v-0.10.1) provides 15 different accounts with 100 ethers allotted for each of the 15 accounts.

Why Remix?

- Remix IDE is a good tool for the initial development and testing of smart contracts.
- It cannot create real user accounts and transfer funds between them, thus making it one of the most preferred tools for beginners to play around with.
- The online version does not require any special installation and can be accessed directly by making use of a web browser. The following URL can be employed to access the IDE: https://remix.ethereum.org/ .
- It gives a complete set of IDE with separate panels for compiling, running and debugging the smart contracts along with a code editor.
- To facilitate the execution of transactions, Remix provides several environments like the JavaScript Virtual Machine. It allows for the emulation of a blockchain for which new instances will be created whenever the page is reloaded.

- Additionally, Remix IDE comes with a number of plugins. Solidity unit testing is one such plugin that can be used for writing contracts for testing purposes.
- Remixd is a NodeJS tool that allows Remix IDE to access the local file system of a computer. It can be made available by using the following command in npm,

```
npm install -g remixd
```

Figure 4. Registration of the user

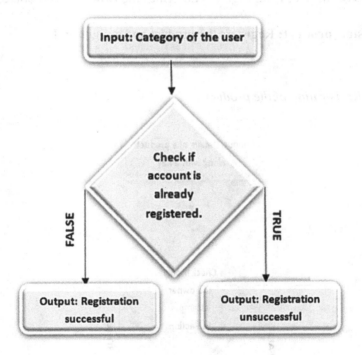

PROTOTYPE IMPLEMENTATION

A prototype of the proposed system is implemented to check for the feasibility of the design, in terms of implementation. The actual flow of the system is made transparent so that we could discern the complete purpose and structure of the system. It will improve the quality of requirements and specifications so that early determination of what the end-user really wants can be made which can result in faster and less expensive software. The flow of the Food Supply Chain Management system along with the pseudocode of the various modules is described below.

Registration

- **register_user**: Adds the user to the list of authorized users.

The input for this module is the category of the user which could be customer, farmer, supplier or distributor. This module checks if the user account already exists. If the account does not exist already, the user is added to the list of authorized users and the registration is successful. If the user is already registered then the registration is declared to be unsuccessful. Figure 4 describes the flow of this module.

- **register_product:** Registers the product and assigns an ID

Figure 5. Registration of the product

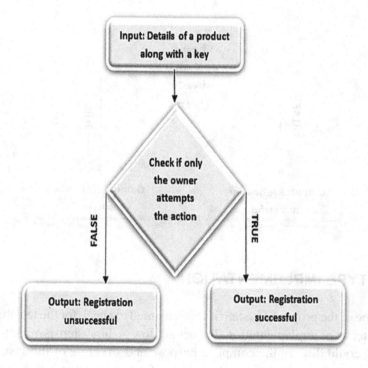

Figure 6. Change of the ownership
Note. The current owner of the product attempts an action for changing the ownership to the destined receiver.

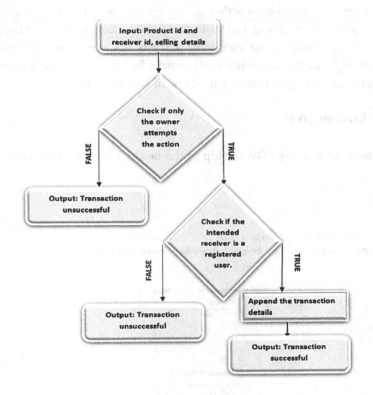

As depicted in Figure 5, this module takes the details of the product as the input along with a key. It checks the account which initiated this action and ensures if it is the product owner. If the product owner has initiated, then the registration of the product is successful. If any other user who is not the owner of the product has initiated the action, then the registration is unsuccessful. This condition makes sure that only the product owner can register a product. Registration of a product is usually done by its initial owner, i.e. the farmer.

Changing Ownership

- **change_ownership**: Transfers the owner of the product from the current owner to the next user in the supply chain.

This module receives Product ID, Receiver ID and selling details such as date and time of purchase as input. It checks the account which initiated this action and ensures if it is the product owner. If it is not the product owner, the transaction is unsuccessful and is terminated. If the product owner initiated the transaction, then the Receiver id is checked whether the receiving party is a registered user. If the receiving party is registered, the transaction ends successfully after the transaction details are appended. If the receiving party is not registered, the transaction is unsuccessful since the receiving party cannot be an illegitimate user and requires prior registration. Figure 6 shows the flow of this module.

Attain Ownership

- **attain_ownership:** Ownership of the product is transferred here.

Figure 7. Attainment of ownership
Note. The ownership is actually being changed here on certain conditions listed.

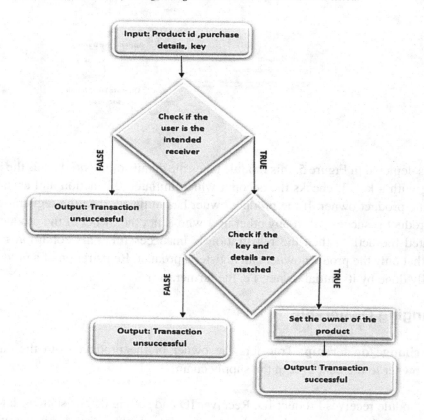

Figure 8. Traceback details
Note. *The details of the product are traced back by the consumer.*

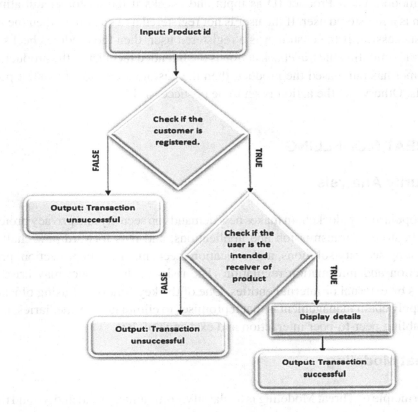

This module takes Product ID and Purchase Details as input along with a key. In Figure 7, the module initially checks if the user initiating the action is the intended receiver. If the user is not the actual receiver of the product, then the transaction is terminated and the ownership of the products still remains with the sender. If the user initiating the action is the intended receiver of the product, then the module checks if the key and the purchase details match. If it matches, the owner of the product is assigned, in this case, the receiver and the transaction is declared to be successful. If the details do not match, then the transaction is unsuccessful.

Traceback Details

- **get_details:** Customers check the history of a transaction along with the product details.

Figure 8 shows how customers can trace back the details of a purchased product. This module takes Product ID as input and checks if the customer initiating the action is a registered user. If the user is not registered as a customer, then the action is unsuccessful. If the customer is a registered user, then the module checks if the customer initiating the traceback action is the intended receiver of the product. If the customer has purchased the product, then the customer can see the entire product details. Otherwise, the action is set to be unsuccessful.

THREAT MODELLING

Security Analysis

The popularity of blockchain makes new demands on security and privacy protection on data storage, transmission and applications, and puts forward new challenges to existing security solutions, authentication mechanisms, data protection, privacy protection and information regulation. The risks in this project may arise from attacks by external or internal entities. One of the key benefits of using blockchain for supply chain management is that it promises to eliminate intermediaries, instead of enabling peer-to-peer interaction and exchange of data.

Threat Modeling

The principle of Threat Modeling is to classify, communicate and understand threats and mitigation to the organization's stakeholders as early as possible. Documentation from this method provides system analysts and defenders with a broad analysis of probable attackers profile, the most likely attack vectors, and the assets most desired by the attacker. Threats can be anything that can take advantage of a vulnerability to breach security and negatively change, erase and damage objects of interest.

Table 1 lists various threats faced by the project at each layer of blockchain on a broad level. Spoofing refers to the ability of the attacker to masquerade as an authenticated entity on the system. Tampering attacks violate the integrity of the data stored on the protected system. Breaches of confidentiality fall under information disclosure. If a user manages to gain unauthorized levels of control over the system, this is a privilege escalation attack. The system is developed in such a way to reduce the attacks as much as possible. Privilege escalation is reduced using product keys, entered during the registration which can be done only by the farmers. The transfer ownership once done can't be reversed and the old owner will lose the corresponding privileges.

Table 1. Threat Model

	Spoofing	Tampering	Information Disclosure	Denial of Service	Elevated Privileges
Cryptographic primitives	Private key		Private key		Private key
Nodes	Malware	Malware	Malware	Failure to update malware	
Networks		Network design	Network design	Network design	Network design
Smart contracts		Arithmetic Bad Randomness Short Addresses Timestamp Unchecked Returns		Access control out of gas	Access control
Blockchain Extension	Insecure APIs				Insecure APIs

Note. Classification of each attack vector based upon its potential effects is done at various levels of the blockchain ecosystem. Each cell shows the different attacks that can occur at a given level of the blockchain ecosystem.

Cryptographic primitives represent the hash functions and public-key cryptography used to ensure data integrity and provide user authentication. The security issues of centralized nodes include the exchanges which involve digital currency transactions and manage large amounts of funds. These nodes are at any point of failure of the entire blockchain network, and the attack yield is high and the cost is low, which is the preferred target of the attackers.

Another attack is Unauthorized Access Attack and it happens in a Smart Contract. A smart contract responds to the message it receives, it can store the received value, and it can send out information and value. This attack is due to the failure to make explicit function visibility or failure to do sufficient permission checks, which can cause an attacker to access or modify a function or a variable that should not be accessed. These attacks are avoided as much as possible in this system by performing the authorization of all stages of users and restricting their capabilities. For example, while transferring ownership, double-check is made from the senders' as well as the receivers' side.

Another important attack includes *malicious information attacks* where the attacker writes malicious information in the blockchain. With the data undelete feature of the blockchain, information is difficult to delete after it is written in the blockchain. If malicious information appears in the blockchain, it will be subjected to many problems.

The basic blockchain technology can be extended by systems built either on top of it or through connections to external systems via APIs. These are the Blockchain extensions.

This blockchain threat model presented in Table 1 represents the classification of the currently known attack vectors against blockchain systems and is designed to be a constant work in progress as no system can be fully secure and blockchain, like any other systems, has new attack vectors being discovered.

51% Attack - Analysis

One of the major attacks that blockchain systems in supply chain management could face is the 51% attack. The 51% attack is an attack against blockchain which occurs when an attacker is in possession or control of 51% of the hashing power. This attack is initiated by creating a chain of blocks privately, that is fully isolated from the original version of the chain. Later on, the isolated chain is added to the network to be established as a genuine chain. This is what enables the double-spending attack. Since the blockchain policy complies with the longest chain rule, if attackers are able to get 51% of the hashing power or more, they will be in a position to drive the longest chain by persuading the network nodes to follow their chain.

Analyzing the nature of the attack and focusing on identifying the vulnerability before it occurs, the best techniques to mitigate 51% attack is the Penalty system for delayed block submission. The penalty system, being a research prototype, proposes increasing the attacking cost extensively so that the potential advantage of gaining 51% attack cannot be achieved towards exploitation. A penalty is applied based on the amount of time an isolated block is hidden from the blockchain network. The time is calculated considering the interval duration between blocks. This security protection technique notifies all the parties including the farmer, the retailer, the distributor etc., about the continuous fork, and during that period, the transactions are restricted from performing fraudulent transactions until the delay is lifted. The prime advantage of this method is the penalty makes the attack much more costly to perform. The delayed block approach sets the attacker to mine a large number of blocks in a sequence before joining the legit chain. This method helps to identify the vulnerability before the genuine chain adopts it.

DISCUSSION AND CONCLUSION

Blockchain technology can be used in food supply chain management in order to set a global standard and to provide quality assurance in food enterprise ecosystems. Introducing blockchain into the food supply chain ensures traceability which is indispensable for tracking back to the source and performing root-cause analysis in case of any contamination in food products. A blockchain environment ensures that each player securely shares data to create an accountable and traceable system. Additionally, a traditional food supply chain system relies on the subjective inputs of individual players when it comes to pricing. Adapting blockchain in the food supply chain system guarantees that the information provided by every player in the value chain is taken into account before quoting a price for a food product, hence making the entire process holistic. Summing up, blockchain's unique properties pave the way for a transparent and decentralized system to warrant verified practices and products in a food supply chain.

Blockchain is, undoubtedly, one of the most promising technologies towards a transparent food supply chain, although many barriers and challenges still persist, which hinder its wider popularity among farmers and food supply systems. The near future will show if and how these challenges could be addressed by governmental and private efforts, in order to establish blockchain technology as a secure, reliable and transparent way to ensure food safety and integrity.

To reduce barriers of use, governments should invest more in research and innovation, as well as in education and training, in order to produce and demonstrate evidence for the potential benefits of this technology. From a law and order perspective, various actions and policies can be taken, such as motivating the growth of blockchain-based ecosystems in agri-food chains, supporting blockchain technology as part of the broader goals of optimizing the competitiveness and ensuring the sustainability of the agri-food supply chain and also designing a clear regulatory framework for implementation of blockchain systems. This system can serve as a foundation for any supply chain management and any number of users or intermediaries can be added or removed based on the scenario.

REFERENCES

Caro, Ali, Vecchio, & Giaffreda. (2018, June 7). *Blockchain-based traceability in Agri-Food supply chain management: A practical implementation.* doi:10.1109/IOT-TUSCANY.2018.8373021

Chen, Xu, Shi, Zhao, & Zhao. (2018, December 10). *A Survey of Blockchain Applications in Different Domains.* . doi:10.1145/3301403.3301407

Divakar, Archana, & Sushma. (2018, May). IoT technology in Smart Farming. *International Research Journal of Engineering and Technology, 5.*

Esmaeilian, B., Sarkis, J., Lewis, K., & Behdad, S. (2020). *Blockchain for the future of sustainable supply chain management in Industry 4.0, Resources, Conservation and Recycling*. doi:10.1016/j.resconrec.2020.105064

Gayatri, M. K., & Jayasakthi, J. (2015). *Providing Agriculture Solution to Farmers for Better Yielding using IoT*. International conference on global trends in signal processing, Chennai, India.

Hongal, A., Jyothi, M. P., & Prathibha, S. R. (2017). *IoT Based Monitoring System In Smart Agriculture*. International conference on global trends in Signal Processing, Bangalore, India.

Karafiloski & Mishev. (2017, July 1). *Blockchain solutions for big data challenges: A literature review.* . doi:10.1109/EUROCON.2017.8011213

Kshetri. (2017). *Blockchain's roles in meeting key supply chain management objectives*. doi:10.1016/j.ijinfomgt.2017.12.005

Nikesh, G. & Kowitkar, R.S. (2016, June 6). IoT Based Smart Agriculture. *International Journal of Advance Research in Computer and Communication Engineering, 5*.

Patil, K. A., & Kale, N. R. (2016). *A Model For Smart Agriculture Using IoT*. International conference on global trends in signal processing, Jalgaon, India. 10.1109/ICGTSPICC.2016.7955360

Queiroz, M. M., Telles, R., & Bonilla, S. H. (2019). Blockchain and supply chain management integration: A systematic review of the literature. *Supply Chain Management, 25*(2), 241–254. doi:10.1108/SCM-03-2018-0143

Saberi, Kouhizadeh, Sarkis, & Shen. (2018, October 17). *Blockchain technology and its relationships to sustainable supply chain management*. doi:10.1080/00207 543.2018.1533261

Shakhbulatov, D., Medina, J., Dong, Z., & Rojas-Cessa, R. (2020). TheBlockchain Enhances Supply Chain Management. A Survey. *IEEE Open Journal of the Computer Society, 1*, 230–249. doi:10.1109/OJCS.2020.3025313

Sunny, J., Undralla, N., & Pillai, V. M. (2020, December). Supply chain transparency through blockchain-based traceability: An overview with demonstration. *Computers & Industrial Engineering, 150*. doi:10.1016/j.cie.2020.106895

Tian, F. (2017). *A supply chain traceability system for food safety based on HACCP, Blockchain & Internet of Things*. IEEE. doi:10.1109/ICSSSM.2017.7996119

Verhoeven, P., Sinn, F., & Herden, T. T. (2018). Examples from Blockchain Implementations in Logistics and Supply Chain Management: Exploring the Mindful Use of a New Technology. *Logistics, 2018*(2), 20. doi:10.3390/logistics2030020

Vujičić, Jagodić, & Ranđić. (2018, April 26). *Blockchain technology, bitcoin, and Ethereum: A brief overview.* . doi:10.1109/INFOTEH.2018.8345547

Wood. (2014). *Ethereum: A Secure Decentralized Generalised Transaction Ledger.* EIP-150 REVISION. (a04ea02 - 2017-09-30)

Wüst, K., & Gervais, A. (2018). *Do you need a Blockchain?* IEEE Zug. doi:10.1109/CVCBT.2018.00011

Yuan, Y., & Wang, F.-Y. (2016). *Towards blockchain-based intelligent transportation systems.* 10.1109/ITSC.2016.7795984

Zheng, Xie, Dai, Chen, & Wang. (2017, September 11). *An Overview of Blockchain Technology: Architecture, Consensus, and Future Trends.* . doi:10.1109/BigDataCongress.2017.85

Chapter 8
Blockchain and PUF–Based Secure Transaction Procedure for Bitcoin

Sivasankari Narasimhan
Mepco Schlenk Engineering College, India

ABSTRACT

In the blockchain, the transaction hashes are implemented through public-key cryptography and hash functions. Hence, there is a possibility for the two users to choose the same private key knowingly or unknowingly. Even the intruders can follow the particular user's bitcoin transaction, and they can masquerade as that user by generating the private and public key pairs of him. If it happens, the user may lose his transaction. Generally, bitcoin technology uses random numbers from 1 to 2256. It is a wide range, but for a greater number of users, there should be one another solution. There is a possibility of digital prototyping which leads to the loss of more accounts. This chapter provides the device-specific fingerprint technology known as physical unclonable function (PUF) to be employed for authentication in a blockchain-based bitcoin environment. The random unique response from PUF ensures correct transaction. In this chapter, a new tetrahedral oscillator PUF has been introduced intrinsically. All the blockchain operations are carried out and verified with PUF response.

DOI: 10.4018/978-1-7998-7589-5.ch008

INTRODUCTION

Bitcoin technology appeared 11 years ago; the decentralized ledger used in Bitcoin is implemented through blockchain technology. The blockchain technique has been proposed in October 2008 by Satoshi Nakamoto (Nakamoto, 2008). Bitcoin technique requires, some cryptographical techniques to control the transactions of Bitcoin among the persons who are involved in it, some hardware instruments to run the software, and the miners who are involved in maintaining the transaction ledgers.

Security issues have become the most challenging problem in Bitcoin, in the sender's point of view. Bitcoin software issues some software challenges to the miners which should be solved within a particular time interval. This challenge makes the miners to find the Nonces for the specified block. The race to solve the challenge starts after the software releases the challenge. After a particular time, this will be closed. Within a stipulated time, who correctly solve the challenge will be rewarded. Other miners validate the answer. The transaction will be added to the blockchain. Most of the threats and blockchain concepts were discussed by Saraju et.al in reference (Mohanty et al., n.d.).

The design of security protocols is complicated due to the problem of creating software challenges and nonces creation. The security of Bitcoin lies in the software challenge; this must be resistant to power analysis attack physical and any side-channel attack. In addition to that, they must be unimaginable by anyone. Moreover, they must be computationally secured and reasonable to produce. The power and memory resources of the bitcoin chain should be less. In this chapter, PUF based blockchain architecture for bitcoin security is presented. Moreover, the enrolment and authentication protocols for the PUF assisted hardware in a blockchain network.

Many types of PUFs have been proposed. It can be categorized mainly into two types: Extrinsic PUFs and Intrinsic PUFs. Both are having its advantages and disadvantages. Based on coating materials, metal components, and memristors, extrinsic PUFs are manufactured. Based on delay properties, in simple logic gates, Intrinsic PUFs are generated. One new category of PUF is introduced in this article to produce the identity of that person. A tetrahedral oscillator (Muthukumar et al., 2019) PUF is proposed in this paper which is used as intrinsic PUF that can be used for the implementation of PUF based blockchain. In some places, PUF is used in place of Hashing operations which avoid more software computation of cryptographic hashes. Elliptic Curve generating module is additionally added with PUF structure to generate public keys. In the case of Proof of PUF-enabled authentication (PoP), the PUF module is responsible for generating the device's unique identification.

Since the response of the PUF element is only known by the device manufacturer and the PUF holder, the behaviors are known only by them. Hence the probability of response duplication and counterfeiting becomes very less. The way that how the intruder is cheating the verifying device lies in the uniqueness and reliability of the underlying device. But in the presence of a PUF device, they can't meet the required conditions expected by the transaction proof chain.

2. RELATED WORKS

A blockchain network hierarchy with Design Authority, contract manufacturer, Distributors, and end-users is described in reference by Cui et al. (Cui et al., 2019). Attack analysis at various levels is described. They suggest PUF as a solution to avoid FPGA cloning. For Decentralized authentication of IoT devices, PUF is used with blockchain. The Trust score has been calculated according to the device performance and the values are stored in the database. If the trust value is greater than or equal to the acceptable level, then the devices start to communicate without expecting the third-party to start. Sensor-based wearable PUFs with blockchain proposed by Rahim et al. (Rahim et al., 2018) are utilized for deciding to accept or reject the person to access a particular device, while the owner is not present in the home. For blockchain environments, PUF acts as a deciding authority. The challenge Response verification procedure has been implemented with hash and MAC algorithms. The design has been implemented in Blockpro by Javid et al. (Javaid et al., 2018). Here one PUF based authentication methodology is proposed along with biometrics. A high-level authentication is proposed for vehicle authentication. The derivation of PUF keys is called Keyless signature technology. The public key can be derived from any of the public key cryptosystems as described in the reference (Intrinsic ID, n.d.). In Key management for blockchain technology Blockchain wallet are discussed in reference Om Pal et al. (Pal et al., n.d.), PUF is used to identify the IoT device. PUF is a function that uses the physical property of the device for generating the desired output. Using generated desired output from the physical property of the IoT device, a unique private/public key pair is generated and the generated pair is used in Blockchain infrastructure. Therefore, IoT nodes are not fully dependent on the nonces. In reference (Patil, n.d.) the attack analysis of blockchain has been exposed and they explain blockchain with PUF and hash algorithm as a solution for some attacks Delgodo et al. (Prada-Delgado et al., 2020) used PUF as a key generator for cryptographic operations. The paper explained digital trust as a physical trust given by PUF.

The remaining section of this paper is organized as follows. In Section 3, PUF based wallets, Bitcoin addresses, and transaction methods are proposed. In Section 4, intrinsic PUF architecture and design were described. The experimental results are presented in section 5, followed by some conclusions.

3. BITCOIN CONCEPTS PROPOSED USING PUF

3.1. Bitcoin Wallets With PUFs

Generally, a Bitcoin wallet consists of secret keys owned by the user. Private keys are generated randomly. Now the secret keys can be generated with PUF response. PUF can be utilized for creating Master Key. By using simple logic circuits consisting of Linear Feedback Shift Registers and Galois field primitives, Child keys can be derived from the Master key. Grandchild keys can also be produced by using simple logic from Child keys. The hierarchy of keys generated from the seed value of PUF is shown in figure 1 (a). The child keys are generated from the Master key, Time Stamp, and Secret information.

The response for the master key which is kept as a secret is treated as a challenge and the response act as the private key (α). The public key is calculated from this private key, from the private key, the public key is calculated as $\beta = \alpha xG$. In the subsequent levels, private and public key pairs are generated in the same way. There may be a problem of two responses from the normal private-public key generation may be the same, but in PUF responses there is no chance for the generation of two responses is the same. It seems to be higher like the number of sands in grain

3.2. PUF Bitcoin Addresses

PUF Bitcoin holder has to generate Bitcoin addresses to send money to everyone. Actually, PUF concept works in the truth of manufacturing variations in one device is not equal to the manufacturing variation in another device even though the same input is applied. This kind of integrated circuit manufacturing variations can't be cloned. PUF-Hashing is a cryptographic algorithm, which produces an entirely different digest even for a single bit variation of input. Moreover, the Hash function is an irreversible one-way function and the process of getting the input from output is generally a tough task. Hence the device-specific PUF module and input specific hash function would make an avalanche effect to distinguish each PUF-Bitcoin chain. Since the hardware module of PUF reduces many complex software execution units, processing time, power consumption, and area are minimized. Collectively, when the same challenge is applied for two PUF devices, the responses from those devices are different. Hence the keys generated from the PUF also different.

Figure 1. (a) Bitcoin Wallet Keys generated from PUF master key; (b) Key derivation from previous Master key

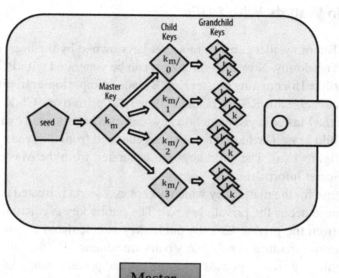

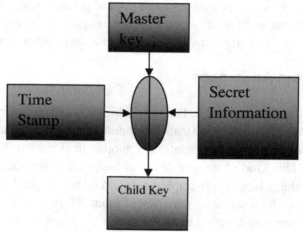

Particular challenge (Challenge may be claimed identity of a person) is applied to the PUF circuit; the response generated from the PUF is termed as the private key of the user (K_{Pr}). The elliptic curve scalar multiplication process is applied to private key K_{Pr} to generate the public key ($K_{Pu} = K_{Pr}xG$). This public key generation process should exhibit one-way property; (i.e) calculation of K_{Pu} from K_{Pr} should be easy and reverse calculation of K_{Pr} from K_{Pu} is a tough task.

Then Public key Bitcoin address is derived from the public key by the following rules:

Figure 2. PUF Bitcoin Address Generation

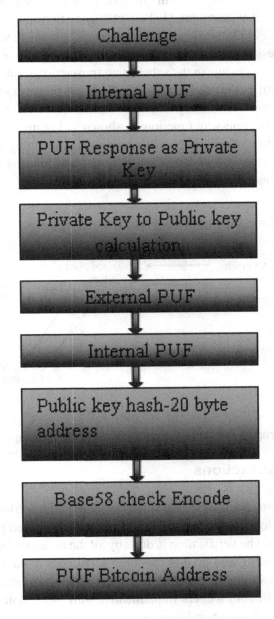

1. First the public key is double hashed by the Extrinsic and Intrinsic PUF hashing algorithm.
2. Then Base58Check encoding operation is done to produce the encoded Public key hash.

The same thing can be provided in QR code form also. Actually, three one-way properties are created at this point. (1) PUF challenge to response (Device Specific level) (2) Private Key to Public key (Public key cryptographical way) (3) Public key to public key address (Hashing level). Hence even a small change in the transaction will cause a complete change in the subsequent transaction hash. Each Transaction hash uniquely identifies the details. The overall process that every PUF should do for the PUF bitcoin address is shown in figure 2. Instead of the software hash function, PUF itself acts as the one-way function. A shown in Figure 2, the challenges are used for the derivation of private keys. Then by using the multiplication algorithm, the public key has been calculated. Then External and Internal PUFs are used as hashing elements instead of a conventional hash.

Figure 3. PUF Private key to Bitcoin Addresses

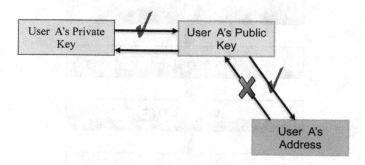

The one-way property of any user address is depicted in Figure 3.

3.3. Bitcoin Transactions

External PUF is considered so strong when compared with Intrinsic PUFs. All the Bitcoin entries are logged into ledgers. Every transaction is used for the creation of the next transaction. The verification is done by all the nodes in the network. Hence the problem of cheating and double spending of Bitcoin money will be avoided. Like the bank transaction, the amount reductions and increments are stored in the form of hashes in Bitcoin ledgers implemented with blockchain. The successive transactions method is shown in Figure 4.

Figure 4. Blockchain Transaction

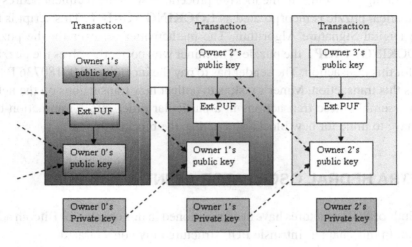

3.4. Bitcoin Transaction Lock With PUF Digital Sign

The transaction hash is generated mainly with four elements (1) The amount for the transaction (2) The recipient address as output (3) the Locking script included with recipient address (3) Timestamp. All the things are hashed together. This is locked by the Digital Signature of the sender's private key. Now in the proposed PUF blockchain technology, the transaction lock is performed by PUF response. Signature is dependent on the transaction. In the Digital Signature creation process, the transaction type and PUF response private key are involved. In the Digital Signature verification process, everyone else in the mining process can participate. The intended receiver only can claim for the transaction. Since nobody can replicate the PUF response.

3.5 Bitcoin Ledgers With PUF

All these transactions are maintained in one Bitcoin ledger as a form of hash codes. If Alice gets money from Jack and Bob, they are indicated in different hashes. Each transaction is maintained in the Bitcoin ledger ((JACK to Alice →)**1021ab3582939214221** and (Bob to Alice→) **ab3582939211231**) as hash functions. The hash functions are unique, case sensitive and punctuations sensitive. For example, if Bob sent the amount 5 Bitcoins (BTC) to Alice then it is recorded in the form-encoded hash form like "**1021ab3582939214221**" in the Bitcoin ledger. As already mentioned, Bitcoin is a decentralized ledger, anybody can mine the transaction between the users. The mining process is happened by additional locking and unlocking procedure. In the locking procedure, with the recipient address, one mathematical puzzle is incorporated as **LOCKING SCRIPT**. This script is based on the Digital Signature Algorithm. The mathematical answer for the puzzle is UNLOCKING **SCRIPT** the puzzle. The miner who correctly solves the puzzle can claim for this transaction. The sender has to pay the incentive (0.00180736 BTC) to process this transaction. Miner's task is to collect new transactions on the network and to assemble these transactions in a particular order into a transaction block. They have to mine for new blocks and update the blockchain.

4. TETRA HEDRAL OSCILLATOR AS INTRINSIC PUF

Two kinds of PUF structures have been mentioned in this chapter for Bitcoin address creation. In this chapter, Intrinsic PUF structure only concentrated.

4.1. Tetra Loop Architecture and Behavior

The proposed Intrinsic PUF is named as tetrahedral oscillator PUF. The tetrahedral oscillator is used as the racing path of logic gates elements. The random and unique pattern creation for one person may utilize different frequencies for each person. The tetrahedral oscillator also utilizes the varying frequency as the person varying phenomenon. The same kind of PUF is used at two different situations of Bitcoin address generation but with different frequencies. The tetraloop is composed of three loops: all loops are made up of simple NOT gates. The first loop consists of four NOT gates and the remaining two loops contain two NOT gates. The oscillatory metastability of logic gates can be utilized for random number generation. In this article, the signal path propagation creates the metastability as well as the unique behavior. Figure 5 shows the loops of the tetrahedral oscillator structure with three loops made up of 8 inverters.

The metastability condition (three loops signal) causes transitory oscillations in the full circuit. This includes jitter conditions in the loop. The traditional ring oscillator loop contains several cascaded inverters. But in the tetrahedral oscillator structure proposed by D.Liu et.al (Liu et al., 2016) contains, nested NOT gate loops with each other, which makes the circuit full of wired-OR logic and signal competitions, resulting in a logic mess and bringing about metastability. Second, the perturbation of noise makes the oscillation to be aroused easier. Furthermore, due to the conflicts among diverse loops, large jitter can be achieved to enhance the randomness of output bits. As illustrated in Figure 5, the number of oscillations is not specific. Also, the final logic levels can differ, ('0' or '1'), which introduces unpredictability.

Figure 5. Tetra hedral oscillator PUF

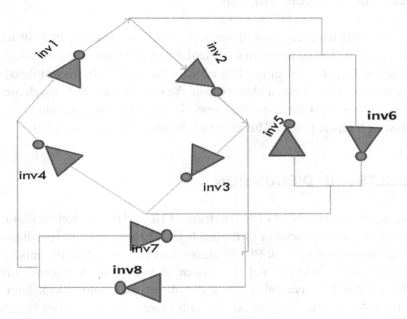

Figure 6. Tetrahedral oscillator PUF

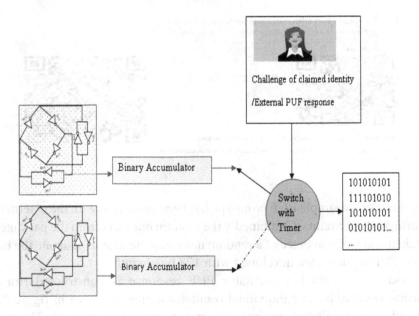

4.2. Tetrahedral Oscillator PUF

The way, how this tetrahedral oscillator is modified to create the PUF structure is shown in Figure 6. The switch with a particular frequency for a person is running to decide whether upper or lower oscillator binary bits have to be accumulated in the output of this module. Claimed identity from the user decides that, which oscillator has to give the output at the respective time. Switch with timer operates with 8 ms, to the flow of 8 bits at a time. This design depends on the user's choice.

5. RESULTS AND DISCUSSION

This chapter considers SRAM PUF as extrinsic PUF and tetrahedral oscillator PUF. The concepts are mainly focusing on the newly introduced tetrahedral oscillator PUF. On the implementation side, for Blockchain implementations, the concepts from the reference (Block Chain Demo, n.d.) have been taken as a model. Instead of Nonce, the PUF response has been taken. Both distributed and single blockchain-based models have been developed. SHA-256 hash function is used. Base56Encoding scheme is utilized in this work.

Figure 7. Single blockchain address generation

For this work, a simple PUF prototype has been generated with the external PUF and intrinsic PUF circuits. Combinedly the random numbers from the package have been taken and given in place of a random number generator to generate the bitcoin address. PUF modules are developed with 128 bits length.

Individually, tetrahedral oscillator PUF response is constructed from two tetrahedral oscillators. The individual oscillator output is shown in figure 8. The upper and lower oscillators are just differing in some time duration. The random oscillated waveform is originally a sine wave. Sine waveform is converted to square waveform first, then it is encoded to a binary number. It can be extended, by increasing the binary accumulator size and encoding size. 64 bits challenge is given to get the response. After collecting a sufficient number of binary numbers, PUF performance metrics have been analyzed. The details about the PUF structure is given in Table 1.

Figure 8. Upper and Lower Oscillator outputs

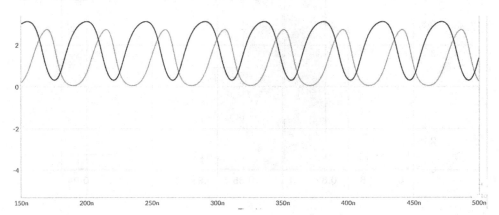

Table 1. PUF performance details

PUF Metrics and Details	Calculated Values
PUF type	Intrinsic Tetrahedral Oscillator PUF
Number of oscillators	2 with each 3 meshes
No of Response bits generated	128
No of Challenge bits	64
Uniqueness	51.07%
Reliability	99%
Randomness	83%

Uniqueness is a measure that every PUF should possesses its characteristics which are explained by Maiti et al. (Maiti et al., 2010) . It is different from other board PUF responses.

Figure 9. Randomness of the produced binary bits

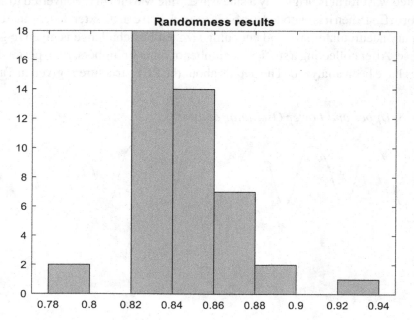

$$Uniqueness = \frac{2}{k\left(k-1\right)}\sum_{i=1}^{k-1}\sum_{j=i+1}^{n}\frac{HD\left(R_i, R_j\right)}{n}\times 100\% \tag{1}$$

It is an estimate of the inter-chip variation in terms of the PUF responses. In this work 9 FPGA boards were taken, hence k=9 here.

Reliability is a measure that how efficiently the chip is reproducing the same response under different environmental situations (Different temperatures, Different voltages, etc.). For doing this, the PUF response (Ri) under normal temperature is determined. At different temperatures, the same instance PUF response (Ri') is calculated up to m times. Hamming distance between the responses is calculated using the formula

$$HD_{INTRA} = \frac{1}{m}\sum_{i=1}^{m}\frac{HD\left(R_i, R_{i'}\right)}{n}\times 100\% . \tag{2}$$

Then the reliability is calculated by

Reliability $=100\%$ - HD_{INTRA} . $\tag{3}$

Figure 10. Histogram of Probability of binary ones to the total bits

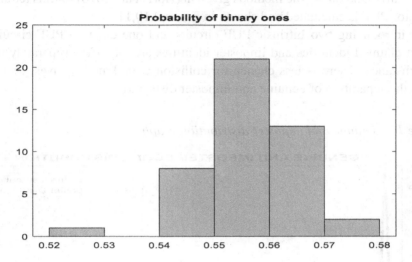

Figure 11. Histogram of Steadiness of the particular bit

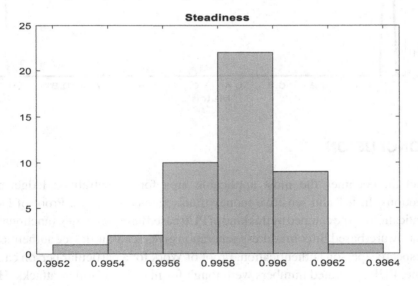

HD_{INTRA} indicates the average number of unreliable/noisy PUF response bits. The value of HD_{INTRA} should be low, and the value of reliability should be high for a particular instance of the chip. In addition to that, PUF responses should be easy to find, and difficult to predict the challenge and the way to prove the device. The probability of binary 1's and 0's should be equally distributed. The histogram metrics are found out by the methods given in (Hori et al., 2010) for this tetrahedral oscillator PUF is calculated and shown in figure 9,10,11.

By introducing two Intrinsic PUF circuits and one external PUF circuit, the correct claimed identities and imposter identities are classified separately with a large distance. There is less chance for collision with True Positives. Figure 12 shows the separation of genuine and imposter distributions.

Figure 12. Genuine and imposter distribution graph

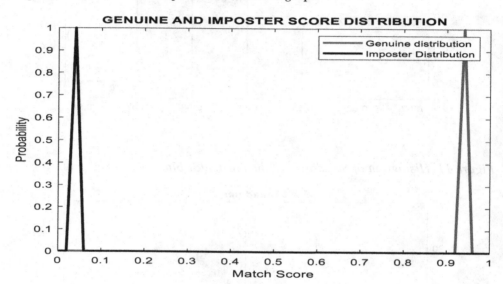

6. CONCLUSION

Blockchain becomes the most applicable area for decentralized ledger-based transactions. In IoT and sensitive money transactions conditions, Proof of Device authentication can be claimed by this kind of PUF based hash generating functionalities. This hardware-based Bitcoin address generation gives accurate device authentication and respective person authentication. Proof of Work for a particular person can also be done. PUF generated numbers were tough for machine learning attacks. Hence it is stronger against side-channel attacks. In the future, for practical applications, specific timing constraints have to be developed for particular applications.

REFERENCES

Block Chain Demo. (n.d.). *Anders Brown*. Retrieved from: https://andersbrownworth. com/blockchain/block

Cui, P., Dixon, J., Guin, U., & Dimase, D. (2019). A Blockchain-Based Framework for Supply Chain Provenance. *IEEE Access: Practical Innovations, Open Solutions*, *7*, 157113–157125. doi:10.1109/ACCESS.2019.2949951

Hori, Y., Yoshida, T., Katashita, T., & Satoh, A. (2010). Quantitative and Statistical Performance Evaluation of Arbiter Physical Unclonable Functions on FPGAs. *ReConFig*, *2010*, 298–303. doi:10.1109/ReConFig.2010.24

Intrinsic ID. (n.d.). https://www.intrinsic-id.com/wp-content/uploads/2017/05/ gt_KSI-PUF-web-1611.pdf

Javaid, U., Aman, M. N., & Sikdar, B. (2018). Blockpro: Blockchain based data provenance and integrity for secure IOT environments. In *Proceedings of the 1st Workshop on Blockchain-enabled Networked Sensor Systems* (pp. 13-18). 10.1145/3282278.3282281

Liu, D., Liu, Z., Li, L., & Zou, X. (2016). A Low-Cost Low-Power Ring Oscillator-Based Truly Random Number Generator for Hash on Smart Cards. *IEEE Transactions on Circuits and Wystems. II, Express Briefs*, *63*(6), 608–612. doi:10.1109/ TCSII.2016.2530800

Maiti, A., Casarona, J., McHale, L., & Schaumont, P. (2010). A large scale characterization of RO-PUF. *Hardware-Oriented Security and Trust (HOST), IEEE International Symposium*, 94–99.

Mohanty, Yanambaka, Kougianos, & Puthal. (n.d.). PUFchain: Hardware-Assisted Blockchain for Sustainable Simultaneous Device and Data Security in the Internet of Everything (IoE). *IEEE Consumer Electronics Magazine, 9*(2), 8-16.

Muthukumar, Sivasankari, & Rampriya. (2019). Anti-aging controllable true random number generator for secured AES-based crypto system. *International Journal of Systems, Control and Communications, 10*(4), 338 – 355.

Nakamoto, S. (2008). *Bitcoin: A Peer-to-Peer Electronic Cash System*. White paper.

Pal, Alam, Thakur, & Singh. (n.d.). Key management for blockchain technology. *ICT Express*.

Patil. (n.d.). *Efficient privacy-preserving authentication protocol using PUFs with blockchain smart contracts*. Academic Press.

Prada-Delgado, M. Á., Baturone, I., Dittmann, G., Jelitto, J., & Kind, A. (2020). PUF-derived IoT identities in a zero-knowledge protocol for blockchain. *Internet of Things, 9.*

Rahim, K., Tahir, H., & Ikram, N. (2018). Sensor based puf iot authentication model for a smart home with private blockchain. In *2018 International Conference on Applied and Engineering Mathematics (ICAEM)* (pp. 102-108). IEEE. 10.1109/ICAEM.2018.8536295

Venkatesan, Srivastava, & Shukla. (n.d.). *Decentralized authentication of IoT devices using blockchain.* Academic Press.

Chapter 9

Blockchain Revolution:
Adaptability in Business World and Challenges in Implementation

Archana Sharma
Institute of Management Studies, Noida, India

Purnima Gupta
Institute of Management Studies, Noida, India

ABSTRACT

As the base of bitcoin, the blockchain has received widespread consideration recently. Blockchain stands for an immutable ledger which permits transactions to occur in a decentralized ways. Applications based on blockchain are numerous for instance financial services, industrial and supply chain services, legal and healthcare services, IoT and blockchain integration, bigdata analytics, and so on. Nevertheless, there are still numerous confronts of blockchain technology like security and fork problems that have to be resolved. This research highlights an inclusive indication on blockchain technology with blockchain architecture in the first phase. And in the second phase, the security challenges and problems associated with blockchain are highlighted. It further proposes and measures up to various typical consensus algorithms used in different blockchains. Research has been concluded with the potential prospects of blockchain as future trends.

DOI: 10.4018/978-1-7998-7589-5.ch009

INTRODUCTION

In the current scenario, Information Technology has been playing a major role in the development of the financial industry. Financial organizations restructuring the way to interact with each other. However, the well-known practice and standards of this segment may face an all-out revamp as incredible innovations such as Blockchain is a maturing stage.

Blockchain was first described by Stuart Haber in the early nineties. In 2008, Satoshi Nakamoto(Nakamoto S.,2008), introduced the blockchain through Bitcoin as a digital cryptocurrency. Bitcoin as a cryptocurrency based on a network protocol permits the users over the network to execute the transaction with digital currency or virtual money in a secure manner that must be present only in their systems. As a sequence of blocks, blockchain register and maintain the details of the transaction in a distributed public ledger crossways with various computers that are connected to peer network. A block records every recent transaction as the present component of blockchain and after completion maintained in blockchain as an eternal database. After completion of each block, another block is created. As a technology revolution of Bitcoin, blockchain maintains proof of every transaction over the network as balance and address. The transactions with Bitcoin are entered in sequential order in a blockchain as the bank transactions are maintained. Due to openness, the entire system sustains security as the public property of blockchain. The transaction is transparent and verifies the authenticity of the owner. Blockchain is considered as decentralized architecture without any verification of the transaction by third parties, it creates a serious distraction to the conventional business procedure which requires centralized architecture or verification from a trusted party. The intrinsic properties of blockchain design and architecture are robustness, transparency, auditability, and network security. Blockchain as a distributed database organizes a sequence of ordered blocks and committed blocks are set to be immutable. Due to the immutable property of the committed block, no one can alter it further. The category of blockchain decides the contents of data stored in a block. For example, Bitcoin maintains the transaction details, the amount transferred, the sender, and receiver information. For authentication, an exclusive hash is associated with each block in comparison to a fingerprint. While the creation of the block, the hash is also calculated concurrently, and in case of any alteration in the same block the hash would also be changed. There are mainly three types of blockChain:

Private Blockchain(Permissioned): Access permissions are restricted in private Blockchain. Network administrator's permission is necessary to join like a participant of blockchain or as a validator. Private organizations in general, may function as private blockchain and won't like the public communication on blocks holding perceptive company details.

Public Blockchain(Permissionless): In oppose to private Blockchain, unlimited members of the open internet can join a permissionless blockchain and perform transactions with validations.

Federated Blockchain: It is a fusion of public blockchain and private blockchain. Though Federated blockchain shares alike scalability and privacy accompanied by private blockchain, a major difference is that leader node (a series of nodes), picked in its place of a single unit for transaction verification processes.

In consideration of the application area of blockchain, renowned execution of public blockchain includes Bitcoin, Litecoin, Ethereum, and broadly the majority cryptocurrencies. The foremost advantages are self-sustained network, self-maintenance, and short of infrastructure costs, radically sinking management overheads. Whereas in private blockchains, the major applications are auditing, database management, and normally, performance-based solutions. For open platforms, Multichain may be considered as an example for constructing and arrange private blockchains. In last, federated blockchains are widely employed in the banking, business organizations, and IT sectors. There are various other application areas also where blockchain has been deployed like healthcare, supply chain, legal services.

Even though the characteristics of blockchain technology may convey additional reliable and expedient services, the security issues and challenges behind this innovative technology is also an important topic that is required to concern. The vulnerabilities include endpoint vulnerabilities,public and private key security, vendor risk, lack of standards, and regulation. Blockchain technology is a grouping of a cryptographic algorithm, peer-to-peer communication, mathematic through a consensus algorithm to determine the synchronization difficulty of distributed database. It's a built-in multi-field infrastructure building (Garay et al., 2015; Gervais et al., 2014; Nakamoto,2013). The blockchain technologies construct of six key elements.

- Decentralized: The basic characteristic of blockchain is that blockchain doesn't require to rely on centralized node any longer, the data can be documented, store, and renew in a scattered manner.
- Transparent: The recorded data by blockchain structure is transparent to all nodes, it too transparent to renew the data, due to this blockchain can be considered reliable.
- Open Source: The majority of blockchain classification is open to all, a record can be ensured publicly and the public can also employ blockchain technologies to produce any application as desired.
- Autonomy: Due to the support of consensus, all nodes on the blockchain organization can reassign or renew data securely, the proposal is to conviction

from a particular person to the complete system, and nobody can interfere with it.

- Immutable: A few records will be set aside evermore, and can't be altered unless somebody can acquire control over 51% of node in the identical time.
- Anonymity: Blockchain technologies resolved the trust, trouble connecting node toward node, therefore data transfer or else transaction can be unidentified, just need to recognize the individual's blockchain address.

THEORETICAL BACKGROUND

Blockchain was introduced through Bitcoin as cryptocurrency. Bitcoin is an organism that controls electronic cash without any support of central power, so certainly there must be a system for the prevention of fraudulence of data, payment repetition, and other kinds of threats and attacks activities possible from unauthorized users. To accomplish this objective, Bitcoin makes use of numerous different essential technologies including, P2P, public-key cryptography, hashing, digital signatures, and Proof of work. The details of these underlying technologies of the blockchain are as follows:

Bitcoin: Electronic Cash in Peer-To-Peer System

As a cryptocurrency, Bitcoin consent to the transfer of digital belongings in the peer-to-peer System without any support of conviction of third parties, Bitcoin is broadly used and exceedingly treasured digital currency across the world (Nakamoto, 2008; Narayanan et al.,2016). In Bitcoin, the complete sequence of a block is vital to maintain possession of each coin. To sustain the ownership of each block, a link has been established through the pointer to form a chain by pointing to the previous correct block in the sequence of the chain. The previous block's hash is maintained to form a linked list structure.

Figure 1. Simplified blockchain

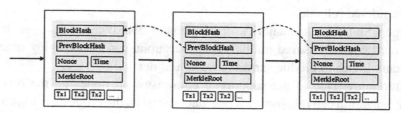

The total count of blocks from starting to end block of the blockchain is known as a block height. Generally, the blockchain persistently grows, and due to this unremitting enhancement of blockchain, there would be a need for a massive amount of computational resources for the validation procedure. To remain the volume and computational attempt reasonable, Bitcoin proposes a simplified payment verification support on Merkle trees (Nakamoto, 2008).

Hash Function

A hash value h is generated in the form of a fixed-size string with the input value I and assigned to hash function H. With the help of this mechanism, a similar hash value will be generated only if the right input is given. Assumption of original input value with the help of hash is tremendously complicated. Bitcoin utilizes the computation of the hash values method to assure the finding of data distortion and verify the persistence of blockchain records.

Figure 2. Hash Mechanism

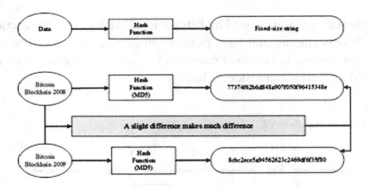

Public-Key Cryptography and Digital Signature

Public, as well as the private key, are significant components of blockchain for digital currency transfer. As asymmetric cryptography, it uses the pair of keys for encryption as well as decryption. Generally, the public key is accessible by anyone in the world and can forward a message to the receiver by encrypting the message using the receiver's public key. The private key of the receiver has been used for message decryption at the receiver's end only (Bergstra & Leeuw, 2013).

Figure 3. Digital Signature

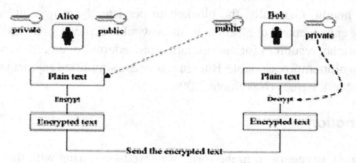

Through public-key cryptography, a digital signature verifies the legitimacy of the message sent digitally. It provides authentication, non-repudiation, and integrity, and including these features, the ownership of bitcoin transactions in addition to the bitcoin wallet addresses has been validated (Badev & Chen,2014).

Timestamp Server

A timestamp server was proposed by Bitcoin to take a block of transactions using a hash for time-stamping and hash publication at a broad level. The timestamp establishes the association chain of transactions, and all timestamp is incorporated in the preceding timestamp inside its hash.

Figure 4. Timestamp Server

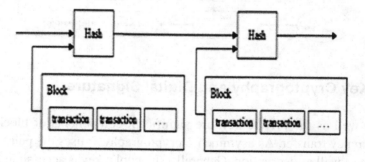

The timestamp server is intended to demonstrate that the data must be present all the time(Nakamoto, 2008).

194

Merkle Trees

Bitcoin's every block with the support of Merkle trees maintains the summing up of each transaction within a block. Merkle tree as a data structure has been used to recapitulate and integrity verification a huge amount of data. As a binary tree, the Merkle tree may also have merely two child nodes (Liu et al., 2015). Merkle tree is created using the hash function and executed recursively on a couple of nodes till there is a single hash identified as Merkle root. Bitcoin's Merkle tree's hash algorithm SHA256 of cryptography has been applied twice, Bottom to top Merkle tree is developed. It doesn't store the transaction, instead of the transaction's data has been hashed and the outcome of the hash will be maintained in each child node. Due to the binary nature of the Merkle tree, in case of an odd figure of transactions, the last transaction will be reproduced to maintain the even figure of child nodes. Merkle tree gives the option to dispose of superfluous transactions without infringement a block's hash because the interior hashes are not maintained.

Figure 5. Merkle Tree

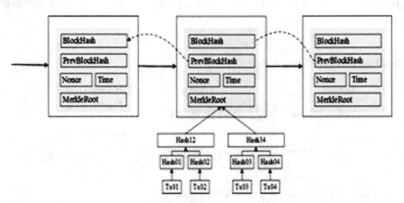

Simplified Payment Verification (SPV) becomes possible in Merkle trees for validation of payment instead of executing a complete network node. A replica of the block header of the longest Proof-of-Work chain is needed to be maintained by the user. The user has no transaction access permission other than network acceptance of it.

As a peer-to-peer network, a network of blockchain also maintains the network of nodes and functions with cryptographic algorithms. The communications and verification process of transactions have been handled by network nodes, and these nodes also resist for revenue (transaction fee) by producing a legitimate block from end to end procedure of getting transactions and determine a resource inducement task (PoW). The bitcoin network runs the following steps:

- Digitally marked fresh transactions are transmitted to every single one node.
- A block contains the fresh transactions collected by each node.
- PoW(Proof-of-Work) is being computed by a node for its block.
- After confirmation of Pow by node, it transmits the block to rest all nodes

Distributed Hash Table

Distributed Hash Table as a disseminated data structure is generally used to accumulate entries related to a key. Moreover, as two major components, the key which is considered to be an address, and value could be the file contents that are linked to that address. Thus, users are permitted to find a key through an entry, as with contacts in a phone as soon as a user looks for a phone number (key) via names (address). DHTs are broadly used to build and manage complex services. For illustration, BitTorrent is employing DHTs for the purpose have hash tables at the top of the mind for any problem as a potential method to resolve the problem." (Figure 6)

Figure 6. Distributed Hash Table

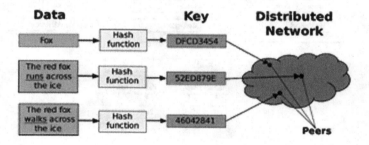

Distributed Ledger Technology

As a catalog, the distributed ledger is to facilitate several locations or along with many participants. Blockchain technology also comes under the name DTL. DLT mentions an innovative and fast mechanism for sharing, recording, and store data beyond multiple ledgers. This technology allows us to share, transact, and recorded the data from different network participants through a distributed network. Each participant can access a shared ledger based on the idea of distributive ledger technology. The idea of Blockchain-based technology was first applied as the fundamental technology of Bitcoin cryptocurrency. It also provides a way to keep your data secure without the interaction of a third party (Mills et al., 2016).

Distributed Ledger Type

Distributed ledger technology can be permissionless (Public) or permissioned (Private) and there are basic differences between the two. Ethereum and Bitcoin are the most popular examples of completely permissionless blockchains, whereas Codra and Hyperledger fabric are a prominent example.

Public Ledger

The public ledger also called the non-permissioned ledger, No one needs permission to create and validate blocks as well as to modify the ledger state by storing and updating data. It provides transparency to everyone for accessing and storing data. In this technique there is no requirement of pre-approval by any entity, network participants can join or leave the network as they will. There is no owner to control it. The homogenous copies of the records are distributed to all network participants. This raises privacy concerns for particular scenarios where the privacy of such data needs to be protected.

Private Ledger

Private ledger, also known as the permissioned ledger, as the name suggests it is restricted that means only trusted and authorized entities are allowed to take part in ledger activities. Distributed Ledgers members are selected prior by someone who is an owner or an administrator of the ledger. They also control network access and sets the ordinance of the ledger. It is restricted unlike its public counterpart in the sense that only authorized and trusted entities can participate in the activities within the ledger. By allowing only authorized entities, a private ledger can ensure the privacy of ledger data, which might be desirable in some use-cases.

Private ledger, also known as the permissioned ledger, as the name suggests it is restricted that means only trusted and authorized entities are allowed to take part in ledger activities. Distributed Ledgers members are selected prior by someone who is an owner or an administrator of the ledger. They also control network access and sets the ordinance of the ledger. It is restricted unlike its public counterpart in the sense that only authorized and trusted entities can participate in the activities within the ledger. By allowing only authorized entities, a private ledger can ensure the privacy of ledger data, which might be desirable in some use-cases.

Table 1. Public ledger vs Private ledger

	Public Ledger	**Private Ledger**
Access	Read & Write public to everyone	Read & Write public to everyone
Central Party	No central owner or administrator	Has some degree of administration or control
Network actors	Don't know each other	Know each other
Speed	Slow	Fast
Identity	User identity anonymous	Identity verification required by the owner
Native Token	Yes	Not necessary
Security	Security through wide distribution in large scale network	Security through access control combined with DLT in small scale network
Openness	Ledger is open and transparent	Different degree of openness and transparency
Level of Trust	Network member is not required to trust each other	A higher degree of trust among members required
Example	• Bitcoin • Ethereum • Manero • Zcash • Steemit • Dash • Litecoin • Stellar etc.	• R3(Banks) • EWF(Energy) • Corda • Hyperledger Fabric Etc.

Hyperledger Fabric

Hyperledger Fabric is emerged by IBM beneath the Hyperleger project. Hyperledger is a project of open-source blockchains. It has been evolved by the foundation of Linux. Hyperledger Fabric was first implemented in 2015. Hyperledger Fabric provides a high privileged network on which members can interact, exchange, and track with digitized data. The fabric is designed to support implementations of a different function, it also allows to use of various programming languages like GO language to implement chain codes, and commonly run within Docker containers. It is a distributed platform for running the chain code. In the hyperedge fabric, transactions follow permissioned ledger and confidential. Since the network is private, every user who wants to participate in the transaction must have registered in the network for getting their corresponding ids. Fabric ledger also provides auditability to meet regulatory needs. The modular architecture delivers a high proportion of resiliency, flexibility, confidentiality in implementation, and design. (Sajana et al., 2018).

Corda

It is a DLT(distributed ledger technology) that focuses on the finance application. It aims to provide support for finance use-cases structure. Various degrees of openness and transparency of the records is possible. It is a permissioned network that means all participants must have corresponding verifiable identities to participant in any transaction. A higher degree of faith among members required. One of the major differences between Corda and other public Distributed Ledger platforms like Ethereum and Bitcoin is the use of a blockchain to record the transaction. Corda is also a DLT platform but does not use a blockchain to record transactions. Corda Govern By private company R3, consortium of over 70 financial institutions. It provides a very high level of trust. One of the powerful features that make Corda different than some renowned financial networks such as Ripple and Stellar is its smart contract facilities. It consists of a large developer community who can write codes in Kotlin and Java to develop DApps in Corda(Chowdhury et al., 2019).

IOTA

IOTA is a freely available distributed ledger designed for the IoT(Internet of Things). It is built to enhance the power of future IoT. It provides secure communications between IoT devices. A distributed technology of IOTA is not a chain of block propel transaction. Its consensus-building structure is made of a DAG (Directed Acyclic Graph) that is based on Tangle. A network of vertices joined by an edge each vertex represents a transaction. IOTA has no cost for transaction and scalability. Its transaction is very fast. IOTA uses Tangle that solving the transaction fee and the scalability both issues faced by most distributed ledgers. IOTA avoids centralization it grows via a transaction, not miners or stacker. IOTa aims to become the backbone of the m2m economy of the Internet of things (Chowdhury et al.,2019).

Blockchain Applications

Digital Currency: Bitcoin

Bitcoin's transaction system and its data structure were developed based on blockchain technologies which built Bitcoin as a digital currency for an online payment system. Funds transfer can be accomplished in a secure manner using an encryption technique without trusting any third party bank. Public keys have been employed for sending as well as receiving the bitcoin, transaction recording, and the individual ID was unsigned. The transaction processes authenticate needs further the user's computing power to acquire consensus and then account for the transaction to the network.

Smart Contract: Ethereum

Smart Contract as a digital contract organize user's digital belongings, devise the participant's right and responsibilities, which will be executed automatically by a computer system. It can be considered as a contract among participants and allow them to receive and respond to messages besides storing the data. Further, a smart contract may send a message to outside also. As a trusted authority or person, a smart contract can also embrace assets for a temporary period and pursue the instructions which have already been programmed (Kosba et al., 2016). As an open-source blockchain, the Etherium platform to handle the contract combines the smart contract and offers a decentralized virtual machine. By the use of ETH, which is called the digital currency of it, users on this platform may create various applications, services, or contracts (Watanabe et al.,2016).

Hyperledger

As Ethereum, Hyperledger blockchain is also an open-source platform to maintain the distributed ledger, initiated by Linux Foundation in December 2015. It is paying attention to ledgers considered to maintain worldwide business transactions, together with foremost financial, supply chain companies and technologies to enhance numerous aspects of performance and reliability. To build up open protocol and set of standards, various independent efforts have been put together to provide a modular framework that maintains dissimilar components for various purposes. This would comprise a mixture of blockchains with their storage models and consensus, and identity, contract, and access control services.

Other Applications

Financial Services

Presently, blockchain technology has been used in a broad level of financial areas, along with business services, financial assets settlements, economic transactions, and prediction markets. An essential role has been expected by blockchain in the global economy's sustainable expansion, consumers benefits in present banking structure and the entire world in common (Nguyen, 2016).

The worldwide financial organizations are looking the procedure of employing blockchain-built application for financial resources, such as fiat money, securities, and imitative contracts (Peters et al., 2016; Fanning & Centers, 2016; Kosba et al.,2016). For example, blockchain technology recommends an enormous alteration to the capital marketplace and a more proficient method for performing processes like derivatives transactions, securities, and digital payments.

Insurance Claims Processing

Claims processing can frequently be an unsolved and a problematical task for the claims processing staff. Insurance workstation requires to go from beginning to end, staged incidents, fake cases, and difficult to deal with clients, etc. which extensively widen the risks of inaccuracy and misclassifications. An ideal framework can be present by Blockchain in such kind of situation administration without any hazard and openness in dealing out with cases. Its encryption (Mota,et al.,2017) feature facilitates guarantor to ensure that dispensation is secure and reliable.

Legal Services

A "Smart Contract" is a computer code for the automation of an agreement, an auto-executing digital agreement that records and implement an agreement between two or more person. Unlike a traditional contract, it is self-enforcing in nature, that is, a smart contract's outcome is inherently and directly coded into the contract itself (Legalwise,2019). A traditional Blockchain allows for a network of computers to build a trusted decentralized and automatic system that is an authority for such Smart Contracts. These digital contracts can be executed more efficiently and without human involvement, resulting in the potential for increased certainty of outcomes.

Healthcare Management

The Healthcare industry is another area of application where blockchain technology could participate an important role in the numerous applications of various regions like public healthcare management, automated health asserts settlement, longitudinal healthcare reports, sharing patients' health check-up data, online patient access, user-oriented remedial research, drug forged, clinical experiment, and precision medicine (Juneja&Marefat, 2018). Normally, blockchain technology along with the SCs could find the solution of problems of the scientific authority of verdict(endpoint switching, missing data, selective publication, and data search) in the clinical examination as well as a matter of patients' informed permission.

Business and Industrial Applications

Blockchain has the prospective to be converted into a significant foundation of troublesome advancements in industry and management through getting better and automate business processes. IoT and blockchain are rising in the current scenario and based on that numerous e-business models have been developed. Blockchain applications materialize to propose substantial performance enhancement and commercialization prospects, recovering reliability in e-commerce and facilitating IoT corporations to optimize their process while reduction of time and cost. blockchain-dependent applications could provide decentralized trade process organization for numerous enterprises. In such examples, all business process illustration may be retained on the blockchain, and the workflow direction-finding could be carried out by SCs, thereby reformation and mechanize intra-organizational procedure and cost reduction (Mendling et al.,2018)

Supply Chain Management

Blockchain technology is likely to raise transparency and liability in supply chain systems, therefore enabling additional flexible worth chains. Particularly, blockchain-dependent applications have the prospective to produce advancements in three areas of the supply chain: optimization, visibility, and demand. Blockchain can be employed in logistics, recognizing bogus products, declining paper load processing, facilitating source tracking, and allow buyers and vendors to perform directly without maneuvering by intermediaries (Subramanian, 2017). Besides, it has been verified that the blockchain-based applications handling within supply chain networks would be able to take care of security, show the way to more vigorous contract management system between 3rd and 4th party logistics (3PL, 4PL) for combating information irregularity, improve tracking system and traceability assertion, offer better information organization across the whole supply chain, offer improved customer facility through highly developed data analytics (i.e. encrypted consumer data) and original recommender system, get better inventory and performance administration across compound supply chains, and at last, it can get better smart transportation arrangement and propose novel decentralized developed design.

VARIOUS PROBLEMS ASSOCIATED WITH BLOCKCHAIN IMPLEMENTATION

Blockchains are digital blocks consisting of records of transactions over public or private networks. The blockchain record security can be ensured through cryptography. The concepts of consensus and immutability are the core security and privacy concern in the blockchain network however blockchain network security depends on the infrastructure of the network. Infrastructure has capabilities like preventing all type of users from accessing sensitive information, preventing illicit data change requests or attempts, and using the highest security mechanism to guard security keys form hackers, are the basic security requirements of infrastructure within blockchain network public, private and hybrid blockchains are different so deliver the different intensity of security. Public blockchains are in communication with public networks like the internet so that any independent node can join it but private networks only let known networks to join. Anonymity is the principle design on which blockchains have typically been designed and identity is the key term that is used by private blockchain to confirm access privileges (Zhang et al., 2019).

Attacks on Blockchain

Majority Attack

An attacker can cause severe network disruption through a majority attack (51% attack), which is a potential attack on a blockchain network, in which the attacker attempts to manage the main part of the hash fee. Transactions over the blockchain network can be prevented if the attack is successful but the attack does not permit the invader to reverse the transactions from other parties. New transaction creation and submission over the blockchain network, cannot be prevented through this attack. However, changing the previously confirmed block gets more difficult when the chain grows because the more confirmation a block gets, it is getting tougher for altering and reverting the transaction. Historical blocks cannot be changed due to the hard coding of the previous transactions. Krypton and Shift are the two blockchain networks based on Ethereum and suffered from majority assault in August-2016. Bitcoin Gold also suffered a majority attack held in May 2018, in which the attacker was successful in double-spend (Lin&Liao,, 2017; Saad et al.,2019).

Double Spending

Double spending is an application-oriented attack, which refers to the spending currency twice through a conflicting transaction in a quick session over the blockchain network which would destroy the trust in the service provider. It is very essential to verify the ownership of the transactions to stop double-spending and other frauds. The outcome of previous researches shows that to execute a double-spending attack over a large blockchain network like Bitcoin would require a very large amount of computational power which would not possible for any individual. the security risk for smaller blockchain networks still exists. The attacker's identity could be revealed after planting this attack over the network and if there are two transactions sequentially generated to impose an attack, then those transactions would be transferred to the unconfirmed transaction pool. the first transaction will be authorized and the second will be flagged as an invalid transaction. in case of both transactions are verified as legal and pulled from the group, then transaction having a maximum numeral of confirmations will be incorporated into the chain, and other would-be discarded(Vokerla et al.,2019).

Finney Attack

Finney attack is launched by the miner in which he mines or controls the content of his block with his transaction and this block is not broadcasted over the network. The coins related to the previous transaction are now used in the second transaction and after that previously mined block is released again. This action would cause some time lag in the rejection of a second transaction by the other miners. If the seller does not wait for enough confirmation, the supply may occur twice. This type of attack gets successful only if the seller accepts the unconfirmed transaction. suppose the time required between finding the block and seller accepts the payment is t, as well as the average time for searching the block is T, then there will be a probability of t/T time unit to find another block on the same network. the attack would not be successful and the attacker will not get any benefit against block B. The standard cost of attempting an attack is (t/T)*B. Suppose V is the value of the transaction, then the seller has to wait at least t=V*T/B before releasing the supply. The Finney attack has a low success probability due to short block intervals and time-sensitive attack procedures. The Bitcoin and Ethereum have 10 minutes and 15 seconds of block time(Saad, et al.,2019).

Brute-Force Attack

In such kind of attack, the invader tries the massive number of possible passwords for digital signature secret keys of existing wallets and checks the returned paint-text for its accuracy. Attack time and the number of attempts depend on the key size. This type of attack is used to steal bitcoins from honest users. First of all, the attacker creates the list of bitcoin addresses having some funds into them using the current set of unused transaction outputs associated with the current status of the blockchain. After that, the attacker selects some set of secret keys from the extracted transaction list and build the secret key list. After that a secret key is selected from the secret key list, and generates a corresponding address. the generated address is then get matched with the addresses from the address list generated in the first stage. If the address is found, then the attacker publishes a transaction to get the benefit of the funds from the compromised address to their address. All these operations are repeated for all secret keys from the list (Vokerla et al.,2019).

Selfish Mining Attack

This attack is also known as Block Withholding Attack. In this attack, an attacker having malicious intentions harms the integrity of the network. In the case of selfish mining, only malicious miners are being referred. The malicious miner hides/ withhold the mined block and harms the other honest miners and lets them loos the trust in the integrity of the blockchain network. In this scenario, honest miners get confused and waste their assets in fruitless courses. It becomes very tough to add valid blocks because of the addition of invalid blocks or withholding the valid blocks by the miners. Selfish miners will maintain their private chain and reveal it for getting more rewards that will be assured because of their contributive approach. A random assignment of blockchain branch to the miners and setting threshold limit for mining pool can eliminate this type of attack (Vokerla et al., 2019; Saad, et al.,2019).

Sybil Attack

An attacker compromises the client system and performs the transaction over the blockchain in this category of attack. A dummy software or multiple fake accounts, nodes, or computers can be treated as a medium to compromise the part of the blockchain. It is a community-based attack performed by a group of compromised nodes. The word "Sybil" comes from the name of a woman having a disease named multiple personality disorder"Sybil Dorsett". If an attacker creates many fake accounts, they can refuse to receive or transmit blocks to prevent other users to perform block transmission. If multiple account creation gives the ability to control the maximum required hash rate of computing strength, then the majority attack can be initiated by the attackers. Elimination of security enforcement against this type of malicious activity over the blockchain association can be performed to make the attack process very impractical by using different types of consensus algorithms like proof of stake, proof of work, or delegated proof of stake. Raising the cost of creating a new identity, implementing trust management protocol before new identity creation, and weighting the user power based on reputation can highly reduce the possibility to launch the attack over a blockchain network (Vokerla et al.,2019).

Fork Problem

Blockchain network is based on a decentralized group of parties (nodes) in collaboration with each other. This problem of Fork comes into existence when blockchain software is involved in an update process. Each node of a blockchain network verifies the public ledger of blockchain and ensures the blockchain network security. When a new software update is launched, the agreement rules also get changed for each node participating in the blockchain system. This event causes the partition of all nodes into two groups. one group accepts the updates and agreed to follow newly updated transaction rules and the other group discards the update and continues to follow the old transaction rules. This conflict arises the chain to be split (Fork) into two parts (Lin, I. C., & Liao, T. C.,2017).

The opinion difference about new protocol in the community results in two different types of approaches (problems). The Hard Fork problem refers to the part of a community that does not agree on the upgraded version of the protocol or new agreement. If there is enough strength of old nodes rejecting software upgrades, they could continue to follow the completely different chain even when the computation power of new nodes is stronger in comparison to old nodes.

Soft Fork can be represented as backward compatible. When the community accepts the new agreement, it is not compatible with the old protocols and refuses to mine the old chain. The majority of nodes should be upgraded with the new protocol to get the Soft Fork work and make the network more secure after Fork. Due to the difference between the computation power of both types of nodes, new nodes never agreed to approve blocks mined by old nodes as well as the same chain is continued to be held by both types of nodes. like a hard fork, the soft fork never reduces the effectiveness and integrity of the system at the time of upgrade. Soft Fork is being used in both Bitcoin and Ethereum blockchain(Lin & Liao,2017).

SUGGESTIONS

Blockchain as a disseminated decentralized network intends to offer immutability and data security. With no central power to authenticate and validate the transactions, all transactions in a blockchain are measured to be protected and validated. As blockchain has been built in a decentralized model and accounts for huge volume transactions in instantaneous, there may be the possibility of the complexity of what is the reality. The key is to obtain consensus on one approach or another, or else malevolent possessions like double-spending assault can occur. Thus, there is a role of the consensus algorithm arrive.

A consensus algorithm is a method in computer science to set up agreement lying on a single data value crossways distributed evolution of systems. As a protocol, in a consensus algorithm, all the team or users of the blockchain network move towards a general agreement (consensus) lying on the current data position of the ledger and be able to believe unidentified peers in a distributed computing background. The consensus algorithms are very much essential in blockchain networks as an essential element because they maintain the integrity and security of these distributed computing systems. In the blockchain, the way to accomplish consensus surrounded by unreliable nodes is a revolution of the Byzantine Generals (BG) Problem(Lamport et al.,1982). In this trouble, a group of generals controls a segment of the Byzantine army on all sides of the city. Various generals are in favour to attack whereas other generals have a preference to retreat. Nevertheless, the assault would be unsuccessful if barely part of the generals assaults the city. Consequently, they have to accomplish conformity (or agreement) to attack otherwise retreat. The way to achieve a consensus in distributed surroundings is a challenge. Same confront for blockchain also due to its network is distributed. There would be a need to make sure ledgers in unlike nodes are consistent.

There are several general approaches to get to a consensus in the blockchain.

Approaches to Consensus

Proof of Work (PoW)

Proof of work is a consensus approach applied in the Bitcoin Net (Nakamoto S., 2008). In a decentralized set of connections, somebody has to be chosen for the documentation of the transactions. The best way is random selection. Nevertheless, a random choice is vulnerable to assault. Subsequently, in case of node desire to bring out a block of transactions, a large number of labor has to be done to establish that the node is not probable to attack the system.

Table 2. Typical Consensus Algorithms Comparison

Property	PoW	PoS		PBFT	DPOS		Ripple			Tendermint
Node identity management	open	open		permissioned	open		open			permissioned
Energy saving	no	partial		yes	partial		yes	nodes	in	yes
Tolerated power of the adversary	<25% computing power	<51% stake	[21]	<33.3% faulty replicas	<51% validators	[22]	<20% faulty UNL	[23]		<33.3% byzantine voting power
Example	Bitcoin [2]	Peercoin		Hyperledger Fabric [18]	Bitshares		Ripple			Tendermint [24]

Figure 7 shows the development of blockchain branches (the branch which would be longest to be admitted as the major chain whereas the shorter one would be abandoned) calculations. In PoW, the network's each node computes a block header's hash. A nonce and miners of the block header would modify the nonce very often to get dissimilar hash values. The consensus has desirable that the computed value necessarily equal to or lesser than a certain specified value. As soon as one node accomplishes the objective, it would transmit the block to additional nodes and every single node must mutually finalize the accuracy of the hash value. In case of the block is validated, supplementary miners would add on the validated block to their blockchain. Nodes that compute the hash describes the miners and the PoW process has been known as *mining* in Bitcoin.

Figure 7. Proof of Work process

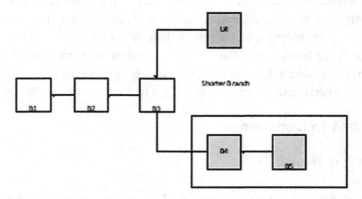

Decentralized network's validated blocks might be produced all together when numerous nodes find the appropriate nonce just about at a similar time. Due to this, branches possibly will generate as shown in Figure 7. Though, it is doubtful that two opposing forks will produce the next block concurrently.

Proof of Stake

Proof of Stake as consensus may be at variance with the PoW mining consensus utilizing a method wherever blocks are authenticated based on the venture of the network applicants. At this time, dissimilar executing hash functions, authenticators stake resources principally in the appearance of tokens or digital money or tokens. Every block's authenticator is further randomly chosen from the stakeholders due to the quantity of computational power owed.

All PoS scheme may put into practice the algorithm in unlike ways, usually, the blockchain is protected by a pseudo-random selection process with the aim of a node's allotment and the distribution— determining the assurance of the party to make sure the network secure. The Ethereum blockchain, which has been considered as largest blockchain network in the world in terms of developer actions, has begun to move from PoW algorithm to PoS to put an effort to improve the network's scalability in addition to reduce unnecessary electricity wastage.

Practical Byzantine Fault Tolerance

It is a replication algorithm to accept byzantine faults (Miguel & Barbara,1999). In this algorithm, Hyperledger Fabric makes use of the PBFT like its consensus algorithm as PBFT could hold upto1/3malevolent byzantine limitation. A novel block is identified in around. In all rounds, a man would be chosen according to a variety of rules. Besides, it is accountable for organizing the transaction. The entire process could be separated into three segments: *pre-prepared, prepared,* and *commit*. In all phases, a node would come into the next phase if it has acknowledged votes from over 2/3 of all nodes. As a result, PBFT has needed that each node is to be recognized to the network. Similar to PBFT, (SCP) Stellar Consensus Protocol (Mazieres D.,2015) is as well a Byzantine fault-tolerant protocol. Within PBFT, all nodes have to inquiry other nodes where as SCP gives contributors the right to select other contributors set to believe. Customers need not be concerned about the fraudulent entrust as they could be designated out without a doubt. DPOS is the spine of bit shares.

Ripple

Ripple is a consensus protocol that makes use of jointly-trusted subnetworks surrounded by the larger network (Schwartz et al., 2014). In this case network's nodes are separated into two categories: *server* for taking part in consensus procedure and *client* for just transporting funds. all servers have a Unique Node List (UNL). It is essential to the server. As soon as determining whether to set a transaction keen on the ledger, the server would inquiry the nodes in UNL, and in case of acknowledged agreements have accomplished 80%, the transaction would be filled into the ledger in support of a node, the ledger will remain accurate provided that the percentage of damaged nodesinUNLisbelow20%.

Tendermint

Tender mint is a byzantine consensus that identifies afresh block in around. A proposer is probably chosen to broadcast the not finalized block in the current round. It might be subcategorized into three steps: 1) *the Prevote step*. Certification authorities choose whether to transmit a pre-vote for the projected block.2) the *Pre-commit step*. In case of the node has received above 2/3 of votes lying on the projected block, it transmits a pre-commit in favor of that block. Otherwise in case of the node has acknowledged more than 2/3 of recommits, it goes through the entrust step. 3) *Commit step*. The node authenticates the block and transmits a commit for the validated block. In case of the node has acknowledged 2/3 of the commits, it admits the block. In distinction to PBFT, nodes need to restrict their coins to turn into validators. Once an authenticator or validator is brought into being to be fraudulent, it would be penalized.

A high-quality consensus algorithm indicates safety, efficiency, and expediency. in recent times, several accomplishments have been over to get better consensus algorithms within the blockchain. Fresh consensus protocols are developed intending to resolve some particular of blockchain. The foremost proposal of PeerCensus(Decker et al.,2016) is to decouple block formation and transaction finalization so that the consensus speed can be significantly improved.

POSSIBLE FUTURE DIRECTIONS

Blockchain has revealed its prospective in business and academia. The research focuses its potential future guidelines concerning four fields: blockchain testing, the tendency to centralization, big data analytics, and IoT with blockchain.

Blockchain Testing

In recent times, a different category of blockchains has come into view and more than 700 cryptocurrencies are recorded in Crypto-currency market capitalizations, 2017 so far. Nevertheless, several developers might forge their blockchain presentation to pull towards investors determined by the enormous profit. In addition to that, as soon as users desire to merge blockchain into trade, It must be clear that which blockchain fits their requirements. So blockchain testing method desires to be in a position to examine dissimilar blockchains.

Blockchain testing could be segregated into two segments: standardization and testing stage. In the standardization segment, every criterion has to be completed and settled. Even as a blockchain is intuitive, it could be experienced with the approved criteria to apply if the blockchain efforts are fine as developer desire. Since for testing segment, blockchain testing requirements to be performed with unlike criteria. For instance, a user who is responsible for online trade be concerned regarding the blockchain's throughput, thus the examination needs investigation of the average time from a client to send a transaction to another transaction and is bundled into the blockchain.

Tendency to Centralization

Blockchain is intended to be a decentralized system. Though, there is a tendency that miners be federal in the mining group. So far, the top 5 mining groups together own superior to 51% of the inclusive hash control in the Bitcoin network. Excluding that, the selfish mining approach demonstrated that groups over 25% of whole computing control could obtain more profits than fair distribution. Balanced miners would be involved in the selfish group and at last, the group could without difficulty exceed 51% of the entire power. Since the blockchain is not projected to serve a small number of organizations, several techniques should be projected to resolve this trouble.

Big Data Analytics

Blockchain could be well shared with big data. Now, it is just about to classify the grouping into two categories: data management addition to data analytics. In support of data management, blockchain could be employed to accumulate important data since it is dispersed and safe. Blockchain may perhaps also ensure the data is novel. For instance, in the case of blockchain is employed to accumulate patients' health details, this information could not have interfered and it would be very difficult to steal an individual's private contents. While as it moves toward data analytics, blockchain transactions could be applied for big data analytics.

IoT and Blockchain

IoT represents the interconnection of disparate things. The term object refers to a human, sensor, or possibly anything that can request or provide a service. The purpose of IoT is to connect an object to object, the object to human, and human to human (Mosenia & Jha,2016). It's convenient for identification, management, and control. Various IoT applications main focus on automating their tasks and empower the objects. Automating the things to perform a different task to support various IOT applications. Main focus to make the object empower, to operate without any human involvement.

IoT Security Goal

IoT applications promise to bring cosmic change into our lives. If we remove the obstacle of security threat then IOT could help to make our life smart and convenient. With the aid of exhaustive computing technology, wireless network, and superior sensor IoT has become the next frontier. The security triad, distinguished technique put into services by use of three main regions which are: data integrity confidentiality, and availability. Data confidentiality is the ability to provide confidence to the user about the privacy of the confidential data by using the different technique so that its disclosure to the unapproved party is prevented and can be ingresses by the authorized users only. Data confidentiality is usually supported through different mechanisms such as data encryption or access control (Zhang et al,,2019). Data integrity refers to the accuracy and consistency of data over its lifecycle. It can be indicated by the absence of modification between two objects or between two upgrades of stored data information. Data integrity can be verified through checksum and cycle redundancy check. Data availability ensures the immediate access of authorized party to their information resources not only in the normal conditions but also in adverse conditions (Sharma et al. 2019; Adat & Gupta,2018)

IoT Security Using Blockchain

Today 5 billion devices have been connected through IoT accounts, and this number will continue to increase and reach 29 billion by 2022 (Reyna et al., 2018). Every object generates and transfers data on the Internet. As IoT has distributive architecture and it is an essential summons for security. Typically, in an IoT network, each node is a possible point of risk that can be utilized to launch cyber attacks. In the presence of a data vulnerability attack, IoT data cannot be exploited properly. Besides, with the involvement of much smart application of IoT where devices exchange data, computational power or other resources, data security becomes critical (Sridhar & Smys,,2017). Blockchain technology has become a very effective solution for all security issues. Blockchain and IoT are two attractive technologies that focus on improving the overall transparency, visibility, level of comfort, and level of trust for the users. The implementation of blockchain into IoT brings some refinements such as decentralization and scalability, identity, autonomy, reliability, security, and market of services The basic idea behind the blockchain is simple, it used distributed ledger technology. The entries in the blockchain are chronological and time-stamped. Each entry in the ledger is tightly coupled with the previous entry using cryptographic hash keys (Panarello et al., 2018).

IoT and Blockchain Integration

IoT can get benefits from the various features delivered by blockchain and can help to further improvement of existing IoT technologies. Blockchain can perform an important role in securing data in IoT applications. At the current time, these two technologies have the most prominent topics in research. The combination of this approach can bring the revolution. (Reyna et al., 2018). Few benefits of IoT and Blockchain integration are as follows:

- Identity: Participants can identify every single device using a common block system. Data provided and store in the system is unchangeable and uniquely recognize actual data that was provided by a device. Subsequently, for IoT applications, a blockchain can provide an authorized and trustful environment.

- Decentralization and scalability: decentralization of the architecture help in the improvement of fault tolerance and system scalability. Other benefits of the shift from a centralized architecture to a Peer-2-Peer distributed will remove central points of failures and tailback.
- Autonomy: Blockchain helps IoT devices to interrelate one device to another without the assistance of any server. Blockchain technology empowers next-generation IOT application features, making it an autonomous object.
- Reliability: With the support of blockchain, IoT information can remain as it has been uploaded. Blockchain systems are capable to check the data integrity and provide the satisfaction that no one has altered the data. The most important aspect of blockchain is to bring reliable IoT.
- Speed: Within a minute, A blockchain distributes the transaction across the whole network and any time throughout the day it can be processed.
- Safely code deployment: Blockchain provides unchangeable storage. Relevant code can be uploaded on the device safely.

Figure 8. Benefits of IoT and Blockchain Integration

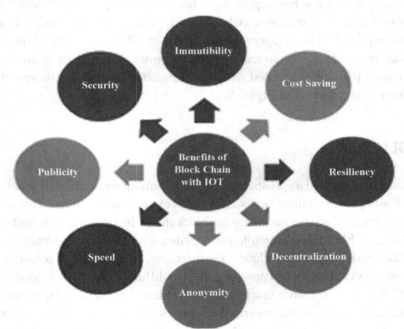

When integrating IoT with blockchain, it has to be determined wherever these interactions will take place. There are varieties of integration scheme:

IoT-IoT

As it can work offline therefore it fastest in terms of security as well as latency. IoT transactions can happen without using blockchain because barely a component of IoT data stored in the blockchain as shown in figure 9. This approach is useful when with secure IoT data where IoT interaction does perform with low data latency.

Figure 9. IOT-IOT to IOT –Blockchain Integration

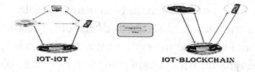

IoT-Blockchain

When this approach has been applied, all interactions happen via blockchain. All selected interactions are traceable as their record can be accessed in the blockchain by using this approach. It also ensures the autonomy of IoT devices. One of the popular complications in blockchain to record all transactions that increase bandwidth and data. Even all IoT data associated with this transaction should also be stored in the blockchain as represented in Figure 9.

CONCLUSION

Blockchain has revealed its prospective for transforming conventional business with its key features: devolution, persistency, secrecy and audit ability. This research explores a comprehensive summary on blockchain. In first phase, it highlights a general idea of blockchain technologies together with blockchain architecture and main characteristics of blockchain.. Furthermore, in next phase research briefs several security challenges and problems that would hinder blockchain development. In addition to that, research discusses the distinctive consensus algorithms used in blockchain to sustain the integrity and security of these distributed computing systems. These conscious protocols were analyzed and evaluated in different perspective. Various potential future directions have been discussed like big data analytics with blockchain, IoT and blockchain integration. At the present time blockchain supported applications are rising up and this research put an effort to conduct in-depth explorations on blockchain-based applications in various business area at present and in the future along with security challenges.

REFERENCES

Adat, V., & Gupta, B. B. (2018). Security in Internet of Things: Issues, challenges, taxonomy, and architecture. *Telecommunication Systems*, *67*(3), 423–441. doi:10.100711235-017-0345-9

Badev, A., & Chen, M. (2014). *Bitcoin: Technical Background and Data Analysis*. Academic Press.

Bergstra, J. A., & de Leeuw, K. (2013). *Questions related to Bitcoin and other Informational Money*. arXivPrepr. arXiv1305.5956.

Chowdhury, M. J. M., Ferdous, M. S., Biswas, K., Chowdhury, N., Kayes, A. S. M., Alazab, M., & Watters, P. (2019). A comparative analysis of distributed ledger technology platforms. *IEEE Access: Practical Innovations, Open Solutions*, *7*, 167930–167943. doi:10.1109/ACCESS.2019.2953729

Decker, C., Seidel, J., & Wattenhofer, R. (2016). Bitcoin meets strong consistency. In *Proceedings of the 17th International Conference on Dis- tributed Computing and Networking (ICDCN)*. Singapore: ACM.

Fanning, K., & Centers, D. P. (2016). Blockchain and its coming impact on financial services. *Journal of Corporate Accounting & Finance*, *27*(5), 53–57. doi:10.1002/jcaf.22179

Juneja, A., & Marefat, M. (2018). Leveraging blockchain for retraining deep learning architecture in patient-specific arrhythmia classification. *2018 IEEE EMBS International Conference on Biomedical and Health Informatics, BHI 2018*, 393–397. 10.1109/BHI.2018.8333451

Kosba, A., Miller, A., Shi, E., Wen, Z., & Papamanthou, C. (2016). Hawk: The blockchain model of cryptography and privacy-preserving smart contracts. *2016 IEEE Symposium on Security and Privacy (SP'16)*, 839–858. 10.1109/SP.2016.55

Lamport, L., Shostak, R., & Pease, M. (1982). The byzantine generals problem. *ACM Transactions on Programming Languages and Systems*, *4*(3), 382–401. doi:10.1145/357172.357176

Legalwise. (2019). *Rise of Smart Contracts with Blockchain Technology in Australia and New Zealand*. Available at: https://www.legalwiseseminars.com.au/news/smart-contracts-and-the-law/

Lin, I. C., & Liao, T. C. (2017). A survey of blockchain security issues and challenges. *International Journal of Network Security, 19*(5), 653–659.

Liu, C., Ranjan, R., Yang, C., Zhang, X., Wang, L., & Chen, J. (2015). MuR-DPA: Top-down Levelled Multi-replica Merkle Hash Tree Based Secure Public Auditing for Dynamic Big Data Storage on Cloud. *IEEE Trans. Comput.*

Mazieres, D. (2015). *The stellar consensus protocol: A federated model for internet-level consensus*. Stellar Development Foundation.

Mendling, J., Weber, I., Aalst, W. V. D., Brocke, J. V., Cabanillas, C., Daniel, F., Debois, S., Ciccio, C. D., Dumas, M., Dustdar, S., Gal, A., García-Bañuelos, L., Governatori, G., Hull, R., Rosa, M. L., Leopold, H., Leymann, F., Recker, J., Reichert, M., ... Zhu, L. (2018). Blockchains for business process management-challenges and opportunities. *ACM Transactions on Management Information Systems, 9*(1), 4. doi:10.1145/3183367

Miguel, C., & Barbara, L. (1999). Practical byzantine fault tolerance. *Proceedings of the Third Symposium on Operating Systems Design and Implementation*, 99, 173–186.

Mills, D. C., Wang, K., Malone, B., Ravi, A., Marquardt, J., Badev, A. I., ... Ellithorpe, M. (2016). *Distributed ledger technology in payments, clearing, and settlement*. Academic Press.

Mosenia, A., & Jha, N. K. (2016). A comprehensive study of security of internet-of-things. *IEEE Transactions on Emerging Topics in Computing, 5*(4), 586–602. doi:10.1109/TETC.2016.2606384

Mota, A. V., Azam, S., Yeo, K. C., Shanmugam, B., & Kannoorpatti, K. (2017). Comparative analysis of different techniques of encryption for secured data transmission. *IEEE International Conference on Power, Control, Signals and Instrumentation Engineering, ICPCSI*. 10.1109/ICPCSI.2017.8392158

Nakamoto, S. (2008). *Bitcoin: A peer-to-peer electronic cash system*. Academic Press.

Narayanan, A., Bonneau, J., Felten, E., Miller, A., & Goldfeder, S. (2016). *Bitcoin and Cryptocurrency Technologies: A Comprehensive Introduction*. Princeton University Press.

Nguyen, Q. K. (2016). Blockchain-A Financial Technology for Future Sustainable Development. *Proceedings – 3rd International Conference on Green Technology and Sustainable Development, GTSD 2016*, 51–54.

Paech, P. (2017). The governance of blockchain financial networks. *The Modern Law Review*, *80*(6), 1073–1110. doi:10.1111/1468-2230.12303

Panarello, A., Tapas, N., Merlino, G., Longo, F., & Puliafito, A. (2018). Blockchain and iot integration: A systematic survey. *Sensors (Basel)*, *18*(8), 2575. doi:10.339018082575 PMID:30082633

Peters, G. W., & Panayi, E. (2016). *Understanding modern banking ledgers through blockchain technologies: future of transaction processing and smart contracts on the internet of money. New Economic Windows*. doi:10.1007/978-3-319-42448-4_13

Reyna, A., Martín, C., Chen, J., Soler, E., & Díaz, M. (2018). On blockchain and its integration with IoT. Challenges and opportunities. *Future Generation Computer Systems*, *88*, 173–190. doi:10.1016/j.future.2018.05.046

Saad, M., Spaulding, J., Njilla, L., Kamhoua, C., Shetty, S., Nyang, D., & Mohaisen, A. (2019). *Exploring the attack surface of blockchain: A systematic overview*. arXiv preprint arXiv:1904.03487.

Sajana, P., Sindhu, M., & Sethumadhavan, M. (2018). On blockchain applications: Hyperledger fabric and ethereum. *International Journal of Pure and Applied Mathematics*, *118*(18), 2965–2970.

Schwartz, D., Youngs, N., & Britto, A. (2014). *The ripple protocol consensus algorithm*. Ripple Labs Inc White Paper.

Sharma, P., Tripathi, S. S., & Panda, R. (2019). *A Survey of Security Issues in Internet of Things*. Academic Press.

Sridhar, S., & Smys, S. (2017, January). Intelligent security framework for iot devices cryptography based end-to-end security architecture. In *2017 International Conference on Inventive Systems and Control (ICISC)* (pp. 1-5). IEEE. 10.1109/ICISC.2017.8068718

Subramanian, H. (2017). Decentralized blockchain-based electronic marketplaces. *Communications of the ACM*, *61*(1), 78–84. doi:10.1145/3158333

Vokerla, R. R., Shanmugam, B., Azam, S., Karim, A., De Boer, F., Jonkman, M., & Faisal, F. (2019). An Overview of Blockchain Applications and Attacks. In *2019 International Conference on Vision Towards Emerging Trends in Communication and Networking (ViTECoN)* (pp. 1-6). IEEE. 10.1109/ViTECoN.2019.8899450

Watanabe, H., Fujimura, S., Nakadaira, A., Miyazaki, Y., Akutsu, A., & Kishigami, J. (2016). Blockchain contract: Securing a blockchain applied to smart contracts. *IEEE International Conference on Consumer Electronics (ICCE'16)*, 467–468. 10.1109/ICCE.2016.7430693

Zhang, R., Xue, R., & Liu, L. (2019). Security and privacy on blockchain. *ACM Computing Surveys*, *52*(3), 1–34. doi:10.1145/3316481

Chapter 10
A Reliable Hybrid Blockchain–Based Authentication System for IoT Network

Ambika N.

ⓘ https://orcid.org/0000-0003-4452-5514

*Department of Computer Applications, Sivananda Sarma Memorial RV College,
Bangalore, India*

ABSTRACT

*IoT is an assembly of equipment of different calibers and functionality working towards
a single goal. A blockchain is a computerized record that contains the whole history
of exchanges made on the system. A multi-WSN arrangement model is structured.
The hubs of the IoT are isolated into base stations, group heads, and conventional
hubs as per their capacities, which encourage the administration and participation
of the hubs. A hybrid blockchain model is proposed. To fit the multi-WSN arrange
model better, as indicated by the various capacities and energies of various hubs,
neighborhood blockchain and open blockchain are sent between group head hubs and
base stations individually, and a crossbreed blockchain model is framed. A shared
validation plot for IoT hubs is proposed. For group head hubs, the creators utilize
the worldwide blockchain for validation, and for customary hubs, they utilize the
nearby blockchain for confirmation. The proposal aims in increasing reliability by
1.17% and minimizes sinkhole attack by 2.42% compared to previous contribution.*

DOI: 10.4018/978-1-7998-7589-5.ch010

1. INTRODUCTION

The Internet-of-things known as IoT (Alaba, 2017) (Ambika N., 2019) is a get together of numerous supplies of various gauge and usefulness progressing in the direction of a solitary objective. The gathering point in speaking with one another using the regular stage gave to them. The gadgets in IoT (Khan & Salah, 2018) control distantly to play out the ideal usefulness. The data sharing among the gadgets at that point happens through the system utilizes the standard conventions of correspondence. The brilliant associated devices or ''things'' extend from preliminary wearable accomplices to enormous machines, each containing sensor chips. The surveillance cameras introduced for reconnaissance of an area can be checked distantly anyplace on the planet. Different shrewd gadgets perform assorting functionalities. An example, observing medical procedure (Ambika N., 2020) in clinics, home surveillance (Al-Ali, Zualkernan, Rashid, Gupta, & Alikarar, 2017), recognizing climate conditions, giving following and availability in autos and ID of creatures utilizing biochips are now serving as the network explicit requirements. The information gathered through these gadgets might be handled continuously to improve the effectiveness of the whole framework.

A blockchain (A & K, 2016) is a modernized record that contains the entire history of trades made on the framework. It is a fundamental purpose behind existing clear outcasts from money trades by bringing in trustworthy progressed cash. It is an assortment of associated blocks that are joined by hash regards made after some time. All information on the blockchain is never-ending and can't be changed. It is arranging worldview utilized for revelation, valuation, and move of quanta is the thing that we characterize as blockchain innovation. The innovation has its job in legislative issues, compassionate, social, conservative, and logical areas.

The invention utilizes to reinforce bitcoin. The blockchain is an open record that decentralizes a trustless framework to move money starting with one point, then onto the next over the web. The innovation intends to take care of the twofold spend issue. The go-between trust is not necessary for the use of the technique. It is a mix of open key cryptography and BitTorrent distributed document sharing. It makes a section of the coin proprietorship affirmed by cryptographic conventions and the mining network. The exchanges that occurred adds to the records. Two components are required – a private key and wallet programming. Utilizing the credentials gives the admittance to the sellers to make exchanges over the web. Wallet programming may record the trading made. The aptitude used in broad daylight record archives includes the report library, the vault of occasions, personalities, and occasions. Any advantage is it controls, follows, and traded. A standard calculation brings innovation into play. The computation acknowledges a document to change over into 64-character code. It guarantees the hash code created can't recover the source record. The exchange utilizes the hash code and timestamp. The source recovers from the proprietor's machine.

The previous contribution (Cui, et al., 2020) uses a hybrid blockchain system. It is a mix of a private and public system. The framework consists of different kinds of devices. Sink nodes gather data for further analysis. Regular devices deployed senses and transmit the processed data to the group heads. The client will be gaining access to the sensed data after authenticating themselves. The sink node and the customers incorporate a public blockchain system. The in-between group heads and regular devices use the local one.

The contribution is an enhancement of the previous suggestion. The nodes use identification and Ethernet address to derive the hashed value. The sink node will be able to map the address of the device to the Ethernet address. Other compromised devices using a similar Ethernet address will come into notice early. The reliability increases by 1.17% in comparison to previous work.

The work divides into seven divisions. The motivation of the proposal is in segment two. The literature survey follows the motive of the contribution. Segment four describes the proposal in detail. The discussion of the analysis of the contribution is in division five. The sixth part discusses future work. The writing concludes in section seven.

2. MOTIVATION

IoT is things made of smart sensors and actuators. These devices are intelligent capable of learning from their experience. These unsupervised devices require security to their network. The previous contribution (Cui, et al., 2020) uses a hybrid blockchain system. It is a mix of private and public blockchain. The framework consists of different kinds of devices. Sink nodes gather data for further analysis. Regular devices deployment senses and transmits the processed data to the group heads. The client will be gaining access to the sensed data after authenticating themselves. The sink node and the customers incorporate the public blockchain system. Local blockchain usage in-between group heads and regular devices.

The adversary can capture the node and make modifications appropriately. A standard device will be unable to detect it at an early stage. Hence reliability is essential for these systems. The proposal is trying to bring trust to the network devices by enhancing reliability and also security.

3. LITERATURE SURVEY

This section discusses the previous contributions towards the domain. A multi-WSN arrangement model (Cui, et al., 2020) is structured. There are numerous hubs in the IoT (Ambika N., 2020). The devices of the IoT isolates into base stations, group heads, and conventional hubs as per their capacities, which encourage the administration and participation of them. To fit the multi-WSN arrange model, better neighborhood blockchain and open-chain are sent between group head hubs and base stations individually, and a crossbreed blockchain model. It suggests a shared validation plot for IoT hubs. To improve the versatility of the IoT confirmation, the authors have received the various leveled blockchain mode. For group head hubs, the creators utilize the worldwide chain for validation. For customary hubs, they use the nearby chain for confirmation.

The general reason for a verification plot is to permit various hubs to convey reliably over a non-confided organizes. In work (Hammi, Hammi, Bellot, & Serhrouchni, 2018), the authors consider a system that claims a lot of things offering and utilizing diverse IoT administrations in an incorporated or an appropriate design. The devices speak with countless different things. Traded messages go through an inconsistent and possibly lossy correspondence organization. The primary objective of our methodology is to make secure virtual zones in IoT situations. Every gadget must discuss just with devices of its zone and thinks about each other gadget as malevolent. It is a structure with a Master of the air pocket that views as an affirmation authority. Some random instruments can be a Master. Besides, each item makes some portion of the framework is called Follower. Every Follower produces an Elliptic Curve (EC) private/open key-pair. Every Follower is given by a structure called a ticket, which speaks to a lightweight testament of 64 pieces.

The contribution presents the out-of-band two-factor confirmation (Wu, Du, Wang, & Lin, 2018) plan to improve the validation and approval measure. The optional validation factor can recognize a home IoT gadget from the pernicious device outside the house, regardless of whether the vindictive instrument imitates the real IoT gadget utilizing the right access token. It solicits the room temperature from the Executor. It can change shading dependent on the current measure. The agent recovers the relationship data of the same from the chain. The agent chooses the related gadget that is in nearness with the unauthenticated device. It sends the activity arrangement to the equivalent. The to-be-authenticated gets and executes the activity arrangement by encoding the succession code to the on/off light switching. The vicinity relative gadget translates the code implanted in the light switching. Vicinity related instrument sends the check result to the chain by summoning the capacity of the Smart Contract on Blockchain. The agent checks chain for the confirmation result through an intelligent contract.

The creators (Huh, Cho, & Kim, 2017) have utilized a couple of IoT gadgets rather than many devices. They have additionally used a cell and three Raspberry Pis. They go about as a meter to monitor power utilization, a climate control system, and light since utilizing genuine gadgets, for example, a climate control frame, would require an excessive amount of overhead. Using a cell phone, the client can set up the arrangement. For instance, a client can set gadgets to turn on vitality sparing mode when power use hits 150 KW. At the point when the client sets up the design through a cell phone, the information sends to the Ethereum arrange. For example, light or forced air systems are recovering estimations of strategy occasionally from Ethereum. Likewise, the meter monitors power use and update it on Ethereum. Accordingly, three unique cycles are going on simultaneously. Ethereum conveyed to the registering stage.

In a multi-hub arrangement (Li, Peng, Deng, & Gai, 2018), the personality data of the gadgets enrolls in the blockchain. Every gadget's ID, open key, a hash of preliminary information, and other data are put away in the blockchain record. Simultaneously, every instrument is a hub in the blockchain arranges, and the agreement system ensures that every hub stores similar data. At whatever point distributed correspondence happens, public-key cryptography utilizes character validation between IoT gadgets. The framework cycle separates into three stages. Everything gadgets require to finish the enrolment in the blockchain before verification. When a device needs to get to the arrangement, it will be confirmed utilizing the enrolment data in the blockchain. After authentication, the gadget checks the honesty of the hash of the primary data to find potential interruption conduct.

The engineering (Almadhoun, Kadadha, Alhemeiri, Alshehhi, & Salah, 2018) is made out of five primary members with admittance to Ethereum contracts through the Internet: admin, end clients, mist hubs, and the cloud workers facilitating IoT information. IoT gadgets do have Ethereum addresses. All different members have of kind Ethereum Address (EA) and interface legitimately with the agreement through an Ethereum customer on account of mist and cloud hubs or through a front-end application/wallet of the Admin and end clients. The Owner of the brilliant agreement can add different clients to be the administrator. The undertaking of the administrators is to oversee the enrolling and de-enlisting of IoT gadgets and haze hubs in the framework. The administrators give consent through the shrewd agreement for end clients to get to IoT gadgets. These consent qualities used by the haze hubs validate clients to get to the IoT gadgets. When the clients are allowed admittance authorization through the intelligent contract, they contact the assigned haze hub liable for dealing with the focused on IoT gadget for verification and access. The keen agreement contains the planning of all the enrolled mist hubs and their related IoT gadgets they oversee. The devices supervise the admittance to IoT gadgets. Each mist hub is regulating and dealing with a gathering of IoT gadgets. Each IoT gadget in the framework plans for one device. The cloud has register and capacity workers total and stores IoT information.

A concentrated keen agreement (Ourad, Belgacem, & Salah, 2018) verifies clients to their particular IoT gadgets. The client authenticates the Ethereum wallet address. If the client is legitimate, the shrewd accord communicates an Access token and the sender's ethereum address. The client and the IoT gadget get the transmitted data from the intelligent contract. The client makes a bundle contains an access token, User IP, Access length, and the ethereum open key. This bundle is marked utilizing the ethereum private key at that point sent with the relating public key. The bundle scrambles whenever needed. Honesty is the thing that is important in this situation marking of the message. When the IoT gadget bundles it confirms its substance. Whenever succeeded, the gadget awards admittance to the client from the sender's IP for the length indicated. Something else, if any of those checks fizzles, the solicitation is dropped.

Toward the beginning of the cycle (Puthal, Mohanty, Nanda, Kougianos, & Das, 2019), singular precipitants/hubs in the system produce exchanges (Trx) with the information and consolidate them into a square. The devices broadcast the squares for additional assessment. The model uses the ElGamal strategy for encryption. Before hub broadcast, the source hub utilizes its private credential to sign and unveils its key, accessible to everybody. It confides instruments inside the system for square approval. With each verification square believed hubs gain trust esteems. It prepares to assess its legitimacy by getting the source hub open key. The mark approves uniquely with the utilization of the credential. In light of the discrete log issue property, one can't process the worth when different qualities are known to them. After mark approval, the believed hub likewise checks the MAC esteem for the second round of assessment. The hubs broadcast the square to the system with PoAh distinguishing proof after confirmation. Following this, device in the system discover the PoAh data from the chain. A singular instrument processes the hash of the square and keeps it to interface the following chain, and the recently figured hash esteem is put away in the current chain to keep up the chain.

The center thought of CertCoin (Jiang, et al., 2019) is to keep up an open record of clients' characters and their related public keys. The framework contains six primary functionalities: enlisting an identification with a relating credential, refreshing the keys, looking through a clue comparing to a given personality, repudiating the open solution comparing to a character, recouping the clue relating to the identification, and mining.

The BATM module (Moinet, Darties, & Baril, 2017) incorporates a trust model called Humanlike Knowledge-based Trust (HKT), given human-like conduct to keep up a notoriety level for every hub. HKT is a trade-off between shared reconnaissances by all devices on the system. It is the nearness of a trusting place. They utilize the payloads contained in the blockchain as a sign of every hub conduct on the system over time. The creators guarantee a hub can't trick others by altering information or professing to be another person. Subsequently, the work assures the dependability of trust assessment without the need for a trusting place. The following advancement will focus on the Network Node trust assessment. The same standards apply to Available administrations, with the distinction that accessible administrations notoriety level is repeated on every hub in the system, subsequently adjusting notoriety level on every device utilizing it. The work performs trust assessment by looking at the current notoriety level of a Network Node to believe him doing certain activities in the network. The contribution uses blockchain-related activities and partners them with a trust level. The level evaluates the base notoriety level for a hub to be trusted to fulfill the result occasion. The work considers two kinds of rules: clocks, key legitimacy breaks, and occasion notoriety factors depicted before.

The cross-area confirmation instrument (Shen, et al., 2020)is running on the head of the blockchain. Personality based Signature (IBS) and Ephemeral Elliptic Curve Diffie-Hellman (ECDHE) credential trade procedures use during the verification and key understanding cycle. In particular, IBS validates gadgets. In IBS-based frameworks, when a device as a petitioner solicitation to be confirmed by another instrument as a verifier, the verifier needs to check the legitimacy of the mark produced by the inquirer utilizing the open key of the inquirer dependent on some fundamental boundaries where the space petitioner lives. A few jobs exist in the proposed instrument, which incorporates IIoT gadgets, Key Generation Center (KGC), Blockchain Agent Server (BAS), and Authentication Agent Server (AAS). They bunch them into various layers by their functionalities. KGC is remembered for the element layer as they are minimal jobs in IBC frameworks. BAS and AAS are two assignment explicit workers presented for specialist missions. The two additional layers incorporate the blockchain layer and the capacity layer. The blockchain layer can be treated as a typical secure channel for area explicit data sharing. Blockchain stores the least data, i.e., area identifier and its coupling esteem comprised of a uniform asset identifier (URI) and hash esteem figured upon the authentic space explicit information. URI focuses on the real stockpiling document situated on the Internet.

IoT gadgets are associated with a passage associates with the blockchain arrangement (Gagneja & Kiefer, 2020). The system administrator confides in a party that has the blockchain on a worker's uses related to processing assets to play out the escalated take a shot for the sake of the IoT gadgets. The blockchain includes squares containing the primary information fields to give a premise to a re-enacted arrange blockchain for IoT. The Sender information field holds the ID of the IoT gadget that is adding the message to the blockchain. The Receiver information field has the open key used to sign communication. This information field is utilized for gadget introduction and shared meeting credential age by the ID of the IoT gadget that is the assigned beneficiary of the message. The Plain Text information field holds messages or directions. The Signature information domain has the mark of the IoT sender utilizing a credential. The information field considers the sharing of open mark confirmation keys with other IoT gadgets uses the blockchain. The Previous Hash information domain uses the past hash-square. The Current information field has the estimation of the current square's hash-value, determined utilizing an SHA work. The Time information category has an hour of square age at a foreordained period. The Proof information subject has the Proof of Work that produces a substantial hash indicated by the blockchain boundaries. The IoT gadgets connect to a door that is associated with a cloud or edge figuring group to do the many hash computations. The blockchain is confirmed utilizing a circle that emphasizes through all squares in the blockchain and checks three conditions for every emphasis. The beginning square sets the blockchain boundaries inside the Plain Text information field.

BCTrust (Tian, Su, & Liang, 2019) is conveyed on the Ethereum blockchain, which gives the best record on the planet, has a network that tails it, and permits to build of an application on it. It guarantees secure exchanges, and, for example, Bitcoin, Ethereum is tried in an enormous scope. In the intelligent contract, just a set of trustful hubs have the composing rights on the blockchain. These favored gadgets are the CPANs of the system. Each CPAN has a couple of private/public keys that permit safely make exchanges with the blockchain. The system has two CPANs and one gadget that has the accompanying qualities: Dresden Elektronik deRFsam3 23M10-R3, have 48 ko of RAM, 256 ko of ROM, and a Cortex-M3 Processor. They sent an Ethereum blockchain duplicate and TestRPC as a customer for associating with the blockchain. The code actualizes using the C language. For associating with the blockchain through TestRPC, they built up an interface that encodes/unravel information to be deciphered per Ethereum. It utilizes JSON RPC for the correspondence, where JSON is a standard printed information arrangement and RPC a far-off methodology call framework. This interface permits programs written in C to speak with TestRPC in a distant strategy call mode, along these lines communicate with the blockchain.

It is a chain-idea (Kim, Kim, & Huh, 2019) dependent on equipment-based and programming-based techniques. The technique for applying the shading range chain to IoT is as per the following: The blockchain utilized in the shading range chain stores the verification status of the gadgets that can get to IoT and works on different workers of the IoT gadget. In the worker, the shading range chain completes the means of affirming the data of the device, putting away the validation condition of the recognized gadget in the blockchain, and checking the verification condition of the put-away gadget. The different gadgets associated with the worker are enrolled in the blockchain through the shading range chain and imparted through the validation step. In the IoT condition, correspondence happens between the worker and the gadget. For secure communication, the worker must confirm that the device confides in an instrument before imparting it. The gadget confirmation measure performs by enlisting the gadget validation status in the shading range chain as follows: as a gadget enrollment technique of the shading range chain, a worker and a gadget create an open key and a private key, for example, an elliptic bend computerized signature calculation (ECDSA)— through a shading range chain for blockchain exchanges. The gadget electronically signs the respective data and the key. It transmits them to the worker, consequently mentioning the enlistment of the device to the shading range chain. The worker thinks about the gotten data with the IoT verification gadget data to affirm that a gadget is a confirmed gadget. A while later, it stores the exchange of proprietorship to the instrument in the blockchain to the worker possessed confirmation token gave by the shading range chain. The put away squares synchronize between the shading range chain workers. If the agreement makes in all workers, the gadget's views as confirmed. An IoT gadget imparts through the confirmation token moved from the worker in the shading range chain. As a gadget validation system of the shading range chain, the device sends carefully marked confirmation data to the worker to speak with the worker. The worker affirms the confirmation status in the shading range chain through the gotten data and checks that it is a verification gadget before playing out the security strategy for secure correspondence. Also, the shading range chain has various validations. The squares production uses the irregular capacity and utilizing the Smart Contract work. It uses a hash convention as opposed to using the current key age convention.

In the proposed framework (Sultana, et al., 2020), various shrewd agreements oversee information and administration sharing among arrange clients. The brilliant accord is Access Control Contract (ACC), Register contract (RC), and Judge Contract (JC). Where ACC deals with the general access control of the framework, the RC enrolls clients (subjects and articles) in the framework. It additionally creates an enlistment table, which stores the data of clients. JC dictates the conduct of the respective. It checks if any misconduct happens. When a subject sends an excessive number of solicitations or drops the created demand, the view is wrong conduct. After the trouble-making conduction, it undergoes the punishment on the subject by the JC. ACC deals with the entrance control between IoT gadgets. At whatever point the respective require any help from the item, it sends a solicitation to the framework. From that point onward, ACC keeps up the entrance control for the subject. It likewise expands the presentation effectiveness of the framework. The object conveys the benchmark structure of numerous ACCs. In this framework, access control is finished by the client rather than the framework itself. The confirmation of clients undergoes finishing by RC by enrolling them in the framework. Making a strategic decision is executed by the JC, which passes judgment on the conduct of clients in the framework. At the point when a subject sends administration demand in the framework. JC checks its doings. It sends a visit, and such a large number of solicitations for help, it is viewed as getting into mischief. Furthermore, if it drops its produced demand, it is otherwise called rowdiness.

4. PROPOSED ARCHITECTURE

The previous contribution (Cui, et al., 2020) uses a hybrid blockchain system. It is a mix of private and public blockchain. The framework consists of different kinds of devices. Sink nodes gather data for further analysis. Regular devices deployment senses and transmits the processed data to the group heads. The client will be gaining access to the sensed data after authenticating themselves. The sink node and the customers incorporate the public blockchain system. Local blockchain usage in-between group heads and regular devices.

The proposed architecture brings reliability compared to. The system uses the following stages –

- Preliminary/Initialization phase – It is the responsibility of the sink node to embed all the credentials into the devices before their deployment. The identities of the instrument are unique. The devices after-deployment transmits the hashed value to the base station for verification. The proposal uses Ethernet details and unique identification to generate the hashed value to enhance trust. The base station will be able to map the Ethernet address to the identity of the devices. In equation (1), the device with identification id_i and Ethernet address Li is hashed using a hashing algorithm and dispatched to the sink node BS.

$$BS \leftarrow hash(id_i \parallel L_i) \tag{1}$$

The other phases are similar to (Cui, et al., 2020). The registration stage consists of group and regular device indexing. The authorization stage is verification between regular devices and customers-regular instruments. The system encompasses the device logout phase.

5. ANALYSIS OF THE WORK

The previous contribution (Cui, et al., 2020) uses Ethernet address to derive the hashed value. This value is verified by the base station. In the proposal, the devices use unique identification and Ethernet address to derive the hashed value. The sinknode will be able to map the unique address to the Ethernet address. This builds in reliability in the system. Other compromised devices using the similar Ethernet address will come into notice early. The work is simulated in NS2. Table 2 provides the parameters used in the study.

Table 1. Parameters used in the simulation

Parameters Used	Description
Dimension of the network	200m * 200m
Number of devices deployed in the network	10
Length of Ethernet address	48 bits
Length of identification	48 bits
Length of hashed value	20 bits
Length of the message	256 bits
Simulation time	60ms

The reliability increases by 1.17% with comparison to previous work (Cui, et al., 2020). The same is represented in the figure 1.

Figure 1. Comparison of Reliability of both systems

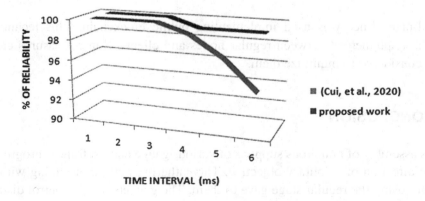

Using the proposal sinkhole attack can be minimized. As the compromised nodes are detected at the early stage, the illegitimate nodes can be detached from the network. The work minimizes sinkhole attack by 2.42% compared to (Cui, et al., 2020). The same is represented in the Figure 2.

Figure 2. Analysis of sinkhole attack

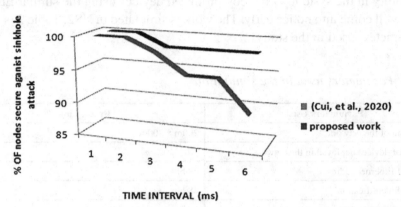

6. FUTURE WORK

In the proposal, the devices use unique identification and Ethernet address to derive the hashed value. The sinknode will be able to map the unique address to the Ethernet address. Other compromised devices using the similar Ethernet address will come into notice early. The reliability increases by 1.17% with comparison to previous work. The work minimizes sinkhole attack by 2.42% compared to (Cui, et al., 2020). The drawbacks of the work –

• Lot of Energy is used implementing public blockchain. This technology is implemented between regular nodes and clients. Some measures can be considered to minimize them.

7. CONCLUSION

IoT is assembly of numerous supplies of various gauge and usefulness progressing in the direction of a solitary objective. The gathering point in speaking with one another using the regular stage gave to them. The gadgets in IoT control distantly to play out the ideal usefulness. The data sharing among the gadgets at that point happens through the system utilizes the standard conventions of correspondence. A blockchain is a modernized record that contains the entire history of trades made on the framework. It is a fundamental purpose behind existing clear outcasts from money trades by bringing in trustworthy progressed cash. It is an assortment of associated blocks that are joined by hash regards that have made after some time. All information on the blockchain is never-ending and can't be changed. It is arranging worldview utilized for revelation, valuation, and move of quanta is the thing that we characterize as blockchain innovation. Both the technologies are combined together to enhance security. In the proposal, the devices use unique identification and Ethernet address to derive the hashed value. The sinknode will be able to map the unique address to the Ethernet address. Other compromised devices using the similar Ethernet address will come into notice early. The reliability increases by 1.17% with comparison to previous work. It minimizes sinkhole attack by 2.42% compared to previous contribution.

REFERENCES

A, B., & K, M. V. (2016). Blockchain platform for industrial internet of things. *Journal of software Engineering and Applications, 9*(10), 533.

Al-Ali, A., Zualkernan, I. A., Rashid, M., Gupta, R., & Alikarar, M. (2017). A smart home energy management system using IoT and big data analytics approach. *IEEE Transactions on Consumer Electronics, 63*(4), 426–434. doi:10.1109/TCE.2017.015014

Alaba, F. A., Othman, M., Hashem, I. A. T., & Alotaibi, F. (2017). Internet of Things security: A survey. *Journal of Network and Computer Applications, 88*, 10–28. doi:10.1016/j.jnca.2017.04.002

Almadhoun, R., Kadadha, M., Alhemeiri, M., Alshehhi, M., & Salah, K. (2018). A user authentication scheme of IoT devices using blockchain-enabled fog nodes. In *IEEE/ACS 15th international conference on computer systems and applications (AICCSA)* (pp. 1-8). Aqaba, Jordan: IEEE.

Ambika, N. (2019). Energy-Perceptive Authentication in Virtual Private Networks Using GPS Data. In Security, Privacy and Trust in the IoT Environment (pp. 25-38). Springer.

Ambika, N. (2020). Encryption of Data in Cloud-Based Industrial IoT Devices. In S. Pal & V. G. Díaz (Eds.), *D.-N. Le, IoT: Security and Privacy Paradigm* (pp. 111–129). CRC Press, Taylor & Francis Group.

Ambika, N. (2020). Methodical IoT-Based Information System in Healthcare. In Smart Medical Data Sensing and IoT Systems Design in Healthcare (pp. 155-177). Bangalore, India: IGI Global.

Balandina, E., Balandin, S., Koucheryavy, Y., & Mouromtsev, D. (2015). IoT use cases in healthcare and tourism. *IEEE 17th Conference on Business Informatics, 2*, 37-44.

Cui, Z., Fei, X. U., Zhang, S., Cai, X., Cao, Y., Zhang, W., & Chen, J. (2020). A hybrid BlockChain-based identity authentication scheme for multi-WSN. *IEEE Transactions on Services Computing, 13*(2), 241–251. doi:10.1109/TSC.2020.2964537

Gagneja, K., & Kiefer, R. (2020). Security Protocol for Internet of Things (IoT): Blockchain-based Implementation and Analysis. In *Sixth International Conference on Mobile And Secure Services (MobiSecServ)* (pp. 1-6). Miami Beach, FL: IEEE.

Hammi, M. T., Hammi, B., Bellot, P., & Serhrouchni, A. (2018). Bubbles of Trust: A decentralized blockchain-based authentication system for IoT. *Computers & Security, 78*, 126–142. doi:10.1016/j.cose.2018.06.004

Huh, S., Cho, S., & Kim, S. (2017). Managing IoT devices using blockchain platform. In *19th international conference on advanced communication technology (ICACT)* (pp. 464-467). Bongpyeong, South Korea: IEEE.

Jiang, W., Li, H., Xu, G., Wen, M., Dong, G., & Lin, X. (2019). PTAS: Privacy-preserving thin-client authentication scheme in blockchain-based PKI. *Future Generation Computer Systems, 96*, 185–195. doi:10.1016/j.future.2019.01.026

Khan, M. A., & Salah, K. (2018). IoT security: Review, blockchain solutions, and open challenges. *Future Generation Computer Systems, 82*, 395–411. doi:10.1016/j.future.2017.11.022

Kim, S. K., Kim, U. M., & Huh, J. H. (2019). A study on improvement of blockchain application to overcome vulnerability of IoT multiplatform security. *Energies, 12*(3), 1–29. doi:10.3390/en12030402

Li, D., Peng, W., Deng, W., & Gai, F. (2018). A blockchain-based authentication and security mechanism for iot. In *27th International Conference on Computer Communication and Networks (ICCCN)* (pp. 1-6). Hangzhou, China: IEEE. 10.1109/ICCCN.2018.8487449

Moinet, A., Darties, B., & Baril, J. L. (2017). Blockchain based trust & authentication for decentralized sensor networks. *IEEE Security & Privacy, Special Issue on Blockchain*, 1-6.

Ourad, A. Z., Belgacem, B., & Salah, K. (2018). Using blockchain for IOT access control and authentication management. In *International Conference on Internet of Things* (pp. 150-164). Santa Barbara, CA: Springer. 10.1007/978-3-319-94370-1_11

Puthal, D., Mohanty, S. P., Nanda, P., Kougianos, E., & Das, G. (2019). Proof-of-authentication for scalable blockchain in resource-constrained distributed systems. In *International Conference on Consumer Electronics (ICCE)* (pp. 1-5). Las Vegas, NV: IEEE. 10.1109/ICCE.2019.8662009

Shen, M., Liu, H., Zhu, L., Xu, K., Yu, H., Du, X., & Guizani, M. (2020). Blockchain-assisted secure device authentication for cross-domain industrial IoT. *IEEE Journal on Selected Areas in Communications, 38*(5), 942–954. doi:10.1109/JSAC.2020.2980916

Sultana, T., Almogren, A., Akbar, M., Zuair, M., Ullah, I., & Javaid, N. (2020). Data sharing system integrating access control mechanism using blockchain-based smart contracts for IoT devices. *Applied Sciences (Basel, Switzerland), 10*(2), 1–21. doi:10.3390/app10020488

Tian, H., Su, Y., & Liang, Z. (2019). *A Provable Secure Server Friendly Two-Party SM2 Singing Protocol for Blockchain IoT. In IEEE Globecom Workshops (GC Wkshps)*. IEEE.

Wu, L., Du, X., Wang, W., & Lin, B. (2018). An out-of-band authentication scheme for internet of things using blockchain technology. In *International Conference on Computing, Networking and Communications (ICNC)* (pp. 769-773). Maui, HI: IEEE. 10.1109/ICCNC.2018.8390280

KEY TERMS AND DEFINITIONS

Blockchain: It is a methodology that brings reliability to the network. The hashed code of the previous and present doings is attached to all the transmitted messages. The messages undergo verification for the same.

Internet of Things (IoT): These are unsupervised devices that are created by assembling sensors and actuators.

Sinknode/Base Station: It is a server that is responsible for collecting and assembling the received data. It also embeds credentials, algorithms into the devices. It also transmits necessary data to the devices of the network.

Chapter 11
The Detection of SQL Injection on Blockchain–Based Database

Keshav Sinha

https://orcid.org/0000-0003-1053-3911
Birla Institute of Technology, India

Madhav Verma
B.I.T Sindri, Dhanbad, India

ABSTRACT

In today's world, the storage of data needs a huge amount of space. Meanwhile, cloud and distributed environments provide sufficient storage space for the data. One of the challenging tasks is the privacy prevention of storage data. To overcome the problem of privacy, the blockchain-based database is used to store the data. There are various attacks like denial of service attacks (DoS) and insider attacks that are performed by the adversary to compromise the security of the system. In this chapter, the authors discussed a blockchain-based database, where data are encrypted and stored. The Web API is used as an interface for the storage and sharing of data. Here, they are mainly focused on the SQL injection attack, which is performed by the adversary on Web API. To cope with this problem, they present the case study based on the Snort and Moloch for automated detection of SQL attack, network analysis, and testing of the system.

DOI: 10.4018/978-1-7998-7589-5.ch011

Figure 1. The Various Development in the Field of Blockchain at Different Time Frame

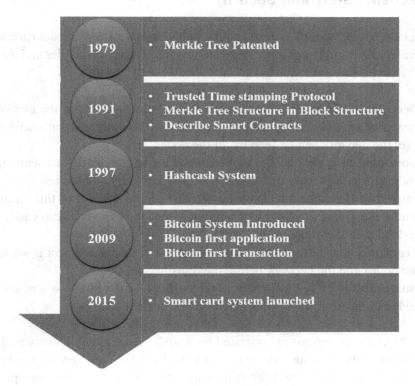

INTRODUCTION

Blockchain has become one of the significant technologies in the field of the IT industry. From the last few decades, blockchain came to the headlines, for the success of crypto-currency and smart contracts technology. After that many companies adopt blockchain technology for their products. Blockchain technology is started in the year 1991, where the trusted time-stamping protocol is used for data privacy (Haber, 1991). Later on in the year 1992, the Merkle tree is proposed for storing the multiple data in a single block (Bayer, 1992). After that researchers are not given much focused to evolve the technology because of the emergence of a centralized system. There is various research that has been done in the field of blockchain in the different time frames which are shown in Figure 1.

Blockchain Safety and Security

The blockchain technology is based on the public ledger, where the data are stored at several nodes for transmission. There are various security principles and features of the blockchain system such as.

1. **Decentralization:** There is no single point failure present in the blockchain system because the nodes are distributed across the internet and all transactions over the network can be seen by all the nodes.
2. **Confidentiality:** Public-key cryptography is used to identify authentic users, and provide the secure transmission of the data over the internet.
3. **Integrity:** Blockchain technology is based on the concept of time-stamped, where every data is signed with a unique time, and any nodes can easily trace and validate the transaction.
4. **Transparency:** In the blockchain system the unique agreement is signed by the nodes and the network before the transmission of data.
5. **Immutability:** The blockchain is the concept of the block, where the data added to the network will not be destroyed or modified.

The blockchain systems are operated by a public ledger, where every node has access to the network data. Any transaction that has occurred on the network is reviewed and validated by the different node members. This creates data transparency and it is not possible to alter the ledger without seeing by any actor within the system network. This concluded that the blockchain systems are resisted against any type of attack. Based on the theory there are no virtual attacks that are possible to the blockchain system. But in the year 2017, there is 10 percent of attacks are executed on the blockchain system (Passeri, 2017). This incident caused a huge loss for the IT industry. Many researchers point that blockchain technology is mainly focused on Cryptocurrency, where the adversaries get huge rewards once the attack is succeeded.

Cryptographic Techniques

The traditional blockchain system is based on the public key cryptography and hash function for the secure transmission of data. The security of data is achieved using the cryptography technique (Darshani, 2018). The most important part of cryptography is to make the data unreadable, in this encryption and decryption plays an important role. The encryption uses the three different type's key selection technique to encrypt the message:

1. **Symmetric-Key Cryptography:** In this, both the sender and receiver use the single key for encryption and decryption (Darshani, 2016).
2. **Public-Key Cryptography:** In this, the pair of keys is used by the client and server for encryption and decryption. The client shares the public key for encryption, where the private key is used by the client for the decryption of the data (Paul, 2019).
3. **Hash Functions:** In this, the arbitrary size data is mapped with fixed-size values (Almuttalibi, 2019). The hash table is used for the storage and retrieval of data in a very small amount of time.

Traditional cryptography uses the permutation technique to scramble the English alphabet in the original text file. Let us see an example, where the ASCII value of alphabet (n) is used for the encryption (Paul, 2019), the original Message (M) is consists of several sets of sub-messages { m_1, m_2, ..., m_n }, where 'm' is the finite set of letters, 'n' is the fixed-length sequences ($n = 2^r$). Here, $n = 2^7$ for the ASCII alphabet. This is how cryptography works for plaintext encryption in a distributed and centralized environment.

The General Structure of Blockchain

The structure of the blockchain is divided into four different sub-section:

1. **Main Data**: It records all the current services for example transactions, bank, and contract records, or IoT data records.
2. **Hash**: The hash is used to secularly broadcast the transaction record to other nodes. The Merkle tree function is used to generate the hash value and it is recorded in the block header. The computational time is reduced by using the Merkle tree function.
3. **Timestamp**: Once the block is created the time is generated for each block and the metadata is stored in the database.
4. **Other Information**: The cryptographic signature and Nonce value are defined by the user for the secure transmission of the data.

The Framework for Blockchain Technology

The blockchain is consist of a public ledger, where every record is added to the lists of transaction. And the collection of various records is known as blocks. Here, every node is responsible for the validation of blocks. Figure 2 presents the framework for the blockchain system. The process is divided into six sub-sections (1) transaction of data, (ii) creation of block, (iii) mining of data, (iv) mining process completion, (v) validation of block, and (vi) creating the chain between the new blocks.

Figure 2. The Framework for Blockchain Technology

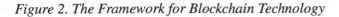
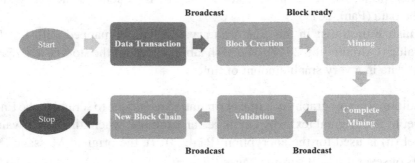

1. **Data Transaction**: The transaction of data between the two nodes is recorded and broadcasted among other connected nodes. In the case of Cryptocurrency, when the transaction is initiated in the blockchain system, then another node is recorded their transaction history. This causes a huge amount of broadcasting between the nodes.

2. **Creation of block**: In the blockchain system the miners validate the global ledger. All the incoming transaction of data is verified based on the blockchain protocol. Once the validity of the block is confirmed then the miner will start organizing the transition. Here, each block has a limited size and the mining process is not stopped until the limit is reached. All the valid transactions are set into the candidate blocks, and the miner will record the timestamp of previous information.

3. **Mining and complete mining of block**: Once the candidate block is completed the mining process is started, this process is called puzzle solving. Here the cryptographic hash is used to obtain the Block ID. The generation of the hash value is very trivial and the miners continue to adjust the nonce value in the candidate block header which creates a security layer and is not be altered by an adversary. Once the puzzle is resolved the mining process is completed.

4. **Validation**: Once the block is mined, the miner sends the block to another node (broadcast) and waits for the confirmation. The other nodes start validating the block and if they find any inconsistency in the block then they reject the block. If the block passes all the nodes without any discrepancy then that block is added to the data chain of the existing network.

5. **New Blockchain**: Once the validation is over the timestamped is added to the block and the final block is added in a linear or chronological order to the chain. The existing chain is broadcast to the entire network and is stored in the public ledgers.

Blockchain System and Automated Detection of SQL Injection Attack

The emergence of blockchain technology provides high secrecy to the data. Besides the concept of temper resistance, the blockchain maintains its logs in the native Database Management System (DBMS). However, in the insider attack, the adversary can alter the transaction logs and login details present in the DBMS. To cope with this problem, we have to push all the database towards the blockchain framework. The storage data are distributed throughout the geographical region and a huge amount of users are present to access those data. Network analysis is a huge challenge for an administrator. According to Frost, 1994; Nikolaidis, 1992, the network traffic is characterized in two ways (i) Stochastic and (ii) Deterministic. The stochastic models are used to track the statistics of the network source in better form, whereas the deterministic model has the worst behavior in the determination of the traffic. There are various stationary stochastic models such as variable bit rate, Markov modulated processes, self-similar, Transform-Expand-Sample (TES), autoregressive models, (etc.) the deterministic models that bound source characteristics include the peak rate model, maximum packet length, and minimum packet inter-arrival time is used to determine the peak rate of each connection. The best example for a large network is an automated teller machine (ATM), which send 53-byte packets or cell through virtual circuits. There are several protocol layers in-between the application protocol and the ATM layer which add complexity, but it doesn't address the issue of Session hijacking. Here, it's come the role of automated detection where it detects the response and event earlier using various stochastic models. The attacks like SQL injection are executed by an adversary on a client-server architecture. The adversary uses the SQL query to inject network traffic which will collect the information. The security of the database is going on in this direction, where BigchainDB integrates Tendermint with MongoDB (NoSQL) to increase the transaction rate of data (Bigchaindb, 2018; MongoDB, 2018; Tendermint, 2018, Kwon, 2014). LedgerDB is another database based on blockchain technology (LedgerDB, 2018). It supports high transaction throughput, single table and it doesn't support the SQL features. The Bitcoin transaction is supported by ChainDB for all general purposes solution (Chaindb, 2018). The blockchain-based DBMS doesn't have much SQL querying interface that increases the concern of data privacy in the public ledger-based blockchain system. The traditional DBMS has more than one administrator, where the inside attack can get full access to the data server. Due to a lack of cryptographic protocol, the traditional DBMS cannot resist the attack. So, our goal is to validate the system before it is used with the blockchain system. The blockchain system only stores the metadata in the DBMS. The hash function is used to map the arbitrary data into fixed-length bit string data (Handschuh, 2005). The hash function is defined as h: $\{0,1\}^{*} \rightarrow \{0,1\}^{n}$, where 'n' is the 128, 256, and 512.

Figure 3. The Cryptographic Hash of Message Block

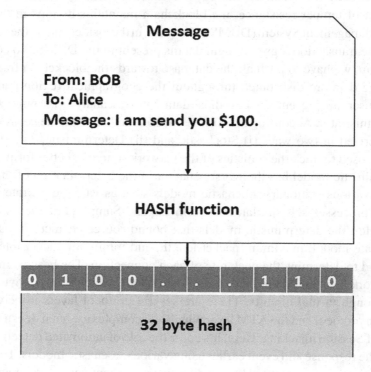

Figure 3 represents the hashing of the original message block and store it in the DBMS. The property of hashing is that the difference between the two values is not relative, which means that the small change in the input provides a huge change in the output value. This creates an advantage for the generation of a unique hash value for all the tuples in the database. The use of existing DBMS with blockchain network is based on metadata. The DBMS tuples are cryptographic hash and then generate the metadata. The DBMS table 'T' is based on the primary key (P_{k}) and tuple with 'r', we have to generate the Row_ID.

$$Row\_ID_{r,T} = h\Big(P_k\big(r\big) \cdot T\Big) \tag{1}$$

Eq. 1 used to concatenate the primary key and tuple with the table name to generate the hash form. The fingerprint of each tuple is stored in the blockchain using the digital signature (private key) on the blockchain node. Every time the changes in the tuple are logged with user information.

Motivation and Proposes of the Work

The motivation of work is to provide secure data storage in blockchain-based DBMS. The tuple of DBMS is updated by any user node in the blockchain and those modifications are stored in the database. Those data come from various fields such as education, military, business, and entertainment. Now the attacks are executed to get the information for the Database. The basic processing of information is called by using the select, update, and delete command in DBMS. Now a day's traditional database is used in the field of blockchain this increased the chance of an attack like SQL injection which exploits the security of the database and retrieves the personal information. To overcome the high percentage of threats it needed to be automated to stop the intrusion or attack on the blockchain network. The administrator has to face lots of security challenges such as:

- **Attack on Personal Information:** At the present date the adversary is waiting on the internet to retrieve the personal information. An attack like SQL injection can retrieve the database table information and login credentials (username, password) to exploit the blockchain network.
- **Replication of Metadata:** In the blockchain network, the database stores the metadata of row and column. The adversary always tries to replicate the details of DBMS.
- **Data Privacy:** The huge amount of data is distributed on the internet. The entertainment company which is based on the blockchain system has always been concerned about data piracy.

These are some of the challenges faced by the blockchain system. But there is a chain of problems present in data security, and we are not able to cover all the problems. There are various ways to provide security on data. But automating the detection of attack is one of the effective ways to stop the tempering of the blockchain database. It provides robustness and effectiveness to securely store the data in the blockchain network.

BACKGROUND

There are various researches has done in the field of blockchain and DBMS security and we found that most of the time the attacker has performed two different types of attack (i) Active and (ii) Passive attack. In an active attack, the adversary modifies the data and sends it to the users, this event causes a serious effect on personnel. In a passive attack, the adversary doesn't harm the system they just watch the traffic of the information. According to w. Jung and S. Park (2017), the blockchain is a P2P system where the adversary applies the DDoS attack to shut down the transaction node. In the blockchain system, all the nodes check the memory pool and the time of the overflood attack. Here, the author proposed the least Mean square method to minimize the creation of a new transaction in the blockchain system. W. J. Lai et al. (2019), proposed the time-sensitive message encryption scheme. Here, the message is encrypted in a decentralized environment, which encourages the participants to share the resource with the network. Bansal and Sethumadhavan (2020), present the prevention technique against name-based attacks. It is a DNS cache poisoning attack in the blockchain system, where the author uses a user-defined port instead of a predefined port for the transmission. In the second step, the author encrypts the port number and the communication is initiated using the decrypted user-defined port number. Tanriverdi and Tekerek (2019), proposed a blockchain-based web attack detection model using signature-based detection. The work is to detect the specific pattern such as Structured Query Language (SQL) Injection, Cross-Site Scripting (CSS), and Command Injection. The author uses the MultiChain application, and the signature list is updated on the blockchain. Anita and Vijayalakshmi (2019), present a brief survey of different types of attacks, challenges, and security feature of blockchain technology. Wang and Li (2019), present a trace analysis technique to detect the various attack in the blockchain. Here, the author captures the sequence of actions based on the running protocol. This will help to detect the attacks like DDoS and triangle. Brown et al. (2020), present a double-spend attack on the established transaction of blockchain. The success of this attack depends on the transaction and computational power. Gochhayat et al. (2019), present a lightweight decentralized encrypted cloud storage model using the blockchain technique. This model provides confidentiality and integrity for storage data. Here, the author has used the hashing and symmetric encryption technique for the security of the data. Saad et al. (2020), explore the attack surface on the public blockchain system. In this, the attribute attack is used to check the cryptographic construct, distributed architecture, and application context. The author also explores how various vectors are connected to the Blockchain system. Holbrook (2020), studied the various security aspects in the blockchain. Here, the author explains that the public ledger is distributed and cannot be modified or deleted. The threats like distributed denial-of-service (DDoS) can expose the security of the blockchain network. The specific feature like Hyperledger, Quorum, (etc.) offers the security to blockchain administrator. Rikken et al. (2019), analyze the various challenges regarding blockchain governance. Here author proposed the framework based on the infrastructure, application, company, and institution/country. Singh et al. (2019), present the blockchain-based DDoS solution to avoid a serious attack on the network. Here the author provides the concern regarding the rapid change of blockchain technology in the field of financial, gaming, and decentralized servers to provide a secure environment for the transaction of the block.

The blockchain system uses the database for storing metadata, where our work is to provide a secure environment for the storage of the data. Based on this fact here we present some of the secure database storage technique which helps in the blockchain environment. According to Sinha et al., (2020), secure storage of data is one of the challenging tasks. Here, the authors present the asymmetric technique for the storage of the data in the cloud data server. Bertino et al. (2007), present the anomaly detection technique, where the author identifies the malicious actions of database application based on the SQL queries. They demonstrate that the proposed model can detect the SQL injection attack on the database. Tajpouret al. (2010), present the various approaches to detect SQL injection. Wei et al., (2006), propose a novel technique to resist various attacks that target the store procedures. They use code analysis and runtime validation to detect the attacks on SQL Server 2005 database. Ntagwabira (2010), proposed the Query tokenization to detect the SQL injection, where the author uses the QueryParser to detect the space, single quote, or double dashes in the strings. The two array string is compared based on the length for the detection of the injection. Sadeghian et al. (2013), presents various detection and prevention techniques for SQL injection which provide confidentiality, integrity, and availability of information in the database. Kumar (2012), presents the survey on SQL injection attacks, detection, and prevention techniques. They found that the poorly coded application affect the organization network. The attackers violate all types of security layers and protocol's to access that information. Singh et al. (2016), discussed attacks and prevention against SQL injection. They proposed the firewall technique for the SQL server which will restrict the privilege of the unregistered users. But for using this service it needed to be the node to node signature authentication. Gudipati et al. (2016), uses the Sp_executesql to execute the syntax in a specific order which replaces the QUOTENAME. It also manages the permission at the time of attacks. Kamtuo (2016), uses the machine learning technique for the analysis of attacks. It also extracts information for training and testing. Zhou (2016), introduced a User Defined Approach (UDA) for mapping the attribute to a specific requirement. It also checks the threshold value for any attacks. Dubey (2016), introduce the filtering mechanism for sending and receiving the request. Aldlaeen (2013), introduced a firewall technique to obstruct the SQL injection attack and provide access control to the authentic users only. Chatur (2015), uses a security-based model for checking the signature of the authentic users. Ghorbanzadeh et al. (2010), introduced the firewall and virtual private network for the prevention of unwanted intrusion on the mobile database. Sallam et al. (2016), introduced a Role-based anomaly detection approach for an insider attack. Fatih (2017) and Mouton et al. (2014), introduced the web-based security approach to protect against SQL injection. Orman (2018), proposed a Blockchain concept to verify the genuine nodes of the webserver.

The blockchain-based database consists of a huge amount of metadata and it needs to organize and optimized before sharing with the network node. Here we present some of the optimization and scheduling technique which reduce the time complexity of the data. According to Priya (2020), the time complexity is reduced by minimizing the makespan of the waited queue. Here the author presents the PA-ACO technique to minimize the makespan of flow shop scheduling problem. Sahana et al. (2018), proposed an optimization and allocation technique for the budgeting problem. The author presents the Genetic Algorithm (GA) and Optimal Computing Budget Allocation (OCBA) technique for the optimization of large scale budgeting problems. Khowas et al. (2016), present the Particle Swarm Optimization (PSO) technique for large-scale budgeting problems. Paul (2019), present the article on voice-based authentication scheme to detect the real world culprits. Verma et al. (2020), present the asymmetric encryption technique for sharing and storage of data in the distributed database. Chaddha et al. (2020), present the real-time image encryption technique based on asymmetric key cryptography. The technique is used for the large scale image encryption and storage of data in the database. Choudhary et al. (2018), proposed multimedia encryption using the asymmetric key for storage. The technique is based on the key management server to store the data in the cloud.

CASE STUDY: AUTOMATED SQL INJECTION DETECTION

After an exhaustive study of different techniques, we would like to propose an automated SQL injection detection using Snort and Moloch. This will help to detect the SQL injection in the blockchain network. The cyber-attacks are one of the buzz problems for any individual. Here the adversary always tries to take personal information like credit/debit card information, passwords from the storage database, and this information are sold on the dark web very easily. On the other hand, the blockchain-based DBMS is used for storing the metadata. Many companies use the blockchain system for multimedia storage and for that they use web APIs. The web interfaces are more vulnerable against (i) weak cryptographic authentication, and (ii) flaws in endpoint connection. The protocols like SOAP provide the security architecture and REST which provide a secure environment for the API implementation. During transmission of data, the adversary secretly intercepts the communications between the two parties, and even though they altered the message. API Injections like XSS and SQLite will inject the malicious code into the software program and create a backdoor in the system. The Distributed Denial of Service (DDoS), is one of his kind of attacks where the attacker will flood the blockchain network with unwanted packets. The API injection or SQL injection is the most common attack which is executed by the attacker. The SQL injection will not need any permission for authentication, instead, it will redirect the information of the database (H. Meyer 1996). In year I988, Computer Emergency Response Team (CERT) is developed a coordination center at Carnegie Mellon University (CMU) that handles the security against network attacks like a worm, virus, malware, etc. (J. Clarke 2009).

Figure 4. SQL Attack on Web API

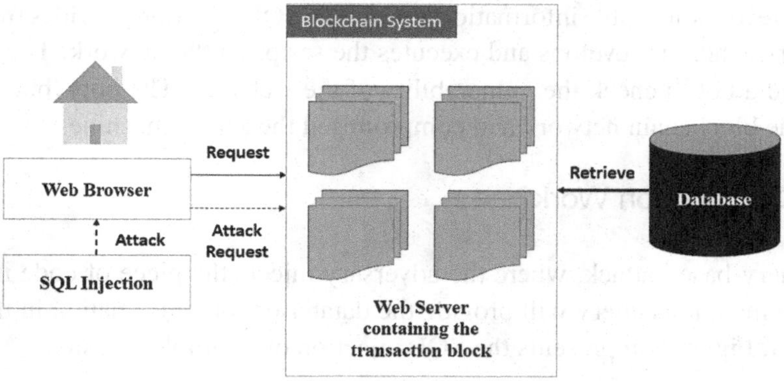

SQL Injection Overview

Mainly the SQL injection attacks are executed on a client-server architecture. The web API acts as a thin-client, where the user sends the query to extract the data from the database. Figure 4 presents the SQL attack executed on the blockchain system having Web API. The web API uses the SQL commands for the extraction of data from the database. SQL is a Structured Query Language that is used for managing and communicating with a relational database. The most common SQL queries are:

- **SELECT:** It retrieves the store entries from the table.
- **INSERT:** It uses for creating entries in a table.
- **DELETE:** It deletes the record from the table.

Here, the authentic user sends the query for retrieval of information from the database. But in the case of SQL injection, the adversary uses the special character and symbols for the authentication. Most of the time adversary uses the 'AND' and 'OR' DBMS condition for the attack.

SQL Injection

SQL injection is a query-based attack on web API and it was first introduced by Jeff Forristal in the year 1998 (Joseph Cox, 2015). The attack mainly consists of an SQL query that exploits and manipulates the database records. SQL injection maintains the position of the top 10 web API attacks on the Open Web Application Security Project (OWASP). The application programmers handle all the types of user input using a scripting language. There is also a programmer's code of conduct, which doesn't believe in user input. Several SQL injection risks are presented such as accessing sensitive data remotely, retrieving the stored information, knowing the database records and table information, (etc.). The SQL injection provides free space to hackers, where it develops and executes the script on the network. The hackers developed a bot to check the vulnerability of the websites. The bots (bots.txt) are run on the blockchain network and compromised the server machine.

How SQL Injection Work?

It is a query-based attack, where the adversary injects the piece of code into web API. The malicious query will provide the database table information in the URL parameter. Figure 5, represents the SQL injection on a simple website.

Figure 5. SQL query-based injection

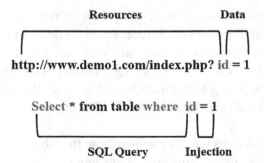

We present several types of SQL injection performed by the adversary to extract the table information from the database (Pollack, 2018).

1. **Boolean-Based Blind Injection:** In this, the logical query is attached with the parameter and the adversary waits for some meaningful search. The malicious query will redirect some result that is related to Boolean operation (True or False). The "WHERE" operator is used to evaluate the tautology of the parameter. Let us consider a Boolean based malicious string (https://abc.com/index1.php?id=1 AND substring (@@version,1,1)=4). Now, the query is used for checking database table information. The "substring (@@version, 1, 1)=4" is used to check the database version. If it is true then it will return one row otherwise it will give the failed "0" result. It means there is no database of version 4. The attacker will do this process again and again to map the logical structure of the database.

2. **Time-Based Blind Injection (TBBI):** It uses the time of the server to access the information of the database. The format for TBBI is applied on any website example (http://example1.com/index.php?id=1; IF User= 'admin' WAIT FOR DELAY '00:00:15'). It evaluates the response by delaying 15 seconds then it sends the information to the attacker.

3. **UNION Based Injection (UBI):** It uses for merging the two different table rows. The only disadvantage of UBI are (i) the structure of the table are same, (ii) the same number of row and column is present. UBI is used the "ORDER BY" operator for finding the column. Example (http://example1.com/index.php?id=1 ORDER BY 1 -> OK & http://example1.com/index.php?id=1 ORDER BY 2 -> Error). The union-based injection is used for testing the 2 columns and only 1 of them is passed.

There are various ways to perform SQL injection attacks on the web API of the blockchain database server. The system firewall is not able to provide that much security against SQL injection attacks. So, our work is to restrict those attacks and provide a secure environment for every user which is connected with the blockchain system. Here, we present the framework for automated detection of SQL injection attacks using Snort (Zhou et al., 2010) and Moloch (Uramova et al., 2017). The outline for the detection system is presented in Figure 6.

Figure 6. The Framework for Automated SQL Attack Detection using Snort and Moloch in the Blockchain System

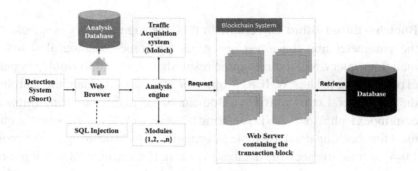

Figure 6 presents the framework of automated SQL attack detection. The framework is divided into several components and each component has specific work such as:

A Detection System (Snort): It uses the Snort technique for the detection of SQL injection. It also analyzes the huge HTTP network traffic. The Snort was first created by Martin Roesch in the year 1988 for network intrusion detection (Roesch, 1999). Here, the packet capture module is used to collect the request and response of the system. The pseudo-code for packet capturing is given below. Here, the genuine user only passes through the authentication process. If there is a SQL attack then it uses the specific keywords to identify the attacks.

Pseudo Code

```
Class Public Signin(request, response)
{
String signin = request. getParameter("signin");
String p_word = request. getParameter("p_word");
String query1 = "SELECT info FROM userTable WHERE";
if ((!signin. equals("")) && (!p_word.equals(""))) query +=
signin = "'+ signin+'" AND pass= "'+p_word +'" elsequery+ =
"'signin= 'Guest''";
ResultSet result1 = stmt. executeQuery(query1) ;
if (result1 != null)
showAccount(result1) ;
else
sendAuthentacationFailed();
}
Here is an example to detect the ICMP packet in ECHO REQUEST.
alert ICMP $ExternalNET
```

248

```
any -> $HOME any (msg:"ICMP PING"; icode:0; itype:8; classtype:
misc-activity; sid:384; rev:5;)
```

The Snort package is divided into two parts Header and Body. The Header is divided into seven different fragments (i) Action, (ii) Protocol, (iii) Source_IP, (iv) Source_Port, (v) Direction, (vi) Dst_IP, and (vii) Dst_Port. These fields are consist of variables or strings to match with the database. The body uses the payload or HTTP headers of the message. The alert is generated by using the fast_output modules. An example is given as:

```
[**] [1:374:5] ICMP PING [**]
[Classification: Misc activity] [Priority: 4]
03/12-02:11:09.359780 10.1.1.10 -> 10.0.1.253
ICMP TTL: 30 TOS: 0x0 ID: 38175 IpLen: 15 DgmLen: 92
Type: 8 Code: 0 ID: 32335 Seq: 1 ECHO
```

The Starting line is used for packet matching. The [**] symbol is used for the starting and end of the sequence. Three values are present inside the brackets which are separated by a colon. (i) Generator_ID (GID) is used in the alert module, (ii) Snort_ID (SID) is used to identify the unique alert, and Revision_No (REV) is used to trigger the alert.

Traffic Acquisition System

It uses the Moloch as a default system to gain the visibility of SQL injection. During the attack, several packets are not logged due to performance reasons. It uses the IPv4 packets for the detection of the intrusion. Moloch session uses the seven tuples: Moloch_Session = (St_Time, Sp_Time, Source_IP, Dstination_IP, Source_Port, Dstination_Port, Protocol).

Figure 7. Moloch Web Interface

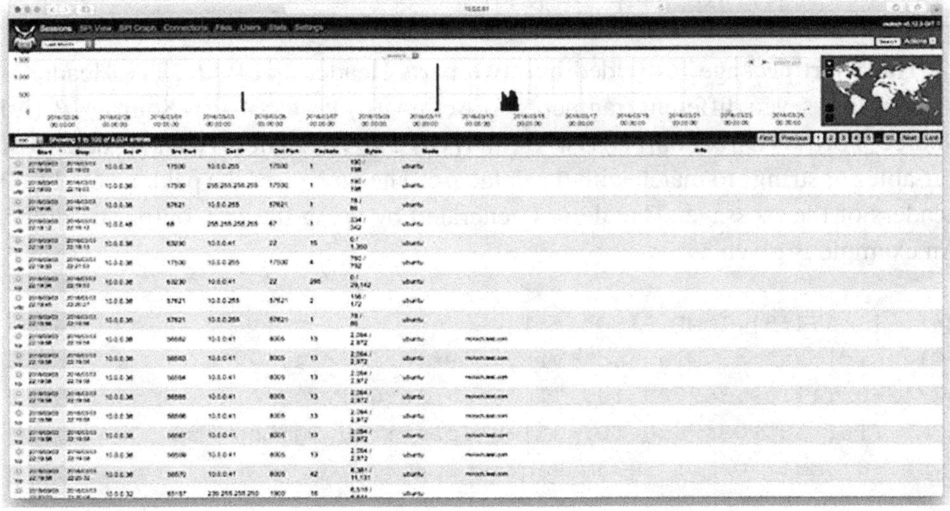

Figure 7 presents the Moloch web interface is used to intercept the network packets. The Moloch is consists of three main parts:

- **Elastic search database:** It is used in indexing stored sessions. It also managed the captured sessions. In real-time, the large volume data is managed by using the network traffic analysis.
- **Capture:** It separates the network between captured and network traffic.
- **Viewer:** It is used for filtering the stored session and it also exports the stored session.

Moloch is used for HTTP session for filtering. The Moloch filtering expression is given as (ip.src == 10.0.0.41 && start_time >= "2019/03/05 22:11:23" && port.dst == 8080).

- **HTTP Tag Filtering:** This is the procedure for Moloch for packet filtering (Protocol = = http && method = = GET && status = = 200 && stop_tm <= "2019/02/05 12:21:03").
- **Analysis Engine:** The work of the analysis engine is to analyze the malicious packets. The PCAP analysis is done by modules. Whereas each module will perform a certain amount of actions on PCAP to return the output from the engine. The database is used to store the information (such as attack investigation) for analysis.

- **Attacker IP Details:** The attacker IP is very trivial to find by any IDS. Attackers often hide their IPs and location server o secure their personal information. According to Cloudflare, there are 90% of the request is came from the Tor browser which is very unpredictable to find genuine requests. The IP address is consist of:
  - The owner IP address,
  - Origin of Internet Service Provider (ISP),
  - CIDR notation,
  - E-mail contact,
  - Tor node check

  All the information is retrieved from Regional Internet Registries (RIRs). All Tor node is present publically and it uses as encrypted traffic to access the HTTPS.

- **Web Server Detail:** It uses to find out the details of the target server. The analysis engine doesn't have access to analyze the web server, so it uses the pattern matching technique for finding the details. The Wappalzer is an open-source tool to detect the web server, content management system (CMS), and JavaScript libraries.
- **Statistical Analysis:** If there is a crime there also evidence, the attacker leaves the fingerprint in the form of the entry point. In statistical analysis, the PCAP pattern is observed to find evidence of the SQL injection. The analysis engine is used to identify the outline in traffic, network endpoints.
- **Database Canary:** The attacker will usually try to retrieve information such as table names and columns. The work of Canary is to add an appropriately long string that replaces the information of the database. It also sends the SQL injection successful message to the server, but instead of the actual table, it sends the empty table to the attacker. Canary is generated by 256 bits string which is placed in the database. This will not provide security against time-based blind injection.
- **Connections:** It captures the network subnet and provides the list of the host. Using Moloch will provide this information in the API panel.
- **Storage and Web Interface:** It uses the RethinkDB document based NoSQL database and API for real-time application. Traditional database will not provide the analysis functionality. RethinkDB will execute on separate machine using remote server or wire. The command for NoSQL database is given as:

```
cursor = r.table('analyses').filter(r.row['dst_ip'] ==
'10.0.0.1').run()
for document in cursor:
print(document)
```

Web Interface: The web interface is used to analyze the results. The visualization of analysis is shown in the web API. The Individual results are offered in the form of a map and table. The implementation is done on the anaconda 3.1, on windows 8.1 x64 platform, having a core i5 processor. The prerequisites for deployments are Snort, Proofpoint, PulledPork instances to generate the signature map. The working of Snort is to generate the intrusion logs in a binary form called unified2. The log is consist of several alerts such as (i) Alert_syslog, (ii) Alert_fast, (iii) Alert_full, (iv) Alert_unixsock, and (v) Log_tcpdump. There are few things needed to set up the Snort log session in Moloch. The Moloch needs the subnet address as a development point, the timestamp in the UTC standard, REST API with self-signed SSL certificate, and PCAP (Packet Capture) which deletes the old unwanted session.

- **Alert forwarding**: Snort is used as the analysis engine to send the alert to the log processing system. The log system is constantly examined the new records. The manual implementation uses the "idstools" package in python to monitor the log record.

  Pseudo Code

```
from idstools import unified2
reader1 = unified2.SpoolEventReader(directory, prefix,
follow=True)
for event in reader:
  # process event
        # ...
```

- **Signature Mapping**: It is a process of setting a numeric signature ID to the textual representation. The pseudo-code for the signature mapping is done by using the "idstools" package.

  Pseudo Code

```
from idstools import maps
sigmap1 = maps1.SignatureMap()
```

```
sigmap1.load_signature_map(open('/path/to/sid-msg.map'))
sigmap1.load_generator_map(open('/path/to/gid-msg.map'))
sigmap.get(gid, sid)
```

An additional task of Snort alert forwarding is (i) Signature filtering and (ii) Bookmarking. In signature, filtering is used to provide the alert of SQL injection Id only. Bookmarking will help to keep track of all the events of the analysis engine.

- **Creating Analysis:** IDS will generate multiple alerts at the time of the SQL injection attack. The analysis engine is used to retrieve the load traffic using the API. The alerts are generated in the form of a time frame and it is a cluster in one analysis. A similar alert is checked with the prescribed cluster. There are three tuples are present in the alert.

$$alert = \left(Source\left(IP\right), Destination\left(IP\right), Destination\left(Port\right)\right)$$

- **Task Queue:** It uses the task in the distributed form means each task is executed in different processors. The Celery is an open-source Python software for parallel processing. Celery is working on the master and slave model, where the master distributes the task for different processors and slaves will run those tasks in parallel. The API will handle the entry of the database. The entry is consists of the timestamp and task status of pending data.

Analysis Engine: It is used for task scheduling. Several steps are present in the analysis engine:

- Status: It monitors the task status such as "PENDING" or "PROGRESS".
- PCAP from Moloch: It analyze the HTTP traffic between source and destination. The alert is generated by using (/sessions.pcap endpoint). Moloch traffic filter is done as (port.dst == {dst_port} && protocols == http && ip.src == {src_ip} && ip.dst == {dst_ip}). In simple the Moloch has observed the initial alert such as Start_Time, Stop_Time, and expression.
- Database entry update: It changes the entry to success or error for the task analysis engine.

Figure 8. Screenshot Of Sqlmap API

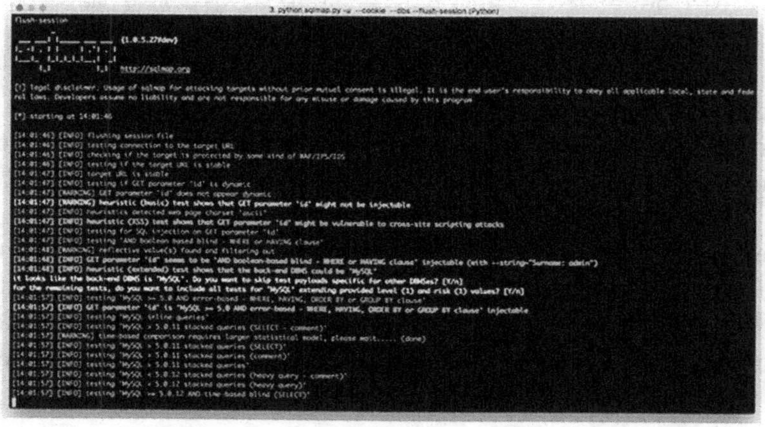

Modules: It uses the command for analyze the analysis_modules: (module_results = module(opts, pcap_path, config).bootstrap())

- **opts** = source IP, destination IP alert.
- **pcap_path:** It retrieves the PCAP store file.
- **config:** It manages the RethinkDB host and port, Celery broker.
- **bootstrap()** return the stored from the database.

The analysis is done by the web interface to analyze the source IP, destination IP. PCAP retrieve the Moloch information. The Snort and Moloch are both monitor host information. It supervised the running task by using the uWSGI, Celery, and Alert forwarder.

Evaluation: For evaluation, the testing is conducted using Ubuntu 18.1, MySQL database, and Damn Vulnerable Web App (DVWA). The Sqlmap is used for the detection of SQL injection (Axinte, 2014). The workflow of Sqlmap's is divided into five steps:

- **Setup:** Sqlmap use as an independent tool for the detection of SQL Injection. It needed some basic configuration such as: Specify the entry pointy of Target URL, HTTP header, Proxy, Tamper Scripts.
- **Detection:** it checks the entry point of the links.
- **Fingerprinting:** It uses the fingerprint of the database server and web server for crucial data. It also detects the Web Application Firewall (WAF) and Protected Web Server (IWS) before the webserver.

- **Enumeration:** It also retrieves the tables and columns of the database using a brute-force attack. It uses the dictionary attack for hash protected data.
- **Takeover:** It tries to access information about the operating system.

For testing, we use the 20 sqlmap (version 1.0.5.27) attacks on DVWA and using the Snort package we able to detect the SQL injection. The alerts are analyzed by using the proper PCAP (packet capture). Sqlmap also identifies the canary string at the response. Snort will generate the 40 different alerts for every sqlmap attack. The sqlmap arguments are used for testing purposes.

```
python sqlmap.py -u
"http://abc.com?id=1&submit=login#"
--cookie "PHPSESSID=[session_id]; security=low"
--dbs --flush-session --tamper=randomcomments --level=5 -v 3
```

The temper script like base64 conversion is not to be detected by using Snort. The Sqlmap also contains functionality to escape IPS/WAF detection using tamper scripts. It only works when the syntax of the input is changed. In most cases (99/100) Snort was able to notice such evasion. This concluded that automation in network-based attack detection use large networks payloads and thousands of system is communicated in very few seconds. The implemented system is used to detect all types of SQL injection attacks.

CONCLUSION

The SQL injection is one of its kind of attacks where the adversary retrieves the personal information from the database. In the current scenario many blockchain-based companies facing the problem of cyber-attack based on SQL injection. To cope with this problem, here we present a chapter that provides a brief idea about the blockchain system and SQL injection. The whole chapter is divided into two parts (i) we started with a brief introduction about the blockchain system and how the data are stored in the public database, (ii) the second part describes the SQL attack performed by the adversary on the database. Here, we present the case study based on the automated detection of SQL injection attacks. For detection, we use the Snort and Moloch package. The system is implemented for large network traffic such as a blockchain system. The Sqlmap is used for the evaluation process and to find out the successful SQL injection. This system doesn't use any new technology for analysis instead, it collects the information based on the timestamp and fingerprinting. It is a Signature-based system that has some limitations at the time of detection. The future scope of this work provides the solution using Splunk technology which provides a huge solution in the field of database threat.

REFERENCES

Chaddha, R., Kumar, A., Sinha, K., Paul, P., & Amritanjali. (2020). Selection on Various Traditional Image Encryption Techniques: A Study. *Lecture Notes in Electrical Engineering*, 219–228. doi:10.1007/978-981-15-2854-5_20

Verma, N., Sharma, S., Sinha, K., Paul, P., & Amritanjali. (2020). Selection on Traditional Cryptographic Algorithm for Real-Time Video Transmission and Storage: A Study. *Lecture Notes in Electrical Engineering*, 229–238. doi:10.1007/978-981-15-2854-5_21

Al-Sayid, N. A., & Aldlaeen, D. (2013). Database security threats: A survey study. *Proceeding of the 5th International Conference on Computer Science and Information Technology.* doi:10.1109/csit.2013.6588759

Anita, N., & Vijayalakshmi, M. (2019). Blockchain Security Attack: A Brief Survey. *Proceeding of the 10th International Conference on Computing, Communication and Networking Technologies (ICCCNT).* doi:10.1109/icccnt45670.2019.8944615

Axinte, S.-D. (2014). SQL Injection Testing in Web Applications Using SQLmap. *International Journal of Information Security and Cybercrime*, *3*(2), 61–68.

Aziz Yousif Almuttalibi, R. (2019). Blockchain Hash Function for Secure Biometric System. *Journal of Engineering and Applied Sciences (Asian Research Publishing Network)*, *14*(11), 3797–3805. https://doi.org/10.36478/jeasci.2019.3797.3805

Bansal, M. K., & Sethumadhavan, M. (2020). DNS Security - Prevent DNS Cache Poisoning Attack using Blockchain. *International Journal of Innovative Technology and Exploring Engineering*, *9*(4), 2151–2162. doi:10.35940/ijitee.d1549.029420

Bayer, D., Haber, S., & Stornetta, W. S. (1993). Improving the Efficiency and Reliability of Digital Time-Stamping. *Sequences*, *II*, 329–334. doi:10.1007/978-1-4613-9323-8_24

Bertino, E., Kamra, A., & Early, J. P. (2007). Profiling Database Application to Detect SQL Injection Attacks. *Proceeding of the IEEE International Performance, Computing, and Communications Conference.* doi:10.1109/pccc.2007.358926

Bigchain, D. B., & Gmb, H. (2018). *Bigchaindb 2.0: The blockchain database.* White paper. https://www.bigchaindb.com/whitepaper/bigchaindb-whitepaper.pdf

Brown, M., Peköz, E., & Ross, S. (2020). Blockchain Double-Spend Attack Duration. *Probability in the Engineering and Informational Sciences*, 1–9. doi:10.10170269964820000212

Chaindb. (2018). *A peer-to-peer database system*. https://bitpay.com/chaindb.pdf

Clarke, J. (2009). *Exploiting SQL Injection*. SQL Injection Attacks and Defense.

Cox, J. (2015). *The History of SQL Injection, the Hack That Will Never Go Away*. Available: https://www.vice.com/en_us/article/aekzez/the-history-of-sql-injection-the-hack-that-will-never-go-away

Dubey, R., & Gupta, H. (2016). SQL filtering: An effective technique to prevent SQL injection attack. *Proceeding of the 5th International Conference on Reliability, Infocom Technologies and Optimization (Trends and Future Directions) (ICRITO)*. doi:10.1109/icrito.2016.7784972

Frost, V. S., & Melamed, B. (1994). Simulating Telecommunications Networks with Traffic Modeling. *IEEE Communications Magazine*, *32*(3), 70–70.

Ghorbanzadeh, P., Shaddeli, A., Malekzadeh, R., & Jahanbakhsh, Z. (2010). A survey of mobile database security threats and solutions for it. *Proceeding of the 3rd International Conference on Information Sciences and Interaction Sciences*. doi:10.1109/icicis.2010.5534685

Gochhayat, S. P., Bandara, E., Shetty, S., & Foytik, P. (2019). Yugala: Blockchain Based Encrypted Cloud Storage for IoT Data. *Proceeding of the IEEE International Conference on Blockchain (Blockchain)*. doi:10.1109/blockchain.2019.00073

Gudipati, V. K., Venna, T., Subburaj, S., & Abuzaghleh, O. (2016). Advanced automated SQL injection attacks and defensive mechanisms. *Proceeding of the Annual Connecticut Conference on Industrial Electronics, Technology & Automation (CT-IETA)*. doi:10.1109/ct-ieta.2016.7868248

Haber, S., & Stornetta, W. S. (1991). How to time-stamp a digital document. *Journal of Cryptology*, *3*(2), 99–111. doi:10.1007/BF00196791

Handschuh, H. (2005). SHA Family (Secure Hash Algorithm). *SpringerReference*, 565–567. https://doi.org/10.1007/springerreference_491

Holbrook, J. (2020). Blockchain Security and Threat Landscape. *Architecting Enterprise Blockchain Solutions*, 323–347. doi:10.1002/9781119557722.ch11

Jung, W., & Park, S. (2017). Preventing DDoS Attack in Blockchain System Using Dynamic Transaction Limit Volume. *International Journal of Control and Automation, 10*(12), 131–138. https://doi.org/10.14257/ijca.2017.10.12.12

Kamtuo, K., & Soomlek, C. (2016). Machine Learning for SQL injection prevention on server-side scripting. *Proceeding of the International Computer Science and Engineering Conference (ICSEC).* doi:10.1109/icsec.2016.7859950

Karuparthi, R. P., & Zhou, B. (2016). Enhanced Approach to Detection of SQL Injection Attack. *Proceeding of the 15th IEEE International Conference on Machine Learning and Applications (ICMLA).* doi:10.1109/icmla.2016.0082

Koçak, S. (2017). A second pre-image attack and a collision attack to cryptographic hash function lux. *Communications Faculty of Science University of Ankara Series A1 Mathematics and Statistics, 66*(1), 254–266. doi:10.1501/commua1_0000000794

Kumar, P., & Pateriya, R. K. (2012). A survey on SQL injection attacks, detection and prevention techniques. *Proceeding of the Third International Conference on Computing, Communication and Networking Technologies.* doi:10.1109/icccnt.2012.6396096

Kwon. (2014). *Tendermint: Consensus without mining.* Draft v. 0.6, fall.

Lai, W.-J., Hsueh, C.-W., & Wu, J.-L. (2019). A Fully Decentralized Time-Lock Encryption System on Blockchain. *Proceeding of the IEEE International Conference on Blockchain (Blockchain).* doi:10.1109/blockchain.2019.00047

Ledger, D. B. (2018). *Github repo.* https://github.com/ledgerdb/ledgerdb

Meyer, H. (1996). A computer emergency response team policy. *Computers & Security, 15*(4), 320.

Mongo, D. B. (2018). *Opensource Document Database.* https://www.mongodb.com/

Mouton, F., Malan, M. M., Leenen, L., & Venter, H. S. (2014). Social engineering attack framework. *Information Security for South Africa.* doi:10.1109/issa.2014.6950510

Nikolaidis, I., & Akyildiz, I. F. (1992). *Source characterization and statistical multiplexing in ATM networks.* College of Computing, Georgia Institute of Technology.

Ntagwabira, L., & Kang, S. L. (2010). Use of Query tokenization to detect and prevent SQL injection attacks. *Proceeding of the 3rd International Conference on Computer Science and Information Technology.* doi:10.1109/iccsit.2010.5565202

Orman, H. (2018). Blockchain: The Emperors New PKI? *IEEE Internet Computing, 22*(2), 23–28. https://doi.org/10.1109/mic.2018.022021659

Passeri, P. (2017). *2017 Cyber Attacks Statistics.* Available: https://www.hackmageddon.com/2018/01/17/2017-cyber-attacks-statistics/

Pollack, E. (2018). *Protecting Against SQL Injection.* Dynamic SQL.

Priya, A., & Sahana, S. K. (2020). A Deterministic Flowshop Scheduling Problem to minimizing the Makespan using PA-ACO. *International Journal of Engineering and Advanced Technology, 9*(3), 1555–1560. doi:10.35940/ijeat.b4573.029320

Priya, A., Sinha, K., Darshani, M. P., & Sahana, S. K. (2018). A Novel Multimedia Encryption and Decryption Technique Using Binary Tree Traversal. *Proceeding of the Second International Conference on Microelectronics, Computing & Communication Systems (MCCS 2017),* 163–178. DOI: 10.1007/978-981-10-8234-4_15

Rikken, O., Janssen, M., & Kwee, Z. (2019). Governance challenges of blockchain and decentralized autonomous organizations. *Information Polity, 24*(4), 397–417. doi:10.3233/ip-190154

Roesch, M. (1999). Snort: Lightweight Intrusion Detection for Networks. LISA. In *Proceedings of the 13th USENIX conference on System administration (LISA '99).* USENIX Association.

Saad, M., Spaulding, J., Njilla, L., Kamhoua, C., Shetty, S., Nyang, D. H., & Mohaisen, D. (2020). Exploring the Attack Surface of Blockchain: A Comprehensive Survey. *IEEE Communications Surveys & Tutorials,* 1–1. doi:10.1109/comst.2020.2975999

Sadeghian, A., Zamani, M., & Manaf, A. A. (2013). A Taxonomy of SQL Injection Detection and Prevention Techniques. *Proceeding of the International Conference on Informatics and Creative Multimedia.* doi:10.1109/icicm.2013.18

Sahana, S. K., Khowas, M., & Sinha, K. (2018). Budget Optimization and Allocation: An Evolutionary Computing Based Model. *Bentham Science.* doi:10.2174/97816810870781180101

Sallam, A., Xiao, Q., Bertino, E., & Fadolalkarim, D. (2016). Anomaly Detection Techniques for Database Protection Against Insider Threats (Invited Paper). *Proceeding of the 17th International Conference on Information Reuse and Integration (IRI).* doi:10.1109/iri.2016.12

Shastri, A. A., & Chatur, P. N. (2015). Efficient and effective security model for database specially designed to avoid internal threats. *Proceeding of the International Conference on Smart Technologies and Management for Computing, Communication, Controls, Energy and Materials (ICSTM).* doi:10.1109/icstm.2015.7225407

259

Singh, N., Dayal, M., Raw, R. S., & Kumar, S. (2016). SQL injection: Types, methodology, attack queries and prevention. In *Proceeding of the 3rd International Conference on Computing for Sustainable Global Development (INDIACom)*, (pp. 2872-2876). IEEE.

Singh, R., Tanwar, S., & Sharma, T. P. (2019). Utilization of blockchain for mitigating the distributed denial of service attacks. *Security and Privacy*, *3*(3). doi:10.1002py2.96

Sinha, K., Choudhary, S., Paul, S., & Paul, P. (2018). Security of Multimedia in Cloud using Secret Shared Key. *Proceeding of the International Conference on Computing, Power and Communication Technologies (GUCON)*. doi:10.1109/gucon.2018.8675031

Sinha, K., Darshani, M. P., Kumari, S., & Paul, P. (2016). Voice Print based Speaker Identification and Verification for Forensic Application. *Imperial Journal of Interdisciplinary Research*, *3*.

Sinha, K., & Paul, P. (2019). Voice Based authentication used in Forensic Lab. *CSI Communications*, *42*(11), 26.

Sinha, K., & Paul, P. (2021a). Network Security Approaches in Distributed Environment. *Research Anthology on Artificial Intelligence Applications in Security*. doi:10.4018/978-1-7998-7705-9.ch061

Sinha, K., & Paul, P. (2021b). Network Security Approaches in Distributed Environment. *Research Anthology on Blockchain Technology in Business, Healthcare, Education, and Government*. doi:10.4018/978-1-7998-5351-0.ch078

Sinha, K., Priya, A., & Khowas, M. (2016). A Framework for Budget Allocation and Optimization Using Particle Swarm Optimization. *Advances in Computational Intelligence*, 149–158. doi:10.1007/978-981-10-2525-9_15

Sinha, K., Priya, A., & Paul, P. (2020). K-RSA: Secure data storage technique for multimedia in cloud data server. *Journal of Intelligent & Fuzzy Systems*, 1–18. doi:10.3233/jifs-191687

Sinha, K., Paul, P., & Amritanjali. (2019). Network Security Approaches in Distributed Environment. *Advances in Computational Intelligence and Robotics*, 174–209. doi:10.4018/978-1-5225-7955-7.ch008

Tajpour, A., & Shooshtari, M. J. (2010). Evaluation of SQL Injection Detection and Prevention Techniques. *Proceeding of the 2nd International Conference on Computational Intelligence, Communication Systems and Networks*. doi:10.1109/cicsyn.2010.55

Tanriverdi, M., & Tekerek, A. (2019). Implementation of Blockchain Based Distributed Web Attack Detection Application. *Proceeding of the 1ˢᵗ International Informatics and Software Engineering Conference (UBMYK)*. doi:10.1109/ubmyk48245.2019.8965446

Tendermint. (2018). https://tendermint.com/

Uramova, J., Segec, P., Moravcik, M., Papan, J., Mokos, T., & Brodec, M. (2017). Packet capture infrastructure based on Moloch. *Proceeding of the 15th International Conference on Emerging eLearning Technologies and Applications (ICETA)*. doi:10.1109/iceta.2017.8102538

Wang, Y., & Li, G. (2019). Detect Triangle Attack on Blockchain by Trace Analysis. *Proceeding of the 19ᵗʰ International Conference on Software Quality, Reliability and Security Companion (QRS-C)*. doi:10.1109/qrs-c.2019.00066

Wei, K., Muthuprasanna, M., & Kothari, S. (2006). Preventing SQL injection attacks in stored procedures. *Proceeding of the Australian Software Engineering Conference (ASWEC'06)*. doi:10.1109/aswec.2006.40

Zhou, Z., Chen, Z., Zhou, T., & Guan, X. (2010). The study on network intrusion detection system of Snort. *Proceeding of the International Conference on Networking and Digital Society*. doi:10.1109/icnds.2010.5479341

KEY TERMS AND DEFINITIONS

Blockchain: It is created by a data block that is connected like a chain, where the data in the chain is consists of a list of records that are inter-linked by using a cryptography algorithm.

Data Security: Protection of digital content in online/offline mode by any kind of attack which is performed by the adversary.

Domain Name System (DNS): It is a collection of computers in the form of hierarchical or decentralized, where the resources are connected with the Internet or a private network.

Hash Functions: In this, the arbitrary size of data is mapped with fixed-size values, where the hash table is used for storage and retrieval.

Intrusion Detection System (IDS): It is a software application to monitor unwanted and malicious activity on the network.

Public-Key Cryptography: In this, the sender and receiver use a different key for encryption and decryption.

SQL Injection: It is a kind of attack which is performed by the adversary by inserting the SQL query in the input data section of the client application.

Structure Query Language (SQL): It is a domain-specific language that is used for managing the data relational database management system.

Symmetric Key Cryptography: In this, the sender and receiver use a single key for encryption and decryption.

Timestamp: It is used to create the time for each data that is stored in the database.

User Interface: It is web-based user interfaces, where applications accept the data at runtime environment.

Compilation of References

A, B., & K, M. V. (2016). Blockchain platform for industrial internet of things. *Journal of software Engineering and Applications, 9*(10), 533.

Abeyratne, S. A., & Monfared, R. P. (2016). Blockchain ready manufacturing supply chain using distributed ledger. *International Journal of Research in Engineering and Technology, 5*(9), 1–10. doi:10.15623/ijret.2016.0509001

Abou El Houda, Z., Hafid, A. S., & Khoukhi, L. (2019). Cochain-SC: An intra-and inter-domain Ddos mitigation scheme based on blockchain using SDN and smart contract. *IEEE Access: Practical Innovations, Open Solutions, 7*, 98893–98907.

Abrams, L. (2018). *Dramatic Increase of DDoS Attack Sizes Attributed to IoT Devices.* https://www.bleepingcomputer.com/news/security/dramatic-increase-of-ddos-attack-sizes-attributed-to-iot-devices/

Adams, J. (2020). *DMX Announces VINblock™ — Blockchain for Everyday Car Business.* https://www.businesswire.com/news/home/20181211005898/en/DMX-Announces-VINblock%E2%84%A2-%E2%80%93%E2%80%93-Blockchain-Everyday-Car

Adat, V., & Gupta, B. B. (2018). Security in Internet of Things: Issues, challenges, taxonomy, and architecture. *Telecommunication Systems, 67*(3), 423–441. doi:10.100711235-017-0345-9

Ademu, I. O., Imafidon, C. O., & Preston, D. S. (2011). A new approach of digital forensic model for digital forensic investigation. *International Journal of Advanced Computer Science and Applications, 2*(12), 175–178.

Adrian, T., Etula, E., & Muir, T. (2014). Financial intermediaries and the cross-section of asset returns. *The Journal of Finance, 69*(6), 2557–2596. doi:10.1111/jofi.12189

Adrian, T., & Shin, H. S. (2010). Liquidity and leverage. *Journal of Financial Intermediation, 19*(3), 418–437. doi:10.1016/j.jfi.2008.12.002

Aitzhan, N. Z., & Svetinovic, D. (2016). Security and privacy in decentralized energy trading through multi-signatures, blockchain and anonymous messaging streams. *IEEE Transactions on Dependable and Secure Computing, 15*(5), 840–852. doi:10.1109/TDSC.2016.2616861

Alaba, F. A., Othman, M., Hashem, I. A. T., & Alotaibi, F. (2017). Internet of Things security: A survey. *Journal of Network and Computer Applications, 88*, 10–28. doi:10.1016/j.jnca.2017.04.002

Al-Ali, A., Zualkernan, I. A., Rashid, M., Gupta, R., & Alikarar, M. (2017). A smart home energy management system using IoT and big data analytics approach. *IEEE Transactions on Consumer Electronics, 63*(4), 426–434. doi:10.1109/TCE.2017.015014

Albanese, M., Jajodia, S., Pugliese, A., & Subrahmanian, V. S. (2011). Scalable analysis of attack scenarios. In *European Symposium on Research in Computer Security* (pp. 416-433). Springer.

Ali, S., Wang, G., Bhuiyan, M. Z. A., & Jiang, H. (2018). Secure data provenance in cloud-centric internet of things via blockchain smart con-tracts. In 2018 IEEE Smart-world, Ubiquitous Intelligence Computing, Advanced Trusted Computing, Scalable Computing Communications, Cloud Big Data Computing, Internet of People and Smart City Innovation (smart-world/scalcom/uic/atc/cbdcom/iop/sci) (pp. 991-998). Academic Press.

Allam, Z. (2018). On smart contracts and organizational performance: A review of smart contracts through the blockchain technology. *Review of Economic and Business Studies, 11*(2), 137–156. doi:10.1515/rebs-2018-0079

Almadhoun, R., Kadadha, M., Alhemeiri, M., Alshehhi, M., & Salah, K. (2018). A user authentication scheme of IoT devices using blockchain-enabled fog nodes. In *IEEE/ACS 15th international conference on computer systems and applications (AICCSA)* (pp. 1-8). Aqaba, Jordan: IEEE.

Al-Sayid, N. A., & Aldlaeen, D. (2013). Database security threats: A survey study. *Proceeding of the 5th International Conference on Computer Science and Information Technology.* doi:10.1109/csit.2013.6588759

Ambika, N. (2019). Energy-Perceptive Authentication in Virtual Private Networks Using GPS Data. In Security, Privacy and Trust in the IoT Environment (pp. 25-38). Springer.

Ambika, N. (2020). Methodical IoT-Based Information System in Healthcare. In Smart Medical Data Sensing and IoT Systems Design in Healthcare (pp. 155-177). Bangalore, India: IGI Global.

Ambika, N. (2020). Encryption of Data in Cloud-Based Industrial IoT Devices. In S. Pal & V. G. Díaz (Eds.), *D.-N. Le, IoT: Security and Privacy Paradigm* (pp. 111–129). CRC Press, Taylor & Francis Group.

Anita, N., & Vijayalakshmi, M. (2019). Blockchain Security Attack: A Brief Survey. *Proceeding of the 10th International Conference on Computing, Communication and Networking Technologies (ICCCNT).* doi:10.1109/icccnt45670.2019.8944615

Appelbaum, D., & Smith, S. (2018). Blockchain basics and hands-on guidance: Taking the next step toward implementation and adoption. *The CPA Journal, 88*(6), 28–37.

Arellanes, D., & Lau, K.-K. (2020). Evaluating IoT service composition mechanisms for the scalability of IoT systems. *Future Generation Computer Systems, 108*, 827–848. doi:10.1016/j.future.2020.02.073

Asharaf, S., & Adarsh, S. (Eds.). (2017). *Decentralized Computing Using Blockchain Technologies and Smart Contracts: Emerging Research and Opportunities: Emerging Research and Opportunities.* IGI Global. doi:10.4018/978-1-5225-2193-8

Ashton, K. (2009). That "Internet of Things" Thing. *RFID.* https://www.rfidjournal.com/that-internet-of-things-thing

Atlam, H. F., Alenezi, A., Walters, R. J., Wills, G. B., & Daniel, J. (2017). Developing an adaptive Risk-based access control model for the Internet of Things. *2017 IEEE International Conference on Internet of Things (IThings) and IEEE Green Computing and Communications (GreenCom) and IEEE Cyber, Physical and Social Computing (CPSCom) and Ieee Smart Data (SmartData),* 655–661. 10.1109/iThings-GreenCom-CPSCom-SmartData.2017.103

Aujla, G. S., Singh, M., Bose, A., Kumar, N., Han, G., & Buyya, R. (2020). BlockSDN: Blockchain-as-a-service for software defined networking in smart city applications. *IEEE Network, 34*(2), 83–91. doi:10.1109/MNET.001.1900151

Axinte, S.-D. (2014). SQL Injection Testing in Web Applications Using SQLmap. *International Journal of Information Security and Cybercrime, 3*(2), 61–68.

Aziz Yousif Almuttalibi, R. (2019). Blockchain Hash Function for Secure Biometric System. *Journal of Engineering and Applied Sciences (Asian Research Publishing Network), 14*(11), 3797–3805. https://doi.org/10.36478/jeasci.2019.3797.3805

Azmoodeh, A., Dehghantanha, A., & Choo, K. K. R. (2019). Big data and internet of things security and forensics: challenges and opportunities. In *Handbook of Big Data and IoT Security* (pp. 1–4). Springer. doi:10.1007/978-3-030-10543-3_1

Badev, A., & Chen, M. (2014). *Bitcoin: Technical Background and Data Analysis.* Academic Press.

Bala, A. (2013). Indian stock market-review of literature. *Trans Asian Journal of Marketing & Management Research, 2*(7), 67–79.

Balandina, E., Balandin, S., Koucheryavy, Y., & Mouromtsev, D. (2015). IoT use cases in healthcare and tourism. *IEEE 17th Conference on Business Informatics, 2,* 37-44.

Banafa, A. (2019). *Ten Trends of Blockchain in 2020.* Open Mind. Retrieved from https://www.bbvaopenmind.com/en/economy/finance/ten-trends-of-blockchain-in-2020/

Bannister, A. (2020). *DDoS suspicions: US health department investigating 'significant increase' in traffic.* https://portswigger.net/daily-swig/ddos-suspicions-us-health-department-investigating-significant-increase-in-traffic

Bansal, M. K., & Sethumadhavan, M. (2020). DNS Security - Prevent DNS Cache Poisoning Attack using Blockchain. *International Journal of Innovative Technology and Exploring Engineering, 9*(4), 2151–2162. doi:10.35940/ijitee.d1549.029420

Bayer, D., Haber, S., & Stornetta, W. S. (1993). Improving the Efficiency and Reliability of Digital Time-Stamping. *Sequences, II,* 329–334. doi:10.1007/978-1-4613-9323-8_24

Bellegarde, M., Orvis, M., & Helba, S. (2010). *Ethical Hacking and Countermeasures: Attack Phases*. EC-Council Press.

Belta, C., Yordanov, B., & Gol, E. A. (2017). *Formal methods for discrete-time dynamical systems* (Vol. 89). Springer. doi:10.1007/978-3-319-50763-7

Bergstra, J. A., & de Leeuw, K. (2013). *Questions related to Bitcoin and other Informational Money.* arXivPrepr. arXiv1305.5956.

Bertino, E., Kamra, A., & Early, J. P. (2007). Profiling Database Application to Detect SQL Injection Attacks. *Proceeding of the IEEE International Performance, Computing, and Communications Conference.* doi:10.1109/pccc.2007.358926

Beyer, S. (2020). *Blockchain Before Bitcoin: A History | Block Telegraph. Block Telegraph.* https://blocktelegraph.io/blockchain-before-bitcoin-history

Bigchain, D. B., & Gmb, H. (2018). *Bigchaindb 2.0: The blockchain database.* White paper. https://www.bigchaindb.com/whitepaper/bigchaindb-whitepaper.pdf

BMW AG. (2020). *How blockchain is changing mobility.* https://www.bmw.com/en/innovation/blockchain-automotive.html

Borhani, M., Liyanage, M., Sodhro, A. H., Kumar, P., Jurcut, A. D., & Gurtov, A. (2020). Secure and resilient communications in the industrial internet. In *Guide to Disaster-Resilient Communication Networks* (pp. 219–242). Springer. doi:10.1007/978-3-030-44685-7_9

Bothos, E., Magoutas, B., Arnaoutaki, K., & Mentzas, G. (2019). Leveraging Blockchain for Open Mobility-as-a-Service Ecosystems. In *Proceedings of the IEEE/WIC/ACM International Conference on Web Intelligence - Companion Volume (WI '19 Companion).* Association for Computing Machinery. 10.1145/3358695.3361844

Boucherat, X. (2020). Interview: Chris Ballinger, CEO, Mobility Open Blockchain Initiative (MOBI). *Automotive World.* https://www.automotiveworld.com/articles/interview-chris-ballinger-ceo-mobility-open-blockchain-initiative-mobi/

Bouri, E., Molnár, P., Azzi, G., Roubaud, D., & Hagfors, L. I. (2017). On the hedge and safe haven properties of Bitcoin: Is it really more than a diversifier? *Finance Research Letters, 20,* 192–198. doi:10.1016/j.frl.2016.09.025

Braeken, A., Liyanage, M., & Jurcut, A. D. (2019). Anonymous lightweight proxy based key agreement for iot (alpka). *Wireless Personal Communications, 106*(2), 345–364. doi:10.100711277-019-06165-9

Brotsis, S., Kolokotronis, N., Limniotis, K., Shiaeles, S., Kavallieros, D., Bellini, E., & Pavué, C. (2019, June). Blockchain solutions for forensic evidence preservation in IoT environments. In *2019 IEEE Conference on Network Softwarization (NetSoft)* (pp. 110-114). IEEE. 10.1109/NETSOFT.2019.8806675

Brown, M., Peköz, E., & Ross, S. (2020). Blockchain Double-Spend Attack Duration. *Probability in the Engineering and Informational Sciences*, 1–9. doi:10.10170269964820000212

Brunnermeier, M. K., & Pedersen, L. H. (2009). Market liquidity and funding liquidity. *Review of Financial Studies*, *22*(6), 2201–2238. doi:10.1093/rfs/hhn098

Cachin, C. (2016, July). Architecture of the hyperledger blockchain fabric. In *Workshop on distributed cryptocurrencies and consensus ledgers* (Vol. 310, No. 4). Academic Press.

Cao, J., Wang, X., Li, Z., Gu, Q., & Chen, Z. (2019). The evolution of open-source blockchain systems: An empirical study. In *Proceedings of the 11th Asia-Pacific Symposium on Internetware (Internetware '19)*. Association for Computing Machinery. 10.1145/3361242.3361248

Caro, Ali, Vecchio, & Giaffreda. (2018, June 7). *Blockchain-based traceability in Agri-Food supply chain management: A practical implementation*. doi:10.1109/IOT-TUSCANY.2018.8373021

Carrier, B. (2003). Defining digital forensic examination and analysis tools using abstraction layers. *International Journal of Digital Evidence*, *1*(4), 1–12.

Cearnau, D. C. (2019). Block-Cloud: The new paradigm of cloud computing. *Economy Informatics Journal*, *19*(1), 14–22. doi:10.12948/ei2019.01.02

Chaddha, R., Kumar, A., Sinha, K., Paul, P., & Amritanjali. (2020). Selection on Various Traditional Image Encryption Techniques: A Study. *Lecture Notes in Electrical Engineering*, 219–228. doi:10.1007/978-981-15-2854-5_20

Chaindb. (2018). *A peer-to-peer database system*. https://bitpay.com/chaindb.pdf

Chamarajnagar, R., & Ashok, A. (2018). Opportunistic mobile Iot with blockchain based collaboration. In *2018 IEEE Global Communications Conference* (pp. 1-6). 10.1109/GLOCOM.2018.8647756

Chandran, R., & Yan, W. Q. (2014). Attack Graph Analysis for Network Anti-Forensics. *International Journal of Digital Crime and Forensics*, *6*(1), 28–50. doi:10.4018/ijdcf.2014010103

Chanson, M., Bogner, A., Bilgeri, D., Fleisch, E., & Wortmann, F. (2019). Blockchain for the IoT: Privacy-preserving protection of sensor data. *Journal of the Association for Information Systems*, *20*(9), 1271–1307. doi:10.17705/1jais.00567

Chen, Xu, Shi, Zhao, & Zhao. (2018, December 10). *A Survey of Blockchain Applications in Different Domains.* . doi:10.1145/3301403.3301407

Chowdhury, M. J. M., Ferdous, M. S., Biswas, K., Chowdhury, N., Kayes, A. S. M., Alazab, M., & Watters, P. (2019). A comparative analysis of distributed ledger technology platforms. *IEEE Access: Practical Innovations, Open Solutions*, *7*, 167930–167943. doi:10.1109/ACCESS.2019.2953729

Chowdhury, M., Kader, M. F., & Asaduzzaman, A. (2013). Security issues in wireless sensor networks: A survey. *International Journal of Future Generation Communication and Networking*, *6*(5), 97–116. doi:10.14257/ijfgcn.2013.6.5.10

Christidis, K., & Devetsikiotis, M. (2016). Blockchains and Smart Contracts for the Internet of Things. *IEEE Access: Practical Innovations, Open Solutions, 4,* 2292–2303. doi:10.1109/ACCESS.2016.2566339

Cimpanu, C. (2020). *AWS said it mitigated a 2.3 Tbps DDoS attack, the largest ever.* https://www.zdnet.com/article/aws-said-it-mitigated-a-2-3-tbps-ddos-attack-the-largest-ever/

Clarke, J. (2009). *Exploiting SQL Injection.* SQL Injection Attacks and Defense.

CloudFlare. (2020). *What is a DDoS Attack?* https://www.cloudflare.com/learning/ddos/what-is-a-ddos-attack/

Cox, J. (2015). *The History of SQL Injection, the Hack That Will Never Go Away.* Available: https://www.vice.com/en_us/article/aekzez/the-history-of-sql-injection-the-hack-that-will-never-go-away

Cui, Z., Xue, F., Zhang, S., Cai, X., Cao, Y., Zhang, W., & Chen, J. (2020). A hybrid blockchain-based identity authentication scheme for multi-WSN. *IEEE Transactions on Services Computing, 13*(2), 241–251. doi:10.1109/TSC.2020.2964537

Daniel, L., & Daniel, L. (2012). Digital forensics for legal professionals. *Syngress Book Co, 1,* 287–293.

Dannen, C. (2017). *Introducing Ethereum and solidity* (Vol. 1). Apress. doi:10.1007/978-1-4842-2535-6

Decker, C., Seidel, J., & Wattenhofer, R. (2016). Bitcoin meets strong consistency. In *Proceedings of the 17th International Conference on Dis- tributed Computing and Networking (ICDCN).* Singapore: ACM.

Dernbecher, S., & Beck, R. (2017). The concept of mindfulness in information systems research: A multi-dimensional analysis. *European Journal of Information Systems, 26*(2), 121–142. doi:10.105741303-016-0032-z

Divakar, Archana, & Sushma. (2018, May). IoT technology in Smart Farming. *International Research Journal of Engineering and Technology, 5.*

Donald, D. C. (2012). *The Hong Kong stock and futures exchanges: Law and microstructure.* Sweet & Maxwell.

Douligeris, C., & Mitrokotsa, A. (2004). DDoS attacks and defense mechanisms: Classification and state-of-the-art. *Computer Networks, 44*(5), 643–666. doi:10.1016/j.comnet.2003.10.003

Dou, W., Chen, Q., & Chen, J. (2013). A confidence-based filtering method for DDoS attack defense in cloud environment. *Future Generation Computer Systems, 29*(7), 1838–1850. doi:10.1016/j.future.2012.12.011

Dubey, R., & Gupta, H. (2016). SQL filtering: An effective technique to prevent SQL injection attack. *Proceeding of the 5ᵗʰ International Conference on Reliability, Infocom Technologies and Optimization (Trends and Future Directions) (ICRITO)*. doi:10.1109/icrito.2016.7784972

Du, X., & Gao, Y. (2020). Blockchain-based intelligent transportation: A sustainable GCU application system. *Journal of Advanced Transportation*, (1), 1–14. https://downloads.hindawi.com/journals/jat/2020/5036792.pdf

Eberhardt, J., & Tai, S. (2017). On or Off the Blockchain? Insights on Off-Chaining Computation and Data. In F. De Paoli, S. Schulte, & E. Broch Johnsen (Eds.), *Service-Oriented and Cloud Computing* (Vol. 10465, pp. 3–15). Springer International Publishing., doi:10.1007/978-3-319-67262-5_1

Elsayed, M. S., Le-Khac, N. A., Dev, S., & Jurcut, A. D. Ddosnet: A deep-learning model for detecting network attacks. In *2020 IEEE 21st International Symposium on "A World of Wireless, Mobile and Multimedia Networks" (WoWMoM)* (pp. 391-396). IEEE.

Esmaeilian, B., Sarkis, J., Lewis, K., & Behdad, S. (2020). *Blockchain for the future of sustainable supply chain management in Industry 4.0, Resources, Conservation and Recycling*. doi:10.1016/j.resconrec.2020.105064

Euromoney.com. (2020). *Blockchain Explained: What Is Blockchain? | Euromoney Learning*. https://www.euromoney.com/learning/blockchain-explained/what-is-blockchain

Faizullah, S., Khan, M. A., Alzahrani, A., & Khan, I. (2020). *Permissioned blockchain-based security for SDN in IoT cloud networks*. arXiv preprint arXiv:2002.00456.

Fanning, K., & Centers, D. P. (2016). Blockchain and its coming impact on financial services. *Journal of Corporate Accounting & Finance*, 27(5), 53–57. doi:10.1002/jcaf.22179

Feghali, A., Kilany, R., & Chamoun, M. (2015). SDN security problems and solutions analysis. In *2015 International Conference on Protocol Engineering and New Technologies of Distributed Systems* (pp. 1-5). Academic Press.

Ford. (2020). *Ford Sustainability Report 2019/20*. https://corporate.ford.com/microsites/sustainability-report-2020/assets/files/sr20.pdf

Fotiou, N., Pittaras, I., Siris, V. A., Voulgaris, S., & Polyzos, G. C. (2019). *Secure IoT access at scale using blockchains and smart contracts*. doi:10.1109/WoWMoM.2019.8793047

Frost, V. S., & Melamed, B. (1994). Simulating Telecommunications Networks with Traffic Modeling. *IEEE Communications Magazine*, 32(3), 70–70.

Gagneja, K., & Kiefer, R. (2020). Security Protocol for Internet of Things (IoT): Blockchain-based Implementation and Analysis. In *Sixth International Conference on Mobile And Secure Services (MobiSecServ)* (pp. 1-6). Miami Beach, FL: IEEE.

Gao, J., Agyekum, K. O.-B. O., Sifah, E. B., Acheampong, K. N., Xia, Q., Du, X., & Xia, H. (2019). A blockchain-SDN-enabled Internet of vehicles environment for fog computing and 5G networks. *IEEE Internet of Things Journal, 7*(5), 4278–4291. doi:10.1109/JIOT.2019.2956241

Gaur, N., Desrosiers, L., Ramakrishna, V., Novotny, P., Baset, S., & O'Dowd, A. (2018). *Hands-On Blockchain with Hyperledger: Building decentralized applications with Hyperledger Fabric and Composer.* Packt Publishing. https://books.google.co.za/books?id=wKdhDwAAQBAJ

Gayatri, M. K., & Jayasakthi, J. (2015). *Providing Agriculture Solution to Farmers for Better Yielding using IoT.* International conference on global trends in signal processing, Chennai, India.

General Motors. (2020). *GM Digital Vehicle Platform Enables Adoption of Future Technologies | General Motors.* https://www.gm.com/content/public/us/en/gm/home/masthead-story/digital-vehicle-platform.html

Ghorbanzadeh, P., Shaddeli, A., Malekzadeh, R., & Jahanbakhsh, Z. (2010). A survey of mobile database security threats and solutions for it. *Proceeding of the 3rd International Conference on Information Sciences and Interaction Sciences.* doi:10.1109/icicis.2010.5534685

Gochhayat, S. P., Bandara, E., Shetty, S., & Foytik, P. (2019). Yugala: Blockchain Based Encrypted Cloud Storage for IoT Data. *Proceeding of the IEEE International Conference on Blockchain (Blockchain).* doi:10.1109/blockchain.2019.00073

Gomes, P. H., Watteyne, T., & Krishnamachari, B. (2018). MABO-TSCH: Multihop and blacklist-based optimized time synchronized channel hopping. *Transactions on Emerging Telecommunications Technologies, 29*(7), e3223. doi:10.1002/ett.3223

Gómez-Arevalillo, A. de la R., & Papadimitratos, P. (2017). Blockchain-based Public Key Infrastructure for Inter-Domain Secure Routing. In *International Workshop on Open Problems in Network Security* (pp. 20-38). Academic Press.

Goransson, P., Black, C., & Culver, T. (2016). *Software defined networks: a comprehensive approach.* Morgan Kaufmann.

Griffin, B. (2019). *MOBI explained: the consortium that's bringing blockchain to vehicles. Decrypt.* https://decrypt.co/10770/mobi-mobility-open-blockchain-initiative-vehicles-explained

Groupe Renault. (2020). *Shared and urban mobility services—Groupe Renault.* https://group.renault.com/en/innovation-2/mobility-services/

Groupe Renault. (2020, May 14). *Groupe Renault has been working on blockchain technology since 2015 to have real-time and secured transactions.* https://group.renault.com/en/news-on-air/news/the-blockchain-transformation-vector-for-the-future-of-the-automotive-industry/

Gruhler, A., Rodrigues, B., & Stiller, B. (2019, April). A reputation scheme for a blockchain-based network cooperative defense. In *2019 IFIP/IEEE Symposium on Integrated Network and Service Management (IM)* (pp. 71-79). IEEE.

Gudipati, V. K., Venna, T., Subburaj, S., & Abuzaghleh, O. (2016). Advanced automated SQL injection attacks and defensive mechanisms. *Proceeding of the Annual Connecticut Conference on Industrial Electronics, Technology & Automation (CT-IETA)*. doi:10.1109/ct-ieta.2016.7868248

Gupta, L. C. (1992). *Stock exchange trading in India: Agenda for reform*. Society for Capital Market Research and Development.

Haber, S., & Stornetta, W. (1991). How to time-stamp a digital document. *Journal of Cryptology*, *3*(2), 99–111.

Hakiri, A., Gokhale, A., Berthou, P., Schmidt, D. C., & Gayraud, T. (2014). Software-defined networking: Challenges and research opportunities for future internet. *Computer Networks*, *75*, 453–471. doi:10.1016/j.comnet.2014.10.015

Hammi, M. T., Hammi, B., Bellot, P., & Serhrouchni, A. (2018). Bubbles of Trust: A decentralized blockchain-based authentication system for IoT. *Computers & Security*, *78*, 126–142. doi:10.1016/j.cose.2018.06.004

Handschuh, H. (2005). SHA Family (Secure Hash Algorithm). *SpringerReference*, 565–567. https://doi.org/10.1007/springerreference_491

Haseeb, K., Islam, N., Almogren, A., & Ud Din, I. (2019). Intrusion prevention framework for secure routing in wsn-based mobile internet of things. *IEEE Access: Practical Innovations, Open Solutions*, *7*, 185496–185505. doi:10.1109/ACCESS.2019.2960633

Hawlitschek, F., Notheisen, B., & Teubner, T. (2018). E limits of trust-free systems: A literature review on blockchain technology and trust in the sharing economy. *Electronic Commerce Research and Applications*, *29*(1), 50–63. doi:10.1016/j.elerap.2018.03.005

Hemdan, E. E., & Manjaiah, D. H. (2018). *CFIM : Toward Building New Cloud Forensics Investigation Model*. Academic Press.

Hendricks, K. B., & Singhal, V. R. (2009). Demand-supply mismatches and stock market reaction: Evidence from excess inventory announcements. *Manufacturing & Service Operations Management*, *11*(3), 509–524. doi:10.1287/msom.1080.0237

Hindia, M. N., Qamar, F., Ojukwu, H., Dimyati, K., Al-Samman, A. M., & Amiri, I. S. (2020). On platform to enable the cognitive radio over 5G networks. *Wireless Personal Communications*, *113*(2), 1241–1262. doi:10.100711277-020-07277-3

Hofmann, E., Strewe, U. M., & Bosia, N. (2017). *Supply chain finance and blockchain technology: the case of reverse securitisation*. Springer.

Holbrook, J. (2020). Blockchain Security and Threat Landscape. *Architecting Enterprise Blockchain Solutions*, 323–347. doi:10.1002/9781119557722.ch11

Hongal, A., Jyothi, M. P., & Prathibha, S. R. (2017). *IoT Based Monitoring System In Smart Agriculture*. International conference on global trends in Signal Processing, Bangalore, India.

Huh, S., Cho, S., & Kim, S. (2017). Managing IoT devices using blockchain platform. In *19th international conference on advanced communication technology (ICACT)* (pp. 464-467). Bongpyeong, South Korea: IEEE.

Huh, J.-H., & Seo, K. (2018). Blockchain-based mobile fingerprint verification and automatic log-in platform for future computing. *The Journal of Supercomputing, 75*(7), 3123–3139.

Ieong, R. S. C. (2006). FORZA–Digital forensics investigation framework that incorporate legal issues. *Digital Investigation, 3*, 29–36. doi:10.1016/j.diin.2006.06.004

Industry Week Staff. (2018). *Major automakers, startups launch Mobility Open Blockchain Initiative.* IndustryWeek. https://www.industryweek.com/leadership/companies-executives/article/22025584/major-automakers-startups-launch-mobility-open-blockchain-initiative

Infosec newsflash. (2019). *Cyber Security Statistics for 2019 By InfoSec Newsflash.* https://www.cyberdefensemagazine.com/cyber-security-statistics-for-2019/

Ismailisufi, A., Popović, T., Gligorić, N., Radonjic, S., & Šandi, S. (2020, February). A Private Blockchain Implementation Using Multichain Open Source Platform. In *2020 24th International Conference on Information Technology (IT)* (pp. 1-4). IEEE.

Jaballah, W. B., Conti, M., & Lal, C. (2019). *A survey on software-defined vanets: benets, challenges, and future directions.* arXiv preprint arXiv:1904.04577.

James, J. I., Shosha, A. F., & Gladyshev, P. (2015). Digital Forensic Investigation and Cloud Computing. In *Cloud Technology* (pp. 1231–1271). IGI Global., doi:10.4018/978-1-4666-6539-2.ch057

Javaid, U., Siang, A. K., Aman, M. N., & Sikdar, B. (2018, June). Mitigating IoT device based DDoS attacks using blockchain. In *Proceedings of the 1st Workshop on Cryptocurrencies and Blockchains for Distributed Systems* (pp. 71-76). Academic Press.

Jeong, B.-G., Youn, T.-Y., Jho, N.-S., & Shin, S. U. (2020). Blockchain-based data sharing and trading model for the connected car. *Sensors (Basel), 20*(3141), 1–20. doi:10.339020113141 PMID:32498273

Jiang, W., Li, H., Xu, G., Wen, M., Dong, G., & Lin, X. (2019). PTAS: Privacy-preserving thin-client authentication scheme in blockchain-based PKI. *Future Generation Computer Systems, 96*, 185–195. doi:10.1016/j.future.2019.01.026

Jiasi, W., Jian, W., Jia-Nan, L., & Yue, Z. (2019). *Secure software-defined networking based on blockchain.* arXiv preprint arXiv:1906.04342.

Jijin, J., Seet, B., & Joo Chong, P. H. (2019). Blockchain enabled opportunistic fog-based radio access network: A position paper. In *2019 29th International Telecommunication Networks and Applications Conference* (pp. 1-3). Academic Press.

Jones, M., Wollschlaeger, D., & Stanley, B. (2018). *Daring to be first - How auto pioneers are taking the plunge into blockchain*. IBM Institute for Business Value, IBM Corporation. https://newsroom.ibm.com/2018-12-12-IBM-Study-Blockchain-Brings-Trust-to-How-Companies-Consumers-and-Cars-Connect

Juneja, A., & Marefat, M. (2018). Leveraging blockchain for retraining deep learning architecture in patient-specific arrhythmia classification. *2018 IEEE EMBS International Conference on Biomedical and Health Informatics, BHI 2018*, 393–397. 10.1109/BHI.2018.8333451

Jung, W., & Park, S. (2017). Preventing DDoS Attack in Blockchain System Using Dynamic Transaction Limit Volume. *International Journal of Control and Automation*, *10*(12), 131–138. https://doi.org/10.14257/ijca.2017.10.12.12

Jurcut, A. D., Ranaweera, P., & Xu, L. (2020). Introduction to IoT Security. *IoT Security: Advances in Authentication*, 27–64.

Jurcut, A., Niculcea, T., Ranaweera, P., & LeKhac, A. (2020). *Security considerations for Internet of Things: A survey*. ArXiv Preprint ArXiv:2006.10591.

Jurcut, A. D. (2018). Automated logic-based technique for formal verification of security protocols. *Journal of Advances in Computer Network*, *6*, 77–85. doi:10.18178/JACN.2018.6.2.258

Jurcut, A. D., Coffey, T., & Dojen, R. (2014). Design requirements to counter parallel session attacks in security protocols. *2014 Twelfth Annual International Conference on Privacy, Security and Trust*, 298–305. 10.1109/PST.2014.6890952

Jurcut, A., Coffey, T., & Dojen, R. (2012). Symmetry in Security Protocol Cryptographic Messages—A Serious Weakness Exploitable by Parallel Session Attacks. *2012 Seventh International Conference on Availability, Reliability and Security*, 410–416. 10.1109/ARES.2012.39

Jurcut, A., Coffey, T., Dojen, R., & Gyorodi, R. (2009). Security Protocol Design: A Case Study Using Key Distribution Protocols. *Journal of Computer Science & Control Systems*, *2*(2).

Kahle, J. H., Marcon, É., Ghezzi, A., & Frank, A. G. (2020). Smart Products value creation in SMEs innovation ecosystems. *Technological Forecasting and Social Change*, *156*, 120024. doi:10.1016/j.techfore.2020.120024

Kaiser, C., Steger, M., Dorri, A., Festl, A., Stocker, A., Fellmann, M., & Kanhere, S. (2018, September). Towards a Privacy-Preserving Way of Vehicle Data Sharing–A Case for Blockchain Technology? In *International Forum on Advanced Microsystems for Automotive Applications* (pp. 111-122). Springer.

Kampik, T., & Najjar, A. (2020). Simulating, off-chain, and on-chain: Agent-based simulations in cross-organizational business processes. *Information (Basel)*, *11*(1), 34. doi:10.3390/info11010034

Kamthe, S., & Deisenroth, M. (2018). Data-efficient reinforcement learning with probabilistic model predictive control. In *International Conference on Artificial Intelligence and Statistics* (pp. 1701-1710). Academic Press.

Kamtuo, K., & Soomlek, C. (2016). Machine Learning for SQL injection prevention on server-side scripting. *Proceeding of the International Computer Science and Engineering Conference (ICSEC)*. doi:10.1109/icsec.2016.7859950

Karafiloski & Mishev. (2017, July 1). *Blockchain solutions for big data challenges: A literature review.* . doi:10.1109/EUROCON.2017.8011213

Karame, G. O., & Androulaki, E. (2016). *Bitcoin and blockchain security*. Artech House.

Karuparthi, R. P., & Zhou, B. (2016). Enhanced Approach to Detection of SQL Injection Attack. *Proceeding of the 15th IEEE International Conference on Machine Learning and Applications (ICMLA)*. doi:10.1109/icmla.2016.0082

Kataoka, K., Gangwar, S., & Podili, P. (2018, February). Trust list: Internet-wide and distributed IoT traffic management using blockchain and SDN. In *2018 IEEE 4th World Forum on Internet of Things (WF-IoT)* (pp. 296-301). IEEE.

Kawaguchi, N. (2019). Application of Blockchain to Supply Chain: Flexible Blockchain Technology. *Procedia Computer Science*, *164*, 143–148. doi:10.1016/j.procs.2019.12.166

Kestenbaum, R. (2017). Why bitcoin is important for your business. *Forbes*. https://www.forbes.com/sites/richardkestenbaum/2017/03/14/why-bitcoin-is-important-for-your-business/#44c5d84741b5

Khan, M. A., & Salah, K. (2018). IoT security: Review, blockchain solutions, and open challenges. *Future Generation Computer Systems*, *82*, 395–411. doi:10.1016/j.future.2017.11.022

Khan, S., Gani, A., Wahab, A. W. A., Shiraz, M., & Ahmad, I. (2016). Network forensics: Review, taxonomy, and open challenges. *Journal of Network and Computer Applications*, *66*, 214–235. doi:10.1016/j.jnca.2016.03.005

Khan, S., Shiraz, M., Abdul Wahab, A. W., Gani, A., Han, Q., & Bin Abdul Rahman, Z. (2014). A comprehensive review on adaptability of network forensics frameworks for mobile cloud computing. *TheScientificWorldJournal*, *2014*, 2014. doi:10.1155/2014/547062 PMID:25097880

Kim, H. S., & Kim, H. K. (2011, May). Network forensic evidence acquisition (NFEA) with packet marking. In *2011 IEEE Ninth International Symposium on Parallel and Distributed Processing with Applications Workshops* (pp. 388-393). IEEE. 10.1109/ISPAW.2011.27

Kim, H., & Feamster, N. (2013). Improving network management with software defined networking. *IEEE Communications Magazine*, *51*(2), 114–119. doi:10.1109/MCOM.2013.6461195

Kim, S. K., Kim, U. M., & Huh, J. H. (2019). A study on improvement of blockchain application to overcome vulnerability of IoT multiplatform security. *Energies*, *12*(3), 1–29. doi:10.3390/en12030402

Kim, T., Goyat, R., Rai, M. K., Kumar, G., Buchanan, W. J., Saha, R., & Thomas, R. (2019). A novel trust evaluation process for secure localization16 using a decentralized blockchain in wireless sensor networks. *IEEE Access: Practical Innovations, Open Solutions*, *7*, 184133–184144. doi:10.1109/ACCESS.2019.2960609

Koçak, S. (2017). A second pre-image attack and a collision attack to cryptographic hash function lux. *Communications Faculty of Science University of Ankara Series A1 Mathematics and Statistics, 66*(1), 254–266. doi:10.1501/commua1_0000000794

Kosba, A., Miller, A., Shi, E., Wen, Z., & Papamanthou, C. (2016). Hawk: The blockchain model of cryptography and privacy-preserving smart contracts. *2016 IEEE Symposium on Security and Privacy (SP'16)*, 839–858. 10.1109/SP.2016.55

Kotobi, K., & Bilen, S. G. (2018). Secure blockchains for dynamic spectrum access: A decentralized database in moving cognitive radio networks enhances security and user access. *IEEE Vehicular Technology Magazine, 13*(1), 32–39. doi:10.1109/MVT.2017.2740458

Kottler, S. (2018). *February 28th DDoS Incident Report.* https://github.blog/2018-03-01-ddos-incident-report

Kreutz, D., Ramos, F. M., & Verissimo, P. (2013). Towards secure and dependable software-defined networks. In *2nd ACM SIGCOMM Workshop on Hot Topics in Software Defined Networking* (pp. 55-60). 10.1145/2491185.2491199

Kreutz, D., Ramos, F. M., Verissimo, P., Rothenberg, C. E., Azodolmolky, S., & Uhlig, S. (2015). Software-defined networking: A comprehensive survey. *Proceedings of the IEEE, 103*(1), 14–76. doi:10.1109/JPROC.2014.2371999

Krivchenkov, A., Misnevs, B., & Pavlyuk, D. (2018, October). Intelligent Methods in Digital Forensics: State of the Art. In *International Conference on Reliability and Statistics in Transportation and Communication* (pp. 274-284). Springer.

Kshetri. (2017). *Blockchain's roles in meeting key supply chain management objectives.* doi:10.1016/j.ijinfomgt.2017.12.005

Kucinski, W. (2019). *MOBI rolls out the first blockchain-enabled Vehicle Identity (VID) mobility standard.* SAE Mobilus. https://saemobilus.sae.org/automated-connected/news/2019/07/mobi-rolls-out-the-first-blockchain-enabled-vehicle-identity-vid-mobility-standard

Kumar, P., & Pateriya, R. K. (2012). A survey on SQL injection attacks, detection and prevention techniques. *Proceeding of the Third International Conference on Computing, Communication and Networking Technologies.* doi:10.1109/icccnt.2012.6396096

Kumar, P., Kumar, R., Gupta, G. P., & Tripathi, R. (2020). A Distributed framework for detecting DDoS attacks in smart contract-based Blockchain-IoT Systems by leveraging Fog computing. *Transactions on Emerging Telecommunications Technologies,* ***, 4112.

Kumar, R., Hasan, M., Padhy, S., Evchenko, K., Piramanayagam, L., Mohan, S., & Bobba, R. B. (2017). End-to-end network delay guarantees for real-time systems using SDN. In *2017 EEE Real-Time Systems Symposium* (pp. 231-242). 10.1109/RTSS.2017.00029

Kumar, T., Braeken, A., Jurcut, A. D., Liyanage, M., & Ylianttila, M. (2019). AGE: Authentication in gadget-free healthcare environments. *Information Technology Management,* 1–20.

Kwon. (2014). *Tendermint: Consensus without mining*. Draft v. 0.6, fall.

Lai, W.-J., Hsueh, C.-W., & Wu, J.-L. (2019). A Fully Decentralized Time-Lock Encryption System on Blockchain. *Proceeding of the IEEE International Conference on Blockchain (Blockchain)*. doi:10.1109/blockchain.2019.00047

Lamport, L., Shostak, R., & Pease, M. (1982). The byzantine generals problem. *ACM Transactions on Programming Languages and Systems*, *4*(3), 382–401. doi:10.1145/357172.357176

Lannquist, A. (2018). Introducing MOBI: The Mobility Open Blockchain Initiative. *IBM Blockchain Blog*. https://www.ibm.com/blogs/blockchain/2018/06/introducing-mobi-the-mobility-open-blockchain-initiative/

Lara, A., Kolasani, A., & Ramamurthy, B. (2013). Network innovation using openflow: A survey. *IEEE Communications Surveys and Tutorials*, *16*(1), 493–512. doi:10.1109/SURV.2013.081313.00105

Le, D.-P., Meng, H., Su, L., Yeo, S. L., & Thing, V. (2018). Biff: A blockchain-based iot forensics framework with identity privacy. *TENCON 2018-2018 IEEE Region 10 Conference*, 2372–2377.

Ledger, D. B. (2018). *Github repo*. https://github.com/ledgerdb/ledgerdb

Lee, Y., Rathore, S., Park, J. H., & Park, J. H. (2020). A blockchain-based smart home gateway architecture for preventing data forgery. *Human-centric Computing and Information Sciences*, *10*(1), 1–14. doi:10.118613673-020-0214-5

Legalwise. (2019). *Rise of Smart Contracts with Blockchain Technology in Australia and New Zealand*. Available at: https://www.legalwiseseminars.com.au/news/smart-contracts-and-the-law/

Li, D., Peng, W., Deng, W., & Gai, F. (2018). A blockchain-based authentication and security mechanism for iot. In *27th International Conference on Computer Communication and Networks (ICCCN)* (pp. 1-6). Hangzhou, China: IEEE. 10.1109/ICCCN.2018.8487449

Li, M., Yu, F. R., Si, P., Wu, W., & Zhang, Y. (2020). Resource optimization for delay-tolerant data in blockchain-enabled iot with edge computing: A deep reinforcement learning approach. *IEEE Internet of Things Journal*, *7*(10), 9399–9412. doi:10.1109/JIOT.2020.3007869

Lin, I. C., & Liao, T. C. (2017). A survey of blockchain security issues and challenges. *International Journal of Network Security*, *19*(5), 653–659.

Li, S., Choo, K.-K. R., Sun, Q., Buchanan, W. J., & Cao, J. (2019). IoT forensics: Amazon echo as a use case. *IEEE Internet of Things Journal*, *6*(4), 6487–6497. doi:10.1109/JIOT.2019.2906946

Liu, C., Ranjan, R., Yang, C., Zhang, X., Wang, L., & Chen, J. (2015). MuR-DPA: Top-down Levelled Multi-replica Merkle Hash Tree Based Secure Public Auditing for Dynamic Big Data Storage on Cloud. *IEEE Trans. Comput.*

Liu, S., Reiter, M. K., & Sekar, V. (2017). Flow reconnaissance via timing attacks on SDN switches. In *2017 IEEE 37th International Conference on Distributed Computing Systems* (pp. 196-206). 10.1109/ICDCS.2017.281

Liu, C. H., Lin, Q., & Wen, S. (2018). Blockchain-enabled data collection and sharing for industrial IoT with deep reinforcement learning. *IEEE Transactions on Industrial Informatics, 15*(6), 3516–3526. doi:10.1109/TII.2018.2890203

Li, X., Jiang, P., Chen, T., Luo, X., & Wen, Q. (2020). A survey on the security of blockchain systems. *Future Generation Computer Systems, 107*, 841–853. doi:10.1016/j.future.2017.08.020

Li, Y., & Liu, Q. (2020). Intersection management for autonomous vehicles with vehicle-to-infrastructure communication. *PLoS One, 15*(7), 1–12. https://doi-org.proxy-bloomu.klnpa.org/10.1371/journal.pone.0235644 PMID:32614893

Liyanage, M., Ylianttila, M., & Gurtov, A. (2016). *Improving the tunnel management performance of secure VPLS architectures with SDN. 2016 13th IEEE Annual Consumer Communications & Networking Conference.*

Luo, C., Zhang, N., & Wang, X. (2019). Time series prediction based on intuitionistic fuzzy cognitive map. *Soft Computing*, 1–16. doi:10.100700500-019-04321-8

Luong, N. C., Anh, T. T., Binh, H. T. T., Niyato, D., Kim, D. I., & Liang, Y.-C. (2019). Joint transaction transmission and channel selection in cognitive radio based blockchain networks: A deep reinforcement learning approach. In *IEEE International Conference on Acoustics, Speech and Signal Processing* (pp. 8409-8413). 10.1109/ICASSP.2019.8683228

Lu, Y. (2018). Blockchain: A survey on functions, applications and open issues. *Journal of Industrial Integration and Management, 3*(04), 1850015. doi:10.1142/S242486221850015X

Ma, J., Huang, X., Mu, Y., & Deng, R. H. (2020). Authenticated Data Redaction with Accountability and Transparency. *IEEE Transactions on Dependable and Secure Computing*, 1. doi:10.1109/TDSC.2020.2998135

Malik, S., Kanhere, S. S., & Jurdak, R. (2018, November). Productchain: Scalable blockchain framework to support provenance in supply chains. In *2018 IEEE 17th International Symposium on Network Computing and Applications (NCA)* (pp. 1-10). IEEE.

Mazieres, D. (2015). *The stellar consensus protocol: A federated model for internet-level consensus.* Stellar Development Foundation.

McKeown, N., Anderson, T., Balakrishnan, H., Parulkar, G., Peterson, L., Rexford, J., Shenker, S., & Turner, J. (2008). OpenFlow: Enabling innovation in campus networks. *Computer Communication Review, 38*(2), 69–74. doi:10.1145/1355734.1355746

Mearian, L. (2018). MOBI adds UEM reporting with new desktop, IoT management tools. *Computerworld.* https://www.computerworld.com/article/3313046/mobi-adds-uem-reporting-with-new-desktop-iot-management-tools.html

Medium. (2020). *Blockchain Architecture Basics: Components, Structure, Benefits & Creation.* https://medium.com/@MLSDevCom/blockchain-architecture-basics-components-structure-benefits-creation-beace17c8e77

Meffert, C., Clark, D., Baggili, I., & Breitinger, F. (2017). Forensic State Acquisition from Internet of Things (FSAIoT): A General Framework and Practical Approach for IoT Forensics Through IoT Device State Acquisition. *Proceedings of the 12th International Conference on Availability, Reliability and Security,* 56:1-56:11. 10.1145/3098954.3104053

Memon, R. A., Li, J. P., Nazeer, M. I., Khan, A. N., & Ahmed, J. (2019). Dualfog-Iot: Additional fog layer for solving blockchain integration prob-lem in Internet of things. *IEEE Access: Practical Innovations, Open Solutions, 7,* 169073–169093. doi:10.1109/ACCESS.2019.2952472

Mendling, J., Weber, I., Aalst, W. V. D., Brocke, J. V., Cabanillas, C., Daniel, F., Debois, S., Ciccio, C. D., Dumas, M., Dustdar, S., Gal, A., García-Bañuelos, L., Governatori, G., Hull, R., Rosa, M. L., Leopold, H., Leymann, F., Recker, J., Reichert, M., ... Zhu, L. (2018). Blockchains for business process management-challenges and opportunities. *ACM Transactions on Management Information Systems, 9*(1), 4. doi:10.1145/3183367

Meyer, H. (1996). A computer emergency response team policy. *Computers & Security, 15*(4), 320.

Miguel, C., & Barbara, L. (1999). Practical byzantine fault tolerance. *Proceedings of the Third Symposium on Operating Systems Design and Implementation, 99,* 173–186.

Mills, D. C., Wang, K., Malone, B., Ravi, A., Marquardt, J., Badev, A. I., ... Ellithorpe, M. (2016). *Distributed ledger technology in payments, clearing, and settlement.* Academic Press.

Miraz, M. H., & Ali, M. (2018). *Applications of blockchain technology beyond cryptocurrency.* arXiv preprint arXiv:1801.03528.

Mirkovic, J., & Reiher, P. (2004). A taxonomy of DDoS attack and DDoS defense mechanisms. *Computer Communication Review, 34*(2), 39–53. doi:10.1145/997150.997156

Mizoguchi, S., Takemori, K., Miyake, Y., Hori, Y., & Sakurai, K. (2011, June). Traceback framework against botmaster by sharing network communication pattern information. In *2011 Fifth International Conference on Innovative Mobile and Internet Services in Ubiquitous Computing* (pp. 639-644). IEEE. 10.1109/IMIS.2011.152

Mlsdev.com. (2020). *Mlsdev.* https://mlsdev.com/blog/156-how-to-build-your-own-blockchain-architecture

MOBI launches Grand Challenge for blockchain in transport sector. (n.d.). *Internet of Business.* https://internetofbusiness.com/mobi-grand-challenge-for-blockchain-in-transportation-launches/

Mobility Open Blockchain Initiative. Home. MOBI. (2020). https://dlt.mobi/

Moinet, A., Darties, B., & Baril, J. L. (2017). Blockchain based trust & authentication for decentralized sensor networks. *IEEE Security & Privacy, Special Issue on Blockchain,* 1-6.

Mongo, D. B. (2018). *Opensource Document Database.* https://www.mongodb.com/

Morgan, S. (2017). *Cybercrime Report, 2017.* Academic Press.

Mosenia, A., & Jha, N. K. (2016). A comprehensive study of security of internet-of-things. *IEEE Transactions on Emerging Topics in Computing, 5*(4), 586–602. doi:10.1109/TETC.2016.2606384

Mota, A. V., Azam, S., Yeo, K. C., Shanmugam, B., & Kannoorpatti, K. (2017). Comparative analysis of different techniques of encryption for secured data transmission. *IEEE International Conference on Power, Control, Signals and Instrumentation Engineering, ICPCSI.* 10.1109/ICPCSI.2017.8392158

Mouton, F., Malan, M. M., Leenen, L., & Venter, H. S. (2014). Social engineering attack framework. *Information Security for South Africa.* doi:10.1109/issa.2014.6950510

Munsub Ali, H., Liu, J., & Ejaz, W. (2020). Planning capacity for 5G and beyond wireless networks by discrete fireworks algorithm with ensemble of local search methods. *EURASIP Journal on Wireless Communications and Networking, 185,* 1–24.

Nakamoto, S. (2008). *Bitcoin: A peer-to-peer electronic cash system.* Academic Press.

Nanthini, S. B., Hemalatha, M., Manivannan, D., & Devasena, L. (2014). Attacks in cognitive radio networks (CRN) - a survey. *Indian Journal of Science and Technology, 7*(4), 530–536. doi:10.17485/ijst/2014/v7i4.18

Narayanan, A., Bonneau, J., Felten, E., Miller, A., & Goldfeder, S. (2016). *Bitcoin and cryptocurrency technologies: a comprehensive introduction.* Princeton University Press.

Narayanan, A., Bonneau, J., Felten, E., Miller, A., & Goldfeder, S. (2016). *Bitcoin and Cryptocurrency Technologies: A Comprehensive Introduction.* Princeton University Press.

Nguyen, Q. K. (2016). Blockchain-A Financial Technology for Future Sustainable Development. *Proceedings – 3rd International Conference on Green Technology and Sustainable Development, GTSD 2016,* 51–54.

Nieto, A., Rios, R., & Lopez, J. (2017). A methodology for privacy-aware IoT-forensics. *2017 IEEE Trustcom/BigDataSE/ICESS,* 626–633.

Nieto, A., Rios, R., & Lopez, J. (2018). IoT-forensics meets privacy: Towards cooperative digital investigations. *Sensors (Basel), 18*(2), 492. doi:10.339018020492 PMID:29414864

Nikesh, G. & Kowitkar, R.S. (2016, June 6). IoT Based Smart Agriculture. *International Journal of Advance Research in Computer and Communication Engineering, 5.*

Nikolaidis, I., & Akyildiz, I. F. (1992). *Source characterization and statistical multiplexing in ATM networks.* College of Computing, Georgia Institute of Technology.

Noura, H. N., Salman, O., Chehab, A., & Couturier, R. (2020). DistLog: A distributed logging scheme for IoT forensics. *Ad Hoc Networks, 98,* 102061. doi:10.1016/j.adhoc.2019.102061

Ntagwabira, L., & Kang, S. L. (2010). Use of Query tokenization to detect and prevent SQL injection attacks. *Proceeding of the 3rd International Conference on Computer Science and Information Technology.* doi:10.1109/iccsit.2010.5565202

Orman, H. (2018). Blockchain: The Emperors New PKI? *IEEE Internet Computing, 22*(2), 23–28. https://doi.org/10.1109/mic.2018.022021659

Ourad, A. Z., Belgacem, B., & Salah, K. (2018). Using blockchain for IOT access control and authentication management. In *International Conference on Internet of Things* (pp. 150-164). Santa Barbara, CA: Springer. 10.1007/978-3-319-94370-1_11

Ou, X., Boyer, W. F., & McQueen, M. A. (2006, October). A scalable approach to attack graph generation. In *Proceedings of the 13th ACM conference on Computer and communications security* (pp. 336-345). 10.1145/1180405.1180446

Paech, P. (2017). The governance of blockchain financial networks. *The Modern Law Review, 80*(6), 1073–1110. doi:10.1111/1468-2230.12303

Panarello, A., Tapas, N., Merlino, G., Longo, F., & Puliafito, A. (2018). Blockchain and iot integration: A systematic survey. *Sensors (Basel), 18*(8), 2575. doi:10.339018082575 PMID:30082633

Passeri, P. (2017). *2017 Cyber Attacks Statistics.* Available: https://www.hackmageddon.com/2018/01/17/2017-cyber-attacks-statistics/

Patil, K. A., & Kale, N. R. (2016). *A Model For Smart Agriculture Using IoT.* International conference on global trends in signal processing, Jalgaon, India. 10.1109/ICGTSPICC.2016.7955360

Pérez Hernández, M. E., & Reiff-Marganiec, S. (2015). Autonomous and self controlling smart objects for the future internet. *Proceedings from 2015 3rd International Conference on Future Internet of Things and Cloud, 301–308.* 10.1109/FiCloud.2015.89

Perumal, S., Norwawi, N. M., & Raman, V. (2015). Internet of Things(IoT) digital forensic investigation model: Top-down forensic approach methodology. *2015 Fifth International Conference on Digital Information Processing and Communications (ICDIPC), 19–23.* 10.1109/ICDIPC.2015.7323000

Peters, G. W., & Panayi, E. (2016). *Understanding modern banking ledgers through blockchain technologies: future of transaction processing and smart contracts on the internet of money. New Economic Windows.* doi:10.1007/978-3-319-42448-4_13

Pilli, E. S., Joshi, R. C., & Niyogi, R. (2010). A generic framework for network forensics. *International Journal of Computers and Applications, 1*(11), 1–6. doi:10.5120/251-408

Pollack, E. (2018). *Protecting Against SQL Injection.* Dynamic SQL.

Pollock, D. (2020, April 3). General Motors applies for decentralized blockchain map patent. *Forbes.* https://www.forbes.com/sites/darrynpollock/2020/04/03/general-motors-applies-for-decentralized-blockchain-map-patent/

Polluck, D. (2019). *BMW Opens Its Doors for Mobility Open Blockchain Initiative's First European Colloquium*. Available at: https://www.forbes.com/sites/darrynpollock/2019/02/15/bmw-opens-its-doors-for-mobility-open-blockchain-initiatives-first-european-colloquium/#618b0c127f1d

Priya, A., & Sahana, S. K. (2020). A Deterministic Flowshop Scheduling Problem to minimizing the Makespan using PA-ACO. *International Journal of Engineering and Advanced Technology*, *9*(3), 1555–1560. doi:10.35940/ijeat.b4573.029320

Priya, A., Sinha, K., Darshani, M. P., & Sahana, S. K. (2018). A Novel Multimedia Encryption and Decryption Technique Using Binary Tree Traversal. *Proceeding of the Second International Conference on Microelectronics, Computing & Communication Systems (MCCS 2017)*, 163–178. DOI: 10.1007/978-981-10-8234-4_15

Puthal, D., Mohanty, S. P., Nanda, P., Kougianos, E., & Das, G. (2019). Proof-of-authentication for scalable blockchain in resource-constrained distributed systems. In *International Conference on Consumer Electronics (ICCE)* (pp. 1-5). Las Vegas, NV: IEEE. 10.1109/ICCE.2019.8662009

Queiroz, M. M., Telles, R., & Bonilla, S. H. (2019). Blockchain and supply chain management integration: A systematic review of the literature. *Supply Chain Management*, *25*(2), 241–254. doi:10.1108/SCM-03-2018-0143

Radware. (2019). *DDoS Attack Definitions - DDoSPedia*. https://security.radware.com/ddos-knowledge-center/ddospedia/dos-attack/

Raghavan, S. (2013). Digital forensic research: Current state of the art. *CSI Transactions on ICT*, *1*(1), 91–114. doi:10.100740012-012-0008-7

Ramezan, G., & Leung, C. (2018). A Blockchain-Based Contractual Routing Protocol for the Internet of Things Using Smart Contracts. *Wireless Communications and Mobile Computing*, *4029591*, 1–14. Advance online publication. doi:10.1155/2018/4029591

Rao, A. R., & Clarke, D. (2020). Perspectives on emerging directions in using IoT devices in blockchain applications. *Internet of Things*, *10*, 100079. doi:10.1016/j.iot.2019.100079

Rathee, G., Ahmad, F., Kurugollu, F., Azad, M. A., Iqbal, R., & Imran, M. (2020). *CRT-BIoV: A cognitive radio technique for blockchain-enabled Internet of vehicles. IEEE Transactions on Intelligent Transportation Systems.*

Reyna, A., Martín, C., Chen, J., Soler, E., & Díaz, M. (2018). On blockchain and its integration with IoT. Challenges and opportunities. *Future Generation Computer Systems*, *88*, 173–190. doi:10.1016/j.future.2018.05.046

Riel, A., Kreiner, C., Messnarz, R., & Much, A. (2018). An architectural approach to the integration of safety and security requirements in smart products and systems design. *CIRP Annals*, *67*(1), 173–176. doi:10.1016/j.cirp.2018.04.022

Rijsdijk, S. A., & Hultink, E. J. (2009). How today's consumers perceive tomorrow's smart products. *Journal of Product Innovation Management*, *26*(1), 24–42. doi:10.1111/j.1540-5885.2009.00332.x

Rikken, O., Janssen, M., & Kwee, Z. (2019). Governance challenges of blockchain and decentralized autonomous organizations. *Information Polity*, *24*(4), 397–417. doi:10.3233/ip-190154

Rodrigues, B., Bocek, T., Lareida, A., Hausheer, D., Rafati, S., & Stiller, B. (2017a). A blockchain-based architecture for collaborative DDoS mitigation with smart contracts. In *IFIP International Conference on Autonomous Infrastructure, Management and Security* (pp. 16-29). Springer.

Rodrigues, B., Bocek, T., & Stiller, B. (2017b). *Enabling a cooperative, multi-domain DDoS defense by a blockchain signaling system (BloSS)*. Semantic Scholar.

Roesch, M. (1999). Snort: Lightweight Intrusion Detection for Networks. LISA. In *Proceedings of the 13th USENIX conference on System administration (LISA '99)*. USENIX Association.

Rosic, A. (2020). *What Is hashing?* [Step-by-Step Guide-Under Hood of Blockchain]. https://blockgeeks.com/guides/what-is-hashing/

Russell, J. (2018). *BMW, GM, Ford and Renault launches blockchain research group for automotive industry*. Techcrunch.

Saad, M., Spaulding, J., Njilla, L., Kamhoua, C., Shetty, S., Nyang, D. H., & Mohaisen, D. (2020). Exploring the Attack Surface of Blockchain: A Comprehensive Survey. *IEEE Communications Surveys & Tutorials*, 1–1. doi:10.1109/comst.2020.2975999

Saad, M., Spaulding, J., Njilla, L., Kamhoua, C., Shetty, S., Nyang, D., & Mohaisen, A. (2019). *Exploring the attack surface of blockchain: A systematic overview*. arXiv preprint arXiv:1904.03487.

Saberi, Kouhizadeh, Sarkis, & Shen. (2018, October 17). *Blockchain technology and its relationships to sustainable supply chain management*. doi:10.1080/00207543.2018.1533261

Sabir, B. E., Youssfi, M., Bouattane, O., & Allali, H. (2020). Towards a New Model to Secure IoT-based Smart Home Mobile Agents using Blockchain Technology. *Engineering, Technology & Applied Scientific Research*, *10*(2), 5441–5447.

Sadeghian, A., Zamani, M., & Manaf, A. A. (2013). A Taxonomy of SQL Injection Detection and Prevention Techniques. *Proceeding of the International Conference on Informatics and Creative Multimedia*. doi:10.1109/icicm.2013.18

Sahana, S. K., Khowas, M., & Sinha, K. (2018). Budget Optimization and Allocation: An Evolutionary Computing Based Model. *Bentham Science*. doi:10.2174/9781681087078118001

Sajana, P., Sindhu, M., & Sethumadhavan, M. (2018). On blockchain applications: Hyperledger fabric and ethereum. *International Journal of Pure and Applied Mathematics*, *118*(18), 2965–2970.

Sallam, A., Xiao, Q., Bertino, E., & Fadolalkarim, D. (2016). Anomaly Detection Techniques for Database Protection Against Insider Threats (Invited Paper). *Proceeding of the 17th International Conference on Information Reuse and Integration (IRI)*. doi:10.1109/iri.2016.12

Satyavolu, P., & Sangamnerkar, A. (2016). Blockchain's smart contracts: Driving the next wave of innovation across manufacturing value chains. *Cognizant 20–20 Insights*.

Saurabh, S., & Sairam, A. S. (2016). Increasing Accuracy and Reliability of IP Traceback for DDoS Attack Using Completion Condition. *International Journal of Network Security, 18*(2), 224–234.

Schinckus, C. (2020). The good, the bad and the ugly: An overview of the sustainability of blockchain technology. *Energy Research & Social Science, 69,* 101614. doi:10.1016/j.erss.2020.101614

Schwartz, D., Youngs, N., & Britto, A. (2014). *The ripple protocol consensus algorithm.* Ripple Labs Inc White Paper.

SEPA for Corporates. (2017). *The Difference between Bitcoin, Ethereum, Ripple & Litecoin.* https://www.sepaforcorporates.com/thoughts/difference-bitcoin-ethereum-ripple-litecoin/

Shah, S. A. R., & Issac, B. (2018). Performance comparison of intrusion detection systems and application of machine learning to Snort system. *Future Generation Computer Systems, 80,* 157–170. doi:10.1016/j.future.2017.10.016

Shakhbulatov, D., Medina, J., Dong, Z., & Rojas-Cessa, R. (2020). TheBlockchain Enhances Supply Chain Management. A Survey. *IEEE Open Journal of the Computer Society, 1,* 230–249. doi:10.1109/OJCS.2020.3025313

Sharma, P., Tripathi, S. S., & Panda, R. (2019). *A Survey of Security Issues in Internet of Things.* Academic Press.

Sharma, P. K., Singh, S., Jeong, Y.-S., & Park, J. H. (2017). Distblocknet: A distributed blockchains-based secure SDN architecture for IoT networks. *IEEE Communications Magazine, 55*(9), 78–85. doi:10.1109/MCOM.2017.1700041

Shastri, A. A., & Chatur, P. N. (2015). Efficient and effective security model for database specially designed to avoid internal threats. *Proceeding of the International Conference on Smart Technologies and Management for Computing, Communication, Controls, Energy and Materials (ICSTM).* doi:10.1109/icstm.2015.7225407

Shen, M., Liu, H., Zhu, L., Xu, K., Yu, H., Du, X., & Guizani, M. (2020). Blockchain-assisted secure device authentication for cross-domain industrial IoT. *IEEE Journal on Selected Areas in Communications, 38*(5), 942–954. doi:10.1109/JSAC.2020.2980916

She, W., Liu, Q., Tian, Z., Chen, J., Wang, B., & Liu, W. (2019). Blockchaintrust model for malicious node detection in wireless sensor networks. *IEEE Access: Practical Innovations, Open Solutions, 7,* 38947–38956. doi:10.1109/ACCESS.2019.2902811

Singh, R., Tanwar, S., & Sharma, T. P. (2019). Utilization of blockchain for mitigating the distributed denial of service attacks. *Security and Privacy, 3*(3). doi:10.1002py2.96

Singh, N., Dayal, M., Raw, R. S., & Kumar, S. (2016). SQL injection: Types, methodology, attack queries and prevention. In *Proceeding of the 3rd International Conference on Computing for Sustainable Global Development (INDIACom),* (pp. 2872-2876). IEEE.

Sinha, K., & Paul, P. (2019). Voice Based authentication used in Forensic Lab. *CSI Communications, 42*(11), 26.

Sinha, K., Choudhary, S., Paul, S., & Paul, P. (2018). Security of Multimedia in Cloud using Secret Shared Key. *Proceeding of the International Conference on Computing, Power and Communication Technologies (GUCON).* doi:10.1109/gucon.2018.8675031

Sinha, K., Darshani, M. P., Kumari, S., & Paul, P. (2016). Voice Print based Speaker Identification and Verification for Forensic Application. *Imperial Journal of Interdisciplinary Research, 3.*

Sinha, K., Paul, P., & Amritanjali. (2019). Network Security Approaches in Distributed Environment. *Advances in Computational Intelligence and Robotics*, 174–209. doi:10.4018/978-1-5225-7955-7.ch008

Sinha, K., Priya, A., & Khowas, M. (2016). A Framework for Budget Allocation and Optimization Using Particle Swarm Optimization. *Advances in Computational Intelligence*, 149–158. doi:10.1007/978-981-10-2525-9_15

Sinha, K., Priya, A., & Paul, P. (2020). K-RSA: Secure data storage technique for multimedia in cloud data server. *Journal of Intelligent & Fuzzy Systems*, 1–18. doi:10.3233/jifs-191687

Sinha, K., & Paul, P. (2021a). Network Security Approaches in Distributed Environment. *Research Anthology on Artificial Intelligence Applications in Security.* doi:10.4018/978-1-7998-7705-9.ch061

Sinha, K., & Paul, P. (2021b). Network Security Approaches in Distributed Environment. *Research Anthology on Blockchain Technology in Business, Healthcare, Education, and Government.* doi:10.4018/978-1-7998-5351-0.ch078

Soleimani, M., & Ghorbani, A. A. (2012). Multi-layer episode filtering for the multi-step attack detection. *Computer Communications*, 35(11), 1368–1379. doi:10.1016/j.comcom.2012.04.001

Sridhar, S., & Smys, S. (2017, January). Intelligent security framework for iot devices cryptography based end-to-end security architecture. In *2017 International Conference on Inventive Systems and Control (ICISC)* (pp. 1-5). IEEE. 10.1109/ICISC.2017.8068718

Statista, R. D. (2019). *Internet of Things-Number of connected devices worldwide 2015-2025.* Statista Research Department. Statista. Com/Statistics/471264/Iot-Number-of-Connected-Devices-Worldwide.

Steichen, M., Hommes, S., & State, R. (2017, September). ChainGuard—A firewall for blockchain applications using SDN with OpenFlow. In 2017 Principles. Systems and Applications of IP Telecommunications. Academic Press.

Stoyanova, M., Nikoloudakis, Y., Panagiotakis, S., Pallis, E., & Markakis, E. K. (2020). A Survey on the Internet of Things (IoT) Forensics: Challenges, Approaches and Open Issues. *IEEE Communications Surveys and Tutorials*, 22(2), 1191–1221. doi:10.1109/COMST.2019.2962586

Subramanian, H. (2017). Decentralized blockchain-based electronic marketplaces. *Communications of the ACM*, 61(1), 78–84. doi:10.1145/3158333

Subramanian, N., Chaudhuri, A., & Kayıkcı, Y. (2020). Blockchain applications and future opportunities in transportation. In *Blockchain and Supply Chain Logistics* (pp. 39–48). Palgrave Pivot. doi:10.1007/978-3-030-47531-4_5

Sultana, T., Almogren, A., Akbar, M., Zuair, M., Ullah, I., & Javaid, N. (2020). Data sharing system integrating access control mechanism using blockchain-based smart contracts for IoT devices. *Applied Sciences (Basel, Switzerland), 10*(2), 1–21. doi:10.3390/app10020488

Sumalatha, M. R., & Batsa, P. (2016). Data collection and audit logs of digital forensics in cloud. *2016 International Conference on Recent Trends in Information Technology (ICRTIT)*, 1–8. 10.1109/ICRTIT.2016.7569587

Sunny, J., Undralla, N., & Pillai, V. M. (2020, December). Supply chain transparency through blockchain-based traceability: An overview with demonstration. *Computers & Industrial Engineering, 150*. doi:10.1016/j.cie.2020.106895

Sutcliffe, M. (2017). *An overview of Blockchain applications—this is just the beginning!* Academic Press.

Swami, R., Dave, M., & Ranga, V. (2019). Software-defined networking-based DDoS defense mechanisms. *ACM Computing Surveys, 52*(2), 1–36. doi:10.1145/3301614

Swami, R., Dave, M., & Ranga, V. (2020). DDoS Attacks and Defense Mechanisms Using Machine Learning Techniques for SDN. In *Security and Privacy Issues in Sensor Networks and IoT* (pp. 193–214). IGI Global. doi:10.4018/978-1-7998-0373-7.ch008

Tajpour, A., & Shooshtari, M. J. (2010). Evaluation of SQL Injection Detection and Prevention Techniques. *Proceeding of the 2nd International Conference on Computational Intelligence, Communication Systems and Networks*. doi:10.1109/cicsyn.2010.55

Tanriverdi, M., & Tekerek, A. (2019). Implementation of Blockchain Based Distributed Web Attack Detection Application. *Proceeding of the 1st International Informatics and Software Engineering Conference (UBMYK)*. doi:10.1109/ubmyk48245.2019.8965446

Tendermint. (2018). https://tendermint.com/

Tian, F. (2017). *A supply chain traceability system for food safety based on HACCP, Blockchain & Internet of Things*. IEEE. doi:10.1109/ICSSSM.2017.7996119

Tian, H., Su, Y., & Liang, Z. (2019). *A Provable Secure Server Friendly Two-Party SM2 Singing Protocol for Blockchain IoT. In IEEE Globecom Workshops (GC Wkshps)*. IEEE.

Tian, Z., Cui, Y., An, L., Su, S., Yin, X., Yin, L., & Cui, X. (2018). A real-time correlation of host-level events in cyber range service for smart campus. *IEEE Access: Practical Innovations, Open Solutions, 6*, 35355–35364. doi:10.1109/ACCESS.2018.2846590

Tiberti, W., Carmenini, A., Pomante, L., & Cassioli, D. (2020). A light weight blockchain-based technique for anti-tampering in wireless sensor networks. In *2020 23rd Euromicro Conference on Digital System Design* (pp. 577-582). Academic Press.

Tripathi, N., Hubballi, N., & Singh, Y. (2016). How secure are web servers? An Empirical Study of Slow HTTP DoS Attacks and Detection. In *2016 11th International Conference on Availability, Reliability and Security (ARES)* (pp. 454-463). IEEE. 10.1109/ARES.2016.20

Tripathi, N., & Hubballi, N. (2018). Slow Rate Denial of Service Attacks against HTTP/2. *Computers & Security*, 72, 255–272. doi:10.1016/j.cose.2017.09.009

Tselios, C., Politis, I., & Kotsopoulos, S. (2017). Enhancing SDN security for IoT-related deployments through blockchain. In *2017 IEEE Conference on Network Function Virtualization and Software Defined Networks* (pp. 303-308). 10.1109/NFV-SDN.2017.8169860

Uramova, J., Segec, P., Moravcik, M., Papan, J., Mokos, T., & Brodec, M. (2017). Packet capture infrastructure based on Moloch. *Proceeding of the 15th International Conference on Emerging eLearning Technologies and Applications (ICETA)*. doi:10.1109/iceta.2017.8102538

Verhoeven, P., Sinn, F., & Herden, T. T. (2018). Examples from Blockchain Implementations in Logistics and Supply Chain Management: Exploring the Mindful Use of a New Technology. *Logistics*, 2018(2), 20. doi:10.3390/logistics2030020

Verma, N., Sharma, S., Sinha, K., Paul, P., & Amritanjali. (2020). Selection on Traditional Cryptographic Algorithm for Real-Time Video Transmission and Storage: A Study. *Lecture Notes in Electrical Engineering*, 229–238. doi:10.1007/978-981-15-2854-5_21

Vokerla, R. R., Shanmugam, B., Azam, S., Karim, A., De Boer, F., Jonkman, M., & Faisal, F. (2019). An Overview of Blockchain Applications and Attacks. In *2019 International Conference on Vision Towards Emerging Trends in Communication and Networking (ViTECoN)* (pp. 1-6). IEEE. 10.1109/ViTECoN.2019.8899450

Vujičić, Jagodić, & Ranđić. (2018, April 26). *Blockchain technology, bitcoin, and Ethereum: A brief overview.* . doi:10.1109/INFOTEH.2018.8345547

Wang, Y., & Li, G. (2019). Detect Triangle Attack on Blockchain by Trace Analysis. *Proceeding of the 19th International Conference on Software Quality, Reliability and Security Companion (QRS-C)*. doi:10.1109/qrs-c.2019.00066

Wang, S., Ouyang, L., Yuan, Y., Ni, X., Han, X., & Wang, F. Y. (2019). Blockchain-enabled smart contracts: Architecture, applications, and future trends. *IEEE Transactions on Systems, Man, and Cybernetics. Systems*, 49(11), 2266–2277. doi:10.1109/TSMC.2019.2895123

Wang, X. J., & Wang, X. Y. (2010). Topology-assisted deterministic packet marking for IP traceback. *Journal of China Universities of Posts and Telecommunications*, 17(2), 116–121. doi:10.1016/S1005-8885(09)60456-8

Watanabe, H., Fujimura, S., Nakadaira, A., Miyazaki, Y., Akutsu, A., & Kishigami, J. (2016). Blockchain contract: Securing a blockchain applied to smart contracts. *IEEE International Conference on Consumer Electronics (ICCE'16)*, 467–468. 10.1109/ICCE.2016.7430693

Wei, K., Muthuprasanna, M., & Kothari, S. (2006). Preventing SQL injection attacks in stored procedures. *Proceeding of the Australian Software Engineering Conference (ASWEC'06)*. doi:10.1109/aswec.2006.40

Weiss, M. B. H., Werbach, K., Sicker, D. C., & Bastidas, C. E. C. (2019). On the application of blockchains to spectrum management. *IEEE Transactions on Cognitive Communications and Networking, 5*(2), 193–205. doi:10.1109/TCCN.2019.2914052

Werbach, K. (Ed.). (2018). *The blockchain and the new architecture of trust*. MIT Press. doi:10.7551/mitpress/11449.001.0001

Wikipedia. (2020). *COVID-19 pandemic*. https://en.wikipedia.org/wiki/COVID-19_pandemic

Wood. (2014). *Ethereum: A Secure Decentralized Generalised Transaction Ledger*. EIP-150 REVISION. (a04ea02 - 2017-09-30)

Wu, L., Du, X., Wang, W., & Lin, B. (2018). An out-of-band authentication scheme for internet of things using blockchain technology. In *International Conference on Computing, Networking and Communications (ICNC)* (pp. 769-773). Maui, HI: IEEE. 10.1109/ICCNC.2018.8390280

Wüst, K., & Gervais, A. (2018). *Do you need a Blockchain?* IEEE Zug. doi:10.1109/CVCBT.2018.00011

Xu, L., Jurcut, A. D., & Ahmadi, H. (2019). Emerging Challenges and Requirements for Internet of Things in 5G. *5G-Enabled Internet of Things*.

Xu, C., Wang, K., Li, P., Guo, S., Luo, J., Ye, B., & Guo, M. (2019). Making big data open in edges: A resource-efficient blockchain-based approach. *IEEE Transactions on Parallel and Distributed Systems, 30*(4), 870–882. doi:10.1109/TPDS.2018.2871449

Yang, J., He, S., Xu, Y., Chen, L., & Ren, J. (2019). A Trusted Routing Scheme Using Blockchain and Reinforcement Learning for Wireless Sensor Networks. *Sensors (Basel), 19*(4), 970. doi:10.339019040970 PMID:30823560

Yang, W., Garg, S., Raza, A., Herbert, D., & Kang, B. (2018, August). Blockchain: Trends and future. In *Pacific Rim Knowledge Acquisition Workshop* (pp. 201-210). Springer.

Yazdinejad, A., Parizi, R. M., Dehghantanha, A., & Choo, K.-K. R. (2019). Blockchain-enabled authentication handover with ecient privacy protection in SDN-based 5G networks. *IEEE Transactions on Network Science and Engineering*.

Yeh, L. Y., Huang, J. L., Yen, T. Y., & Hu, J. W. (2019, August). A Collaborative DDoS Defense Platform Based on Blockchain Technology. In *2019 Twelfth International Conference on Ubi-Media Computing (Ubi-Media)* (pp. 1-6). IEEE.

Yeh, L. Y., Lu, P. J., Huang, S. H., & Huang, J. L. (2020). SOChain: A Privacy-Preserving DDoS Data Exchange Service Over SOC Consortium Blockchain. *IEEE Transactions on Engineering Management*.

Yuan, Y., & Wang, F.-Y. (2016). *Towards blockchain-based intelligent transportation systems.* 10.1109/ITSC.2016.7795984

Zawoad, S., Hasan, R., & Skjellum, A. (2015). OCF: an open cloud forensics model for reliable digital forensics. *2015 IEEE 8th International Conference on Cloud Computing,* 437–444.

Zawoad, S., & Hasan, R. (2015). A trustworthy cloud forensics environment. *IFIP Advances in Information and Communication Technology, 462,* 271–285. doi:10.1007/978-3-319-24123-4_16

Zeng, Y., Zhang, X., Akhtar, R., & Wang, C. (2018). A blockchain-based scheme for secure data provenance in wireless sensor networks. In *2018 14th International Conference on Mobile Ad-hoc and Sensor Networks* (pp. 13-18). 10.1109/MSN.2018.00009

Zhang, R., Xue, R., & Liu, L. (2019). Security and privacy on blockchain. *ACM Computing Surveys, 52*(3), 1–34. doi:10.1145/3316481

Zheng, Xie, Dai, Chen, & Wang. (2017, September 11). *An Overview of Blockchain Technology: Architecture, Consensus, and Future Trends.* . doi:10.1109/BigDataCongress.2017.85

Zheng, Z., Xie, S., Dai, H. N., Chen, X., & Wang, H. (2018). Blockchain challenges and opportunities: A survey. *International Journal of Web and Grid Services, 14*(4), 352–375. doi:10.1504/IJWGS.2018.095647

Zhou, Z., Chen, Z., Zhou, T., & Guan, X. (2010). The study on network intrusion detection system of Snort. *Proceeding of the International Conference on Networking and Digital Society.* doi:10.1109/icnds.2010.5479341

Zhu, Z., Qi, G., Zheng, M., Sun, J., & Chai, Y. (2020). Blockchain based consensus checking in decentralized cloud storage. *Simulation Modelling Practice and Theory, 102,* 101987. doi:10.1016/j.simpat.2019.101987

Zia, T., & Zomaya, A. (2006, October). Security issues in wireless sensor networks. In *2006 International Conference on Systems and Networks Communications (ICSNC'06)* (pp. 40-40). 10.1109/ICSNC.2006.66

Zoria, S. (2019). *How is Blockchain Technology impacting the automotive industry.* Medium. https://medium.com/datadriveninvestor/how-is-blockchain-technology-impacting-the-automotive-industry-728875a7c940

About the Contributors

Surjit Singh received his Ph.D. degree in Computer Engineering from National Institute of Technology, Kurukshetra, Haryana, India. He is currently working as Assistant Professor with the Computer Science and Engineering Department, Thapar Institute of Engineering and Technology, Patiala, India. He has served as Assistant Professor with NIT Kurukshetra before joining TIET, Patiala. He has served as Guest Editor for IEEE Transactions and other journals of repute. He has three books to his credit. He has also published many research papers in journals of high repute including IEEE Transactions, Elsevier, Springer, Wiley, and Taylor & Francis. He has done extensive research work in the area of Wireless Sensor Networks, Computational Intelligence, Information Security, Blockchain Technologies, and the Internet of Things.

Anca Delia Jurcut is an Assistant Professor in the School of Computer Science, University College Dublin (UCD), Ireland, since 2015. She received a BSc in Computer Science and Mathematics from West University of Timisoara, Romania in2007 and a PhD in Security Engineering from the University of Limerick (UL), Ireland in 2013 funded by the Irish Research Council for Science Engineering and Technology. She worked as a postdoctoral researcher at UL as a member of the Data Communication Security Laboratory and as a Software Engineer in IBM in Dublin, Ireland in the area of data security and formal verification. Dr. Jurcut research interests include Security Protocols Design and Analysis, Automated Techniques for Formal Verification, Network Security, Attack Detection and Prevention Techniques, Security for the Internet of Things, and Applications of Blockchain for Security and Privacy. Dr. Jurcut has several key contributions in research focusing on detection and prevention techniques of attacks over networks, the design and analysis of security protocols, automated techniques for formal verification, and security for mobile edge computing (MEC). Since 2015, she has collaborated on many international research projects as a principal/co-PI/funded investigator. Dr. Jurcut is an active chair as well as a reviewer for many key conferences and journals in related disciplines. She is an expert evaluator and reviewer of several Union

European projects in the area of cybersecurity and network communications. (More Info: https://people.ucd.ie/anca.jurcut)

* * *

Indika Balapuwaduge is a Senior Lecturer in the Department of Electrical and Information Engineering at University of Ruhuna. He received the B.Sc. Engineering (First Class Honors) degree from University of Ruhuna, Sri Lanka, in 2008, and the M.Sc. and the Ph.D. degrees in Information and Communication Technology (ICT) from University of Agder (UiA), Norway in 2012 and 2016, respectively. His Master thesis was awarded as the Best Master's thesis in ICT at UiA in 2012. From March 2017 to March 2020, he served as a Post-Doctoral Research Fellow at the Department of ICT, UiA. He spent one year as an engineer at Huawei technologies, Sri Lanka, from Oct. 2008 to Aug. 2009 and he worked as a lecturer at the Department of Electrical and Information Engineering, University of Ruhuna from Aug. 2009 to Aug. 2010. Moreover, he has served as a Session Chair for IEEE ICC conferences, and on the TPC of several international conferences. Dr. Anuradha's current research interest covers various areas of mobile and wireless communications, including cognitive radio networks, ultra-reliable communication, massive MTC, Internet of Things, modeling and performance analysis of modern communications systems and networks.

Sonam Bhardwaj received MTech Degree from UIET Kurukshetra for conducting research in Big Data. Research interests are Network Forensics, Cybersecurity, Information Privacy, Evidence Preservation.

Purnima Gupta is working as Assistant Professor. She has qualified 4 times UGC NET and 2 times AWES PGT exam. She has been awarded by 2 times Eastern Central Railway Mughalsarai Division for developing their five projects (Pension Senitization System, Central Receipt & Dispatch Mangement system, LAR, RMS and TROMGS). She has done M.tech (CSE) and Master of Computer Applications. She is having a rich experience of teaching and research in the field of Computer Science & Engineering. She has published and presented a large number of research papers in International as well as national journals/conference. Her area of interest is C/C++, Compiler Design, Artificial Intelligence, Data Structure, Network Security, DBMS (Oracle/PL-SQL), HTML, CSS, Java Script, Python(Pandas, Numpy, Matplotlib), R language, Tableau, IOT, etc.

Michalina Hendon has always had an interest in computers and how users interact with technology. As a problem solver, Dr. Hendon always seeks to explore how technology can aid in the easy of information and lifestyle. With more than ten years of instruction in Higher Education, courses in Information Technology have been her focus.

Eranda Harshanath Jayatunga is a Senior Lecturer attached to the Department of Electrical and Information Engineering, Faculty of Engineering since 2013. He obtained his Bachelor Degree in Electrical and Electronics Engineering from University of Peradeniya, Sri Lanka in 2003 and Master's Degree in Information and Communication Technology (ICT) from Asian Institute of Technology, Thailand in 2007. He worked as a research assistant in Memorial University of Newfoundland, Canada also. His research interests include but not limited to Internet of Things (IoT), Cooperative Communication, MIMO Systems, Modulation Classification and Digital Signal Processing. He is also a Certified CCNA Instructor Trainer in CISCO Network Academy, Sri Lanka. Webpage: http://eie.eng.ruh.ac.lk/team/eranda-jayatunga/.

Abhijith Kalayil completed Bachelor of Engineering in Mechatronics. Has 3-year experience in Networking as a Network Engineer/Administrator. Currently pursuing Masters in Digital engineering.

Karpagam Manavalan is a Professor and Associate Head with 23 years of experience in Computer science and Engineering in PSG College of Technology. She obtained her B.E, M.E, and Ph.D. in Computer science and Engineering. Areas of Specialization include Database Management System, Data Structures and Algorithms, Service Oriented Architecture, Cloud Computing, Cyber-Physical Systems Model Driven Architecture, and Security.

Ambika N. has completed her MCA in the year 2001 and M.Phil in the year 2008. She completed her Ph.D. from Bharathiar University, Coimbatore in the year 2015. She has 13 years of experience. She has published a significant amount of papers in International papers, books and Journals. She has guided significant number of students in their projects which include under-graduate and graduate students. Her areas of interest include Wireless sensor network, Internet-of-things (IoT), and Cyber Security. She is working as faculty in the Department of computer applications, SSMRV College, Bangalore.

Sivasankari Narasimhan completed B.E. in Anna University in 2005. and completed M.E. in 2008. Currently pursuing Ph.D degree from Kalasalingam University. Her area of interest includes VLSI and Security.

Loreen M. Powell is a tenured professor of Information Technology and Analytics at Bloomsburg University of Pennsylvania. Her research areas are information technology, programming, analytics, security, and pedagogy. She has authored over 50 scholarly refereed journal publications, 100+ conference presentations, and several mini research grants.

Soundarya R. completed her Bachelor's in Computer Science and Engineering at PSG College of Technology, Coimbatore. She is an ardent lover of technology and is a philomath.

Pasika Ranaweera is currently pursuing his PhD studies in School of Computer Science, University College Dublin, Ireland. He obtained his Bachelor Degree in Electrical and Information Engineering in 2010 from University of Ruhuna, Sri Lanka and Master's Degree in Information and Communication Technology (ICT) in 2013 from University of Agder, Norway. Pasika is focused on enhancing the security measures in Multi-access Edge Computing (MEC) and Internet of Things (IoT) integration. His research directives extend to the areas of lightweight security protocols, 5G, MEC, NFV, SDN integration technologies, Privacy preservation techniques and IoT security. Web: https://ucdcs-research.ucd.ie/phd-student/pasika-sashmal-ranaweera/.

Virender Ranga has received his Ph.D. degree in 2016 from Computer Engineering Department of National Institute of Technology, Kurukshetra, Haryana, India. He has published more than 80 research papers in various high Impact factor International SCI Journals in the area of Computer Communications. Presently, he is Assistant Professor in the Computer Engineering Department since 2008. He has been awarded by Young Faculty Award in 2016 for his excellent contributions in the field of Computer Communications. He has acted as member of TPC in various International conferences of repute. He is a member of editorial board of International Journal of Advances in Computer Science and Information Technology(IJACSIT) and Journal of Science Engineering and Technology (JSETEC). He is an active reviewer of many reputed journals of IEEE Transactions, Springer, Elsevier, T & F and InderScience. His research area includes Wireless Sensor & Adhoc Networks.

Jessica Schwartz is a blockchain certified educator, having worked in a variety of educational institutions focusing on instructional design and implementing courses in new technologies, such as machine learning, artificial intelligence, and blockchain technology. As a wife and mother, she enjoys traveling with her family and walking her three dogs.

Archana Sharma is presently working as Associate Professor at IMS Noida. She has over 25 years of experience spanning the IT industry and academia in different capacities and has published 40 research papers of which 14 are in international journals. She has also authored one text book for MCA and B.Tech. students, besides that published book chapter with IGI Global. She has organised and attended various conferences, Faculty Development Programmes, workshops and seminars during her stint in different organisations and has been credited with awards and commendations. Her major areas of competencies include Blockchain, IoT, Advanced Database, Mobile Commerce, Distributed systems, Operating systems and Data Science.

Thamizhi S.I. completed her Bachelor's in Computer Science and Engineering at PSG College of Technology, Coimbatore. She is currently working in the Computer Networks domain.

Keshav Sinha was born in Dhanbad, India, in 1991. He received the B.E. Degree in Computer Science and Engineering from Sri Chandrasekharendra Saraswathi Viswa Mahavidyalaya, Kanchipuram, India, in 2013, and M.E. Degree in Software Engineering from the Birla Institute of Technology, Mesra, India, in 2016. Currently, as a research scholar, he is doing a Ph.D. from Birla Institute of Technology, Mesra, India in the field of Cryptography and Network security. In the future, this work provides a secure environment for multimedia transmission. As a research scholar, he published several papers in various conferences and journals. His current research interest includes Soft Computing, Cryptography, and Network Security which provides flexibility in the computer science society.

Dhana Srinithi Srinivasan completed her Bachelor's in Computer Science and Engineering at PSG College of Technology, Coimbatore, India. She is currently exploring through various opportunities and technologies in the field of research in Computer Science, with a keen passion for data. Her eventual goal is to develop tools and technologies for the benefit of the society.

Rochak Swami is a PhD research scholar at the Department of Computer Engineering in National Institute of Technology, Kurukshetra, Haryana, India. She received her B.Tech degree (2012) in Computer Science and Engineering from Rajasthan Technical University, Kota, India and M.Tech degree (2015) in Computer Science from Birla Institute of Technology Mesra, Ranchi, Jharkhand, India. She is an ACM and IEEE student member. Her current areas of interest include cyber security, security issues in Software-defined networking, and DDoS attacks.

Nikhil Tripathi is working as a security researcher at the Technical University of Darmstadt, Germany in close collaboration with the Fraunhofer Institute for Secure Information Technology (SIT), Germany. He earned his Ph.D. from the Department of Computer Science at the Indian Institute of Technology Indore. Prior to the current role, he was briefly with IIT Indore working on a cloud security project. His research interests include network and system security. In particular, he primarily works on vulnerability assessment of application layer protocols to explore vulnerabilities that can be exploited to launch DoS/DDoS attacks. He is also working towards devising cloud-based DDoS defense mechanisms. He has published several research papers in the area of security and is a regular reviewer for various journals and conferences and also served as a TPC member of conferences such as CANS and ANTS.

Madhav Verma was born in Dhanbad, India, in 2001. He is currently pursuing his Bachelor's degree in Computer Science and Engineering from B.I.T Sindri, Dhanbad. His major interest in the field of Mathematical Formulation and Security.

Index

A

B

C

D

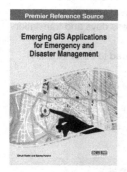

IGI Global Author Services

Providing a high-quality, affordable, and expeditious service, IGI Global's Author Services enable authors to streamline their publishing process, increase chance of acceptance, and adhere to IGI Global's publication standards.

Benefits of Author Services:

- **Professional Service:** All our editors, designers, and translators are experts in their field with years of experience and professional certifications.
- **Quality Guarantee & Certificate:** Each order is returned with a quality guarantee and certificate of professional completion.
- **Timeliness:** All editorial orders have a guaranteed return timeframe of 3-5 business days and translation orders are guaranteed in 7-10 business days.
- **Affordable Pricing:** IGI Global Author Services are competitively priced compared to other industry service providers.
- **APC Reimbursement:** IGI Global authors publishing Open Access (OA) will be able to deduct the cost of editing and other IGI Global author services from their OA APC publishing fee.

Author Services Offered:

English Language Copy Editing
Professional, native English language copy editors improve your manuscript's grammar, spelling, punctuation, terminology, semantics, consistency, flow, formatting, and more.

Scientific & Scholarly Editing
A Ph.D. level review for qualities such as originality and significance, interest to researchers, level of methodology and analysis, coverage of literature, organization, quality of writing, and strengths and weaknesses.

Figure, Table, Chart & Equation Conversions
Work with IGI Global's graphic designers before submission to enhance and design all figures and charts to IGI Global's specific standards for clarity.

Translation
Providing 70 language options, including Simplified and Traditional Chinese, Spanish, Arabic, German, French, and more.

Hear What the Experts Are Saying About IGI Global's Author Services

"Publishing with IGI Global has been *an amazing experience* for me for sharing my research. The *strong academic production* support ensures quality and timely completion." – **Prof. Margaret Niess, Oregon State University, USA**

"The service was *very fast, very thorough, and very helpful* in ensuring our chapter meets the criteria and requirements of the book's editors. I was *quite impressed and happy* with your service." – **Prof. Tom Brinthaupt, Middle Tennessee State University, USA**

Learn More or Get Started Here:

For Questions, Contact IGI Global's Customer Service Team at cust@igi-global.com or 717-533-8845

IGI Global
PUBLISHER of TIMELY KNOWLEDGE
www.igi-global.com

Printed in the United States
by Baker & Taylor Publisher Services